9/00

W9-CZJ-710

3 1323 00963 5953

ML

WITHDRAWN
NEWTON

No Room of Their Own

GENDER AND CULTURE
Carolyn G. Heilbrun and Nancy K. Miller, Editors

דירג'יניה וולף, סופרת אנגליה פרוקת ופיוחרת פמינה, ואחת המפרשות החשובות בתקום הייטף הפורהני.

העיגול ליד וירג'יניה

Deganit Berest, "The Circle by Virginia" (1975), 24" x 20",
black and white photo and chinograph.

NEWTON FREE LIBRARY
NEWTON, MASS.

No Room of Their Own

Gender and Nation in Israeli Women's Fiction

YAEL S. FELDMAN

Columbia University Press   NEW YORK

NEWTON FREE LIBRARY
NEWTON, MASS.

892.43
F33N
1999

COLUMBIA UNIVERSITY PRESS
Publishers Since 1893

New York   Chichester, West Sussex
Copyright © 1999 Columbia University Press
All rights reserved

Library of Congress Cataloging-in-Publication Data
Feldman, Yael S.
No room of their own: gender and nation in Israeli
women's fiction / Yael S. Feldman.
p.   cm. — (Gender and culture)
Includes bibliographical references and index.
ISBN 0–231–11146–0 (cloth)
ISBN 0–231–11147–9 (pbk.)
1. Israeli Fiction—Women authors—History and criticism.
2. Feminism and literature. 3. Feminist literary criticism.
I. Title. II. Series.
PJ5029.F35   1999
892.4'3099287—dc21   99–31641
                                                      CIP

Casebound editions of Columbia University Press books
are printed on permanent and durable acid-free paper.

Printed in the United States of America
Designed by Audrey Smith

c 10 9 8 7 6 5 4 3 2 1
p 10 9 8 7 6 5 4 3 2 1

To the beloved memory of my mother
whose untold story
shines through the pages of this book

Contents

Preface

This book has been long in the making; so long, in fact, that it has accumulated more than one beginning.

The most recent is the one that determined its final conceptualization and title. That beginning took place on a typically gloomy English morning a few years ago, when Steve discovered in one of those quaint Oxford bookshops—his favorite pasture during our sabbatical there—a first edition of *A Writer's Diary*, the first posthumous selection of Virginia Woolf's diary. Little did we know at the time that his chance find would eventually offer me precisely what I was looking for—an appropriate framing for my story of the long and difficult gestation of Israeli literary feminism. The setting could not have been any more congenial, as I spent the rest of our stay in Oxford immersing myself in the enchanting yet conflicted world of this quintessentially English writer. More than any contemporary author or theorist, I felt, Woolf—especially the later Woolf, the one who struggled to hold onto her sanity, life, and feminist dream in the besieged London of World War II—offers a relevant perspective on the Israeli story I was attempting to tell. For the crux of this story—told here for the first time—is the nexus of feminism and nationalism, the difficulty of achieving the one while remaining loyal to the other in a country that has been under siege (psychological when not military) ever since its inception.

How I wandered into this particular project is itself a long story. Perhaps it began, ironically, in the late 1970s, when a group of students of Hebrew at Columbia University surrounded me, greatly agitated, asking what I—the token Israeli newcomer—thought about the charges voiced in a new book, *Israeli Women: The Reality behind the Myth*.

I had no need to read Lesley Hazleton's book, of course (or so I felt), to brush off her critique. As far as I was concerned, Israeli women (that is, myself) were liberated and in no need of feminist enlightenment. Was I not confidently mastering just then a variety of meta-narratives, the *grands récits* of the time—semiotics, cultural systems, modernism, postmodernism? Women's liberation may be relevant to American bourgeois culture, I thought, but not to us "socially aware" Israelis.

I have often revisited that moment in my mind—the primal scene (sin?) of my feminist journey. For, in a few years, soon after obtaining my doctoral degree (and while pursuing another meta-narrative, psychoanalysis), I was about to make a "discovery": the new Israeli fiction of the early 1980s was echoing my own personal "denial," engaging feminism while expressing ambivalence about it. Apparently, the problem was not mine alone. I slowly realized that a recalcitrant Hebrew literary tradition, one that was blatantly lacking in women novelists throughout this century (the first of its modern phase), was finally making room for women as both authors and subjects. As I learned in retrospect, this transformation was one of the ripple effects of the Yom Kippur War (1973), which made Israeli women (some of them, at least) sharply aware of their marginal position in a society under siege.

My initial explorations of these developments (as well as my early publications) had a personal angle as well. They were accompanied by endless arguments with my late mother, Clara Keren-Or. That staunch individualist, a strong-willed pioneer and a fiercely freethinking Zionist—a "natural" feminist if there ever was one—would not readily accept my newly evolving view of feminism. For me, that so-called American import was a contemporary version of her own youthful rebellion, the dream she erroneously believed to have materialized in the state she had helped to build. It took her a long time to see it my way. By the end of that decade, however, my research into the literary non/representation of the mythical New Hebrew Woman of my upbringing intensified, while my mother's objections began, slowly but surely, to loosen their grip . . . Once "converted," she watched the changing map of Israeli fiction with great interest and excitement, closely following the virtual explosion of Hebrew fiction by women throughout the 1990s. Unfortunately, she passed away last summer, just before this study reached completion, and it is lovingly dedicated to her memory: her warm, rich spirit dwells among these chapters just as her insatiable intellectual curiosity has forever inspired my own.

No Room of Their Own is the final product of this entwined journey. It tells about the times and art of the "foremothers" of the current boom in Israeli women's fiction—and of some of their Western models. Major among these models is the life and art of Virginia Woolf, but no less intriguing are the analogues and influences of other staple feminist authors, from Simone de Beauvoir and Marie Cardinal to Jean Rhys and Marilyn French.

While some of these connections surfaced through my own research, others required "my" authors' active cooperation. I wish to thank them all for generously giving me of their time, and especially for the gift of their imagination, creativity, and daring. I greatly enjoyed my sojourns in their fictional realities and hope that my own narrative does them justice.

Next on my list of thanks are my close friends and colleagues, as well as my students at New York University (in the Skirball Department for Hebrew and Judaic Studies, the Departments of English and Comparative Literature, and the Liberal Arts Program). Knowingly and unknowingly, in formal and informal ways, they all helped me think through many of the issues that inform this study. Over the years their interest, expertise, and support, both practical and moral, were crucial in this lengthy journey.

Just as crucial were the lessons I learned in my course of studies at the Columbia University Center for Psychoanalytic Training and Research. I wish to thank my teachers and colleagues-classmates and especially Dr. Ethel Person, then director of the center, for encouraging my forays into their field and for helping me learn a new language.

My research greatly benefited from the work done by two Israeli institutions: Genazim, the literary archives of the Hebrew Writers Association in Israel, and the Institute for the Translation of Hebrew Literature. I wish to express my thanks to Rosa Hasson and Nili Cohen, respectively, and to their resourceful staff, for making research an exciting adventure. I am grateful also to the librarians at the Hebrew University and the Bodleian, where different portions of this research were carried out. Special thanks goes to Evelyn Ehrlich, the head of Humanities Reference at Bobst Library (NYU), who went beyond the call of duty to help with last-minute searches for misplaced references and other indispensable data.

Several fellowships supported my research trips to Israel and England over the years: a Columbia University Junior Faculty Fellowship, an NEH Summer Fellowship, a Lucius Littauer Foundation Travel Grant, the Koerner Fellowship at the Oxford Centre for Hebrew Studies, and the NYU Research Challenge Award. I am indebted to them all, and especially to the directors and staff of the Oxford Centre for generously providing a congenial sabbatical retreat, an ideal environment for thinking and writing.

Portions of this manuscript-in-process were presented in professional meetings and invited lectures; my thanks go to my hosts and the participants in these gatherings for their input and comments. Earlier versions of several sections were published in scholarly forums, and I am grateful to these journals for permission to use this material here.

Drafts of different chapters benefited from the informed reading of Eve

Tabor Bannet, Janet Handler Burstein, Nurit Gertz, Nili Gold, Anne Golomb Hoffman, Tzippi Keller, Hava Tirosh Samuelson, Alice Shalvi, Ellen Handler Spitz, and Ellen Tremper. I wish to express my profound gratitude to all of them (and to others whose names I may have overlooked), and especially to the readers from Columbia University Press—their critiques as well as enthusiasm made the publication of this book possible. Any lacunae or errors of judgment are my own responsibility, however.

Above all, I am deeply indebted to the dedicated staff of Columbia University Press, whose concerted effort gave this book its final shape: to Jennifer Crewe, for her faith in my project and for her patience and amiable encouragement throughout all its permutations; to her assistant, Mary Ellen Burd, on whose resourceful assistance I could always count; to my manuscript editor, Susan Pensak, who, with an assured hand, removed my Israeli commas and gave my English an American inflection and whose genuine interest, expertise, and friendship sustained me through many a nerve-racking moment; and to the anonymous graphic designers who graciously accommodated my requests, even at short notice. I also thank my graduate student, Jill Aizenstein, for the ardor, care, and long hours she invested in preparing the bibliography and index.

Last but not least, endless love and thanks to my small family circle: to my sister Leah Shulman and her family, my home away from home, for selflessly adopting my project and for nurturing me through the rough times we experienced together; to Tami and Shai, for lovingly sharing with me their private spaces and for their surprisingly attentive ears; and to my dear spouse, Steven Bowman, for making it all possible. This work is suffused with traces of his love and active support in more ways than I can count—from a *Writer's Diary* to "A Woolf in the Holy Land," his original naming of my project-in-process, conceived amidst the green pastures and woolly lambs of Yarnton Manor.

New York
June 1999

A Note About the Artist

"The Circle by Virginia," featured as the frontispiece and on the cover of this book, is a collage conceived in 1975 by Deganit Berest, one of the most original contemporary Israeli artists. It seems to respond to the first wave of Hebrew translations of Woolf, illustrating my own outline of the reception of Woolf in Israel (see my introduction).

Virginia Woolf's most famous profile is "cited" here from the Israeli press. The accompanying caption reads: "Virginia Woolf, an unusually fascinating English author, and one of the most important innovators of the modernist novel." Not a word about her contribution to feminism, in keeping with the climate in Israel of the mid-1970s.

Deganit Berest's graphic intervention seems to subvert this consensus, however. By placing "the circle *by* Virginia"—more accurately in front of her implied gaze—she turns her from (the spectators') object of beauty and admiration to a subject in her own right, one who owns her own gaze, which seems to contemplate "the circle," itself a classic symbol of perfection and eternity. Berest, however, would have none of this canonic representation. Her circle "deepens" under our very eyes, exposing its dark shadowy underside. Visually reflecting the black and white contrast of Woolf's profile, this double circle—potentially representing such binarisms as center/margins, male/female, known/unknown—now undergoes another transformation, a "deconstruction," so to speak. Virginia's gaze seems to liberate the dark side of the moon (= circle?), perhaps a representation of the unknown eternal feminine. By giving the crescent moons their autonomous space on the page, she (Virginia? the artist?) endows them with their own subjectivity. Most important—these "new moons," former parts of the hegemonic whole, are now perceived as neither black nor white but rather as an (androgynous?) admixture of both.

In 1990 Berest contributed a later version of "The Circle by Virginia," dated 1976, to "Feminine Presence," the first exhibition dedicated to Israeli women artists at the Tel Aviv Museum of Art. In this later version the crescent moons are represented as large three-dimensional sculptures, giving them even more weight and autonomy than in her earlier version. Berest also contributed an essay to the catalogue. In contrast to the heavily Lacanian/postmodern tone of other essays (see my afterword), she chose to revisit Woolf's *A Room of One's Own*, working through her own doubts about the sexuality of the artist's mind and the limits and possibilities of the "feminine identity/presence."

A similar mood prevails in another work by Berest, which is displayed on p. 103. "Orlando" (1975) is a wonderful visual joke, captivating in its surface simplicity and perfectly fitting Woolf's own whimsical spirit in *Orlando*. Although the latter is presumably only a footnote (*) to a bookshelf of an Israeli artist (the Hebrew titles include several books on photography as well as some representative literary classics, from Swift's *Gulliver* to Agnon's *Shira* and Solzhenitsyn's *The First Circle*), it clearly occupies a good position at the center. Moreover, the asterisk in fact marks this slim and modest volume as outstanding, thereby unsettling the cultural hierarchies we would "naturally" construct when viewing this "weighty" bookshelf. The significance of *Orlando* for the artist's (postmodern) perception of her own gender identity and fluid subjectivity may be readily inferred from my discussion in chapter 4.

No Room of Their Own

Introduction

> We were not suffragettes. . . . The Palmach was suffragist—self-declared
> suffragist. The Palmach inscribed "sexual equality" on its flag, along
> with other issues, while we, the girls, were expected to realize this prin-
> ciple. So we accepted this—and ate shit.
>
> —Netiva Ben Yehuda, *1948—Between Calendars*

1. *"Running with She-Wolves"*?

Although the modern Hebrew woman writer has yet to find her literary
historian, her first century may be demarcated as spanning the years 1897
to 1997. This periodization will perhaps come as a surprise to any reader
familiar with Hebrew letters. The late entry of women into the renaissance
of Hebrew literature—a vital aspect of the Jewish national revival at the
turn of this century—is a fact long recognized by both consumers and
scholars of this culture. My choice of dates thus demands an explanation.

While not motivated—as feminist scholarship has perhaps conditioned
us to expect—by new findings of hitherto unknown spurts of female creativity, it is meant to outline the unusual history of reception of the
Hebrew woman writer by her male peers. Unlike analogous histories in
other cultures, women writing in Hebrew were received with open arms a
century ago, when—and probably because—they were few and far
between. By contrast, a recent, ostensibly unexpected, proliferation of fiction by women, marked by their topping the 1997 Israeli best-seller lists
(that is, women's commercial success), elicited much ado in the Israeli
media, triggering—within the space of one month—expressions of both
exuberance and alarm.

In October 1997 *Ma'ariv*, the popular daily, featured an extensive
interview in its cultural supplement, provocatively grouping ten women
authors and four male editors under the American-inspired title, "Running with She-Wolves." For the informed reader, however, any connection between this press coverage and Clarissa Pinkola Estés's popular
Women Who Run with the Wolves was sorely missing. (Pinkola Estés's

volume, a "handbook" that maps out the Jungian wild woman arche-type, had been translated into Hebrew earlier that year.)[1] Raising basic questions about the possible definitions and desirability of "women's lit-erature," or "feminine writing," the *Ma'ariv* interview investigated the contemporary flourishing of Israeli women's fiction without so much as casting a sidelong glance at the archetype of its provocative title. The rival daily *Yediot Aḥaronot* did not lag behind: On October 15 Yaron London, one of the most senior Israeli journalists, interviewed the "Four Religious Women Novelists Who Topped the Best-Seller Lists," as the sensational heading announced. Ironically, the leading best-seller was a Hebrew translation of Naomi Ragen's American best-seller, *Sotah*, whose Hebrew title, *Ve-'el 'ishekh teshukatekh* (based on Genesis 3:16: "Unto your husband shall be your desire"), supplied the title of the interview. The apparent contradiction between the references of the two interviews (the Jungian she-wolves and the biblical husbanded wife—particularly when we recall the second half of the Genesis verse, "and he shall rule over you") obviously calls attention to one of the major rifts in Israeli culture today. Nevertheless, given the first group's consensus (though not without some dissension) that what they have in common is a preoccupation with the thematics of "love" and "personal relation-ships," it would seem that, rather than running with wolves, their wildest exploit would be their "success in overrunning—and confidently so—the Israeli literary scene."[2]

As mild as this feat may seem from this side of the ocean (and notwith-standing the controversy about its causes), it no doubt has had a different meaning in Israel, given the short history of Israeli "best-seller lists" (which were introduced only in 1993 by the prestigious daily *Ha'aretz*). Typically, any new book by a canonic author would be rated high on the list. In other words, Israelis are not only avid readers, they are consumers of "good" literature. Moreover, since Hebrew (= original) popular or casual fiction is a recent business in Israel, its commercial success has not yet completely overshadowed that of canonic fiction. Consequently, the distinction between canonic and noncanonic may be lost on the average reader, as both segments of contemporary Hebrew literature successfully gain access to these lists.

This confusion may explain male paranoic response, apparently caused by the "feminization" of the 1997 lists and the media's celebra-tion of this achievement. The counterattack was not slow to appear: "[Israeli] male writers have been absolutely silenced, and who knows when they will regain their eloquence . . . ," panicked a librarian of a veteran kibbutz (!) in a letter to *Sfarim*, the book review supplement of *Ha'aretz*.[3] Echoing infamous nineteenth-century American complaints, this literatus was obviously frustrated at what seemed to him a preference for women's fiction on the part of Israeli publishers and readers. His frustration was premature, however. Within a few months the pendulum swung again: balance has been restored, argued *Sfarim*'s editor, Michael Handelsaltz, with the publication of new books by veteran, "canonic" male writers.[4]

A century ago, however, the picture was quite different. In contrast to the American woman writer, who "has entered literary history as the enemy,"[5] the Hebrew woman writer seems to have entered her literary history sister, as bride, as comrade in arms. Already in 1897—an early date for a literature that came of age in that very decade—Eliezer Ben-Yehudah (1858–1922), the propagator of spoken Hebrew, openly invited women (and particularly his wife, Hemda, who happened to be a chemist) to contribute to his journals. His chivalrous invitation is a precious document, reminding us once more that even with insight and goodwill one may still be unable to escape the snares of gender essentialism: "Only women," he argued, "are capable of reviving Hebrew, this old, forgotten, dry and hard language, by permeating it with emotion, tenderness, suppleness and subtlety."[6]

So the door seemed to have been wide open. Yet women were slow to enter, perhaps intuitively sensing that double bind of which recent scholarship has made us aware—the fact that Ben Yehudah's benign encouragement was circumscribed by his gender bifocals. For although a number of women graced his journals, none left her mark on the canon of Hebrew literature. No Hebrew male writer could ever have complained, as did American author Nathaniel Hawthorne,"about the 'damned mob of scribbling women' whose writings . . . were diverting the public from his own."[7] In contrast to other literary traditions (e.g., English, French, Japanese), Hebrew did not develop a line of women novelists, either within or without the canon.[8] For the first century of its modern phase (or even for its first 150 years, depending on the periodization used) Hebrew prose fiction was primarily the domain of male writers, while women generally found their expression in poetry—an apparent gender preference whose implications will soon concern us.[9] In fact, one can frame the difference between the historic poetics of the Hebrew and English traditions (the Jewish component of the latter not excluded)[10] with a paraphrase of

Virginia Woolf's well-known question, But why . . . were they, with few exceptions, all poets?[11]

This cultural difference is no doubt highly significant for any discussion of gender essentialism, as I shall argue in chapter 1. For now it is only necessary to recall that the first woman to enter the canon as fiction writer, Dvora Baron (1887–1956), wrote short stories and novellas, mainly in the lyrical-impressionist mode,[12] thereby fulfilling the "feminine" role devised for the second sex by the arbiters of the Hebrew renaissance. In a different vein, the first Hebrew *novels* women published were each the first prose fiction of a *poet*: *Simta'ot* (Alleyways; 1929) by Elisheva [Bihovsky] (1888–1949) and *Vehu ha'or* (It/He Is the Light) by Leah Goldberg (1911–1970). In the latter the impact of the poet's innate lyricism on the novel's prose style is unmistakable. Yet, while to contemporary readers Goldberg's poetic flourishes may seem outdated and totally misplaced in an otherwise realistic novel, this hybrid style was not uncommon for its time (1946).[13] In this specific case, however, it was perhaps also meant to provide a softening counterpoint to the "hard" thematics of this narrative, whose young protagonist painfully grapples with her father's traumatic nervous breakdown and with her own fear of its hereditary potential.[14] In any case, as Hebrew prose matured it slowly outgrew its youthful stylistic hybridity. Yet this style did linger on—though in different, updated guises—in women's prose fiction, thereby prolonging the gender stereotyping begun by Eliezer Ben-Yehudah.[15]

With few exceptions, it is only recently that women have begun to overcome this stylistic feature, often considered gender specific.[16] Since the early 1980s their prose fiction has emerged as a substantially diverse phenomenon, including such traditionally hard-core male genres as the historic novel or fictional autobiography, and even a genre as popular as the mystery novel.[17] However, notwithstanding the popularity of this literature, it has proliferated too quickly for scholarship to catch up. Thus, among contemporary women writers, only veteran author Amalia Kahana-Carmon was included in the pioneering feminist studies of the late 1980s, despite the generalizing claims of their subtitles.[18] On the other hand, the first volume specifically devoted to *Gender and Text in Modern Hebrew and Yiddish Literature* (1992) still preserved the old balance: while both Israeli writers whose essays sign off the collection are prose fiction writers who have graduated from short stories to novels (Ruth Almog and Amalia Kahana-Carmon, to whom we shall return), the critical articles themselves are neatly divided between women's poetry and men's fiction.[19] Ironically, this traditional generic division between the genders is crossed over only in Naomi Sokoloff's annotated bibliography, which makes visible the new gender studies (in modern Hebrew literature) budding in the early nineties.[20]

The centrality and diversity of women's *prose* was thus established only with the publication, in Israel, of *Hakol ha'aḥer* (The Other Voice), the first ever collection of Hebrew prose fiction written by women (1994, edited by Lily Rattok). The significance of this volume notwithstanding, it foregrounded women's short stories while relegating their long fiction to comments in the accompanying editorial essay (261–349). Whereas this choice is of course technically unavoidable, it adds to the particular slant of the editorial essay—the focus on the difference underlining the female experience, particularly as it is highlighted by the biological life cycle and traditional gender roles.[21] I would argue, however, that this acceptance of the politics of sexual difference eclipses some interesting rewritings of Western feminisms produced by Israeli novelists in the last two decades, an eclipse that has been further reinforced by another factor—the imbalanced representation of women's fiction in translation. To date, the English reader has more access to Israeli women's short fiction than to their novels.[22]

There is no doubt, however, that the new literary map drawn by Israeli women novelists deserves readers' full attention, not only because of its inherent interest as a phenomenon in Israeli culture but also because it brings into sharp focus a general point of contention that has been raging among scholars since the late 1970s: the relationship between modernist feminism (both literary and social) and postmodern theories.[23]

Zeroing in on the "death of the [Enlightenment] subject" as the major loss announced by postmodern thinkers (other "deaths"—those of philosophy and history—are secondary in this argument), feminist theorists on both sides of the Atlantic have embraced or mourned postmodernism as either "useful" or "damaging" for their project. Although the demarcation line between these two positions may overlap the French/Anglo-American divide (as suggested, for instance, by Alice Jardine's *Gynesis*), recent reviews yield a picture that is ever more complex.[24] This picture commands our attention in the third section of this introduction as well as in chapter 2. It is enough now to cite just one of the critics of postmodernism, the American scholar Jane Flax, who eloquently expressed her frustration at the accidental coincidence of the postmodernist death of the subject with the very time in which "women have just begun to re-member their selves and to claim an agentic subjectivity available always before only to a few privileged white men."[25]

Bearing this problem in mind, we should not be surprised by the low profile of *conscious* postmodernism in the work of the Israeli writers analyzed in the present study. Inasmuch as they were selected precisely because of their grappling with the representation or construction of female "agentic subjectivities" (self-consciously autonomous women, acting intentionally and purposefully as their own agents) in a society *still* inhospitable to such a project, their work understandably falls within the boundaries of modernism proper. Yet since they are writing during the very decades in which Israeli culture has been opening up (slow as this process may be) to postmodernist mistrust of the modernist project, their prose predictably reflects a rather careful selection of *issues* (rather than *poetics*) from the postmodernist repertory.[26] In this they differ entirely from the wholesale absorption of postmodernism evident in works written during the same decade by other (mostly male) authors, e.g., David Grossman, Avram Heffner, Yoel Hoffmann, Anton Shammas, Yuval Shimoni (and also by the younger female author Orly Castel-Bloom, to whom we return in the afterword).[27]

First and foremost among these issues is the problem of gender difference, which—though permeating all their oeuvre—reaches its fullest expression in the writings of Amalia Kahana-Carmon—a major Israeli writer, leading feminist, and long-recognized exponent of Virginia Woolf's modernist poetics in Hebrew. Despite this perception, however, I argue that Kahana-Carmon embeds gender difference in a deconstruction of one of postmodernism's arch-enemies—the general category of binarism and specifically the binarism of subject versus other. This preoccupation, especially in her later work, paradoxically involves her in a dialogue with the tradition of Simone de Beauvoir's existential feminism, thereby decentering her commonly agreed upon "filliation" with Virginia Woolf.

The debate over gender essentialism is another postmodernist theme evoked by these writers. This issue is explored via a gendered analysis of Israeli fictional autobiographies. The peculiar correlation between gender and genre that this material reveals is attributed not only to Israel's Jewish legacy but to its specific contemporary circumstances as well, concomitantly supporting *cultural* definitions of gender.

No less intriguing is the insight this body of work offers into the problematic relationship between feminist and nationalist ideologies. This burning issue, universal as it may sound, carries a particular urgency in a country bending under the yoke of siege (psychological when not military) for as long as it can remember. And although Israel's is perhaps a special case of postcolonial nationalism, ironically the distant voice of Virginia Woolf may be heard in the Israeli working through of this problem. Written under the threat of the Nazi invasion, her later feminist psychopolitical admonitions serve as a perfect paradigm for writers who constantly find themselves torn between feminist aspirations and nationalist constraints.

Finally, this corpus covertly poses (though never openly articulates) a specifically Israeli/Jewish problem, one that may be framed within the overarching postmodernist questioning of canon formation: Why has the "New Hebrew Woman," supposedly fostered by early Zionism—as our epigraph so starkly delineates—disappeared on her way to literary representation?[28]

2. The "New Hebrew Woman"

In a way, the following study constitutes an attempt to grapple with this very question; to "grapple" in order to "come to terms with" rather than arrive at a satisfactory answer. For, more than anything else, what follows reflects the unease with which contemporary new Hebrew women (the novelists studied here as well as the author of this study) have processed and transformed the anxiety-provoking tradition they/we inherited. So, before we approach the present-day scene, a brief review of this contradictory inheritance is in order.

The revival of modern Hebrew literature in the late 1800s was conceived and developed on Russian soil; as such, it was bound up with nineteenth-century socialism and nationalism. The former had openly propagated—at least in theory—both social and sexual equality for women. However, as recent sociohistoric studies in Israel have shown, not a little was lost in the translation from ideological platform to lived experience. In the view of contemporary scholars, cogently recapitulated in the term *Equality Bluff,* the prestate Zionist women's movement had not fulfilled its own expectations either in the urban settlements or in the kibbutzim.[29] Nor did the legendary Palmach, apparently, despite the long-held perception to the opposite. As told only recently by one of its most notorious fighters, Netiva Ben Yehuda (b. 1928), the distance between the inscription on its "flag" and the reality in the ranks of Israel's War of Independence in 1948 was immense (see the epigraph to this introduction and chapter 7).[30] Still, hindsight should not allow us to ignore the ethos (some would say mythos) of equal rights, as it was experienced by both fathers and mothers of the pioneering founding generation. Nor should it permit us to belittle the early political as well as cultural "conquests" made by some of these women, Manya Schohat (1880–1959) and Rachel Katznel-son-Shazar (1885–1983), for example, and, of course, the better-known writers Dvora Baron and Rachel (1890–1931).[31]

The force of this ethos was still felt in the early decades of the state, at least in some segments of Israeli society. English readers may be familiar with this ethos through the much publicized image of the Israeli female soldier, often photographed with a gun in her hand. In the late 1950s this image found its fictional expression in the popular, rather facile novel *New Face in the Mirror.*[32] Written (in English) by Yael Dayan—today the chair of the Israeli Knesset (parliament) Committee on the Status of Women, then better known as the young daughter of Israel's charismatic chief of staff, victorious commander of the 1957 Suez Campaign, and symbol of Israeli male chauvinism, Moshe Dayan—this novel projected a female macho stereotype that in reality was neither "feminist" nor all that common. It reflected, however, precisely that paradoxical Israeli ethos that made feminism, as it came to be known in the United States in the sixties, seem redundant, as if it were something "*we* have *always* known" (albeit under the rubric of the woman question), a latter-day product of a Western "luxury" culture that had finally awakened to some of its social(ist?) blind spots.[33]

If this paradoxical position does not make sense to us in the 1990s, we may recall that, well into the seventies, even Simone de Beauvoir similarly refused to label herself a feminist—*The Second Sex* of 1949 notwithstanding—believing that the woman question would be resolved by the socialist platform. The analogy between French and Israeli new women is not accidental. Just recall Karen Offen's contention that "Beauvoir's arguments were received with greater enthusiasm in English-speaking countries than in her own," apparently because of the socionational legacy of French feminism.[34] If Offen is correct in anchoring this legacy in "France's seemingly perilous demographic position," exacerbated early in this century by the great loss of men's lives in the Great War (147), we should have no difficulty in understanding the isomorphy between the early feminisms of post–World War I France and wartorn Israel.

On the other hand, we should not forget that by the sixties, socialism (or social Zionism) had already lost its broad popular base in Israeli society. The post–World War II immigration from Europe and the Middle

East countries had more than doubled the population of the young state and drastically changed the country's demographic and cultural makeup.[35] From that point on a large portion of the Israeli population was *un*affiliated with prestate ideologies. For this community both "old" and "new" feminisms were anathema, a forthright subversion of their traditional (mostly Oriental and/or Orthodox) ways of life. When the pressures of life under constant military siege are added to this sociocultural complex, it becomes clear that, socially speaking, Western feminism could not have had a warm reception in the Israel of the sixties and the seventies, despite a pro forma adherence to the indigenous, social Zionist women's movement. As described in chapter 6, this new trend was introduced by recent Anglo-American immigrants but was typically considered alien in Israeli culture.[36]

But what about the literary arena? Here we do well to remember that until recently most Hebrew *writers* were allied—either biographically or politically—with the ethos of the prestate community, with all its ideological trappings. Neither the Oriental nor the Orthodox section of Israeli society was proportionally represented in the canon of Hebrew literature. (The contemporary picture is significantly different.)[37] Yet despite its ideological "baggage," the Israeli literary mainstream (some would say "malestream")[38] seems to be curiously lacking when it comes to fictional representation of women. Bending under the yoke of its national narrative (the "meta-Zionist paradigm," as it has been called recently), Israeli literature has been shown to have a warped balance sheet when it comes to the representation of women. Israeli culture, as modern and secular as it is, has relegated its women, argued Kahana-Carmon, to their traditionally secondary position in the synagogue, in the women's gallery (*'ezrat hanashim*).[39] With one glaring exception, the new Hebrew woman, or, in postmodern parlance, the "female subject," was destined to remain a rhetorical construct, mostly excluded from works by both male and female authors.

The exception was the audaciously revolutionary poetry of Yona Wallach (1944–1985), whose legacy—despite her premature death—no doubt laid the foundation for a self-conscious Israeli woman subject. The problem was, however, that Wallach was ahead of her time. Except for a small circle of readers, Israel of the 1960s (and even the 1970s) was not yet ready for her brazen destabilization of the sociosexual value system. Conversely, by the 1990s the time was ripe. Wallach has recently been transformed from the object of public scandal, following her "pornographic" use of phylacteries in her poem "Tefilin" (1982), into an Israeli cult figure. This strong and idiosyncratic artist has been appropriated by the postmodern present, the subject of a biography, popular plays and exhibitions, and academic explorations.[40]

The timing is not surprising. It was preceded by the literary debut of the new Israeli woman—a debut engendered by the wave of women's prose fiction that had begun to sweep Israel in the early 1980s and is still going strong. Precisely this debut—its belatedness, its specific literary shape, and its sociopolitical implications—is the subject of the following inquiry. I follow its meandering narrative through the work of five Israeli prose writers: Shulamit Lapid (chapter 1), Amalia Kahana-Carmon (chapter 3), Shulamith Hareven (chapters 5 and 6.3), Netiva Ben Yehuda (chapter 7), and Ruth Almog (chapter 8). Although they began publishing in the 1960s (except for Ben Yehuda), it is generally their more recent novels (with the exception of Hareven, see chapter 5) that hold the key to the belated emergence of their precarious subjects and no less troubled feminisms. The journey will end with an overview of the work of the younger writers of the post-Zionist/postmodernist 1990s (the afterword). From this contemporary perspective the construction of a new Hebrew woman is just one more *grand récit* (Lyotard) whose time is over.[41] These young women either bypass this model of feminist narrative or parody it altogether, thus bringing my search to a wistful yet perhaps inevitable close.

But before I set off on this winding cultural journey, I will need to chart a path, narrow though it may be, through the maze of modern/postmodern theories, so that I can later gauge their impact on the Israeli reconceptualization of classical feminism.

3. The Subject of Postmodernism

A full exploration of postmodern theory is quite beyond the scope of this study. The following overview will briefly summarize fundamental positions and attitudes common to Derrida, Lacan, Foucault, Lyotard et al.[42] At the center of attention here is the relationship between feminism and postmodernism. That this relationship is not simply a matter of rejection or acceptance was already alluded to above. On the one hand, feminism (and especially its later permutation, gender theory) is clearly implicated in postmodernism's deconstruction of basic dichotomies in Western systems of thought. One of the major casualties of this project is the philosophical notion of the subject and its related opposition, the other.[43]

Thus, while postmodern philosophy has generally decentered the human cogito from its privileged position in Western tradition, gender theory has used this decentering to question the historic identification of the subject with heterosexual masculinity, thereby opening a (theoretical) door for female subjectivity.[44] On the other hand, while helping feminists question historic and contemporary perceptions of sexual and gender differences, postmodernist critiques of the Enlightenment (pronouncing the fictiveness of a unitary self and of reason's truth, among other things) seem to threaten and undermine the very foundation of and justification for women's quest for autonomous subjectivity. This aspect of contemporary thought is clearly problematic for the modernist-based strands of feminist theory, known as equal rights or liberal individualism feminism. For, if the subject is only a cultural or linguistic inscription to begin with, who is there to be "oppressed" or "liberated" in the first place?

Responses to this dilemma are polarized, to say the least (as we explore in detail in chapter 2). At one extreme we find Jane Flax's psychoanalytically based suspicion that the postmodernist death sentence on the subject is motivated by a *fear* of the "return of the suppressed," by "the [male] need to evade, deny or repress the importance of early childhood experiences, especially mother-child relationships, in the constitution of the self and the culture more generally."[45] At the other extreme we find a feminist reevaluation of the concept of female "otherness." This may take the form of "the simple device of making Other into Subject," as suggested by Alicia Ostriker, by means of dismantling and reversing literary conventions and social codes.[46] But it may also take the form of a postmodern destabilization of the automatic identification of otherness with threat, demonization, marginalization, or any other exclusionary attitudes (as described and codified by Simone de Beauvoir). In some sense (and only in some quarters, one may add) otherness has entirely shed its pejorative connotation and is alternatively viewed as a new definition of female selfhood. This ostensibly new, positivized perception of female *otherness* is often named sexual *difference*, particularly in France or by French-inspired theorists.

Not all of this reevaluation is new, of course. As was already argued by Toril Moi (in *Sexual/Textual Politics*), Jane Marcus (in *Virginia Woolf and the Languages of Patriarchy*), and Catharine Stimpson (in "Woolf's Room, Our Project"), at some level (and with much less theoretical jargon) it was begun by the arch-modernist Virginia Woolf, whose work anticipated all the paradoxes animating contemporary feminism: "Because of its inventiveness," summarizes Stimpson, "*A Room* foreshadows a strain of post-modernism; because of its self-division, a conflict with feminist criticism about post-modernism."[47] Of particular interest for our study is the relationship between Woolf's much-debated "androgyny," which I explore and reinterpret in chapter 4, and the just as problematic recent resurrection of the maternal metaphor in contemporary gender theories. Among the latter, Julia Kristeva's "Semiotic" is of special importance (see chapter 2), because she is the only one among contemporary female theorists who seems to have accepted postmodernism's death sentence with impunity, suggesting different strategies of action for women (not feminists) of the "third generation." For this generation, she avers, identity is an essentialist notion that should be relegated to metaphysics.[48]

The above is just a small sampling of the paradoxical tensions—even contradictions—that have energized debates over the Woman Question for the past half-century. What may have seemed in the first half of the century a relatively simple issue of social and psychological emancipation to be achieved by educational and economic equal opportunity (represented by a surface reading of Woolf's *A Room of One's Own*, 1929), seems hopelessly entangled today with philosophical challenges to a long, even ancient tradition, that of woman's alterity (as documented in Beauvoir's *The Second Sex*, 1949).

With postmodernism, however, the philosophical and psychological dualisms underlying this tradition (the logic of either/or) have been undergoing severe revisions.[49] For one thing, the other can be seen as negative, as the obverse side of the self, only by the objectivizing gaze of a subject—that very construct which, for the past few decades, postmodernism has been undoing, unraveling, decentering, deconstructing. In the absence of a stable subject this dichotomy should have been thrown into question, and with it its gendered hierarchy (the male subject versus the female other/object). Yet, as we shall see in the following chapters, this is not always the case.

The dilemma faced by contemporary feminist/gender scholars has been often framed in terms of positionality: should they refuse the perspective of a privileged male/subject by refuting, denying, explaining, correcting the negative alterity attributed to the female/object? Or should they answer this gaze by upholding, defending, celebrating their [essentialist?] "difference" as their own gynocentric subjectivity? And, beyond pragmatics, how are these strategies to be theoretically conceptualized— as a reversal of an androcentric legacy, or as a step beyond its essentialist categories? Put differently, does difference just mark otherness as privileged, or does it create a new space beyond the self/other (or subject/object) dichotomy? And can it function as a third term, as the coveted *elsewhere* beyond gender, outside the male/female binarism?[50]

Baffling questions abound. As do postmodern solutions, to no less baffling effect. Some of these solutions have recently been imported into Israeli academic discourse, in the attempt to synchronize Israeli feminism and postmodernism with contemporary—particularly continental—theories (e.g., Kristeva).[51] So far, however, this interpretative effort has shed little light on the genesis and evolution of Israeli feminism as a unique cultural phenomenon, anchored in its own time and place. The truth is that, to date, there are no Hebrew translations of any of the leading postmodern/feminist theorists. Scholars may read them in the original or in English translations. Here and there Hebrew excerpts are available in academic journals (mostly since the 1990s, though). But all this is a far cry from a widerange dissemination that would have a meaningful impact on writers and intellectuals—especially of the first generation—outside the narrow confines of academe. The questions aroused by contemporary theory would not suffice, then, if we want to understand Israeli literary feminism on its own terms. To do that, we need to place it within its own sociocultural context and to locate the intellectual and literary sources that may have inspired it—both within and without Hebrew letters; in the words of a great precursor of contemporary theorists, Mikhail Bakhtin: "It is only on a concrete historical subject that a theoretical problem can be resolved."[52]

The search for "a concrete historical subject" evidently constitutes part and parcel of the following chapters. One more point, however, is appropriate to conclude this introduction, namely, a presentation of the European models whose indisputable presence in Israel makes them a convenient prism through which to focus the belated emergence of feminism in Israeli literature and the particular shape of its evolution in the last two to three decades.

4. Israel and the European "Woman Question"

Probing the Israeli cultural climate for traces of "foreign" feminist presence, one would readily come to the not so surprising conclusion that the works discussed here generally follow one or two paradigmatic European feminist classics, Simone de Beauvoir and Virginia Woolf. Indeed, for a generation that came of age in the 1950s (including most of our writers), these were readily available paradigms, accessible both directly—in French and English, respectively—and indirectly, first by word of mouth and later in translation. More recently, the humanist (that is, prepostmodern) framework of these earlier signposts of the Woman Question have no doubt offered a relatively stable space in which Israeli feminists could ground the easily shifting terms of contemporary gender theory. In addition, these models obviously had both the advantage of intellectual status and the backing of literary traditions that scored highly with the Israeli intelligensia.

This was especially true for Simone de Beauvoir, whose authority originally stemmed not so much from her feminist masterpiece, *The Second Sex* (never translated into Hebrew!) but rather from her socialist and existentialist identity.[53] Left-wing existentialism was de rigueur for the young intellectuals of nascent Israel, for whom the Paris Left Bank was the first home away from home on their "voyage out."[54] Sartre and Camus were cultural heroes (they still are—as these pages are being written Camus's *Letters to a German Friend* has just appeared in Hebrew),[55] while such key concepts as authenticity and alienation could be heard everywhere in good company and read in Op-Ed articles (which—unlike today—used to occupy a sizable portion of the dailies). Beauvoir traveled in this company, especially after her roman à clef, *The Mandarins*, received the 1954 Goncourt Prize. The journalist Uri Keisari, for example, seized upon the occasion and wrote a detailed encomium enthusiastically supporting the Académie's choice. Pointing out that literary reviewers were divided over the merit of the novel itself (which he could not yet have read), he interpreted the prize as recognition of this woman's outstanding life as an intellectual. Half of his essay was devoted to *The Second Sex,* Beauvoir's "most important contribution," in his opinion.[56] By 1958 *The Mandarins* was available to Hebrew readers (produced, predictably, by a left-wing publishing house), eliciting much voyeuristic interest, to which a host of reviews in the daily newspapers attest.[57]

The next phase of Beauvoir's "presence" in Israeli letters is less clear-cut, challenging any attempt to limit cultural presence to the availability of translations. On the one hand, no other translation of Beauvoir's work appeared until the 1980s—a gap of a quarter-century, to be exact. To date, only four of her books are available in Hebrew—but a scant representation of her rich legacy, especially when compared to the availability of her work in English.[58] Yet, paradoxically, this scant representation does not imply a lack of interest. Indeed, the Israeli press followed Beauvoir's literary career quite closely, reporting on her new publications, from *Memoirs of a Dutiful Daughter* (*Ma'ariv,* May 29, 1959), through *The Force of Old Age* (*Al Hamishmar,* February 27, 1970, and March 6, 1970), to *Farewell to Sartre* (*Yediot Aḥaronot,* February 28, 1981), naming just a few. As recently as 1998 her posthumously published *Lettres à Nelson Algren* was reviewed in detail (*Ha'aretz/Sfarim,* March 18, 1998, p. 4).

Throughout the years the extensive coverage seems to have been divided between two foci: while the feminist message of her life and work (her being a woman writer) was clearly behind some of it, her political activism had its share too.[59] The latter gained momentum in 1966, when she visited Israel, with Sartre, in preparation for a special issue of *Les temps modernes,* which they dedicated to the Israeli-Arab conflict. Within a decade Israel formally acknowledged Beauvoir's devotion to the issue of human (and Israeli) rights by awarding her the prestigious Jerusalem Prize. Since this was 1975, the International Year of the Woman, we should not be surprised that this choice was instigated by Alice Shalvi, then a budding feminist, who within a decade would become the founder of Israel's Women's Network (see chapter 6.2). Serving on the panel of judges in 1975, she "both composed and read the judges' citation"; Beauvoir, she says, "fell in love with Jerusalem and Teddy Kollek [the mayor], and spoke very warmly of the city in her response to the award."[60]

By the 1980s, however, it is Beauvoir the feminist (rather than the humanist-socialist political activist) that takes over center stage. This is the decade, as we shall see, in which Israeli feminism came into its own. Accordingly, between 1983 and 1985, three of her books were translated: *An Easy Death,* her 1965 astonishing report of coping with her mother's death;[61] *A Woman Destroyed,* three stories originally published in 1967, whose emphasis on women's dependence and lack of agency was perceived as outdated, out of sync with the time (of publication in Hebrew: 1984!), and—most significantly—in contrast to her own public "feminist" stance even in the 1960s (an important issue that will be treated in chapter 3);[62] and, finally, *The Blood of Others,* one of her earliest novels (1945), an existentialist exposition of questions of life and death (and one's personal responsibility in these matters) in World War II Paris.[63] The difference between the recent lukewarm (and at times ironic)[64] reception of these works and the one written some thirty years earlier by Uri Keisari is telling; it illustrates the transition from hero worship to sober revisionism—a process that had been initiated by Beauvoir's own tell-all autobiographical writings but was exacerbated by the posthumous publication of her letters and diary as well as the less-than-flattering biographies published since her death in 1986.[65] Despite this erosion, however, Israeli media of the last decade has come back to Beauvoir, celebrating her once again as the "breaker of myths," as "the pioneer of women lib," and, above all, as the author of *The Second Sex*—the woman who taught other women (and men) that "no man is God,"[66] yet who was sadly unable to act upon her own words.

This recent Israeli return to Beauvoir's "most important contribution," the urtext of the woman as other, is not accidental. As we shall see in chapter 2, this text, although predating postmodernism by a quarter of a century, holds some intriguing clues to the mushrooming polarities evident among its offshoots.[67] More significantly, it will prove helpful with Israeli feminism, even in its besieged form. For this source sheds light on a central chapter in the Israeli struggle with female otherness and explains its inability to shake off woman's dependence, even while aspiring for personal agency (chapter 3).

For other chapters in the Israeli saga, however, it will be necessary to dig even deeper into the past of European feminism. Perhaps predictably, it is the modernist (at least nominally) feminism of Virginia Woolf that seems most congenial—in a variety of ways, to be sure—for the interpretation of the authors selected for this study. Woolf's presence in Israeli culture, however, has had quite a different history from that of Beauvoir's.

To begin with, for many years Virginia Woolf's image was that of the English modernist, the author of difficult experimental novels, a challenge to the small elite of English-reading literati (and some college English majors). It was not until the 1970s, however, when Western feminism rekindled interest in Woolf, that translation of her work into Hebrew began. Between 1973, when *Flush*—her humorous (and much neglected) "biography" of Elizabeth Barrett Browning's dog—made its appearance in Israel, and 1995, when her early novel *Night and Day* received a lukewarm reception, most of Woolf's fiction has been translated, including Quentin Bell's 1972 biography (see the appendix for a full list).[68] Thus Hebrew renditions of Woolf's modernist classics, *Mrs. Dalloway* and *To the Lighthouse*, were published in 1975 (most of the latter was published serially in the first three issues of the then new cutting-edge literary journal *Siman Kri'ah*, 1972–1973). Woolf's late novel, *The Years*, in its time (1937) a commercial (though not a critical) success, especially with the American readership, had a rather cool reception in the Israel of 1979. The next decade opened, significantly enough, with *A Room of One's Own*, coupled with *Between the Acts*, Woolf's last will and testament (1981). In a few years the translator of these two books, Aharon Amir (a writer of clear ideological stance in his own right) followed suit with *Three Guineas* (1985). With the latter the Hebrew rendition of Woolf's overtly feminist legacy was complete, ushering in, symbolically, the decade in which feminism emerges in Israeli discourse. The same years also show a growing awareness of the Woolf industry overseas, as attested, for example, by its frequent appearance in Ruth Almog's weekly column in *Ha'aretz* (more about this in chapter 8). Other translations published in the 1980s included the experimental novels *The Waves* and *Jacob's Room* as well as Bell's biography. The 1990s picked up the slack with a collection of short stories and the early novels *The Voyage Out* and *Night and Day*.

This picture will not be complete, however, without mentioning *Orlando*. Curiously, the translation (in 1964) of this audacious fantasy, the most irreverent of Woolf's flights of imagination, preceded by a full decade what in retrospect emerges as a two-decade translation project.[69] Since I discuss this 350-year biography in some detail in chapter 4, I will just tentatively reflect here on the appeal *Orlando* may have held for Israeli literati of the 1960s. That so-called State Generation, best known for its representative writers Amos Oz, A. B. Yehoshua, and Amalia Kahana-Carmon, was then in the throes of rebellion against the literary (socialist) realism of their predecessors, the writers who witnessed (and described) the birth of the state. *Orlando* may have offered them another model of the "fantastic," another paradigm of breaking the realistic code. As for *Orlando*'s feminist argument, its androgynous vision—this seems to have generally passed unnoticed (except, perhaps, for the writer Shulamith Hareven, and our frontispiece artist, Deganit Berest). Thus even as late as 1980 *Siman Kri'ah*, Israel's cutting-edge journal, could publish a (scathing) book review (of *The Years*) in which *Orlando* was grouped with *Flush* as "Woolf's works whose value is doubtful."[70]

As may be expected, this extensive body of translations generated its own industry of critical reviews and commentary, too numerous to be described here in detail. What does stand out, however, is the difference between the enthusiastic reviews that address issues of aesthetics and style, admiringly placing Woolf in the context of Proust's and Joyce's modernisms or defining her impressionism in relation to psychology or cinematography,[71] and the less-than-enthusiastic commentaries that take issue with her feminist polemics, and especially with the pacifism of her later

years. While the sometime severe critique of the early novels is not surprising (*The Voyage Out* in particular was viewed as a boring, didactic document, having historic, but no aesthetic value),[72] the reaction to *The Years*
(see note 70), in its time an American "best-seller" of sorts, does raise
questions about the effect of cultural difference on literary reception.

This difference is doubly felt in the area of academic scholarship. As late
as the mid-1980s, when, in the West, feminist scholarship of Virginia
Woolf had already reached its zenith, shifting into a postmodernist phase
(with Toril Moi's 1985 reevaluation), a first-rate Israeli scholar published
an exhaustive analysis of the principles of Woolf's poetics and ideology
without so much as mentioning her gender trouble (to borrow Judith
Butler's title).[73] In other Ph.D. dissertations written in the seventies and
eighties Woolf is usually yoked together with other modernists for a discussion of "the tragic," "concepts of the novel," or "child-parent relations"; when she is the major focus, her narrative and stylistic techniques
command attention.[74]

The celebration of Woolf the feminist did not catch on in the Israeli
popular imagination until the 1990s. The extensive media coverage of the
fiftieth anniversary of her death (1991), including a television program
and new retellings of her life story, finally shook up the modernist edifice
that had been built around Woolf in the Israeli mind. Significantly, an
interview with Professor Alice Shalvi highlighted Woolf's feminist take on
issues of sex and gender as never before.[75] Continuing through the 1990s,
this process can be said to have reached an apex with the apparent reversal in the fortunes of *Orlando*: in 1997 it was perceived in the media as the
"greatest of Woolf's books," as a work that deserves a high place in the
history of "postmodern fiction," because "women's history still cannot
be written—regrettably—except through flights of imagination and daring that transport us to the heights of fantasy, precisely as it is done in this
book."[76] This shift from modernism to postmodernism is evident in the
academic perception of Woolf, too, as the titles of recent dissertations
make clear;[77] her "feminism," however, yet awaits Israeli academic
expression.

Despite this belated recognition of Woolf's feminism in Israeli culture
(to be further explored in chapter 4.3), I argue in the following chapters
that Woolf's hard-won transition from her modernist "Ivory Tower," that
legacy of nineteenth-century symbolism, to a postmodernist blend of feminism and psychopolitics may be detected in the work of contemporary
Israeli novelists. And no wonder: the paradigmatically passionate (albeit

naive) feminist-political positions she adumbrated in her *later* work (*The Years, Three Guineas,* "The Leaning Tower," and *Between the Acts*) were generated as England was gearing up for a possible Nazi invasion, even for the destruction of Civilization with a capital *C*—a state of siege well familiar to Jews living then in Palestine and still alive in Israel a generation later.[78] Tragically, her warning was drowned out by the cacophony of the German Blitz. Yet her voice can be heard (even heeded)—some fifty years later—not only by contemporary scholars but by contemporary Israeli novelists, who cautiously apply it to their own circumstances.[79]

Among the modernist/postmodernists paradigms that concurrently animate and undermine Israeli literary feminism are the subversion of the modernist elitism of "pure art" by the pressure of historic exigencies and the use of Freudian insights in the forging of a specific female/feminist response to these exigencies (see chapters 6 and 8). One of Woolf's modernist paradigms, androgyny, proves to be more problematic. Despite its recent popularity among Israeli writers (both female and male), some of its social implications conflict with basic tenets of Jewish culture, past and present, as I will explore in chapters 4.3, 5, and 7. The most significant issue, however, to "benefit" from the Woolfian legacy is the intriguing relationship between feminist and nationalist ideologies. It is within this familiar postmodernist questioning that Woolf's subversion of her own modernism may serve as a crucial guide in our exploration of Israeli literature. As I will show in chapter 1, the meta-Zionist narrative, as it is now fashionably called, is the indispensable matrix for an understanding of the unhappy history of Israeli feminism. It is precisely because the authors assembled here "under one roof," so to speak, are both Zionists and feminists that they need to mask their feminist discontent. As part of the mask, of the compromise formation, "nation" is secondary to the analysis of "gender" in their novels. Yet its presence grows very gradually from being a muted background, hardly articulated, as in chapter 1, or sublimated into generalities (race and class), as in chapter 3, to the recording, in this study's later chapters (5–8), of a long inner conflict, lasting over thirty years, in which the national agenda only recently has been overcome—hesitantly as it may be—by gender considerations. Typical Woolfian themes, from the solidarity of the "Outsiders" to female critique of male aggression,[80] and from the deconstruction of gender roles via androgyny[81] to the use of insanity as social critique,[82] reverberate throughout this corpus—begging, I would argue, to be recognized not only for their similarity but also for their postmodernist difference.

The different spin that some of these analogies put on their European precursors derives from the special position contemporary Israel holds between the Western (European) intellectual tradition and its own political and cultural realities in a postcolonial, third world region. We should not be surprised, then, that the juxtaposition of the two narratives—the Israeli and the European (including the Anglo-American), the fictional and the theoretical—creates a third narrative, a critical retelling of Western literary feminism.

This retelling, while honing the analytical tools used in our textual analyses, also tests the validity of feminism's modernist/postmodernist schism in an arena that is itself both inside and outside the system. Aspiring to be part and parcel of the contemporary intellectual West yet suffering from an acute burden of the distant and not so distant Jewish past, Israeli culture is both of the "West" and tangential to it. As such, it constitutes a fertile testing ground, an Archimedean point from which one might be capable of unveiling (if not cutting) the Gordian knot of Western essentialism, feminism being one of its major points of contention. It thus helps frame the questions one may ask about the meaning and possibilities of Western notions of female subjectivity under sociopolitical constraints exemplified by the Israeli situation but not limited to it. At the same time, however, Israel's alignment with the West allows for a critique of the very systems of thought it has habitually borrowed and transformed, as my final chapters clearly bear out.

This conceptual framework is reflected structurally in the organization of the following chapters. A critical review of representative gender theories, from Beauvoir to Kristeva (chapter 2), and my rereading of Virginia Woolf's androgyny (chapter 4), as well as of her feminist psychopolitics (chapter 6.1), alternate with textual analysis of the story of Israeli literary feminism (chapters 1, 3, 5, 6, 7, 8), generating an intertwined narrative whose two strands both shed light on and critique each other.

I begin my entwined inquiry with a preliminary excursus: a look at the precarious emergence of Israeli subjectivity—both male and female—from the group identity typical of its earlier literature and a closer probing into the even more anxious fictional construction of women's autonomous subjects.

Chapter 1

Emerging Subjects

"All these men will be coming home from wars now," said Professor Barzel. "They'll all have learned to fight. The country will change again. Everything will become more professional, the fighting too. The individual won't count any more, only the stupid plural. The plural is always stupid. . . . "

"And what will be then, Elias?" asks Hulda worriedly.

"We will be then," said Elias, so quietly that they couldn't be sure they had heard right. "For better or worse, we will be."
—Shulamith Hareven, *City of Many Days*

The binary opposition anxiously projected into the future in this dialogue is age-old and universal—the individual versus the collective, the personal versus the national. What gives the almost stock opposition a particular twist is its clearly defined cultural and historical grounding—the experience of the protagonists of the novel *City of Many Days* (1972), in which Shulamith Hareven reconstructs life in Jerusalem under the British mandate, before and during World War II.[1] Against the background of that period's polyphony of voices, the characters "worriedly" foresee the forthcoming replacement of the "first-person singular" by the "first-person plural," the voice of the private self by that of the communal self. This is not a universally existential or otherwise symbolic construction. It is, rather, a fictional representation of a palpable, historically anchored reality—the notorious WE of the Palmach, the 1940s underground combat units of the Haganah (the Jewish military organization in prestate Palestine) that spearheaded the struggle for Israeli independence ("We are everywhere the first/ we, we, the Palmach," as their song proudly proclaimed).

By having her characters "explain away" the creation of this group self as the consequence of a historical moment (war and national strife) while they simultaneously grieve the loss of their individual voice, Hareven demonstrates some of the tensions underlying Israeli society from its very inception (see chapter 7 for further discussion). Situated as it is a few pages before the end of the narrative (182, 182–83), this dialogue may be read as an interpreting sign, almost a closure.[2] It retrospectively highlights the cultural code underpinning this novel—the troubled existence of the personal and the psychological within a society of national persuasion.

This inherent ambivalence is not unique to Hareven's novel. The national and ideological nature of Hebrew/Israeli letters is a critical axiom rarely questioned by scholars. Recently this strand of the literature has been labeled the "meta-Zionist narrative"; earlier, however, it was more often explained away by the attenuating circumstance of the national state of *siege,* a noun that has been prevalent in titles of Israeli literary studies.[3] It is the power of this national narrative that has been put on the analyst's couch, so to speak, in Israeli fiction of the last two to three decades. Yet this analysis, characteristic of a whole range of contemporary Israeli novels, has its limits too. As a rule, these novels come very close to introspection and self-analysis but exhibit ambivalence when approaching the "forbidden zone."

Indeed, although the intriguing history of the reception of modern psychology by Israeli culture has yet to be written, it is clear that, almost from the beginning, Zionist ideology and Freudian psychology were locked in uneasy coexistence. The tension between these two competing solutions to the Jewish malaise—both products of turn-of-the-century Vienna—has been traced back to the pioneers of the 1920s, who tried, although not very successfully, to reconcile them both.[4] Later historical developments (e.g. World War II, the Holocaust, the War of Independence, and the continuous state of siege in which Israel has found itself since its establishment in 1948) strengthened the national and collective identity of the young state while marginalizing Freudian or other modes of personal introspection practiced in the West. Recently, however, Israeli writers have begun to question and problematize this state of affairs by appropriating the hitherto "banned" luxury for their literary critique of national ideology; obviously, not without the ambivalence predictable in such cases, as I explore in more detail in chapter 6.

This is particularly true of a group of novels (mostly the product of the 1970s) that I have elsewhere suggested treating as "arrested" fictional autobiographies.[5] As a rule, novels classified in this category are not the paradigmatic first books of budding artists, nor are they recollections from the tranquillity of old age. Rather, these are the products of writers in their mid-career who try to make sense of their life and art by constructing a real or fictive self whose life story they tell in retrospect, as viewed from the vantage point of the present, of the narrating moment.[6] The distance between the real-life authors and their narrated subjects differs greatly from novel to novel. In addition, these are not necessarily first-person narratives. In fact, their surface heterogeneity is so great that I have proposed labeling them as a *modality* rather than a genre, thereby cutting across issues of presentation (fictional versus factual) or formal features (first- versus third-person narration).[7] Thus if I preserve use of the term *genre* in the following discussion it is for the sake of its long-discovered playful affinity with *gender*: for it is this genre (or modality) that holds the initial clue to the gender difference among the Israeli subjects that emerge from these fictional constructions.

1. The Masked Autobiography: Genre and Gender

If there is anything outstanding about these constructions, it is their challenge at large to some basic tenets of classical (often [nick]named metaphysical) theory of autobiography. Although a relatively young field (blossoming in the postmodern climate of the 1980s but having roots in the more serene 1950s), this theoretical field has quickly evolved along the lines of the modernist/postmodernist fault. Whereas earlier debates raged over the truth claims of the genre, measuring the text against its author's ostensible *bio* (fact and fiction, truth and design), later arguments predictably cast doubt—following Derrida—on the ontology of the subject itself (its *auto*), or—following Lacan—on its status outside or beyond the linguistic system (its *graphe*).[8] Some of the more celebrated titles along this route may reveal this development: what has begun as an inquiry into "Conditions and Limits of Autobiography" (Gusdorf, 1956) has evolved into de Man's subversive (and by now suspect) "Autobiography as Defacement" (1979), and later into *The Art of Self-Invention* (Eakin, 1985), which altogether challenges the "metaphysics of the subject," the unquestioned presupposition of classical autobiography.[9]

Interestingly, very little of all this postmodernist burden is palpable in the Israeli fictional autobiographies published during the same years. Generally, their subjects are neither threatened by Lacan's "alienation through language" nor by Derrida's "decentering."[10] Rather, what impinges on these personal narratives is the pressure of sociopolitical realities, condensed into particular historical moments. While this pressure, often in the shape of an ideological crisis, is the moving force behind the need to construct a self and fix it in language, it is also what "arrests" their attempts to live up to the ideals of Western autobiography—autonomy, agency, and individualism.

To the extent that these life stories collapse the conventional opposition between the individual and the national, the private and the public, they exhibit a certain "pull towards ideology," an impulse that Janet Gunn sees as a "threat" to "experiential autobiography":

> The pull towards ideology is all the more difficult for autobiography to resist because the ideological impulse has so much in common with the autobiographical impulse. Both arise from . . . a need for acknowledging a meaningful orientation in a world. . . and both represent an effort to take hold of something in the process of vanishing or disintegrating.[11]

Whether or not this pull toward ideology is conceived as a threat or a blessing is, of course, a matter of one's politicocultural conviction. The interesting question, however, is precisely under what conditions the ideological impulse does compete with or take over the psychologically oriented autobiography. Gunn does not ask this question, possibly because she treats—like most critics before her—only the tradition of Western male autobiography. Yet it is in theories of female and non-Western autobiography that a redefinition of the genre has been tacitly taking shape.

Corroborating the claims of certain strands in gender psychology,[12] these theorists see the female subject as relational rather than autonomous. They claim that woman's identity—in life and on paper—is mediated through "others," that her "self" is communal and collective rather than purely individual.[13] The logical conclusion of these psychological suggestions is perhaps Shoshana Felman's recent theorizing of the "resistance to autobiography" she traces in the *mothers* of feminism—from Woolf to Beauvoir to Adrienne Rich.[14] Yet we should not forget, by contrast, the challenging question posed by Domna Stanton in her pioneering essay, "Autogynography: Is the Subject Different?"[15] in which she argued that *textually*, she could not find any distinctive female signature in autobiography, despite fundamental gender differences. Whatever the case, the argument for gender difference (and there is room for dissension, see note 48), opens up a two-fold hornet's nest: 1. Is the gender difference we observe "essentialist" or "culturalist," constitutional or acquired? and 2. What is the effect of this difference on the presuppositions of "classical" Western autobiography (as defined, say, by Gusdorf, Olney, Lejeune, Spengemann, Jay, Eakin et al.)?

That these questions are directly related to the postmodernist debate over the subject is no doubt clear. If gender difference can be shown to be culturally/historically/ideologically determined, then the ontology of the subject in general should be similarly understood. And if features of the "female subject" can be found in male autobiographies (as Germaine Brée has claimed for Michel Leiris and Roland Barthes) and vice versa, then perhaps some of our most cherished (essentialist) concepts should be reconsidered.[16]

To this theoretical debate Israeli fictional autobiographies may add a new dimension, for they problematize not only conventional oppositions deemed inherent to the genre but also some popularly accepted gender distinctions. Surprisingly, there is a clear correspondence between certain aspects of the so-called typical female autobiography and contemporary Israeli fictional autobiographies, and, unless all Israeli autobiographers are women, this fact alone should cast grave doubts on essentialist definitions of gender, both within and without the genre. Indeed, by demonstrating how gender boundaries may be crossed over—given a similar pressure of sociocultural conditions—this material will no doubt contribute to cultural definitions of gender.[17]

To complicate matters even further, there is hardly a woman among the Israeli (fictional) autobiographers I have in mind. This absence is doubly surprising in view of the intimately autobiographical Hebrew prose written by women at the beginning of the century.[18] In this they did not differ, of course, from their sister autobiographers in English, and perhaps the world over.[19] But this resemblance is only superficial, pertaining to noncanonic texts. For unlike the English tradition, the Hebrew canon has featured a long list of women poets but no women novelists. As I argue in the introduction, until the last decade only few women excelled in fiction, mostly in the short forms (stories and novellas), and mainly in the presumably "softer" lyrical-impressionistic mode.

Does this mean that we have come full circle to bedrock gender differences? I suspect not. Rather, as early as the turn of the century women were cast in a well-defined "feminine" role by the arbiters of the renaissance of Hebrew (see Eliezer Ben Yehudah's invitation quoted in the introduction). It is thus not surprising that the breakthrough of women into the canon took place—two decades later—in poetry, where it was easier to accommodate the stereotypic ideal cut out for them by their male patrons. It was perhaps also easier to write verse, given its poetic license (or freedom), without the training in classical Hebrew traditionally reserved for males. It is no coincidence that the first modern Hebrew prose writer, Dvora Baron, had been raised "as a son," that is, instructed in the sacred sources, by her father, a rabbi. Indeed, the similarity to Virginia Woolf's home training by her father is not accidental—the two women belong to the same generation, born only five years apart in a decade of transition in women's education ("by 1884, women had the right to do degree-level work at both major British universities," say Sandra M. Gilbert and Susan Gubar in *No Man's Land*).[20] The divergence in their later development is therefore instructive: Sir Lesley refused to let go of his daughter, denying her the privilege of academic education (and personal independence) enjoyed by her brothers—a fact she never forgot nor forgave. By contrast, the young Baron was allowed to leave home and pursue her course of studies in the "big city," soon making her way to the Promised Land, where she was hailed as the first accomplished woman writer in Hebrew.[21]

Still a different rationalization for women's generic choices was offered by the contemporary writer Shulamith Hareven, for whom woman's life rather than language seems to be the problem: "When I had babies I wrote poems in between diapers; when they went to school I had time enough for short stories; only when they grew up could I take the time to write a novel."[22] As attractively antiessentialist as this formulation sounds, it has at least one problem—its resemblance to Virginia Woolf's explication of the *opposite* phenomenon, the novelistic tradition of English literature. Citing Florence Nightingale's complaint that "women never have an half hour . . . that they can call their own," and building on her own call for "a room of one's own," Woolf goes on to claim, "Still it would be easier to write prose and fiction there [in the common sitting room] than to write poetry or a play. Less concentration is required."[23] From this it is but a short step to recasting this social circumstance as a universal, perhaps an (culturally?) essential, mark of female creativity: "Women's books should be shorter, more concentrated than those of men, and framed so that they do not need long hours of steady uninterrupted work. For interruptions there will always be."[24]

These diverging evaluations are not arbitrary; they reflect different traditions and in their difference remind us once more of the historical relativity of our horizon of expectations about genre and gender. For it is only within the particular historical poetics of Hebrew literature that the mastery of prose fiction in general and fictional autobiography in particular (rather than the elevated poetic forms of the Greek and Latin legacy) would be deemed a desirable conquest for women writers.

As it transpired, it took more than half a century for this conquest to begin to materialize. Indeed, it is in the last two decades that a number of women made the shift from short stories to novels, some of which are of almost epic proportions. Until very recently, however, none of these narratives came close to the fictional autobiography, even in its "arrested" form, as found among Israeli male writers.[25] I would nevertheless argue that at least some of these novels are nothing less than "masked autobiographies," reflecting—in different degrees of displacement—their authors' struggles with the question of the female subject.

There is nothing new, of course, in this literary device. It fits into a larger category of palimpsestic writing, the one attributed by Gilbert and Gubar, in their pioneering study, to works by women writers from Jane Austin to Emily Dickinson, "whose surface designs conceal or obscure deeper, less accessible (and less socially acceptable) levels of meaning."[26] The fictional autobiography is a special case of this general class, continuing well into the twentieth century, as novels by Virginia Woolf would readily illustrate.[27] Unlike her, however, Israeli women writers don a much "thicker" mask: they transpose their autobiographies, hiding behind historical displacement.

I first suspected that this was the case when I saw the term *feminist* on the jacket of *Gei oni*, a historical novel, published in 1982, whose narrated period is 1882. The transparent anachronism of the usage set me on the detective trail.[28] I soon discovered a pattern. Several recent novels by Israeli women are in fact novels of education, in which contemporary concerns are projected onto "liberated" heroines of another time or another place. In fact, one can point to a process of regression in the choice of historical settings, from Jerusalem of the 1920s and 1930s in *City of Many Days* (1972, quoted in the epigraph to this chapter)—a period the author, Shulamith Hareven, could not have experienced directly, since she arrived in Palestine as a child only in 1940—through Palestine of 1882 in Shulamit Lapid's *Gei Oni* (1982), to the vaguely and poetically defined European past (seventeenth century) in Amalia Kahana-Carmon's novel(la), "The Bridge of the Green Duck" (in *Lema'lah bemontifer* [Up in Montifer], 1984). However, this regression is counterbalanced by a diametrically opposite *progression* in the "feminist" consciousness of the protagonists of these novels. As a group, they move from traditional, essentialist gender roles in a patriarchal society to a utopian new womanhood, paradoxically projected back into the historico-mythical past. (A fourth novel, Ruth Almog's *Shorshei 'Avir* [Roots of Air], 1987, both continues and transcends this narrative modality, as I argue in chapter 8.)

If this analysis is correct, then these writers are still at the stage that Carolyn Heilbrun charted out almost two decades ago in *Reinventing Womanhood*: "Women are only recently taking up autobiography in the attempt to show themselves . . . (though the autobiographies are often in the form of novels)."[29]

But why should this be so? Why should contemporary Israeli women be incapable of facing their personal selves directly? Moreover, why can't they, to quote Heilbrun again, "imagine women characters with even the autonomy they themselves have achieved"?[30] Why isn't one of these *Bildungsromane* cast in the mold of the *Künstlerroman*? And why isn't there even one "portrait of an artist" among these novels of development?[31] Or at least why isn't there even one Hebrew equivalent of Lily Briscoe, that self-portrait of the artist in Woolf's *To the Lighthouse*? Is it because of the precariousness of these writers' self-image as "artists"? Or is it because this aspect of their recently gained autonomy is subsumed by national—and perhaps more basic—concerns and achievements?

The answer is, "Yes," I'm afraid, to both questions. The first will take us back to woman's problematic place in the Jewish tradition, which by and large has all but excluded her from participating in man's public roles.[32] The second yes, on the other hand, will highlight the *cross-gender* correspondence apparent in the Israeli corpus. For, just like their male counterparts, the four novels of development (or masked autobiographies) mentioned above are governed by national concerns; they are motivated by sociopolitical pressures and organized around major historical events. The latter function as pivotal moments in the heroines' "voyages in,"[33] thereby embedding their subjective experience within a larger, and presumably more demanding, national narrative.

2. What Does A Woman Want? Gei Oni *and the Feminist Romance*

To demonstrate the above claim, this chapter offers an analysis of the second (by order of publication) of these masked autobiographies, the highly popular historical novel *Gei Oni* (1982). Its fascination stems partially from the unprecedented manner in which it engages issues of gender and national ideology. One must add, however, that this is done by a dis-

Shulamit Lapid

placement to the nineteenth century, to the beginning of the Zionist movement and the modern resettlement of the Land of Israel.

Stylistically, this is not a novel of great sophistication. Written in a rather coarse realistic style, it is crowded with dialogues and interior monologues that are barely distinguishable (from each other as well as from the narrative voice); the third-person narration weaves its way through a maze of "relationships" that easily rivals those of any Hollywood or TV melodrama. Nothing is implied here, not even the characters' most intimate reflections. Thoughts, emotions, ideology, and popular psychology are all evenly spread out, lit by the strong flashlight of the authorial voice, as if illuminated by the bright Israeli sun.

Yet despite its limitations (and perhaps because of them—the book was often classified as a novel for young readers), *Gei Oni* caught the imagination of Israeli readership. In the first place, it played right into the wave of nostalgia that swept the country in the 1980s, when the first centenary of the earliest Jewish *aliyah* (immigration) to Palestine was celebrated. Indeed, Shulamit Lapid—until then a rather obscure short story writer (1969, 1974, 1979), but since then a prolific novelist, dramatist, and literary activist—wrote her first novel *in anticipation* of 1982. In that year the Galilean settlement Rosh Pinah, whose earlier name had been Gei Oni (a hebraization of the Arabic name Ja'uni), celebrated one hundred years of its existence. Judging by the reception the book enjoyed, the timing was right; readers exhibited great hunger for the richly documented panorama of that distant past, filtered as it was through a fictional prism.

This was not the only reason, however. Readers were no doubt responding to the novelty of being introduced to a "serious" historical reconstruction through the eyes and mind of Fania—a young Russian immigrant who joins Gei Oni in the opening scene and remains the central consciousness through which the narrative is focalized to the end of the novel.

But why should this be considered such a novelty? Wasn't the pioneer movement—indeed, the Zionist ethos in general—supposed to have promoted the equality of women? In fact, wasn't the "woman question" one of the basic issues debated—and deemed solved—by the early communes and kibbutzim?

The answer is yes, of course, to all of the above; but only as long as we remember to add the qualifier—in theory. As pointed out in the introduction (section 2), recent research has shown that, in practice, neither the early settlers nor the second wave of immigrants at the turn of the century had transcended the patriarchal norms of their home communities in Europe.[34] And as Shulamit Lapid herself has recounted, she could find no historical model for her heroine in the archival records of Gei Oni, later named Rosh Pinah.[35]

As the book jacket states, the names of those "giant women" who were part and parcel of the early settlement wave "are absent from history books because the records of the saviors of the motherland list only men." Even among the figures of the second aliyah Lapid could make use of one exceptional personality—Manya Schohat (1879–1959; see introduction). Fania had to be invented, then: a woman who "did not know she was a feminist" but whom the contemporary reader recognizes as such.

We are in a better position now to appreciate the source of the great appeal that *Gei Oni* exerted on its readership. The book was a bold attempt to do justice to the founding mothers, to rectify by fiction the wrongs of a (male-dominated) national narrative. And it was no small challenge. For how does one create a narrative frame that would authentically preserve the patriarchal way of life of the 1880s while at the same time accommodating a fictive protagonist whose own norms would satisfy contemporary "feminist" expectations?

The solution came in the form of a collage, welding together two novelistic genres—the first-settlers epic and the romantic melodrama. On one level, *Gei Oni* is a typical settlement drama, almost a western ("The Wild East," as one of its reviewers labeled it),[36] realistically depicting the struggles against all odds of the small Galilean group in the early 1880s. The chief antagonist of this plot is nature itself, the mythical mother earth. In this story she is no welcoming bride; as we join the narrative she has been holding back her gifts for two consecutive years. Severe drought has chased away most of the pioneers, leaving behind a few tenacious and idealistic families, including that of Yehi'el, the male protagonist of the novel.

On another level, this is a typically euphoric "heroine's text," as defined by Nancy Miller.[37] It is a predictable love story whose models are not only the canonic texts adored by the protagonist (*Anna Karenina*, just imported from Russia, and books by Jane Austen, Fania's favorite; see p. 161), but also popular romances à la Rudolf Valentino that Shulamit Lapid herself ridiculed in one of her journalistic forays.[38] Despite her ridicule, Lapid utilizes the popular genre with great dexterity: Fania is the self-conscious budding young woman who struggles to preserve her independent spirit while falling in love with her enigmatic "dark prince." The latter, for his part, is "handsome like the prince of Wales" (34, 69, 85), "wise like king

Solomon" (117), and the envy of all women. Predictably, he is also proud, reticent, and distant—the very qualities Lapid has enumerated in her brief article ("preferably a widower/divorcé/bachelor, thirty years old, tanned, dark hair, a sneering look")—which means, of course, that although he falls in love with Fania's looks the moment he sees her, he keeps the secret to himself. Since neither the reader nor Fania gets to know the truth before half the story is over, a chain of romantic misunderstandings and jealousies constitute the better part of the plot. To add insult to injury, there are echoes of Daphne du Maurier's *Rebecca*: Fania is "welcomed" to her "prince's" abode by the picture of his deceased wife, whose two sisters are conveniently present to evoke her beauty and otherworldly qualities whenever they can—all of which naturally makes the denouement that much sweeter.

But before we get there, a question arises: Haven't we wandered too far afield from "founding mothers" and "inadvertent feminism," as I have elsewhere called it?[39] Can the conventions of the romance, of the heroine's euphoric text, which Lapid herself declared "obsolete," indulge a fighting, independent spirit in the mold of Manya Schohat? Hardly, of course. Lapid could not have sustained her model *and* satisfy her feminist quest had she kept the model intact. Nor could she write a true historical novel (fully omniscient narration, authorial perspective into general historical processes) while staying as close to Fania's consciousness as she did. She resolved the first of these problems, at least, by splicing the two models together just at their respective points of cracking. In other words, the meeting ground between them is that of deviation, where their generic conventions are violated. As we shall soon see, it is from the intersection of two *frustrated* genres that a new hybrid model emerges, one that generously accommodates contemporary expectations.

To begin with, Fania's romance deviates from its imputed model in one crucial detail—its denouement does not coincide with the closure of the novel. Nor does it lead to a marriage proposal or an engagement. For all this typical "heroine's text" takes place *within* the boundaries of a marriage. And our two protagonists are atypical as well: Fania is not only an orphan, as suggested by Lapid in the quote above ("an English orphan, preferably penniless"); she is a sixteen-year-old survivor of a Russian pogrom (the infamous Ukrainian pogroms of 1881–1882 that are credited with inspiring the first wave of immigration to Palestine), who finds refuge in the Promised Land, accompanied by an old uncle, a deranged brother, and a baby—the initially unwanted fruit of her rape in that pogrom.

Yehi'el, who happens to see her upon her arrival in Jaffa, is a twenty-six-year-old widower and a father of two, one of the few courageous souls left in the nearly desolate Gei Oni.

As the narrative opens, we are privileged to Fania's reflections after a hasty betrothal in Jaffa. While Yehi'el's motives are not disclosed, it soon becomes clear that for Fania this is not merely a marriage of convenience but also a marriage of appearances. Upon arrival in Gei Oni she insists on separate sleeping arrangements: a rather unexpected turn within the conventions of the romance, but a perfectly plausible step for a psychologically conceived character still smarting from her traumatic past. The attentive reader will notice, however, a structural and symbolic analogy in this otherwise realistically motivated action. It is not only the human bride who denies her husband her favors; because of the continuing drought, the fertilization of mother earth is also thwarted.

There is a perfect symmetry, then, between the two plots—the psychological and the mythic, the romantic and the historico-national. In both the male principle is initially defeated and no consummation is possible. This symmetry does not escape Yehi'el himself, who, unaware of Fania's trauma, reacts to her refusal by saying: "When you change your mind, let me know. I ask for favors only from the land" (*'adama*, lit. "earth," fig. "land"; 45). To get the story rolling again, both female protagonists must give in. It is against the background of the long-awaited rains (117, 121, 123)—a pioneers' version of the notorious Romantic storm?—that the passionate (and confessional) reunion between Fania and Yehi'el finally takes place (119–128) and the euphoric plot seems to have reached its happy ending.

But not quite. For in the second part of the narrative the settlement plot comes back with a vengeance, leaning heavily on the delicate balance of the new romantic attachment. The Galilee or mother earth (or perhaps the pioneering quest itself) "pressures" the human subjects of this story, limiting their freedom of choice and forcing them into its mold. But, unlike her predecessors, Lapid is not willing to accept the verdict of the national narrative, of the Zionist "dream of redemption, burning like fire in the bones" (103–4, 144, 175). She does not have Fania "skip over her own self," as does Sara, the heroine of *A City of Many Days* (see chapter 5, this volume) but rather allows her to develop her female subjectivity despite and against the pressures of the collective vision, with all the tragic consequences of this choice. In so doing, Lapid has unwittingly blended her two models into a third one, a bildungsroman that may be rather fanciful for the 1880s but totally satisfying to readers one hundred years later.

I have elsewhere suggested naming this hybrid model after Erich Neumann's 1952 analysis of *Amor and Psyche*, labeled "The Psychic Development of the Feminine."[40] The heuristic convenience of this choice stems from the story's origins, as Neumann brilliantly shows, in the myth of the Great Mother, the archetypal mother earth. It is this archetype that has nourished all myths—old and young—of a return to the motherland, Zionism not excluded. And it is this nexus of images and metaphors that has been recently questioned in the attempt to explain the problematic place of woman in the Zionist narrative.

Only a few years before the publication of *Gei Oni* writer Lesley Hazleton deconstructed the familiar Zionist image of sons-lovers returning to motherland/earth *livnot ulehibanot bah*, "to build and be built in her" (notice the effect of Hebrew's genderized grammer: "land" as well as city, country, state, are all grammatically feminine in Hebrew!). She did this by a literal, almost ad absurdum analysis of the psychoanalytic ramifications of this language:

> But while Zion played Jocasta to the male pioneers' Oedipus, where was the Agamemnon to the women pioneers' Electra? What value could all this libidinous attraction have for them? What archetypal images could it arouse in a woman's mind? What role was there for women in this scenario of sons and fathers fertilizing the motherland?[41]

As startling as this query is on first reading, it loses some of its persuasive power once we recognize one small oversight: except in songs, has Zion ever played Jocasta to her returning sons? *Was* she a welcoming bride? Or has she been mostly an earlier Jungian archetype—the Great Mother?

The difference is crucial. In the primitive myth the female figure had not yet undergone what Neumann calls "the process of secondary personalization"; she had not yet functioned as a human representation, but as an impersonal blind principle of fertility.[42] In fact, this is the *negative* aspect of the great mother, the "Terrible Mother" that Neumann has unearthed in the ancient myths and fertility rituals.[43] In these myths the male had more to lose than to gain, for the impregnation of the female principle was achieved only through the perennial death of her "consort," her son/lover/savior, later incarnated in the myths of Tammuz, Osiris, and Dionysus.

We can now return to the plot of *Gei Oni* and discern that its scenario does not support Hazleton's feminist worries. Here it is not Electra who is excluded from the game but rather Oedipus. The deep structure of the historical plot is therefore not a Freudian triad but an earlier, Neumannesque dyad, that of the Terrible Mother and her doomed consort. In Yehi'el's failure to conquer mother earth (he eventually dies of malaria), primitive fertility myths play themselves out once more. The essence of myth, we are reminded, is endless repetition. Standing alone, then, the settlement script would have come to an impasse, if not for its dynamic intersection with the second plot, the heroine's text.

In this text Yehi'el is a "passive accomplice" in Fania's long and often bewildered search for her own identity as a woman and as an autonomous subject. As in the myth of Amor and Psyche, the main psychological thrust of our story is the liberation of the female protagonist from the yoke of the social norms imposed on her by Aphrodite-like representatives of the community. "Psyche's act of rebellion," says Neumann in his interpretation of *Amor and Psyche* (the Hebrew translation of which happened to appear in 1981!), "signals the end of the mythic era. . . . From now on it is the era of human love, when the human soul knowingly undertakes all fateful decisions for its own life" (60).

It is interesting to note that Neumann speaks about the maturity of the human soul in general. That this process is symbolized for him precisely in the process of individuation of the feminine principle should come as no surprise. After all, it is the latter that has to liberate itself from the blind collective principle of fertility and veer toward the "light"—the archetypal symbol of masculine consciousness in Neumann's (as well as others') conceptual system (68). Although this genderized reading has its problems (particularly for feminist critics),[44] it can readily accommodate the *Bildung* plot of our story. Fania "develops" from a scathed teenager who acts under duress, and runs away from a new relationship at the first eruption of pain and frustration, to a mature woman who stays on, consciously choosing to realize the pioneer's dream of her dead husband-lover.

Predictably, Fania achieves her independence by a process of individuation in which she transcends the norms dictated to her by mother figures who try to teach her "her natural place" (117, 144, 175, 234). Like Psyche, she reaches maturity after a series of tasks she undertakes to save her husband and home from the devastation wrought by mother nature. We find her breaking into the male-dominated world of commerce, political discussion, even armed self-defense. At the same time, she does not deny her femininity (cf. Psyche's care to preserve her beauty), her difference from the male world surrounding her: the fun of lighthearted chatter, good romantic novels, some childlike pranks (104, 144, 175). Her personal code is defined, then, as the freedom to choose the best of both worlds, to move freely from one to the other in a kind of Woolfian androgyny.[45] Although we are never told precisely how, even motherhood, that (unsurmountable?) hurdle of liberal feminism, poses no serious problem, somehow being woven into Fania's busy schedule. This heroine fully embodies cross-gender equality as she shuttles between home and "world," Gei Oni and Jaffa, taking care of husband and children while trading, gypsylike, on the road.

As for Yehi'el, he turns out to be just as exceptional. Although he does not fully approve of Fania's androgynous tendencies, he does not stand in her way, which is more than can be said for any of his peers (109, 172–73, 188, 236). The result is a virtual reversal of conventional gender roles (with Yehi'el staying close to home and Fania going into the world) and, more important—the transformation of Fania from a child-bride into a mature wife-companion, fully aware of her choices, sexual as well as social.

It is only natural, then, that as the novel comes to a close, and Yehi'el succumbs to exhaustion and malaria, the reader is ready to embrace Fania's Bildung as a necessary training for her ultimate task—the perpetuation of the historico-mythical quest. But, in an ironic twist on Hazleton's critique, Fania, although ready to undertake the role, perceives it as something alien, not her own script:

> Should she sell their home? Driving Yehi'el out of his dream? This home and this land were the purpose of his life. Once again fate had decreed that she realize others' dreams. Had she ever had her own dreams? But perhaps everyone is like this? Everyone realizes someone else's dream? (256)

Is this a feminist protest, lamenting the lot of women in general? Or is this a specific charge against the androcentric Zionist dream? And who is the "everyone" of the final questions: Women? All people? The lines seem to blur here, leaving the reader with a sense of an unfocused grievance. What was read throughout the novel as a critique of a male-engendered national ideology now takes on an existential turn, possibly hiding behind the "human condition." Fania's frustration—"her father's dream of rebirth turned into a sacred insanity that was now consuming her youthful years, her life" (102, cf. 142, 194, 202–3, 226)—inadvertently brings to the fore a contradiction that may have been inherent in the Zionist enterprise from its inception, but was rarely made overt before the 1970s (especially before the so-called post-Zionist scholarship of the last decade)—the potential incommensurability between private salvation and communal redemption.[46] However, by marking as negative the "dreams" of the two father figures in her life, in language that clearly echoes Beauvoir's charge that women "still dream through the dreams of men,"[47] Lapid may be lending this general critique a feminist coloring, problematizing the role of the individual subject—woman in particular—within the framework of collective ideology (whether socialist or nationalist or both).

Yet this potential feminist protest loses its edge just as we might expect it to fully materialize. Fania's shift to universal generalizations ("Everyone realizes someone else's dream?") illustrates Beauvoir's complaint about women's "deep-seated tendencies towards complicity" (*The Second Sex*, xxiv–xxv), which we explore in more detail in the next chapter. In the language of contemporary feminism it is an attempt (prevalent in women's life writing, as demonstrated by Heilbrun in *Writing a Woman's Life*) to rationalize away the justified rage against a social system that in the guise of a new ideology has reinscribed traditional double standards toward women. More often than not Fania's feelings remain unexpressed. Typically, her frustration and hurt are reported to the reader ("Fania wanted to scream: And I? And I? but she kept silent" [176, cf. 105, 144, 164, 187, 217]), but they always remain confined within the seething turmoil of her narrated inner monologues. When they are actually verbalized, it is only in the framework of private female discourse. Fania may have penetrated male praxis, but not its *public discourse*. The prevailing ideology remains untouched by her feminist critique. In the final analysis Fania's quest for subjectivity inscribes itself only as a comment on the margins of an androcentric system.

We should not be surprised, then, that Lapid does not give her heroine the chance to try to make it on her own. In the last page the plot of the euphoric text prevails, promising a romantic betrothal beyond the boundaries of the book. Sasha, an old acquaintance, himself a survivor of the Ukrainian pogroms, reappears, asking permission "to help and be helped" (a phrase clearly reminiscent of the Zionist quest "to build and be built"). With this new beginning the novel reverts to its two original models: the mytho-historical and the romantic. Subjective experience is again embedded in Jewish collectivity, symbolized throughout the story by the legendary Phoenix ("This is what we Jews do. Start all over again. Again. And again. And again."), only to be overtaken by an old/new romantic closure: " 'I need you, Fania! Will you allow me to help you?' Fania looked at him wondering. Then she thought that if he hugged her, her head would barely reach his shoulder. And then her eyes filled with tears" (266).

One need not be a devotee of Harlequin romances to recognize the style. The New Hebrew Woman, to the extent that she is constructed in this text, collapses back into a romantic figure. As such, this popular novel, Lapid's first (she was born in 1935), may serve as the most extreme example not only of women's masked autobiography but of what I would call the feminist romance as well. Through this hybrid form a compromise formation is worked out between feminist aspirations for masculinist autonomy—the very Enlightenment ideal pronounced fictive by some and labeled individualist by others—and stereotyped feminine patterns of psychological dependency, generally expressed through romantic attachment. My emphasis here is on *stereotyped*, since these narratives rarely question this received dichotomy nor the hierarchical value judgment it implies.[48]

As mentioned above, there is nothing new or particularly Israeli about this conflict, nor even about the specific novelistic form it takes. Still, the displacement of the feminist concerns of *contemporary* authors that transpires in these historical narratives tells us about the cultural status of Israeli feminism. As late as the 1980s the feminist agenda still collided with the larger political issues that have always been at the center of attention. Israeli women writers were therefore trapped in a double bind. Unwilling to relegate themselves to marginalized "women's journalism" or "female thematics," they were obliged to enter the mainstream "in disguise." More often than not they registered their critique of the national narrative vicariously, by having their presumably historical protagonists struggle with the national agenda of their distant past.

In the case of *Gei Oni* there are obviously no direct biographical ties between the author, our contemporary, and the pioneers of a century ago. (Except, perhaps, for the fact that Lapid was born in Romania, the native country of some of the settlers in Rosh Pinah.) But at the same time her authorial intention is quite transparent: to project into the historical past feminist concerns and expectations that present-day Israeli reality cannot satisfy. This intention grows suspiciously palpable when we consider a peculiar technical aspect of the novel. Although it is told in a straightforward third-person narration, information is mostly limited to that which is available to the heroine. Fania is not only the protagonist of the action but also its point of focalization. Her inner world is too close to that of the narrator (to the exclusion of all other figural perspectives) to do justice to the narration of a *historical* novel. This lack of (ironic or other) distance, as well as the narrator's narrow point of view, undermines the work's claim to be a purely historical narrative, generating the impression that the development of the heroine's consciousness is a projection of a contemporary bildungsroman, or spiritual autobiography, masqueraded as a more acceptable genre. Not unlike her nineteenth-century English precursors, analyzed by Gilbert and Gubar (1979), Lapid obviously felt that a feminist subjectivity would not be socially acceptable to her Israeli audience in the early 1980s; they *would* accept it as a historical projection but find it difficult to digest as a realistic proposition for the here and now.

This palimpsestic layering is not, however, the only feature shared by the novels under discussion. They also share an unarticulated doubt—usually evidenced only in their plot structures—concerning the limits of the feminist project. Conceived purely in terms of Enlightenment-type emancipation, this project is generally represented here as a modernist attempt to synthesize (rather than deconstruct) the two sides of the coin of gender difference. The heroines of these narratives try to bridge the two terms of the by now familiar binary opposition—to be individualist yet relational (Offen), autonomous yet interdependent (Johnson), separate yet bonded (Flax). In short, they try to live by the popular maxim, conventionally attributed to Freud—the ability to work and love.

"The communal life of human beings had, therefore, a two-fold foundation: the compulsion to work, which was created by external necessity, and the power of love," says Freud.[49] Indeed a poignant definition of human mental health and happiness! Yet despite its attraction, some caution is called for here. For immediately following the inclusive language of his opening statement ("human beings") Freud's gender essentialism reasserts itself, positing two different love objects for the two sexes: "[The power of love] made the man unwilling to be deprived of his sexual object—the woman, and made the woman unwilling to be deprived of that part of herself which had been separated off from her—her child."[50]

Viewed from this perspective, it could be claimed that by adopting Freud's well-known universalized slogan the feminist revolution was using Freud against himself, reading him—in the best revolutionary tradition—"against the grain," against his ubiquitous sexual double standard. A new feminist subjectivity, abundantly propagated in the West in the 1960s and 1970s, was to be forged by appropriating a Freudian androcentric equilibrium between work and *erotic* (rather than *maternal*) love. The effect of this goal on the position of motherhood within early feminist thought is well known, and Israel is no exception: the low profile of motherhood in the early stages of the Israeli feminist romance (and masked autobiography) is a remarkable phenomenon to which we will later return. Yet even this erasure does not seem to solve the problem. In the final analysis the Israeli protagonists of our corpus experience work and love more as a dichotomy than as an equilibrium.

What I am arguing, then, is that a close reading of the deep structure of the narratives under consideration reveals their authors' (perhaps unconscious) distrust of their heroines' ability to live up to the work and love ideal of classical feminism. The resulting ambiguity puts them squarely within the category of "minority discourse," in the specific definition that Deleuze and Guattari give to this concept.[51] These authors' unresolved tension between subscribing to or undermining their own agenda, as well as their techniques of masquerade and displacement, are typical, according to Deleuze and Guattari, of minority literature. The latter is obviously defined not by its numerical value but rather by its distance from the base of political power, thus making it applicable to the numerous postcolonial others (women included) theorized by Homi Bhabha.[52] We shall later see, however, that the specific feminist conflict between aspiring to and subverting the hegemonic order and the canon preserving it (in this case constructions of psychological and/or ideological [national] subjectivity) is in fact the legacy of Virginia Woolf's modernist feminism, with all its inner contradictions (see chapter 6). But before we get there, a deeper probe into our Israeli corpus is in order.

The first item on the agenda is the way in which these Israeli novelists respond to the conflict aroused by the minority position of their feminist romance. As a rule, their solutions differ in two respects: in the understanding of the "source" of the conflict (whether it is internal, that is, conceptually or psychologically gender-specific, or external, that is, sociocultural or deriving from national circumstances) and in the degree to which the conflict is finally perceived as solvable or at least negotiable. As such, these narratives address a question that is crucial to the postmodernist debate over gender identity and sexual difference. The perceptions they offer vary, as do the limits and boundaries they envision for feminist emancipation.

The ambivalence expressed in Shulamit Lapid's first novel obviously reflected her own ambivalence as well. To judge from her public pronouncements, she then neither considered herself a feminist nor believed in "women's literature" as a category per se. At the same time, she has mostly limited herself to "women's subjects." With one novel as exception (1984), her subsequent work features female protagonists. Her first play, *Abandoned Property* (1987), explored the psychological dynamics between mother and daughters in a broken family on the margins of the social system, while her second play engaged the contemporary issue of surrogate mothering by deftly rewriting a biblical model (Abraham, Sarah, and Hagar; *Surrogate Mother*, 1990). By 1989, however, in an interview outside Israel, this "happily married mother" (by her own admission) described herself as "small, delicate, and becoming more and more aggressive" at her "ripe fifty-four."[53] The timing of this "transformation" is not arbitrary. In 1987 the Israel Women's Network hosted the International Women Writers' Conference, an event that no doubt contributed to the "awakening" of some of the writers discussed in this study.[54]

By the end of the decade Lapid had resolved her ambivalence by shifting from the "canonic" historical narrative and the female euphoric text (the romantic betrothal plot), to a different genre—the spinster detective story. In a series of popular thrillers,[55] all set in a contemporary provincial town, she has constructed a New *Israeli* Woman, a lower middle-class journalist whose first priority is work and for whom love is divorced from matrimony. Thirty-something years old and single, Lizzie Badiḥi, who is proud of her "professionalism" and work ethic, is not a descendant of the New Hebrew Woman of the Zionist revolution (Fania and her like); rather, she is a throwback to the turn-of-the-century spinster detective of English literature.[56] In Lapid's version of this genre motherhood is rejected firsthand ("I have seen my sisters," Lizzie explains), and masculine autonomy is appropriated without any equivocation. The novel's final question, repeated twice, "What do you want, Lizzie?" reads like a wry parody of Freud's notorious question "What does a woman want?" What this woman wants is apparently work and a new kind of romance (male-modeled, of course, no strings attached). The latter makes its appearance—once again—only at the close of the story. Like Fania, Lizzie gets her reward in the form of a "dark prince," updated for the 1980s: a tawny, handsome, rich, and worldly divorcé whose timely "information" rescues Lizzie from the imminent danger of . . . losing her job.[57]

It is hard to ascertain whether the simplicity with which sexual difference is overcome in these plots is an indicator of naive conceptualization or a projection of a collective fantasy (given the noncanonic nature of the genre, on one hand, and the totally *un*autobiographic characterization of the heroine, on the other).[58] Whatever the case, it is clear that the feminist romance produced here is an essentialist mirror image of its masculinist counterpart. While the sociocultural antagonism it may encounter is given cursory attention, any possible complication by psychosexual difference is blissfully ignored.[59]

The same goes for some of Lapid's later short stories in which romance is replaced by aggression. A straightforward reversal of roles in a violent rape scene, for example, is the subject of "Neḥitat 'oness" (Forced Landing; published in English as "The Bed" but better rendered as "Forced Entry").[60] The painful experience of what I would call "counter-rape" is focalized through the eyes of the victim—a young *man*, whose bewildered incomprehension is utterly ignored by his female attacker. Gender difference is again turned upside down: here the female grotesquely "redeems" her alterity by donning the dark face of masculine subjectivity, aggression.[61]

More sophisticated dramatizations of these issues are to come in the following chapters. But in order to do justice to their rich fictional webs I need to pick up the thread of theoretical narrative. The question I expect it to answer is, to put it crudely, How are we to cut—if at all possible—the Gordian knot of gender essentialism, of difference and otherness? In pursuit of this inquiry, I will first turn to the mother of "woman's alterity," Simone de Beauvoir, and her contemporary daughters. In view of Beauvoir's significant presence in Israeli culture since the 1950s (see the introduction), her special blend of existentialist feminism should offer some valuable insights into the work of authors who began writing in the 1960s. In a brief visit to the origins of gender theory—as well as to its contemporary offshoots—I therefore outline the "solutions" offered by both while highlighting those that are particularly relevant to the Israeli authors explored in this study.

Chapter 2

Alterity Revisited: Gender Theory and Israeli Literary Feminism

Half the people in the world
love the other half
half the people
hate the other half . . .
Half the people love,
half hate.
And where is my place between the two tightly fitting halves . . .
—Yehuda Amichai

It is difficult for a woman to define her feelings in language which is chiefly made by men to express theirs.   —Thomas Hardy

1. Beauvoir's Drama of Subjectivity

Woman's primordial otherness—as represented in ancient myth and ritual as well as in interpretations of them by twentieth-century (mostly male) scholars—is one of the deep structures we encountered in our mythological reading of *Gei Oni*. These are the very myths that Simone de Beauvoir set out to expose in her pioneering study, *The Second Sex*. One of the major points made by Beauvoir in her work is that the single common denominator of different myths and other narratives about woman's alterity (as indeed of alterity in general!) is that of *ambivalence*. Whether filtered through Freud's individual psychology or Erich Neumann's "archetypology" (*The Great Mother*) or through Simone de Beauvoir's own exposition of myths about the second sex, the ambivalence of alterity is a constant: woman is other as both virgin and harlot (Freud), as the Good Mother and the Terrible Mother (Neumann), as the giver of both life and death (186), as bountiful Nature incarnate and as the menacing embodiment of untamed Nature (223).[1] In Beauvoir's succinct summary, woman, "the fearsome other" (191), "is all that man desires and all that he does not attain" (223).

It is this position of duality or ambivalence that makes the other (in general) a *necessary* foil in the constitution of subjectivity. "The subject can be posed only in being opposed," says Beauvoir, openly reflecting (pun intended) Hegel's speculations on the agonistic formation of self-consciousness (xx): "He sets himself up as the essential, as opposed to the other, the inessential, the object." (To anticipate later formulations [mutatis mutandis], "The subject comes to be(ing) in the field of the Other.")[2]

Yet, generally speaking, the subject, whether collective or personal, is not alone in the world: "But the other consciousness, the other ego, sets up a reciprocal claim," says Beauvoir, continuing her Hegelian narrative. If there is any potential here for a psychological interpretation (that is, an understanding of this confrontation as internal, as taking place in some mental space), Beauvoir is unaware (or perhaps unwilling?) to acknowledge it, highlighting instead its external, "foreign relations" function. Encounters between cultures, tribes, classes, and private individuals "deprive the concept *Other* of its absolute sense" and make manifest its relativity and reciprocity, thereby opening the path to a mutual, intersubjective recognition (xx).

Couched here in the language of philosophical abstraction is the tension between self-centeredness and reciprocal reflection that is more familiar to us in the garb of the mirror metaphor. This age-old classical image (magnificently traced and critiqued in Martin Jay's *Downcast Eyes*) has always had a double function, representing both narcissism (Greek myth, revived by Freud) and mutual specularity (Aristotle). Attended by its obligatory gaze, or look, that second meaning was resurrected by Lacan in 1936 (*le stade du miroir*) and newly reinterpreted by Sartre in 1943 (*L'Etre et le néant*). The latter is of particular significance for us because it dramatizes by way of metaphor the Hegelian point that Beauvoir is making here: that the looked-upon, objectified other has the ontological ability to return the gaze, to say No to the objectifying look, thereby gaining his (or her?) own subjectivity.[3] Curiously, none of this Sartrean drama is even hinted at here. Staying close to Hegel's philosophical discourse, Beauvoir shies away from its metaphorical descendants, especially those coined by Sartre. She does cite Lacan's gaze briefly in the discussion of the nursling's mirror stage ("It is especially when he is fixed by the gaze of other persons that he appears to himself as being one," 303), unaware, however, of the potential danger to her Hegelian (should we say Cartesian?) Subject harbored by this gaze. Neither is she aware, apparently, of the gender trouble concealed behind her innocent formulation, "other persons." Using ungendered terms (nursling, infant, child—and parents), Beauvoir weaves a seamlessly neuter narrative in a balancing act between subjectivity and otherness, separation and attachment. The grammatical subject of this narrative is—naturally enough—the ostensibly all-inclusive humanist "he." And although Sartre's existentialism lurks behind her formulation of the "autonomous subject, in transcendence toward the outer world" (ibid), the Sartrean warfare, his "duel of looks," is never mentioned. Was Beauvoir returning the look of her lifelong companion, whose magnum opus preceded hers by a few years?

We will never know for sure, except for the clues she has left in her conceptualization of the particular case of Woman's alterity. As she keenly reminds us, "[this] reciprocity has not been recognized between the sexes. . . . One of the contrasting terms is set up as the sole essential, denying any relativity in regard to its correlative and defining the latter as *pure otherness*" (xxi; emphasis added). Significantly, this anomaly is further sharpened by comparing women's otherness to that of (who else?) "American Negroes" and the Jews. On one hand, women are not a numerical minority like these two groups; on the other, they lack even the "memory of former days," before disrecognition (or oppression) had set in, to which the two other groups have recourse (ibid). It is the memory of this past (a foundational myth or collective memory, we would say today) that makes a change possible, "as the Negroes of Haiti and others have proved." Interestingly, the proof of the "Jews of Palestine" had not reached her yet in 1949 (!), although she made up for it in later years, as documented in the introduction to this volume. Her next observation, however, has a familiar ring: "Regarding themselves as subjects, they transform the bourgeois, the whites into 'others' " (xxii).

Several points of this argument deserve our attention: first and foremost, the classification of women's alterity in the same category as racial/religious marginalization (women = blacks = Jews; cf. xxvii). From the perspective of Jewish feminism, this is an important early (perhaps the first) act of inclusion, one that does not ignore or exclude the Jewish problem from a general discussion of marginalization. Sadly, such exclusion does reinscribe itself into later studies of Beauvoir. In her recent study (1994), in a chapter entitled "Narratives of Liberation" (204–213), Toril Moi pays special attention to Beauvoir's treatment of the "negro question" (*négritude*), placing it within the context of Sartre's and Frantz Fanon's writings on this issue. The Jewish question seems to have dropped from the equation. It is precisely this equation, however, that was picked up by Israeli arch-feminist Amalia Kahana-Carmon, who inventively used it in constructing her own "narrative of liberation" (1984), analyzed in detail in chapter 3.

Other issues worth highlighting are the importance of a past (or at least a memory of one) for restoring balance, and, finally, the unquestioned premise that by assuming subjectivity one automatically transforms the other party into an other . . . a rather pessimistic perception of the human subject that will concern us later.

In any case, women have not had this option or the problem it arouses; having never shared the world in equality with the "first" sex, they are likened to the slave in the notorious master-slave paradigm, that corner-stone of human relations according to Hegelian (and Marxist) theories (xxiii). It is this primordial otherness that needs to be repaired if women are to reinvent themselves as authentic autonomous subjects. Daunting as it may sound, this is not a (theoretically) impossible task if we remember that the slave of this paradigm is presumed to progressively gain more access to the means of production and thereby to freedom. Yet Beauvoir's prognosis for women's liberation is guarded, given the "deep-seated ten-dencies towards complicity," later called "alienation," that she detects in her peers. As we shall see, this paradigmatic divergence between the progress of the slave in the Hegelian narrative and Beauvoir's own pes-simistic rereading of it for woman constitutes the core of the Israeli liber-ation narrative that is unraveled in chapter 3. In that story Kahana-Carmon juxtaposes three categories of otherness, woman, black, Jew, in their attempt to regain subjectivity. Although she does use the Hegelian gaze metaphor with impunity, the woman of her script succumbs precisely to what Beauvoir called her "tendency to complicity." Yet this is only a tem-porary lapse, for the final moment of triumph is imagined by Kahana-Car-mon in a typical existential formula: the ability to say no to one's oppres-sor . . . (a verbal image revisited in chapter 6).

Needless to say, from the vantage point of the 1990s not all of Beau-voir's answers and explanations seem satisfactory. While charged by some with "essentialism" (namely, her acceptance of biology as a determinant factor of sexual difference, and her concomitant rejection of motherhood as "the crown of a woman's life" [582ff]), others have championed her as the first theorist of gender *avant la lettre*[4]—a title that really belongs (as I argue in chapter 4) to Virginia Woolf. On the other hand, she was criti-cized for holding up a so-called masculine ideal—existential transcen-

dence—as the goal of woman's liberation. "Being like a man" is not politically correct anymore, nor is the insistence on the power of willed, ratio-
nal intelligence to overcome acquired *unconscious* (namely, psychoanalytic) behavioral patterns (Beauvoir, 50ff). So if I have quoted *The Second
Sex* somewhat generously, it is not for the strength of the solutions it offers
as much as for the power of its exposition and its diagnostic relevance.
Indeed, it is commonly agreed that the various feminisms that have developed in the West in the past decades have all responded, in their different
ways, to Beauvoir's challenge. Moreover, her "presence" in Israeli culture
(see the introduction) makes her ideas a crucial tool for the interpretation
of a central chapter in Israeli literary feminism.

I would further suggest, however, that by grouping together "the eternal feminine," "the black soul," and "the Jewish character" as three categories of oppressed alterity (xxvii) Beauvoir anticipated the recent explosion of multicultural and postcolonial studies, in which minority discourse
has been redefined, following Foucault, to include any cultural challenges
to the dominant canon, thereby "erasing" the numerical meaning of the
concepts minority (or other).[5] This nexus is also present in other contemporary paths of inquiry, all tangentially relevant to our topic: the historical confluence of racism and misogyny (as in Sander Gilman's work on
gender in antisemitism and its impact on Freud's theories),[6] the sociological and theological genderism within Judaism (as in the work of Jewish
feminists, mostly American),[7] and, finally, the symbolization and artistic
sublimation of these issues by Jewish creative writers.[8] It is to the latter
that I will eventually return, finding in the work of Amalia Kahana-Carmon, the subject of chapter 3, direct traces of Beauvoir's take on the
woman question and its relation to the two other others—the Jew and the
black. But, before arriving there, another question is in order: How did
Beauvoir's legacy—and her conceptualization of woman as other in particular—survive the feminist upheavals of recent decades?

2. Beauvoir's "Daughters": Otherness as Difference

An interesting clue (already cited in the introduction) is offered by historian Karen Offen, who in 1988 traced the reception history of *The Second
Sex* as part of her outline of the changing definitions of the term *feminism*:
"Beauvoir's arguments were received with greater enthusiasm in English-
speaking countries than in her own," apparently because of the socionational legacy of French feminism.[9] Thus, while France developed what

Offen labels relational feminism, featuring "the primacy of a companion-
ate, non-hierarchical, male-female couple as the basic unit of society" and
emphasizing women's rights as *women* (defined mainly by their *nurturing*
capacities; emphasis added), Anglo-American feminists followed Beauvoir's individualist feminism, emphasizing the abstract concept of human
rights and "celebrating the quest for personal independence (or autonomy) in all aspects of life, while downplaying . . . childbearing and its
attending responsibilities" (136).

It is the latter, of course, that won the day with the 1960s "explosion"
of second-wave feminism in the English-speaking countries. Beauvoir's
anatomy of woman's otherness has inspired a feminism whose goal was the
eradication of all those inequalities blamed on the sociopolitical alterity of
women. In due time (a decade or so is the usual delay in importing American ideas to Israel) it also infiltrated Hebrew literature, but not without
some typically Jewish modifications (see chapter 6). This orientation,
alternatively called equal rights, individualist, humanist, or liberal feminism, reduced—as followers often do—the duality and ambiguity of
woman's alterity as described by Beauvoir, preserving only the pejorative
connotation of the concept. Like Beauvoir, however, it equally applied
itself to other underprivileged groups: racial and ethnic minorities, as well
as social classes. The dubious nature of the latter (given the a priori middle-class pigeonholing of any theory-producing feminist) is in fact an
ironic repetition of Virginia Woolf's last-ditch attempt to enlist the solidarity of the working class on the eve of World War II. Building on *her*
version of female difference, the identity of the "Outsider" she had developed throughout the 1930s ("codified" in *Three Guineas*, 1938), she now
tried to reach the commoners. That her valiant address to "commoners
and outsiders like ourselves" had a rather meager success is apparently a
historical lesson still not learned by contemporary feminism.[10]

For a more successful unfolding of Beauvoir's legacy we need to look
at the contemporary reinvention of *gender*. Following her famous statement "One is not born, but rather becomes, a woman" (*The Second Sex*,
301)—yet in contrast to her ostensible biologism—Anglo-American feminism developed the concept of gender to distinguish between given (biological) sexual differences and those gender *relations* that are constructed
by social and cultural processes. The aim was to tease out the "socially
imposed division of the sexes" from the web of natural difference (hence-
forth labeled sex), as Gayle Rubin had initially defined it.[11]

The transformation of gender from a grammatical to a social science category, and the study of the sex-gender system that this category has made possible, were perceived as an antidote to the narrowness of feminist studies, a corrective allowing for the analysis of "masculinism" in analogy to feminism. It thus promised to "liberate more than women. . . . It would liberate human personality from the straightjacket of gender,"[12] that very jacket that *produces* perceived disymmetry and perpetuates *representations* of otherness. In due time, however, followers were encouraged to "go beyond gender,"[13] or to find a third term elsewhere, outside the masculine/feminine dyad, because gender, no less than its precursor, sex, was found implicated in binarism, that major culprit in the annals of postmodern critique.[14] Indeed, recent studies explicitly alert us to the "slippage between 'sex' and 'gender,' "[15] cautioning that " 'gender' is silently replacing 'sex' as the referential base for postmodern theories."[16] In short, within less than two decades the sex/gender distinction is already losing its edge, while gender has been redefined as a "technology" or a "performance" (masquerade).[17]

The importing of gender to Israel, meanwhile, has had a particularly interesting history. Though as a sociocultural category of analysis it has slowly infiltrated Israeli feminist research of the last two decades, it did not leave much of a mark on feminist literature. In fact, a Hebrew translation of "gender," *migdar*, was not even invented until a year or two ago. I explore in chapter 7 the psycholinguistic reasons for this difficulty. It merely suffices to point out here that the only Israeli writer who directly wrestled with this issue—and not out of any theoretical concerns—was Netiva Ben Yehuda, the Palmach fighter whose impassioned conflict between sexual equality and Zionist loyalty is recorded in the epigraph to this study (see the introduction and chapter 7). In a typically Israeli way she had to invent *gender* (using her own linguistic ingenuity) in order to grapple with the sexual discrimination she experienced as a distinguished fighter in the 1948 War of Independence.

But, to return to our narrative of gender theory, ironically, the continuous search for the *roots* of the gender straightjacket led back to the realm of psychoanalysis—the very discipline whose explanatory power had been dismissed—and for good reasons—by the foremother of feminism ("All psychoanalysts systematically reject the idea of *choice* and the correlated concept of value, and therein lies the intrinsic weakness of the system," Beauvoir, 50). This was not, however, a return to Freud, whose female psychology had been found lacking, to say the least (58), but to post-Freudian psychology. Thus, while Beauvoir herself tried to account for male ambivalence toward the female by the somewhat circular argument that "the source of these ter-rors lies in the fact that in the Other, quite beyond reach, alterity, otherness, abide" (191), recent explanations rely on psychoanalytic assessments of early *pre*oedipal family dynamics, where the mother rather than the (oedipal) father plays a major role. This so-called object relation theory, developed mainly in England (Fairburn, Guntrip, Winnicott), helped Nancy Chodorow, for example, to question Freud's oedipal masterplot. Since it is this paradigmatic transition from the oedipal masterplot to the maternal nar-rative that we will encounter at the heart of the feminist project in Israeli women's (and some men's) fiction, I want to take a closer look at Chodorow's study and its repercussions on subsequent scholarship.

In *The Reproduction of Mothering: Psychoanalysis and the Sociology of Gender* Chodorow offers a new definition of woman's alterity. Arguing that, in contrast to girls' identification with their mothers, boys develop their sense of self in defensive *opposition* to the mother, she conceptualized their later denigration of the feminine as a *defense* against their earlier iden-tification with the phallic *pre*oedipal mother. Despite the explicitly psy-choanalytic language, the legacy of Beauvoir's "fearsome other" is quite clear here, as is the (Hegelian) agonistic perception of the construction of (masculine!) subjectivity. What is new, however, is the (quite disturbing) transformation of philosophy's generalized abstract other into a flesh and blood, sociologically (if not biologically) necessary female (m)other. Motherhood is again (as for Beauvoir) the culprit, but on a deeper, *uncon-scious* level. Since it perpetually reproduces psychological differences between the sexes, it of necessity reinforces female alterity: the presumably relational, easily malleable ego of woman, the result of mother-daughter identification (and the cause of her attachment needs), in opposition to man's fixed, inflexible ego boundaries, the expression of a separation anx-iety caused by fear of an ostensible identification with the maternal.

Widespread as Chodorow's theory is, it is not without its problems, and not only for its inadequacy in explaining "male domination" as it purports to do.[18] No less troubling is the substitution of bedrock psychological dif-ferences for biological ones. Recent revisions critique the principle of gen-der polarity altogether, showing its binarisms to be false and culturally constructed. Thus Jessica Benjamin concludes her study of the problem of domination, *The Bonds of Love*, with the statement that "ironically, then, the ideal of freedom carries within it the seeds of domination—freedom *means* fleeing or subjugating the other; autonomy means an escape from dependency," while Miriam Johnson challenges the presumed separation versus attachment dissymmetry between the genders by arguing, "Whereas a woman's relational needs get defined as her 'dependency,' men may disguise their dependency needs because they are being met everyday by women. . . . [Financial] dependence must not be confused with psychological dependency."[19]

These critiques notwithstanding, Chodorow's study has had a decisive impact on the perception of female otherness precisely because it made possible a shift in the valorization of otherness from negative to positive. Despite her indictment of the institution of mothering (which Chodorow suggests fixing by a change in child-rearing arrangements),[20] her analysis brought to the fore aspects of female psychological growth that allowed for the beginning of a new trend—the celebration of mother-daughter bonding and its concomitant "female" identity.

This change of perspective should come as no surprise. Beauvoir's valorization of male subjectivity had come under attack by the 1980s, and, with it, "liberal" feminism. Derogatorily labeled masculinist or assimilationist, it has recently been charged with making masculinity a universal norm of liberation and achievement, thereby perpetuating traditional phallocentric dichotomies. Between the publication of Carol Giligan's *In a Different Voice* (1982) and Sara Ruddik's *Maternal Thinking* (1989) Anglo-American gender studies was transformed.[21] Refusing the perspective of the male gaze (which had been explored by feminist cinema theorists since the mid-seventies),[22] these "separatist" feminists now *embraced* their otherness rather than deploring it. If black was beautiful, so was the feminine. Beauvoir's wish for reciprocity was finally taking shape, at least in theory; although probably not the one she was looking forward to. For now American women—though not exactly a minority—extolled their *difference* under the banner of cultural pluralism. As for Israeli feminists— as usual, there was a delay in catching up with their Western sisters, but we can hear some echoes of separatist feminism in the Israel of the late 1990s (as I argue in chapter 6).

For the inspiration of this global change we need to cross back, ironically, to the continent, to meet Beauvoir's own unfaithful daughters. If we recall the tradition of French matrimonial (relational) feminism described by Offen, we should not wonder at its latest phase. Here woman's alterity has totally shed its pejorative meaning and has come to signify her particularly embodied and engendered being in the world. These sexual difference theorists (Hélène Cixous, Luce Irigaray, Monique Wittig) celebrate their otherness by privileging the very negativities traditionally attributed to women in Western civilization. Beauvoir's priorities are turned upside down, one by one, in what could be best described as an oedipal agon (in the spirit of Harold Bloom's *Anxiety of Influence* [1975] and contra Gilbert and Gubar's objections).[23]

In a massive rewriting of the history (or at least selected chapters thereof) of the mirror and gaze metaphors, those traditional emblems of subjectivity (avoided by Beauvoir, we may recall!), Luce Irigaray has exposed the complicity of philosophy itself in the perpetuation of sexual binarism and hierarchy, in the privileging of the masculine, and in the production of female alterity. Her *Speculum of the Other Woman* (1974) is a parodic feminist/deconstructive reading of Freud (and—indirectly—Lacan), Plato and Aristotle, Hegel and Decartes. Identifying the specular/speculative tradition as phallocentric ("Yes, man's eye—understood as substitute for the penis"),[24] she rejects its terms altogether, dismissing the theory of her mentor (Lacan) in the process. Through this dismissal Beauvoir's invitation to women to attain subjectivity is interpreted as another reobjectivization, because "Any Theory of the 'Subject' Has Always Been Appropriated by the 'Masculine.' "[25] "Woman has no gaze, no discourse for her specific specularization that would allow her to identify with herself (as same)."[26] Self-identity, self-consciousness, subjectivity are rejected by Irigaray as a masculinist obsession with sameness and oneness, the expression of fear of *multiplicity* and *fluid* ego boundaries. The latter, metaphorized by female sexuality and anatomy (or, more accurately, by selected parts thereof; see *This Sex Which is Not One,* 1977), are the very markers of female difference she invites us to applaud.

Although Irigaray is hard to pin down, the source from which she derives (more often than not) this positive female difference is none other than the *maternal*—precisely that biological function that Beauvoir saw as the obstacle in women's route toward equality, subjectivity, and transcendence. Like Chodorow's followers—albeit with different emphasis and for differing aims—Irigaray privileges the mother-daughter symbiotic bonding as the root (at least metaphorically) of female empathy and psychological fluidity; unlike them, however, she used this otherness to deconstruct the heterosexual paradigm. Much like Adrienne Rich on the other side of the Atlantic, who moved from the problematization of motherhood (*Of Woman Born,* 1976) to a "lesbian continuum" (1980),[27] Irigaray moved from a critique of phallocentric essentialism to the idealization of gynocentrism, female sexual multiplicity, and homoeroticism. This progression was reflected also in her style of writing. Associative, richly allusive and metaphoric, at times even ungrammatical, it challenged from within the logocentric expository prose of philosophical discourse that *The Second Sex* had so dutifully sustained. This is *écriture féminine* par excellence, the ultimate exaltation of sexual difference.[28]

The foundational essay of this orientation is Hélène Cixous's 1975 "The Laugh of the Medusa," which advocated experimental, disruptive, and unsettling "writing through the body." The declared purpose of this mode of writing is precisely to inscribe an other language, that female language for which Hardy's exceptional heroine was unwittingly searching a century ago but could not yet name (see the epigraph to this chapter). Now women's tongue is alternately named the "(m)other's voice" or the "discourse of the hysteric,"[29] and is highly valorized and idealized. Feminine writers—among whom, in an anti-essentialist move, some major male authors are counted— are presumed to lift the lid of repression off female otherness (symbolized by the body and the hysteric's desire), thereby challenging the mind-body split and other logocentric binarisms. That by so doing they in fact maintain the very dichotomy that *The Second Sex* had set out to undo is, of course, one of the ironies of the recent history of female difference.

Another irony awaits us on the other side of the Mediterranean. As I show in chapters 5 and 6, the exploration of some of the major issues fore-grounded by sexual difference feminists—sameness versus difference, the nexus of mother-daughter relations and the lesbian continuum, and, finally, the writing *of* the body (rather than through the body)—was car-ried out in Israel by the novelist and journalist Shulamith Hareven, who more than any other writer raised the flag *against* the category of women writers and the identification of women's style as different or recognizably feminine. Conversely, some of the most traditional, essentialist character-izations of female alterity are to be found in the ostensible epitome of Israeli écriture féminine, the works of Amalia Kahana-Carmon (chapter 3). These paradoxes are resolved, finally, in the work of Ruth Almog (chapter 8), who explores the mother-daughter continuum without abandoning the oedipal plot and grafts the discourse of the hysteric onto a masculinist narrative—successfully challenging many boundaries, old and new.

3. Postmodernism's Other: Mother's Body, Mother's Tongue

The irony of this multifaceted picture increases as we probe a little deeper into the ostensible analogy between theories of difference on both sides of the Atlantic.

In the United States gender was originally conceptualized as an anthropological category, never losing sight of its political implications. Inspired by Foucault's analysis of the structures of power and domination operating within the sociocultural system, this orientation has recently yielded ever growing differentiation, demanding to speak the particularity of more narrowly defined social groups. Woman was replaced by women, feminism by womanism (black women). Third world women and women of color, social classes and diverging sexual orientations—each group insists on a historical and cultural particularism that generic feminism or even gender studies cannot address.[30] Responding to the postmodern crisis of representation by eschewing the universality of the traditional discourses of subjectivity (philosophy and psychoanalysis), these others nevertheless redefine their social space in terms of collective selfhood, often "transforming some other group into 'an other,' " to paraphrase Beauvoir again. In this case the reproduction of the American scene on the Israeli stage did not lag behind: recently, Oriental (*mizraḥiot*, rather than Sephardi) feminists have created their own organization, attuned to the familiar politization of American gender theories and goading the apologetic mea culpa of leading Ashkenazi feminists.[31]

The conceptualization of sexual difference in France is quite different, almost diametrically opposed. To begin with, the basic concepts of sexual difference and écriture féminine are not as originally female products as they may seem to be, and neither is the celebration of woman's alterity. As convincingly demonstrated by Alice Jardine in *Gynesis* and Teresa de Lauretis in *Technologies of Gender*, postmodernist discourse habitually named as *la femme* or *le feminin* all those spaces external to the (metaphysical, psychoanalytic, social) system from which it tried to deconstruct or unhinge the "humanist" metanarratives of the West (Truth, History, Man). Thus, for Lacan, the "Subject comes to be in the field of the Other" precisely because the Cartesian (and Hegelian-Sartrean-Beauvoirian) subject has lost its mastery, priority, and stability; he is subject to (that is, subjected to) the system into which he is initiated, rather than the subject of it (that is, its agentic manipulator).[32] That power is attributed to the Unconscious, the Other with a capital *O*, which Lacan genders as feminine. (Hence: "The woman—she does not exist." The Other is by definition that which is beyond the symbolic, outside our system of representation.) As for Derrida, his other is writing, écriture—his arch-metaphor for the endless play of signifiers, the deferral of closure and the dissemination of meaning—in short, the locus of all the revisionary and subversive energies deployed in the deconstruction of logocentric signification and phallocentric binarisms. Less consistently but nevertheless in a tangible way, écriture is naturally gendered as feminine (and not only because of its French grammatical inflection).[33]

In a paradoxical way, then, while women as such are almost absent from the theories of the leading spokesmen of postmodernism, the abstract notion of the female other has come to occupy center stage in their discourse. Yet, even more paradoxically, this presumed transvaluation (Nietzsche) does nothing for the deconstruction of the hoary dichotomy of male-female. Whether or not we see the revolutionary deployment of the feminine as a (dangerous?) reification of Hegelian negativity, as has been recently claimed,[34] we can agree, I believe, that this teleology does not expunge the feminine of its original negativities; although marked positively by Derrida (and Lacan, Foucault, Lyotard), the feminine remains entrapped in the old binarism. It is exclusion, absence, lack, unarticulated matter and unrepresentable body, nothingness and even god, in short, the ultimate Other, "all that [postmodern] Man desires and all that he cannot attain" (again, citing Beauvoir).

In (women) theorists' attempts to explain this paradox we can predictably detect shades of the demonized female other, the so-called phallic mother. While Alice Jardine has implied male paranoia, Jane Flax has gone so far as to take Chodorow's suggestions to their logical extremity (absurdity?), claiming that postmodernist deconstruction of subjectivity derives from "the need [of its male theorists] to evade, deny or repress the importance of early childhood experiences, especially mother-child relationships, in the constitution of the self and the culture more generally."[35] If we take Flax's "diagnosis" seriously (which I am not sure I can bring myself to do), we are compelled to face an unflattering scene of competition, a tragicomic or even grotesque pathology that cruelly undercuts deconstruction's aspiration to revise the phallocentric discourses of Western metaphysics and epistemology.

But even if we do not go that far, we may now be in a better position to appreciate the impasse in which French female intellectuals have found themselves. With no recourse to Cartesian subjectivity, and with the feminine taken up by their male peers, they have opted to seize those revolutionary spaces of *abstract* feminine otherness and make them their own by re*embodying* them. Hence the exaltation of female anatomy and female homoeroticism, the hystericization of feminine writing, and the exuberant celebration of female desire and the maternal function—precisely that demonized, unrepresentable ghost *still* lurking beyond the confines of androcentric postmodern metaphysics. As we have already implied, this aspect of continental theory is the least developed in Israeli fiction, save for some experiments in the 1990s by mostly (but not only) younger writers; some traces of it can be found, however, in the latest work by both Kahana-Carmon and Hareven (chapters 3, 6) as well as in Almog's major novel (chapter 8).

Although claimed to be symbolic and iconic rather than literal, this glorification of feminine difference exposes its propagators (on both sides of the Atlantic) to charges of reverse essentialism. In a paradoxical way it is not a Derridean *différance* (that is, a third term outside the traditional binarism of male subjectivity and female otherness) that has been constructed in French feminine writing but an exaggerated version of traditional representations of female otherness, the only difference being the reversal of its valorization (from negative to positive).

Moreover, the feminine (in fact, hysterical) exuberance of this writing blurs the often thin line between description and prescription. Is it claimed that the other sex indeed exhibits all the feminine traits idolized by sexual difference writers, or are these traits cited as models of femininity to be imitated or adopted across gender lines? If meant descriptively, this portrait will no doubt fail the test of reality, if meant prescriptively, then another alterity has been created, and with it a new binarism, that of homoeroticism versus heteroeroticism.Would it be terribly politically incorrect to ask (following Yehuda Amichai; see the epigraph to this chapter) where heterosexuality would find its (theoretical) space, "between the two tightly fitting halves" of the suggested new order?[36] And would it be too intellectually retrograde to remind ourselves at this juncture of the veteran Freudian concept of bisexuality?[37] Of Virginia Woolf's androgyny? Of the even older Hegelian "*internal* dialectic" of self and other? In short, of the various attempts to contain difference rather than project and eject it?[38]

4. Empowering the M/Other?

A solution of sorts awaits us in the work of Julia Kristeva, who supposedly conceptualizes the other beyond gender dichotomy altogether. Dismissing écriture féminine and sexual difference as reinforcing received binary oppositions, she considers as other that revolutionary impulse which fractures the symbolic order by introducing preverbal, preoedipal, and unrepresented patterns of signification that she names the "Semiotic."[39] Although descriptively and functionally similar to the generic feminine other of postmodern discourse, its closest conceptual relative is Lacan's Imaginary, again with the predictable reversal of its valorization. Like the Imaginary, the Semiotic is derived from infantile bodily and emotional experience, which is naturally available to *both* genders; similarly, it is *contained within* the symbolic order rather than projected beyond its boundaries (as is the other of postmodernism); unlike it, however, it is perceived to be the source of subversive creativity, a potentiality highly situated on Kristeva's scale of priorities. Furthermore, by identifying this maternal other in the avant-garde writing of Artaud, Mallarmé, Joyce, and other (mostly male) writers, Kristeva insists on its genderlessness. Her theory seems to transcend gender alterity, then, by positioning otherness within subjectivity itself (decentered as the latter may be), irrespective of gender.

Have we finally reached our destination or, rather, that of gender theories? Is Kristeva's maternal Semiotic the third term that goes beyond binarism, beyond essence by, paradoxically, diving inside? An archimedean point within the system rather than without? Has she managed to counteract the paranoic marginalization of the (m)other by including rather than excluding maternal otherness and difference?

If the reception and dissemination of her ideas are any measure, she may indeed have done just that,[40] ironically at the expense of feminist political correctness. Her notorious declaration—that the task of "third generation" women [*sic*], not feminists, is the "de-dramatization of the 'fight to the death' between rival groups and thus between the sexes"—readily supports both sides of the irony.[41] But, beyond the pragmatic gripe of political feminism,[42] her conceptualization does not get around the (by now predictable) charge of complicity with received representations of feminine (or, in her case, maternal) otherness. By relegating, as she does, the question of gender difference to the realm of metaphysics (an altogether suspect discourse in her frame of [postmodernist] thinking, as her "Woman's Time" makes clear), she does not get rid of it. It returns through the kitchen door, so to speak, through the unresolved tension between the commonality of human (infantile) experience and the biological one-genderedness of maternity. Taking both as unquestioned givens, Kristeva is unable to allow both genders an *equal* use of the Semiotic other. It is not by chance that the models of her "revolutionary poetics" are male writers. Their sex/gender distance (difference?) from the maternal protects them, she says, from the risk of psychotic disintegration that would threaten a woman under the same circumstance. We encounter an illustration of this dogma in Kahana-Carmon's early writing, in the figure of Tehila (chapter 3).[43]

The psychoanalytic underpinnings of this logic are tiresomely familiar. So is the old adage about the madwoman in the attic.[44] But how are we to account for women's creativity? For instance, for Julia Kristeva's protean fecundity?

It is not my intention to grapple with this question here. Fortunately, Kristeva's amazingly rich and multifaceted creativity seems to belie her own theory. For this visit to the promised land "beyond gender" of her making turns out to be quite disturbing. Even if we do not go so far as to endorse the criticism that her "concept of the subject in process, which dissolves female subjectivity entirely, fails to answer—indeed it does not attempt to answer—the question of the engenderment of subjectivity as feminine. Rather, it leaves no place for it,"[45] it is no doubt clear that under the guise of a progressive theory, which attractively names its most privileged term after the maternal, Kristeva once again conceptualizes women's creativity as achieved only at a high cost. The inclusion of gender difference within the system fails to obliterate women's partial exclusion. If their access to the site of artistic agency is not totally blocked, it is fraught with grave danger (ironically—because it is too close for comfort). "In her case studies," argues one psychoanalytic study, "the mother is defined as *the* problem for her female patients. This way of defining the mother works to restrict the agency of women. . . . For Kristeva, avantgarde writing only offers the *man* a chance to be in touch with his primal femininity while safely transcending this deadly force."[46] In the final analysis Kristeva's system, presumably beyond gender, allows woman to buy her way into its maternal site of energy and excitement only at the cost of preserving intact the existing paternal order.

Once again the maternal is at the heart of this paradox, as observed by Domna Stanton in her insightful critique of the "maternal metaphor" employed by contemporary gender theorists.[47] Indeed, it is the ambiguous position of this female-feminine excess that emerges as a major parameter for the conceptualization of gender alterity. In some sense the analysis of female otherness carried out by gender theorists for the past fifty years may be reduced to just that: the anchoring of the general ambivalence toward woman—as summarized by Beauvoir—to its ostensible origin, motherhood. Whether demonized or idolized, concretized or metaphorized, it is this Derridian (biological? cultural?) *excess* that has replaced Freud's anatomical female *lack* (castration) as the marker of sexual difference.[48]

United around this single shared premise, gender scholars are nevertheless divided by their evaluation of its theoretical and pragmatic implications. In fact, the distance traveled by gender studies may be measured by the distance between Beauvoir's and Kristeva's positions on this issue. While the first critically views maternity as the social institution that hinders woman's journey toward autonomy and transcendence, the latter valiantly grapples with the constricting ambivalences of the Catholic tradition she has inherited,[49] attempting to recast the maternal as the psychological locus of androgynous revolution and creativity. There is even room to ask, I believe, whether Kristeva's thematizing of Maryology in the midst of the atheist (to the exclusion of Lacan?) discourse of postmodernism does not signify a return of the repressed, does not bring to the surface yet another dimension of anti-universalist difference, adding religion to the coordinates (sex, race, class, etc.) deployed in recent gender analysis.

Indeed, the addition of this parameter may explain some of the differences among the various feminist strands followed here, including the Israeli. For one of the conclusions to be drawn from our brief detour through the landscape of postmodernist gender theory is that the position held by motherhood in a given cultural system may be crucial for the attitudes developed in that system toward the woman question. Contemporary psychosocial analyses of this institution may merely be scratching the surface as long as they do not take into consideration the ethnoreligious systems underlying their object of research. There is a world of difference, as we know, between the respective institutions of motherhood in the Christian and Jewish traditions.[50] To do full justice to these differences, a wide-scale comparative analysis is needed. Such a probe, which is obviously beyond the boundaries of the present study, could perhaps begin with the observation that the most extreme positions on both sides of motherhood were conceived in Catholic France, by French-writing women (who have often rejected feminism proper). Conversely, writers in English, self-acknowledged feminists, seem to have favored middle-of-the-road compromises, perhaps following the example of Virginia Woolf, whose own struggle with motherhood is described and reinterpreted in chapter 4.

That the latter tradition is naturally more congenial to Israeli feminism should come as no surprise. My readings of Israeli literature in the following chapters are therefore mostly framed within the legacy of Virginia Woolf, focusing on those parts of it that Israeli feminists have reshaped in their own image. This legacy sheds light on the attempts of contemporary Israeli women authors to negotiate the impasses and conflicts beleaguering contemporary gender theory as well as feminist practice.

First among these authors is Amalia Kahana-Carmon, a long-acknowledged practitioner of Woolf's poetics in Hebrew literature, who, I argue, single-handedly foregrounded both otherness and difference in Israeli culture, weaving together Woolf's modernist poetics and Beauvoir's existential feminism. If the feminist horizon of expectations in this recalcitrant culture has somewhat changed during the last two decades, it is due, in no small measure, to the creative tenacity of Kahana-Carmon, whose fiction and nonfiction continuously streamlined the message.

Chapter 3

Empowering the Other:
Amalia Kahana-Carmon

Gentiles and Jews, they're like men and women, my father used to say. "Why," I once asked.

"Only because of preconceived judgments. Of each side: about one-self; about the other, too." My father smiled. Each side has its own picture, my father always said, its portrait of the other. Therefore, when addressing someone from the other side, it is to the portrait and not to the person that one would speak.

—Amalia Kahana-Carmon,
The Bridge of the Green Duck, Up in Montifer

"It is to the portrait and not to the person that one would speak"—a rather intriguing definition of *otherness* to find in a work of fiction.[1] In this extended metaphor Amalia Kahana-Carmon, one of Israel's leading prose fiction writers, points out the tragic source of otherness—the unavoidable split between signified and signifier, the person and the portrait, the subject and one's predetermined perception of what it/he/she might be.

At the same time, this is a paradoxical definition, as it cancels the uni-directionality usually associated with otherness. If "*each* side has its own picture. . . its portrait of the other," then there is no Other with a capital *O*. And there is no privileged Self either—with a capital *S*, one might say—no center stage against which one is to weigh the otherness of the other. By having *each* side functioning *equally* as the other's other, Amalia Kahana-Carmon seems to highlight sameness within otherness. What she has achieved by this maneuver is not only a cancellation of the easy identification of the other with the marginal and the inferior but also the problematization of the notion of privileged subjecthood.

That this repositioning of self and other would be penned by a woman should come as no surprise. After all, "reading against the grain" has long been identified as a feminist ploy.[2] What is striking, nevertheless, about *The Bridge of the Green Duck* is that it embeds the woman problem—in the spirit of both Beauvoir and contemporary minority discourse—within the *general* paradigm of otherness, successfully questioning all its major categories—gender, class, and race.

Yet, with all the admiration that such a sophistication justifiably arouses, we may also ponder its timing. Nineteen eighty-four, the publication year of *Lema'lah bemontifer* (Up in Montifer), the triptych of which *The Bridge of the Green Duck* is the major narrative, is a relatively late date in the career of its author (b. 1926), a prolific writer since the late fifties,[3] winner of several prestigious literary prizes, darling of academe (the only one among contemporary female authors) and subject of several scholarly monographs, and a writer-in-residence at both Tel Aviv University and the Oxford Centre for Post-Graduate Hebrew Studies (more recently, the Oxford Centre for Hebrew and Jewish Studies). Moreover, although Kahana-Carmon is known as *the* outspoken feminist critic of Israeli literature and Jewish culture, a close look at the dating of her feminist lectures and essays shows that they have, predictably, gained momentum only since the mid-1980s.[4] A significant bridge was apparently crossed by her in that decade, a turning point that is crucial to understanding the meandering narrative not only of her own fiction but also of the Israeli feminist romance, or masked autobiography followed here. To better appreciate this point, we begin by searching Kahana-Carmon's earlier work, looking for clues to the tensions animating the later work as well.

1. Feminine, Feminist, or Modernist?

Most of Kahana-Carmon's oeuvre—a collection of stories (1966), two novels (1971, 1992), a monodrama (1976), and two "triptychs" (three novellas, 1977, 1984)—has been perceived as thematizing women's marginality in an androcentric society, on a scope and in a style unrivaled in Hebrew literature. On both counts, but especially for the uniqueness of her poetics, she has long been associated in the Israeli literary mind with Virginia Woolf.[5] That her heavy reliance on syntactical effects is reminiscent of Woolf's insistence on rhythm as the major device of prose writing is no doubt true;[6] so is her utilization of the visual arts, the pictorial quality of her prose,[7] and, to no less effect, her use of interior monologue and stream of consciousness.

When it comes to thematics, however, the picture is more complex.

On the one hand, Kahana-Carmon seems to be preoccupied with precisely that subject matter literary theory (particularly on the Anglo-American side) has come to expect of the "first stage" of feminist literature—a subversive exposition of overt and covert biases that lurk behind the representation of women in a male-dominated system.[8] On the other hand, her lyrical stories and novels, mostly focalized through the perception of a female protagonist, are generally structured around an epiphanic vision, a moment of a (sometimes mutual) enchantment, that somehow "lifts" her narrative above and beyond a narrow feminist angle. Hebrew literary scholarship has interpreted this aspect of her poetics in light of the dialogic philosophy of Martin Buber, his existential search for an "I-Thou" relationship.[9] This attribution makes even greater sense when we place Buber himself within modernism's general yearning for spirituality in a universe devoid of it. Framed this way, Kahana-Carmon's models would no doubt be the great modernist novelists of the early twentieth century, Virginia Woolf not excluded, who were pursuing, each in his or her own way, involuntary memories (Proust), elusive epiphanies (Joyce), or visionary "moments of being" (Woolf) in order to redeem a world cut loose from its spiritual anchors.[10]

Yet even this broader context would not do full justice to an important aspect of Kahana-Carmon's epiphanic encounters: the fact that her visionary moments come, more often than not, in the form of a cross-gender interaction. More significantly, her narratives in a way subvert Buber's notorious formula because they often replace his generically masculine "I" with a spirituality-seeking female subject. This substitution is possible only within a narrative, because, like most languages, Hebrew features just one word for "I," which is morphologically unmarked but habitually perceived, especially in historical and philosophical discourses, as representing a male subject. It is this substitution that gives her heroine's spiritual longings, whether perceived as Buberian or modernist, a feminist twist. A closer look at this presumably feminist quest would reveal that it is underlined by a typical heroine's dysphoric script: the unrequited romance. Thus the potential for spiritual/romantic fulfillment is always checked, leaving the protagonists (usually women, although not exclusively so) with little more than a sense of a missed opportunity. Moreover, in most cases they accept their "fallen" reality with a resignation that paradoxically places them too close to traditional gender essentialism.

We should note, however, one major exception to this rule: Kahana-Carmon's most often taught and reprinted tale, in Hebrew as well as in translation, "Ne'ima Sasson Writes Poetry."[11] This early story, at the center of which is a young schoolgirl's infatuation with one of her teachers, may be regarded as Kahana-Carmon's signature piece. Despite the heavy displacement (the story takes place in a [Sephardi] school in Jerusalem; the author, a daughter of veteran pioneers of European extraction, spent her childhood on a kibbutz—a subject matter totally absent from her oeuvre, a fact I revisit in chapter 8), it contains the major elements we have come to expect of a Kahana-Carmon narrative: a female narrator whose absolute attraction to the "stronger" sex is habitually frustrated by his insensitivity, lack of empathy, or other characteristics that render him unattainable (difference of age, marital status, cultural and social setting, or simple lack of interest). However, while in most of Kahana-Carmon's stories and novels this frustration results in female resignation and submission (Beauvoir's infamous "women's complicity"), in this early story the young heroine precociously learns to sublimate her drives, using her attachment to fuel her creativity. Although totally unbelievable as a realistic representation of Ne'ima's imputed age, this story is no doubt an expression of one of its creator's more optimistic moments. For buried under the emotional dependence is the promise that an object of desire, as unavailable and unresponsive as he may be, can be imaginatively turned into a source of inspiration. With this gender reversal of the topos of the traditional (f.) muse, Kahana-Carmon made a feminist statement that would elude her in many subsequent works. In fact, it is her belated recapturing of this momentum that is the story of the present chapter.

Yet before we get there, a look at how Kahana-Carmon complicates the scenario of her early fiction is in order. She undercuts this scenario with a dense network of analogies and figurative connections (particularly in the longer works) that universalize the major themes and thereby subvert or at least problematize whatever gender-specific "meaning" they may seem to hold. With the help of a bit of hindsight, one could claim that not only the women but *most* of Amalia Kahana-Carmon's characters enter the scene *other*wise. They are fully aware of their otherness as women and wives, as mothers or children, as artists or new immigrants (*Bikhfifah 'aḥat* [Under One Roof], stories, 1966), sometimes as 1948 Israelis (of either sex) marooned in the Tel Aviv of 1967 and after (*Veyare'aḥ be'emek 'ayalon* [And Moon in the Valley of Ayalon], 1971), sometimes as an artist (male!) trapped in a "masculinist" system, ironically represented by a young, goal-oriented American female scientist (!) who frustrates *his* dream of "work and love" ("Sham ḥadar haḥadashot," in *Sadot magnetiim* [Magnetic Fields], 1977). Theirs is a disabling otherness of the worst kind—almost crippling—that is rendered, however, with the most powerful literary mastery; a mastery that should warn us against confusing the fictional creation with its creator.

Take, for example, the case of Tehilah (fame, praise),[12] the only character in Kahana-Carmon's first novel, *And Moon in the Valley of Ayalon*, who tries to combine love and work, who dares to cross the line and enter the (ostensibly phallocentric) world of artistic creativity.[13] Not only is her story presented negatively—almost grotesquely—filtered through the eyes of a narrator who admits to having been infatuated with her for years; before long her aborted foray into the Symbolic Order (Lacan) stereotypically terminates in "an institution."[14] Yet this oppressive story does not fail to elicit the protagonist's identification (*sippur ḥayay*, "the story of my life").[15] Kahana-Carmon seems then to exact on her heroine(s) a heavy price; this is the same price with which Julia Kristeva "threatens" women who take the risk of subverting the (male-dominated?) Symbolic by way of the (maternal) Semiotic (see chapter 2). At the same time, Kahana-Carmon simultaneously constructs and deconstructs both male and female essences, forever placing differences not within gender dichotomy but outside it (namely, within each gender).

And Moon in the Valley of Ayalon poignantly concludes with an imaginary interview of an eccentric author (male, of course). The focus of this interview is the knotty problem of "what enters into" the creative process. Predictably enough, the first item on the agenda is the writer's sex (or gender—there is no lexical distinction in the Hebrew of the seventies); except that it is followed by a list of other personal factors that carry equal weight. More important, Mr. Hiram, the author, both denies and affirms, in the same breath, the role of all these parameters—ethnic, social, economic, political—in the artist's creation:

> When you [m. *'atta*] write, you speak about what to you seem to be suprapersonal truths. Your sex, ethnic roots, social standing, income, or the party you vote for have no relevance.
>
> Your personal point of view—the one you cannot escape—your scale of values, but first and foremost your motivation, whatever has originally moved you to tell this particular story in this specific way—all these are, *unfortunately*, [representations of] you in the story; formed, among everything else, by your sex, ethnic roots, social standing, income, etc.[16]

The key word here is "unfortunately." It encodes a modernist aspiration to transcend the personal. Not unlike Virginia Woolf, this fictional author would like, we may presume, "to look beyond the personal and political relationships towards the wider questions which the *poet* tries to solve—of our destiny and the meaning of life" (emphasis added).[17] As we shall see in chapter 4, this drive toward the mystical and the abstract, the expression of what Woolf called "poetry" and "reality" at one and the same time, is at the heart of Woolf's paradoxically modernist feminism.[18] Apparently, similar tensions animate Kahana-Carmon's artistic universe. Her list of the parameters that make up one's subjective experience is clearly reminiscent of her predecessor's list: "Consciousness of self, of race, of sex, of civilization have nothing to do with art," argued Woolf.[19] Except that Kahana-Carmon is well aware, as the imaginary interview quoted here illustrates, that this ideal of the suprapersonal, the romantic/modernist legacy that has come down to us in many garbs (i.e., Keats's "Negative Capability" or T. S. Eliot's "Objective Correlative") is no longer viable.[20] Her fictional author acknowledges, albeit grudgingly, the impossibility of leaving one's subjective reality behind.

A feminist reader/critic may question, however, the choice of a male writer to echo both the convergence with and divergence from the mother of modernist feminism, Virginia Woolf. Anticipating this challenge, Kahana-Carmon concludes the novel with her female protagonist's agitated reflection following Mr. Hiram's interview: *sippur ḥayay*, "the story of my life."[21] In a typical Kahana-Carmon manner, Mrs. Talmor finds her life reflected in the life stories of both the would-be (insane?) writer Tehilah (f.) and the professional author (nearing the end of his career) Mr. Hiram (m.).

So on which side of gender essentialism does this leave us? On which side of subjectivity and otherness? If a writer's gender (among other parameters) is both crucial and not crucial to the artistic process, why should Kahana-Carmon, like Julia Kristeva, penalize her heroines (Tehilah is not alone in her lot, only in the greatest extremity) for their attempt to cross boundaries, to partake in the very freedom she herself has enjoyed as an artist? Clearly, there is an ambiguity here that calls for deconstruction—the very ambiguity, I would argue, that has contributed to a certain miscommunication between the author and her Israeli readership.[22]

One of Kahana-Carmon's major complaints in her 1980s essays is that the warm reception of her work hinged on its artistic excellence rather than on its "substance." To English readers this should sound familiar: Virginia Woolf similarly agonized over the reception of her later experimental books, contrasting "solid meaning" to "accomplished writing." Except that she kept her grievance within the confines of her diary, often sublimating her nervous expectation by way of parody. Here is what she registered on the eve of the publication of her first feminist "manifesto," *A Room of One's Own*:

> I forecast, then, that I shall have no criticism, except of the evasive joc-
> ular kind . . . that the press will be kind and will talk of its charm and
> sprightliness. . . . I am afraid it will not be taken seriously. Mrs. Woolf is
> so accomplished a writer that all she says makes easy reading.[23]

She did not always, however, manage to sublimate her anxieties; after the *warm* reception of *The Waves* (her most experimental novel), which greatly surprised her, she admitted: "What I want is to be told that this is solid and means something."[24] What these and other diary entries reveal is Woolf's intuitively felt opposition between serious criticism (or solid meaning) and the charm of accomplished writing. However, these and similar misunderstandings of her work are only sometimes related (as in the case of her "feminist manifesto") to her "feminine logic," to "a shrill feminine tone" (Oct. 23, 1929); at other times the critics simply miss the point, she avers: they "praise my characters when I meant to have none" (Oct. 5, 1931).

Amalia Kahana-Carmon's use of her critics' misunderstanding is quite different. Claiming that "artistic excellence" is a standard never applied to male writers (a claim not easily supported by fact), she has persistently rejected its terms. Her argument, framed within a universal gender dichotomy, supposedly declares an unambiguous feminist allegiance, openly challenging her male readers:

> This reader will react to the *tools* of the woman writer as if they were
> objects ("every sentence of hers is a pearl"); he will not respond to the
> *substance*, contained in her words, that created the need for these tools
> in the first place and then shaped their *form*.
>
> Indeed, this *content* is hidden from his eyes . . . much as you and I,
> unfortunately, cannot enjoy the highly perfected song of the bats in
> flight. . . .
>
> If so, the problem for the woman writer, apparently, inheres in the
> *subject matter* about which she attempts to speak. In the world of
> Hebrew fiction, such *material* has low visibility.[25]

The emphasis added here is meant to underline an opposition between two sets of semantic fields, the classical distinction between tools and sub-stance, or content. In the original the dichotomy is much stronger, as all the different synonyms used in the translation in opposition to "tools" or "form" represent, in fact, a single Hebrew term, *tokhen* (or the plural, *tekhanim*). Kahana-Carmon's distinction between *tokhen* and *tzurah* thus echoes the platonic dualism of matter and form that has recently been shown to be heavily implicated in gender symbolism.[26] Except that in her complaint this symbolism is involved in a gender reversal, one of which she may not be aware. As the philosophical tradition would have it, form is the privileged term, "naturally" associated with maleness, while "debased" matter (or body) is the realm of the female. The deconstruction of this essentialist dichotomy, by one reversal or another (either associating femaleness with form or privileging matter and substance) is of course the dream of any feminist, Anglo-American or French, respectively.

Yet Kahana-Carmon the polemicist is blind—as so often is the case—to options created by Kahana-Carmon the artist.[27] Does her charge that (male) readers "see" only the form of her art because its matter—female inwardness—is *in*visible to them (namely, unrepresentable) reject the terms of "gynesis," the French idealization of female attributes tradition-ally viewed as negative (otherness, lack, even absence), or does it approve of it?[28] Does her clamoring for cross-gender legitimization of her highly feminine "subjects" (pun intended) position her on the side of Virginia Wolf's androgyny (see chapter 4), Beauvoir's liberal, Enlightenment-based feminism, or on the side of the (French) sexual difference feminism that was explored in chapter 2?[29] Does she deplore her heroines' exclusion from male-made history? Does she privilege their otherness? Or perhaps she espouses Julia Kristeva's third generation ideology, whose task is, among other things, "the de-dramatization of the 'fight to the death' between rival groups and thus between the sexes"?[30]

As we shall see, this ambivalence is not accidental. On the contrary, it is deeply rooted in the paradoxes underlying Kahana-Carmon's writing. For the fact is that any reader, male or female, initiated into her artistic world—the early fiction in particular—cannot help but be struck by the impact of her unconventional, innovative style (i.e., *kelim* or *tzurah*, that is, "form"). Her idiosyncratic use of Hebrew syntax and semantics (which I have tried to preserve in my translations), of colloquialism and scriptural allusion, and her unique manipulation of narrative and textual expecta-tions—all these are too powerful to ignore. To treat this aspect of her artis-tic achievement as "just tools" is obviously a misjudgment, an outdated separation between art and artifice. Yet to consider it an Israeli version of écriture féminine, as recently suggested, has its own problems as well.[31] For, on the continent, where the concept originated, feminine writing has been propagated as a logical conclusion of sexual *difference*, a position much too unambiguous to accommodate the special blend that is Kahana-Carmon's feminism. For hers is definitely not the hysterical language of the body (although she thematizes the "poetics of the body" in her latest novel, as I will discuss further on in this chapter). In fact, her prose features a heavy concentration of scriptural allusions, a rich compendium of sources in the spirit of the best male-stream of Jewish tradition. On the other hand, loosely strung together and postmodernistically ungrammatical, the colloquial syntax of these citations clearly fractures the system (Symbolic Order?) from which they are borrowed.[32] So why doth the lady protest so much?

The answer may lie precisely in the effect her tools have on the perception of her substance. In fact, the artistry she has invested in the evocation of the female condition is so powerful that the line between grievance and glorification tends to blur.[33] It is not always clear, for example, whether woman's private sphere, her inwardness, is her prison or her mansion; whether feminine "passivity" is viewed as a social evil, imposed by patriarchal pressures, or as a deliberate choice, an intentional withdrawal from public action (thereby clearing a path for female creativity); finally, whether the penchant of her heroines for the dysphoric plot, for dependent, unrequited love attachments, is to be censured as a disruption of their capacity for masculinist work and autonomy or lauded as a unique, gender-specific endowment, a sort of existential transcendence.

Kahana-Carmon's feminist romance seems, then, to be torn among several contradictory demands. Her desire to represent an authentic female subjectivity, which she understands exclusively in terms of oppression and passivity, is undercut by two opposing forces: the temptation to idealize or even essentialize femininity or sexual difference and the yearning for universal, cross-gender, feminist equality, for an idealized state of grace before the Fall.

It is in the latter, of course, that the New Hebrew Woman is to be expected. But she is not readily available in Kahana-Carmon's early canon; at least not in the reality of her fictional universe. She inheres in her protagonists' imagination, partly fantasy, partly trace memory. As an actual reality she is limited to a single time period—to the 1948 War of Independence, in which the author participated as a wireless operator, or to the year preceding it at the Hebrew University in Jerusalem. The experiences of the war were recorded in Kahana-Carmon's early story, "The Whirling Sword" (1956), and then reworked, expunged of the stylistic hallmarks of the Palmach literature to better fit the new style she was developing in the

1960s. The protagonist of her first novel, on the other hand, like other women fighters of World War II (such as the British heroine of David Hare's play *Plenty* [1978]), perceive the "morning after" as a fall from the grace (the "highest point," *hasi'*) of autonomy they experienced in the war years.[34] The postwar protagonist is often conceptualized as an impoverished version of her former self, a frustrated housewife who has lost her capacity for work—and even for love.[35] Though she is fully aware of her dependency and depletion, she is unable to act, or, at best, she sublimates the loss by the celebration of female inward subjectivity—an essentialist strategy of survival that seems to have exhausted its usefulness by the beginning of the 1980s.

2. A Brotherhood of Outsiders: Women/Jews/Blacks in Up in Montifer

Apparently aware of the danger of essentialism lurking in this strategy of survival, Kahana-Carmon has finally made an effort to break away from the confines of her own making and construct a female subject liberated from the yoke of passivity and dependent attachment. Predictably, this experiment coincided with the publication, in 1984, of the first in a series of programmatic essays, "To Be a Woman Writer," a kind of an Israeli feminist manifesto.[36] (As we shall see, 1984 happened to be a very good year for feminism in Israel.) Just as predictably, it took the form of a quasi-historical narrative, ostensibly for "young adults" (that is, a *non*canonic genre).[37] Even more than Shulamit Lapid in *Gei Oni*, Kahana-Carmon felt compelled to transpose her protagonist into the past—in her case, all the way back to seventeenth-century Europe—in order to both subjugate her to and emancipate her from the yoke of Jewish/feminine victimhood. And as if such chronotopical displacement would not suffice, she further distanced both herself and the reader from the issue at hand by embedding it within a general paradigm of otherness.[38] In fact, the novel(la) *The Bridge of the Green Duck*, the centerpiece of *Up in Montifer*,[39] is a typical postmodernist inquiry into essentialism, testing "difference" in the areas of gender, class, and race.

The author herself characterized the book as "a breakthrough . . . a different direction, a different approach," comparing its role to that of "The Ladies of Avignon" in Picasso's artistic development.[40] Here, she argued, "my characters try, for the first time, to do something about their reality..' . . . [They try get out of] their stoic inaction."[41] Whether or not this is indeed a meaningful turning point is a question to which I shall return. For now it may be noted that this new experiment was received more enthusiastically by female readers than by male readers, who were rather critical of the novel on thematic as well as aesthetic grounds.[42] But first let us explore the broader implications of the central topos of this narrative, exile and captivity.[43]

The Bridge of the Green Duck is not only the story of a woman's life in exile and captivity in seventeenth-century Europe, it is also an experiment in entering the subjectivity of the other. On the one hand, it takes place in a heavily androcentric society in which social boundaries are tightly drawn. The social hegemony of the white, male Christian horsemen is firmly established from the opening line, as is their agentic subjectivity. On the other hand, this internal subjectivity, this self-identity, is reported to us through the retrospective narration of a young Jewish woman, a former captive of these very horsemen. It is through *her* perspective that we get to know the horsemen's inner world; more accurately—through the ador-ing *imagination* of the child she had been many years ago, before they killed her father and took her prisoner to Montifer; before one of them fell in love with her and saved her life only to enslave her, abuse her, force his attentions (as well as his mastery) upon her;[44] and before she slowly grew into her own, shaping her own subjectivity, separating from her admired "other," and escaping into freedom.

I am not sure that this brief synopsis conveys the intricacy of perspec-tives permeating this novel. Self and other constantly shift places, not only among the characters but between reader and text. Like the young child, the reader is compelled (as we shall soon see) to enter into the subjectiv-ity of the other, only to experience the relativity of perceived dichotomies.[45]

My contention is that the young protagonist's immature infatuation with Peter, her captor-lover, should be read not merely as an exercise in popular Freudian psychology (the mechanism of identification with the aggressor, etc., as suggested by critics)[46] but rather as a literary probing of the philosophical question of difference, effectively deconstructing the binary opposition of self and other.[47] The fascinating tools executing this deconstruction are the focus of the following close analysis.

The opening of the novel unexpectedly plunges us into the as yet unnamed narrator's inner monologue, describing the mysterious "they" of the first sentence: "Not on the road they were galloping" (61). A quick external glance invites the reader to admire their energy, laughter, appetite, and self-confidence; the latter is amplified by the narrator's observation that "they" have never lost their awareness of being *kat segurah, kat 'ila'ah 'overet lifnei hamaḥaneh hemah, 'am levadad yishkon shel 'anshei ḥalutz kovshim* (a closed, superior caste, one that "passes over armed before the camp," "people who dwell alone," a sect of pioneers who clear the way) (61).

In Hebrew the biblical and national resonance of *'over(et) lifnei hamaḥaneh* and *'am levadad yishkon* is inescapable. It marshals a host of allusions to the status of a chosen people and its sense of uniqueness and vocation (see especially Numbers 22 and 32). When the (Hebrew) reader realizes—a few pages into the narrative—that this all too familiar description is attributed here to the other—and that the gentile (and of course male) dark horsemen are in fact the enemy, the captors of the (then twelve-year-old) narrator—it is too late. A miracle of sorts has already taken place: By providing a new signified for the biblical signifiers, the text has triggered a process of identification/projection, thereby assisting the reader in imagining the other subjectively. The "preconceived judgment," the portrait we usually have of the other (particularly of a different gender, nationality, or class, as illustrated in this story—see the epigraph to this chapter) has been partially or temporarily bracketed so that self and other may exchange places, at least for a short while.

But there is more. Not only is the social positionality of otherness subverted, so is its psychological makeup. The dichotomy of "inside-outside," central to otherness both psychologically and physically (e.g., the inability to leave Montifer) is thematized in numerous ways, from the folksy fables about the cuckoo fledgling in its host nest and the family romance of the duckling, to the allusions to the biblical Dinah and to biblical laws that sanction marrying a gentile (female) war captive. Thus, Rabbi Zefaniah, whose marriage proposal is rejected by the heroine, uses a phrase from Deuteronomy 21:11 ("If you see a woman of beauty among the [war] captives and take a liking to her, you may marry her") to justify the attraction she holds for him. Although technically she is neither a captive nor a convert, her beauty and otherness (after years of a reverse captivity among the gentiles) are enough for him to relate to her as to an other, so that the Deuteronomy laws "permit" him to marry her (84).

The protagonist, on the other hand, retroactively recognizes that her long captivity on Montifer was not strictly that. She was not just part of the spoils of war, as others may think, because in her heart she had yearned after the alien, the enemy, for a long time before that moment:

Because I know this was not so. Because the arena of my heart was a bird's nest; many days before my captivity an alien egg had been placed there. A cuckoo's egg. And this is the story of a cuckoo's egg. . . . The trouble is, however, that [in the end] the fledgling itself does not know any better, and sees his nonparents, and only them, as his real parents. Possibly something of this kind happens in a human's heart, when it turns into an arena of war.   (86–87)

The Beauvoirian ambivalence of the other is demonstrated here in all its complexity; as is the basic doubleness of the self, of the split subjectivity of postmodern discourse, from Lacan to Homi Bhabha. This split is articulated by the heroine in her retrospective imagined conversation with her captors on Montifer: "With you I was always absent there. However, I was tamed by force to accept, to believe that this I, the absent one, was the real I" (150). The major metaphor, however, for this split is the image of a second wagon, a "double" that the protagonist sees moving alongside her own wagon on the way to the fair in the big city (chapter 8). Transparently used as a stand-in for the self, this metaphor marks several stages of a major transformation in the heroine's consciousness:

And only outside, along [my wagon] another wagon seems to move, a double [wagon]. There, straight and silent, I sit, I-the-double, I-the-fruitful.   (159)

I turned to roll up the curtain a bit. But I was not looking out. As if only watching, keeping eye contact. Contact with the double [wagon]. Inside it [was] the other me. The watchful, the wistful.   (163)

I was silent: like someone hanging on, climbing on a moving wagon, or like a butterfly on the other side of a window glass, it seemed that the I who was in the double wagon was trying to get in. To come, solemn and sorrowful, finally to sit down with me. "Strange developments," I said [to myself].   (166)

These "strange developments" speak for themselves. By stages, they mend the long split I, dissolving the unseen "window glass" that separates the present self from the absent self, finally bringing together the wistful I and the fruitful I, canceling the need to ride in two parallel wagons.

Moreover, the porous boundaries between self and other also dissolve—when the biblical allusion to the chosen people, quoted above, is attributed by the (still unnamed) narrator to . . . herself (176). Not only to herself, however. At this stage of the plot she is equipped with a recently acquired friend who is (surprise! surprise!) . . . a *black* ex-captive. What has been earlier perceived then as the domain of the elect, the chosen other (the male, European, gentile conqueror) is now triumphantly attributed to a new signified—the self-awareness of the formerly subjugated Jewish female (*Judea Capta?*) and the formerly enslaved black, Eved Hakushi.[48] With this reversal a whole range of boundaries is subverted and crossed over—race, class, and gender—so that the marginalized other is allowed the privilege of her or his own subjectivity. That this self-awareness is expressed in precisely the same figurative language as that of the oppressor's makes the point all the more transparent.

An uninformed reader might perhaps ask how a liberated black slave shows up in seventeenth-century Northern Europe. While not that uncommon (as Shakespeare's *Othello* should remind us), the historical accuracy of this otherwise lyrically wrought narrative is indeed impressive. (This is by no means to detract from the power of its poetic mimesis: that century's special blend of violence and humanism, of dark fanaticism and the stirring of liberalism is masterfully evoked here, its verisimilitude established by the most lyrical yet lifelike landscapes of both wo/man and nature.) In a kind of uncanny coincidence, Kahana-Carmon anticipated in this story two of the components that make up another reconstruction of "Seventeenth-Century Lives"—Natalie Zemon Davis's historical study of *Women on the Margins*: the life story of a fiercely independent Jewish [female] merchant, Glikl of Hamlin,[49] and the role of Surinam, the South American slave colony, in the life "metamorphosis" of a no less independent Protestant (female) artist-naturalist, Maria Sibylla Merian of Amsterdam.[50] Although Kahana-Carmon claims to have heard about Glikl's diary only after her own story had been completed,[51] this coincidence between fiction and history is no doubt striking. Was she aware of the slave plantations in Surinam? Perhaps not. Yet this fictional/historical connection is no less intriguing.[52] For Doovdevan Surinam (the Cherry of Surinam), Eved's "botanical" nickname, enigmatically alludes to a past he is reluctant to reveal. Could he be one of those Surinam slaves who, despite the imminent threat of punishment, "got away successfully"?[53] We will never know for sure, nor is this knowledge crucial for our understanding or appreciation of Eved's characterization. What I might argue, though, is that his function in the symbolic structure fashioned by the novelist is greatly illuminated—in retrospect of course—by the conclusions of the historian. For Davis's conclusion is that the "secret" behind the unique empowerment of her three "women on the margins" was their encounter with the

Amalia Kahana-Carmon

other: "In the cases of all three women we looked at their connections, imagined or real, with non-European people."[54]

This observation is no doubt true for Kahana-Carmon's fictional universe as well. Rather unexpectedly, the ex-slave comes to represent the most profound subjectivity and agency. In a move that clearly resonates with Beauvoir's analogy between women, "Negroes," and Jews, and as well as with contemporary postcolonial or minority discourse (see chapter 2), his double otherness (both race and class) mirrors that of his Jewish friend, unobtrusively assisting in her own transformation.

To begin with, before the curtain comes down Kahana-Carmon treats us to a last act in which the Hegelian-Sartrean warfare of intersubjectivity is dramatized in all its tension, finally leading the narrator to appropriate her first name, that sacrosanct hallmark of the construction of subjectivity. (That this name is accompanied by her patronymic—"Clara, the daughter of Avigdor the merchant," 179—is, however, an ironic undermining of this very construction.) Clara—as she is finally named (significantly late in the narrative)—is taught to "look back" and "take" her autonomy. To do so she needs to give up her presumed position of physical frailty vis-à-vis her black friend—a script that smacks not only of the Beauvoirian solution for female otherness but also of the Zionist solution for Jewish otherness. What sets this scene apart, however, is the ironic fact that Clara is forced into this step by *his* refusal to accept the position of strength she stereotypically attributes to him.

With this final scene Kahana-Carmon brings ad absurdum a psychological pattern that in fact controls Clara's life: her neurotic attachment to the father figures of her life. While her mother plays a small (rather ambivalent) role in her life (a psychological feature typical of the Israeli feminist romance in its infancy),[55] her psychological growth, her Bildung, is represented mostly through her object relations with male figures: her own father, 'Avigdor (*'avi* meaning "my father" in Hebrew), Rabbi Tzefaniah (whose name connotes both an enigma and a conscience, *matzpun*, and who functions as a Freudian superego, the addressee of Clara's introspective letters throughout the narrative), her captor-lover (whose name, Peter, particularly in its Hebrew pronunciation, nicely puns on "patron," in its secular meaning: "boss," not "patron saint");[56] and finally Eved Hakushi, the black ex-captive.

From a psychological perspective Clara's life story is the unfolding of an inner conflict between an all-devouring urge for transference love/dependency and a conscious struggle against it. The obsessive character of her need becomes particularly transparent in the last part of the plot, when, after successfully releasing herself not only from her physical bondage in Montifer but also from an emotional attachment to her captor, she is all but ready to repeat the same pattern in her relationship with a new authority figure, the liberated Eved Hakushi. The contrast between chapter 7 (Clara's encounter with Peter) and chapter 8 (her encounter with Eved) is a masterfully rendered drama (oddly neglected by scholarship) that bristles with metaphoric references to key chapters in the philosophical literature on subjectivity and otherness.

Chapter 7 finds Clara at a relatively safe distance from Peter. She has escaped captivity, now living "*harḥek mimontifer*" (far away from Montifer, the iron mountain), in the house of a Jewish innkeeper. But the predator (Peter's major epithet throughout the text) does not give up on his prey so easily. "*Miketz yamim rabim*" (the fablelike "after many days" adding to the presumed ahistoricity of the narration), Peter reappears, sowing fear all around, even though he enters this time with a peace offering: he wants to start a new phase ("*hagilgul haba*"), magnanimously asking (in fact, almost commanding) Clara to accompany him in his flight north; now not as a slave, of course, but as a free companion. Surprisingly, Clara is able to resist his feline predatory charm: "The answer is no," she says, repeating it twice, delighting in Peter's disbelief and celebrating her "liberation": "The day I said no. It passed my humble lips (*dal hasefataim*). And my own ears heard it" (143). Peter's total shock ("The words froze on his lips: 'What did I hear,' he asked") attests to the measure of her accomplishment. As if following a Hegelian script, the constitution of the other (his ex-object) as a subject finally brings forth an admission of his own intersubjectivity:

> "What is there to explain, you fool. You set the tone [*ta'am*], didn't you?" . . .
> "With you, everything had some purpose [*ta'am*] too . . .
> Perhaps I was pushed to this against my will, perhaps," his voice faded, "but it is a fact. Another man, I believe, I've become. With you."
> *(146)*

Still, this admission does not sway Clara from her decision. She had been objectivized by Peter's gaze for too long to be persuaded by his inadvertent recognition of her separate subjectivity. Her true test comes only in the next chapter, in her encounter with a different kind of other, Eved Hakushi.

In this penultimate chapter the slave-turned-master (Hegel), although engaged by Clara as a handyman, teaches her a lesson not only in the empowerment of otherness but in existential transcendence as well. This lesson is intriguingly composed of two seemingly unrelated intertexts, one Shakespearian and the other Beauvoirian. At the opening of the chapter we find Clara, by now an independent single woman and a successful merchant, sitting in a wagon on her way to the annual fair in the nearby "big town." Accompanying her is Eved Hakushi, who has recently begun to work for her and whom she considers her only "friend" in this place. . . . As they ride in the wagon, Eved is patching a coat Clara gave him: "My father's old black coat, which I gave him today as a gift . . . " (161). The repair done, Eved takes off his own old coat,

> in order to put on my father's coat. And I saw, turning my head to look inside [the wagon], and I was struck with amazement at the sight of his black flesh. I saw that, except for his faded pants he wore nothing under his coat. Not even socks. . . .
>
> But I, since when did I forget that Eved Hakushi was black . . . the reality hit me in the face. That is, his face [is] not at all that of local peasants in the summer's heat, [it is] darker, Eved Hakushi's face, his hands and his feet. The man is black all over. *Black and different* . . .
>
> "How terrible," I murmured.   *(164; emphasis added)*

In response to Eved's bland incomprehension (" 'What's so terrible,' wondered Eved Hakushi"), Clara attempts to explain the source of her horror, elaborating even further on her "horrifying discovery":

> "As if someone took and encased you in a black tight stocking, as it were, a second skin. What a misfortune . . . "
>
> "As if by force," I tried again, "without consulting you, they tattooed your whole body. And there's no removing it."

Now Eved is amused: "No removing and no concealing. . . . Remember, no concealing either." To drive his point home, he calmly translates what she perceives as color otherness into subjective race consciousness, equating—in the most postmodernist fashion—his race subjectivity with her gender subjectivity:

> "But you're mistaken, you know," he said. . . . "Take a look and tell me. You. Are you a man in a woman's body? You're not. Is this such a misfortune? Why a misfortune. With you, with me, it's the same thing, more or less. And why a tight stocking. Why a tatoo. A black man. This is me and this is what you see."   *(164)*

This lesson in the empowerment of otherness allows Clara to engage in a dialogue that surreptitiously "bridges" the differences between them, leading them onward to the symbolic bridge of the green duck (175), the very location where epiphanic moments in the relationship with her father and Peter had taken place in the past. But before reaching this stage a whole comedy of errors is enacted, the core of which is another set of binary differences that are negotiated and deconstructed in a variety of ways.

With the question of racial alterity seemingly resolved, the next issue to be faced by our protagonists is that of class difference. This seems to be neutralized with relative ease, starting with Eved Hakushi's friendly kiss on Clara's cheek (165). Her observation, "Eved Hakushi does not obey my orders. He is just intent on walking behind me as a walking tower" (167), is then followed by a reversal in which the social difference blends into gender difference, thereby anticipating the denouement of this encounter: when Eved leads the way through the dangerous streets, "where a woman cannot walk alone" (!) (170), Clara "silently admits: now it is I who steps behind him" (171).

Next comes the issue of social communion, typically negotiated via a shared meal, a code automatically recognized by both parties. Handing Clara half his bread, Eved apologizes: " 'Forgive my eating with my hands,' said [Eved], tearing the bread with his teeth." To which Clara teasingly responds: " 'Forgive my eating with knife and fork,' said I somberly, tearing the bread with my fingers" (171).

When it comes to the code of emotional communion, however, things become somewhat more complicated. The description of the embrace (initiated by Eved) is represented through Clara's stream of consciousness as a veritable web of erotic and incestuous allusions:

> He opened my father's coat which he was wearing and wrapped me inside it, humming quietly, then clasped me to his chest, pushing me against the wall.
> Already freely I'm rushing toward him, willingly accommodating him, pressing, rubbing forcefully the tough smooth dark skin, I could feel his scraggly beard, fluttering outlandishly over the skin of my face, and the back of his thumb tightening on the scar on my cheek,[57] and then reversing itself, kneading into the scar with the pad of the thumb, "I am not sure who is more insane," I said in a small voice, realizing I wasn't speaking to the point, "Nobody's insane," Eved Hakushi said, his face pressed in me, realizing he [too] was not speaking to the point,

> yet I could feel the haft of a knife concealed on his left, perhaps sewn
> into the lining of his large pants.   (*159*)

The rising rhythm of this scene is unexpectedly brought to a halt with
Clara's (almost adolescent) question: "Why do you hug me?" only to be
answered by Eved's even more unexpected reply: " '—I am your
brother.'—'My brother?' I said with a jolt. I lifted my face to him, *shaken*:
'So, OK, I have a brother in the world,' I said *shaken*" (172; emphasis
added). Why is Clara shaken, perhaps even shocked (*nir'eshet*, repeated
twice)? Was she wrong? Has she misread the code of intimacy? Or perhaps
we should translate her emotional response as "deeply moved" or "pleas-
antly surprised" by Eved's brotherly response?

Answers to these questions are not immediately forthcoming. For a
while Clara's agitation remains unexplained, except for her emotional
(and lengthy) exploration of this new sense of familial bonding (172–175)
in which she happily learns more about Eved's life and beliefs. Yet when
by the end of this process she declares, "Hurrah, for the first time in my
life I have a brother in this world," the positive valorization of this "label"
begins to crystallize, finally culminating in the privileged self-consciousness we mentioned above:

> And my brother is a free man, free like a bird, aware, I felt.
>   Both of us are aware, aware of being *kat segurah, 'ila'ah, 'overet lifnei
> hamahaneh, 'am levadad yishkon, 'anshei halutz kovshim.*   (*176*)

What precisely is the source of this brotherly bond is never made clear.
Nor is there any explanation for the sudden exaltation inspired by this
bond. Is it familial? Is it erotic? Is Eved's declaration, *'ahikh 'ani* ("I am
your brother"), a gendered reversal of the biblical " *'ahotenu 'at*" ("You
are our sister," Genesis 24:60), echoing the blessings of Rebecca's family
when she departs from home on her betrothal trip? Or is it an answer to
the "sister bride" of the Song of Songs, who once, and once only (8:1),
wishes for her lover to be her brother (*'ah*) rather than her beloved (*dod*)
so that she could publicly kiss him without censure?

To fully understand Kahana-Carmon's use of the term we have to wait
patiently for our analysis of her next novel. For, in the present text, this
moment of brotherly recognition does not last long. In a typical Sartrean
fashion Clara immediately (though unintentionally) lapses into "other-
ing" her "brother." Asking him to cut off a branch of a prickly bush
because "You do not get scratched," she receives a well-deserved
reproach, which is a paraphrase of (who else?)—*Shylock*'s famous mono-

logue: " 'Don't we scratch? Won't we scratch?' he turned around to me as if to threaten, the backs of his hands stretched forward. And I saw the blood stains, lighter than the color of his skin" (176). The allusion to Shylock's "Don't we bleed?" faint though it may be, implies Eved's racial sensitivities, which make him jump to a conclusion about Clara's racist "slur." Clara's rushed apology, however, makes clear that hers is gender rather than racial "bias" (or "preconceived judgment," in her father's formulation): " 'Not because of your color . . . because of your strength' " (176). With this move the author succeeds in turning otherness into an all-inclusive paradigm.[58] Exclusionary attitudes toward race and gender—stereotypes of Jews and blacks, of masculinity and femininity—are all decentered and subverted. Beauvoir's side show—the analogies between the demonization and exclusion of women, blacks, and Jews—has moved to the center of attention only to be ideally debunked and hopefully reversed.

But this is of course more easily said than done, even in the fictive universe created in this novel. Because for Clara the terms of the argument have shifted. Admitting to her ostensibly gendered weakness, she has in fact forfeited her potential subject transcendence. Furthermore, her clinging attachment to the "stronger sex" is interpreted by Eved as an absolutely repulsive "search for power" (179). We should not be surprised then that the next stage of their encounter is marked by a sort of an agon, a Sartrean duel of gazes. Repeated twice (as is almost every key motif or metaphor in this narrative), the enigmatic expression *'eino haletushah be-'eini haletushah* ("His piercing eye [fixed] on my piercing eye," 179, 180) calls for interpretation.

Intratextually, it is not difficult to place it within the context of similar locutions, describing—earlier in the narrative—young Clara's infatuation with the dark horsemen; except that there the metaphor was slightly extended, developing the *difference* between the two piercing eyes. While her eye was described as the curious and searching eye of a seriously minded young child, the horseman's (or Peter's) eyes were perceived as arrogant predator's eyes. The balance of power is quite clear. It was this arrogance that kept Clara entrapped, feeding on her infatuation with otherness and her eagerness to partake in it (117, 119, 153). By now, however, this distinctive feature seems to have faded. The present duel of gazes presents us with a metaphorical balance between the two eyes (both of them piercing, with no distinctive features). This "repetition in variation," a familiar trait of biblical poetics,[59] naturally arouses our expectation; does this balance foretell the future? Does it guarantee an equal standing to both sides?

It should have, if this were a purely Sartrean drama. But Clara is still not ready. She soon fully recapitulates. Relinquishing the opportunity to rejoin the Jewish community from which she was kidnapped as a child, she chooses to follow Eved, the other who has become her new "br/other." Ironically, she acknowledges the audacity of her choice with the help of a classic Jewish source: "I have crossed a covert boundary. Now I am clearly beyond the pale" (181). "Like the young Moses I am, who between gold and coals has chosen the coals" (182). The allusion to the midrashic "explanation" for Moses's speech impediment is startling indeed. It raises questions about the self-image of the protagonist and the unconscious motivation of her decision.[60] For, consciously, she may be aware of the social meaning of her move, of the identity choice it implies, but not of its existential implications. Her inward plea ("Where are you, Eved Hakushi, my heart kept hoping. Wouldst I found you, that I might return home with you," 182) ironically dramatizes—much more glaringly than did the final recapitulation of Fania in *Gei Oni* (see chapter 1)—Beauvoir's analysis of women's complicity in their own subjugation.[61] No wonder, then, that Kahana-Carmon parts here with the Hegelian narrative that underlies her Beauvoirian script.

In an unexpected move the ex-captive refuses to fulfill the role of the master. In contrast to Peter, the young captor-lover who has taken advantage of Clara's dependency (and in the end fallen in love with her himself), Eved Hakushi is "older and wiser." His recently gained freedom, both social and emotional, is his most cherished possession (but also the source of his ambivalence). In the last chapter we find him at the inn, light-headed and totally deaf to Clara's imploring. Chapter 9 is a masterfully rendered dialogue of miscommunication between her pathetically self-conscious "need for encouragement" and his obstinate "Am I a father to you?" (184). And although this rejection obviously deals a sharp blow to Clara's spirits, it would be erroneous to read it as merely another illustration of the ubiquitous male betrayal of the weaker sex, as some critics have done.[62] To read it in this way is to identify entirely with Clara's point of view—a "natural" position for a reader of a first-person narration but not a sophisticated maneuver for a critic. For only by distancing ourselves from the narrative perspective are we able to piece together the (implied) authorial position, the one suggested in Kahana-Carmon's most celebrated early story, "Ne'ima Sasson Writes Poetry" (see section 1)—despite the pain involved, Eved's rejection of Clara is instrumental in her internalization of his "lesson" in freedom/autonomy/subjectivity.

Such is precisely the conclusion. In the last episode of the novel Clara "declares" her maturation and self-reliance by demanding (and receiving) the *key* to a case of merchandise. When Eved removes the key from "her father's coat pocket" (191), which he is now wearing, the Freudian-Lacanian symbolism becomes quite transparent. While Eved's role as substitute father is over, the protagonist herself moves into the paternal position. The case's key is in fact her key to the very trade that Jewish folklore, via the celebrated lullaby, foretells to the (male) babe—commerce in "raisins and almonds" (= dried fruit, in the language of this story).[63]

The narrative thus concludes with a verbal agon that seems to achieve what the specular duel has failed to do:

> "I'm staying. To find out. Here, at this place, tomorrow. Concerning trading in dried fruit in our place. Also to shop for myself. This is what I came here for," I said. "After all, this was the plan."
>
> Eved Hakushi shrugged his shoulders. But when I turned away, he stopped me, laughing:
>
> "How do you plan, tell me, to find a place for the night by yourself, a woman alone, in this city."
>
> "We'll see."
>
> "And how do you plan, tell me, one woman alone, to confront all this city's great dried fruit merchants."
>
> "We'll see."
>
> "You have no idea what you are talking about."
>
> "We'll see."
>
> "And how do you plan to draft a porter tomorrow, tell me."
>
> "We'll see."
>
> "We'll see" he repeated after me, with jeering eyes.   (*191–192*)

The contrast between this closing dialogue and the closure of Lapid's *Gei Oni* could not be any greater. With her insistent declaration of independence, Clara seems resolved to flee the feminist romance, giving up love for the sake of work. Yet the wry irony underlying this final scene cannot be mistaken. Even her own mentor doubts the viability of her newly acquired autonomy.[64] Once again, we are faced with the ubiquitous double standard; except that this author, unlike her predecessor, ironically acknowledges its subversive power. It would seem that although she has taken this heroine a step further toward masculinist autonomy, Amalia Kahana-Carmon too, as Shulamit Lapid before her, could hardly envision a feasible reality for her New Hebrew Woman. Framed by the anaphoric repetition "We'll see," this reality is still only a promised land, beckoning the heroine beyond the closure of the text.

What remains unanswered is the question concerning the source of this deferral. Is emancipation just an act of self-will, or is it subject to internal and/or external obstacles? Stripped of all former dependent relationships with male figures, would not a typical Kahana-Carmon's character find herself at a loss? And would not the dominant social power deny her the "privilege" it had granted to her black friend? More important, is it a privilege? Should she/can she forego love for the sake of 'work'? Questions abound. But satisfactory answers are not readily available. And it was probably this ambiguity, wrapped as it is in a thick layer of allegorism, that perplexed the readers of *The Bridge of the Green Duck*. Their waning enthusiasm might have echoed the author's own quandary, contributing to a long hiatus in which programmatic essays took the place of creative writing.

3. *The Brotherhood That Cannot Hold*

Only in Kahana-Carmon's later novel, *Liviti 'otah baderekh leveitah* (With Her on Her Way Home, 1992), published almost a decade after *Up in Montifer* (1984), has the fog somewhat dissipated.[65] Foregoing historico-allegorical displacement, Kahana-Carmon has courageously woven a contemporary story of romance and artistic creativity (a nice substitute for work), matrimony, and divorce. Working much closer to home, autobiographically speaking, she boldly portrays the ups and downs of two decades in the life and loves of a (fictionally) famous Israeli . . . theater actress.[66] A passing allusion to Katharine Hepburn in her regal role in the film "The Lion in Winter" ("a lioness in winter," 56), conveys both her celebrity status and the pathos of the decline of this status.

Me'ira Heller, whose name is in fact a Hebrew (and Yiddish) rendition of Clara,[67] seems to pick up where Clara left off. She actually manages to have a successful career, be a mother (though in a totally unproblematized way),[68] and—at the crucial moment of approaching midlife—find the love of her life. Unlike Clara, however, she is not in possession of her story. Her story is narrated by Mossik, her lover, who is (rather predictably) an Israeli synthesis of Clara's two "loves": the irresistible attraction of his *bon physique*, countlessly reiterated throughout the dialogue (as if paying homage to the "body politics" of postmodernism and to the French paean to "writing the body"; 71, 276, and passim), is reminiscent of Peter's predatory hold on Clara. Unlike Peter, however, Mossik is not "white"; he is a "dark Adonis," resembling "a giant from the N.B.A." (49, 115), whose "silky brown" skin, associated with "perhaps" some "Ethiopian genes" or "negroid blood" (ibid.), clearly aligns him with Eved Hakushi. Except that here this "racial" otherness is not a cause for alarm but for adoration. In a deconstructionist move Me'ira mockingly declares herself a "racist" because she cannot see herself with "anyone who is not an 'oriental' Israeli" (*me'edot hamizrah*). This mock-racism says it all: *With Her on Her Way Home* is, on some level, a contemporary "actualization" of the allegorical bond between the others essayed in *The Bridge of the Green Duck*. Two internal Israeli others—Israel's "minorities" in the Deleuze and Guattari sense—a "white" female (Heller) and a "dark" *mizrahi* male, a representative of *Israel hashniah*,[69] overcome their marginalization by entering into a singular relationship, one that is blithely labeled, once and again, "our infamous bond": *ha'ahvah hayedu'ah leshimtzah* (36, 48, 73, and passim).

To make sense of this almost untranslatable locution, a biblical subtext is necessary: As constructed in this text, *'ahvah*, literally "brotherhood," is a contemporary transformation of Abraham's peace offering to Lot in Genesis 13:8, *halo' 'anashim 'ahim 'anahnu* ("for we be brethren" [KJ], or "for we are close kinsmen" [NEB]). This biblical prooftext is cited early on in the narrative (36) as the basis for the protagonists' relationship. However, the frequent use of the allusion tends to obliterate two ironic moves that operate in the transformation of the subtext.[70] First, in the case of Abraham and Lot, this statement of fact introduces a proposal for a peaceful solution for a sibling *rivalry* (parting or separate coexistence) rather than *cooperation*—perhaps an ironic foreshadowing of the denouement of our plot; second, it assumes two *male* siblings, which is precisely what the "translation" into the contemporary idiom *'ahvah* seems to undo. Generally translated as "brotherhood," this nongenderized abstract noun carries a strong connotation of egalitarian friendship (created no doubt by the contiguity of *shivyon ve-'ahvah*, the Hebrew for the slogan *egalité et fraternité* of the French Revolution). As English does not offer any satisfactory equivalent, I have translated *'ahvah* as "brotherly bond," a translation preserving the grammatical root of the noun, *'.h.h.*, its biblical intertext (the "brethren" of the Genesis allusion), as well as its modern, nongenderized connotation. (This translation fails, however, to capture the homophonic pun on the word *'ahavah*, "love" proper.)

We may now be able to better understand, retrospectively, the use of the label *brother* in *The Bridge of the Green Duck*. Unlike the earlier narrative, however, here "brotherly bond" is the backbone of the relationship, expounded and elaborated throughout the narrative. Moreover, its attribute, *hayedu'ah leshimtzah* (infamous), mockingly acknowledges the lovers' self-awareness of its rarity and unconventionality. Implying cross-gender equality, it is in fact a modern version of the common topos of the lover as soul mate or twin, which resonates with Aristophanes' androgynes or the biblical *'ezer kenegdo* (when properly understood).[71] In a sense, it is the very condition on which the joyful erotic love of this story is founded.[72]

The exquisite portrayal of this unconventional love—spanning twenty years and two lengthy cross-continental breakups—is one of the most authentic in the author's oeuvre and unprecedented in Hebrew fiction. I cannot do justice here to its nuanced stylization, intricate structure, and psychological insights, nor to the rich web of intertextuality that links it to the rest of Kahana-Carmon's work. I will also forego the temptation to map this novel's numerous "citations" (not only from the canon of Hebrew poetry, but from works of art, music, and other literary traditions as well), which place it in the orbit of postmodernist poetics.[73] Suffice it to say, for the purposes of our immediate argument, that on the surface this singular love seems to offer an antidote to the "feminist romance," constructing its own version of the New Hebrew Woman.

Paradoxically, the narrative bearer of this new configuration is the male counterpart, a maneuver that may be construed as problematic, if not subversive for a feminist project of this kind. That this is not the case attests to the imaginative strategy of indirection deployed by our author. Me'ira's voice does reach us, because Mossik's narration is in fact a mechanical replay of past telephone conversations, recorded by him (without the knowledge of his interlocutor). In other words, the modernist art of recollection (Proust) has undergone here a postmodernist metamorphosis. By substituting mechanically produced memories for the human process of (involuntary) remembering, this narrative casts doubts on the subject's ability to collect his fragments into a meaningful whole *on his/her own*. Along the way, it also "updates" a veteran theme, giving a contemporary twist to one of the major preoccupations of all literature, the inexorable effect of time on love and life.

Unique as this narrative frame may be, it in fact reflects the uniqueness of the story it unravels, at least in the corpus we are surveying. For, like

Clara in our earlier novel, Mossik compulsively tries to "decode a secret," to make sense of a relationship gone wry. Structured *in opposition* to marital bliss, the dynamics of this relationship seemingly explode the captivity narrative of female dependency and gender inequality. Its earlier stages, at least, effect a synthesis between work and love, enhanced by a strong dose of *jouissance*, in the best French tradition (both critical and otherwise). The liberating power of shared intimacy ("the poetics of the body," 43), both physical and spiritual, is explored here with all its playfulness and humor,[74] but all its pathos as well. For this idealized brotherly erotic bond (not to be confused with incestuous love) is undermined by its very catalyst—the human body. And although the betrayal of the body is a lament of old standing ("The body is the cause of love," says Yehuda Amichai, "Later, the fortress guarding it, / Later, the prison of love"[75]), here it has a special poignancy. "Twenty years" is not only the duration of this romance; it is also (roughly) the age difference between the lovers—although not the one we would expect.

On the face of it, it is the difference in the aging process of our two lovers that stands in the way of happiness. For when Mossik has finally outgrown his adolescent fear of "codependency" ("My rebellion without cause against you is over, like measles and whooping cough," 52); when after seven years of absence he is ready to acknowledge the mutuality of their attachment ("This story of ours, it is only now beginning. We are invincible," 51)—it is precisely then that Me'ira reaches the "eclipse of her light" (in Hebrew the play on her name is quite clear; 276), entering a stage of parting, of farewell, of the "body's swan song" (43). "Twenty years later," says Leah Goldberg, in a poem that may be declared, in Riffaterre's terminology, the semiotic subtext of this novel, "Emotions are not like old wine: / They do not become more perfect, nor more sublime."[76] Time, "all that has happened in the world," is clearly the culprit in this poem (published in 1955). Four decades later Kahana-Carmon is able to cut closer to the bone; it is not (or at least not only) what happened in the world, she seems to be saying, but what happened with us, in our bodies (and souls) that makes the river of time so menacing.

Yet in this particular case it is not only the truism of the transitory nature of love (and life!) and the decline of the body that is at stake. What Me'ira is concerned about is the violation of the equilibrium (*'anaḥnu kevar lo' koḥot shavim*, 276) their relationship had enjoyed earlier. With the realization that this condition is gone, arrived at late in the story and in the narration, Me'ira is struggling with her own verdict to give up the relationship despite her continued attraction to Mossik's physique (295). At the close of the novel Me'ira paradoxically finds herself at a crossroad not that different from Clara's, mutatis mutandis. She has to choose between the unhappiness of dependent love and the unhappiness of lonely aging. In fact, it is the obsessive evocation of her coming to terms with the latter that renders this narrative both powerful and exasperating. For this is a grim prospect in a relationship that had earlier been described in glorious terms by both parties (e.g., the rarified flight of the condor over the Andes, 51–52).

One of these terms is of particular interest to our topic, as it uncovers the author's inadvertent transformation of a Freudian metaphor, a core concept in his (anti)feminine psychology: the discovery of Africa, the uncharted continent (49, 74 and passim). While for Freud the "dark continent" was a negative symbol of the female psyche, of its unknowability ("What does a woman want?"), Kahana-Carmon insists on the vitalizing element of self-discovery in her metaphoric use of "Africa": "The utopian yearning to dig into yourself as if into another country, a country of mystery; a mystery of power, of magic, that is inside you . . . but about which you somehow were not aware."[77] With this Kahana-Carmon seems to have transformed Freud's negative "unknowability" of the female in the same way as Julia Kristeva has transformed Lacan's maternal Imaginary (and Derrida's female otherness and absence) into the semiotic locus of creativity.[78]

This creative transformation notwithstanding, the question "What went wrong?" is always at the heart of Me'ira's reflections. Nevertheless, she never questions the nature of her glorious past, the ostensible equilibrium now lost. It is left to the attentive reader to ask, What is wrong with this picture?

We can begin by reconsidering the nature of the "infamous equilibrium." The fact is that despite the idealization the two parties were never on an equal footing. At the time of their fateful meeting—which occupies the middle section, the longest of three that make up the narrative (79–219)—Me'ira Heller was at the peak of her career while Mossik was young and socially uninitiated, a kind of an Israeli Rastignac (see Balzac's *Le père Goriot*), groping his way in the metropolis. But it was precisely this reverse hierarchy that enabled Me'ira to feel equal in some way to Mossik. Theirs was the bond of the weak, producing a false sense of egalitarianism. As long as his low social status compensated for her basic "feminine weakness" (the need for dependency and the worshipping of masculine "strength," which are the same for the immature and disadvantaged Clara and the celebrity of the Tel Aviv stage), the illusion of equilibrium could hold. But this illusion eventually gives way to sexual otherness: While social realities change, psychological structures do not. Even in this best of all possible relationships, Kahana-Carmon is unable (or unwilling?) to imagine a truely nonhierarchical male-female interaction. In the final analysis the change of scenery has not affected the fundamental dynamics of her feminist romance. When all is said and done her latest protagonist is the victim of gender essentialism just like her predecessors, despite the clamoring for cross-gender equality. Once again, Kahana-Carmon has carved out the most touching, insightful, and compelling dramatization— not of the New Hebrew Woman (that is, feminist emancipation) but of the unresolved tensions between sexual difference and female otherness. The persistence of these tensions in her work, throughout all its permutations, seems to attest to its deep-seated source. Small wonder that Kahana-Carmon's critique of the national narrative as an impediment to feminist liberation is relegated to the wings of her fictional stage, or—more eminently—to her extraliterary pronouncements. As in other cases, artistic intuition seems to better articulate psychological realities than do programmatic essays.

Nevertheless, one should not lose sight of the liberating vision that has motivated Kahana-Carmon's literary career. In this vision it is Clara and not Meira who has the last word. In an unusual act of fictional recreating, Kahana-Carmon has recently (1996) reissued a selection of her works in which she carefully organized some of her short stories and novellas into what she named, in the subtitle of the book, "Five Novels." *Kan nagur* (Here We'll Live) recants the old age resignation of *With Her on Her Way Home*, stringing together a life-affirming narrative that moves us from stories of frustration and emotional paralysis (part 1) through narratives of mature adjustments and accommodation within the family (parts 2, 3). In parts 4–5 we are back to young heroines, all smarting from the pain and insult inflicted on them by their idolized male object. The last "installment" in the journey of this collective heroine is, not surprisingly, Clara's narrative. Reproduced here in its entirety, signing off the four-hundred-page book with its hopeful refrain, "We'll see," it stands as Kahana-Carmon's emancipatory manifesto, foregrounding a future that holds a promise for the precarious Israeli feminism of today.[79]

Chapter 4

Who's Afraid of Androgyny?
Virginia Woolf's "Gender"
avant la lettre

> Undeniably, the maternal metaphor exemplifies women "getting within," seizing, powerfully manipulating male discourse on women. . . . But the maternal metaphor, in my view, does not herald the invention of a different poetic or conceptual idiom. Indeed, it underscores not "the ease" but the unease of "springing from within" to a radical elsewhere.
> —Domna C. Stanton, "Difference on Trial"

The impasse in which we have left Amalia Kahana-Carmon's characters is not much different from the one encountered by Beauvoir's daughters (see chapter 2). The attempt to use female otherness as a strategy for subjectivity seems to be as problematic as the endeavor to deny it altogether, and the postmodernist valorization of difference—of any variety—turns out to sustain, ironically enough, the very dichotomy that Beauvoir (and Kahana-Carmon's recent protagonists) set out to undo. The attempt to dissolve this dichotomy led our next writers to compromise formations similar to those suggested by Virginia Woolf's androgyny. As we shall see in the following chapters, they put this idea to different uses, cautiously adapting it to the Jewish tradition and Israeli circumstances. The invention of Israeli androgyny coincided, interestingly enough, with the controversies that erupted within Western (mostly Anglo-American) feminism over Woolf's own legacy. The terms and arguments of this controversy are crucial for an understanding of both the similarities and the differences between Woolf's paradigmatic androgyny and its distant descendant recently forged in Israel. This chapter is therefore devoted to a close look at the Woolf controversy and to a bioliterary retracing of the genesis of androgyny in her work. The latter will enable me to offer a new psychological interpretation of its role in Woolf's artistic evolution; more important, it will reclaim Woolf's androgyny for general consumption as a counterbalance to the contested maternal metaphor of contemporary feminist discourse.

1. Untangling the Homoerotic Web: Between Orlando *and* A Room of One's Own

Given the scholarly industry that has evolved around Virginia Woolf since the 1970s, there seems to be no lack of information about her life and art. Yet it is precisely because of this plethora of data that there is still room for new ways of putting the puzzle together. For a puzzle she remains, all our learned disputations notwithstanding.

The first piece in the puzzle may be stated by paraphrasing the title of Edward Albee's notorious play: "Who's afraid of Woolf's androgyny?" This question is triggered by recent developments in the literature on Woolf, developments that have sown more confusion than is necessary. In order to clarify my take on this issue, let us begin by briefly tracing the reception history of the term from the 1970s to the present.[1]

The starting point of our inquiry is not arbitrary, of course. Although already celebrated during her lifetime ("I am in danger, indeed, of becoming our leading novelist, and not with the highbrows only," Woolf confided to her diary on October 17, 1931; less than a year later she noted coyly: "I am going to be photographed. Three more books appearing on Mrs. Woolf," August 20, 1932), very few new studies appeared between Woolf's death in 1941 and the publication of Quentin Bell's biography of his aunt in 1972.[2] This biography (and others), along with Leonard Woolf's autobiographical volumes (published in the sixties), apparently paved the way for the torrent of scholarship of the 1970s, much of it naturally inspired by feminist criticism, then in its prime. While both *Orlando* (1928) and *A Room of One's Own* (1929)—her two books in which androgyny is "practiced" and theorized, respectively—continued to enjoy unprecedented popularity with the lay readership,[3] the concept itself seems to have aroused much disagreement. If in the early seventies it still featured in at least two book-length studies, by the 1980s the allure began to diminish.[4] The scholarly offensive was led by Elaine Showalter's critique, "Virginia Woolf and the Flight Into Androgyny." Speaking in the name of "gyno-criticism," Showalter denigrated androgyny as a denial of women's (mostly though not only biological) experience, as a sexual sublimation in which the specificity ("difference" in postmodern parlance) of the female writer is once more absorbed into the experience of the male writer: "There is an eerie hint that in the androgynous solution Woolf pro-vides there lurks a psychological equivalent of lobotomy" (!).[5] The fierce postmodernist objection to this American pragmatism has been voiced time and again in recent scholarship, following Toril Moi's 1985 pioneer-ing study. The terms of this argument are largely familiar by now, rehears-ing in one way or another the postmodernist anxiety over essentialist def-initions of identity and its questioning of the precarious boundaries between sameness and difference, self and other. But along with this overt debate another discontent, of quite a different nature, was brewing. A measure of it may have been voiced by Lyndall Gordon, a biographer writ-ing in the mid-eighties:

> While writing *Orlando* and *A Room of One's Own*, between 1928 and 1929, Virginia Woolf toyed with the notion of an ideal composite of opposite sexes. But such a composite . . . was based on social stereotypes of masculinity and femininity and Virginia Woolf, at her most searching, questioned these in favor of natural attributes as yet obscured. *Her flir-tation with androgyny was short lived.* *(emphasis added)*[6]

This paragraph is the only reference to Woolf's "androgyny" in a biogra-phy of 280 pages—a scant allowance indeed.[7] Despite Gordon's terseness, however, it is not difficult to detect a certain discomfort between the lines, and the source is not indecipherable; in fact, it hides behind the ellipsis I created in the second sentence of our quotation. It consists of four words only but alludes to a long story: "as exemplified by Vita."

Implied in this parenthetical phrase is an unfortunate conflation (appar-ently not uncommon) of two related (but in my opinion not identical) themes in Woolf's life and art: androgyny and homoeroticism.[8] That this conflation is the product of the 1980s is only too obvious; it is the result of the "coming out" of gay studies (especially on the American campus) and the concomitant appropriation of women's studies by lesbian orienta-tion, and its recent sibling/rival, "queer theory."[9]

Indeed, for lesbian-oriented critics Virginia Woolf's rich yet enigmatic life and loves are a veritable gold mine. At the heart of the enigma is her puzzling sexuality, an issue that is, to my mind, still unresolved. The cen-tral piece in this puzzle is her liaison with the author Victoria (Vita) Sackville-West and the way their long and abiding friendship was inte-grated into their unconventional marriages.[10] Much ink has been spilled in the attempt to illuminate the sexual mores and psychological complex-ity of this and other bisexual relationships among and around the Blooms-bury group.[11] But Woolf's enigma still stands: whereas Sackville-West, while presumably enjoying (as did Woolf herself) a long and mutually sat-isfying marriage,[12] lived as an openly active lesbian, Woolf's sexuality appears to be overly repressed and sublimated. She was possibly one of those overdetermined cases on whose defensive armor astute psychoana-lysts thrive.[13] It is, therefore, not surprising that the nature of this friend-ship would lend itself to different interpretations.[14] Yet we would be mis-taken to believe that what is at stake here is only biography. Far from it. In the guise of questions (among others) of whether or not the in/famous liaison was sexually consummated, or how erotically intimate it was throughout, another battle is being fought: first, over the meaning of the sexual parody in *Orlando*, and, second, over the homoerotic connotations of *A Room of One's Own*.

Recent lesbian criticism (which should not be automatically identified with lesbian critics) is adamant not only in interpreting *Orlando* as a model of homosexuality but also in appropriating *A Room of One's Own* for the same purpose. What has been lost in the process is the last chapter of *A Room of One's Own* in which Woolf develops—via Coleridge's "marriage of opposites"—her own version of platonic androgyny, that disarmingly charming dream of the *supra*sexuality of the creative *mind*. Although she cites only Coleridge, there is no doubt that Plato's *Symposium* was not far from her mind, as the formulation "man-womanly" and "woman-manly" may attest.[15]

The analogous myths of the Jewish tradition, expounded in Genesis Rabbah, interpret Genesis 1:27 ("Male and female He created them [Adam]") in a way that brings it close to Platonic androgyny. Although underplayed throughout much of Jewish history, this interpretation was resurrected in the recent feminist attempt to counteract traditionally misogynist readings, in both the Christian and Jewish traditions, which ignore Genesis 1 and base themselves on Genesis 2:21–22 (woman as Adam's rib) and on a mistranslation of 2:18 (the famous "helpmeet" of the King James translation). I suspect that the presence of these Jewish myths in the minds of midrashically oriented writers may explain the ease with which contemporary Israelis embraced the idea of androgyny, as I will show in chapters 5 through 8 (and see pp. xiii–xiv and 103).[16]

The American reception of Woolf's androgyny has been more tempes-tuous, however. Whereas in the early 1970s Carolyn Heilbrun's *Toward the Recognition of Androgyny* could still advocate androgyny as a symbol of complementarity, or of "complete human possibility" (34), and while Catharine Stimpson warned against the derogatory identification of "The

Androgyne and the Homosexual," by the end of the decade Jane Marcus read *A Room of One's Own* as "Sapphistory," a text signaling (rather than openly speaking) "female desire."[17] That the textual strategies ostensibly effecting this signaling—allusions, question marks, ellipses, silences—are in fact the hallmarks of Woolf's prose in general is a fact conveniently ignored by this approach. So are the inner tensions (whether conscious or not) animating Woolf's feminist tract, her conflicted image of woman's nature, the contradiction between her sometimes embarrassing essentialisms ("That is a man's sentence," 64), her "postmodernist" deliberations about sexual difference ("Ought not education to bring out and fortify the differences rather than the similarities?" 73), her almost Marxist materialism (from the farcical first chapter through her motto of "a room and 500 a year of one's own"), and her (post?)modernist dream to go beyond sex ("It is fatal to anyone who writes to think of their sex," 86).

As in the case of *The Second Sex*, a rich, multivalent text, seething with all the fascinating paradoxes of postmodern gender theory, is reduced to just one of its possible readings, the muffled expression of "women's sexuality" (which in Jane Marcus's reading means female homoeroticism). This reading, focusing on the fifth, penultimate chapter of the book, disregards Woolf's own choice of closure. By shifting the emphasis from the androgynous myth of the last chapter (the crescendo toward which the whole manifesto builds) to the fictitious novel developed in chapter 5, Marcus generates a new script, one that interprets Woolf's carefully phrased "Chloe liked Olivia" (68) as "women in love" (with each other).

What makes this shift possible, and allows for this reading between the lines, is the conflation of life and art. Without "the example of Vita," to paraphrase Lyndall Gordon again, that reading would be much harder to accomplish. Without Vita, indeed, even *Orlando* would lose its strictly homosexual raison d'être. If we could engage momentarily in a speculative exercise, suppose we were to imagine reading *Orlando* without Woolf's diary, without the privileged information it allows us. Would not Orlando lose her homosexual specificity, "exemplified [indeed!] by Vita" (and her other lesbian conquests)?[18] In fact, Orlando's fantastically time-stretched (some 3.5 centuries) "biography," and her science-fiction-like sex change, enable Woolf to hilariously unmask gender essentialism (in the best postmodernist spirit) without necessarily endorsing homoeroticism.[19] On the contrary. Orlando's awakening from her earlier masculine dream(?) life equips her with precisely the gift that her creator most valued in the heterosexual artistic mind: "Men were no longer to her the opposing faction." How could they be, indeed, if she had been one of them herself?

The above quotation is culled, of course, not from *Orlando* but rather from *A Room of One's Own* (76). It is the link that helps Woolf move from her fable (in chapter 5) about Mary Carmichael, the new novelist writing about Chloe and Olivia (who, by the way, also shared a laboratory together, "although one of them was married and had . . . two small children," 69), to the analysis, in the last chapter, of the androgyneity of the truly creative mind. That the two are linked is quite clear: the imaginary Mary Carmichael is finally "complimented" for precisely the same quality later attributed to the androgynous mind: "She wrote as a woman, but as a woman who has forgotten that she is a woman" (77). The final chapter turns this observation into a recommendation: "It is fatal to be a man or woman pure and simple; one must be woman-manly or man-womanly" (86).

In the biography of Orlando Woolf made good her later admonition. Orlando's fantastic sex change is, in a way, a playful literalization of a metaphor, a dramatic externalization of an abstract mental identity. If fe/male synchronicity is a concept that runs against one of the most deeply set human "reality principles," namely, our "natural" recognition (according to Freud) of the difference between the sexes, then she would make it more palatable by presenting it as a diachronic process, fantastic as this may be. Although requiring suspension of disbelief to a high degree, the change from one sex to another along a time axis seems to exert a popular appeal that anticipates the creation of later literary androgynes.[20] A deadly serious joke, this fantastic creature pokes fun at social institutions, sexual mores, and fixed gender roles.

Although he/she was consciously inspired by Vita, as amply documented in Woolf's letters and diary (between March and October 1927), there is still room to question the nature of this inspiration. In what way was Vita the "example" of *androgyny*, as defined in *A Room of One's Own*; by virtue of her flagrant homosexuality? Or perhaps by virtue of her great creative mind? The latter is obviously impossible, given Woolf's (warranted) opinion about her friend's literary gifts.[21] In the absence of any other evidence, one can only surmise that she has become so by the conflation—apparently via *Orlando*—of homoeroticism and androgyny, by reading the latter through the lens of the former.

That this identification would be welcome to some readers but not to others is all too natural. And it seems plausible that it is this identification that Gordon was unconsciously defending against (given her general view of the Vita and Virginia affair, e.g., 255). Indeed, her scoffing at Woolf's "short-lived flirtation" would undoubtedly make more sense (and not only metaphorically!) if we make Vita (rather than androgyny) its object. For the picture that emerges from recent scholarship suggests precisely this—that the erotic intimacy between the two women was indeed short-lived, taken over by deep, even maternal, friendship, one among the many that kept Woolf's emotional life afloat. (The idealized aspect of this kind of relationship was fictionally represented already in *Mrs. Dalloway* (1925), to which I will return in chapter 5.3.)

But how about androgyny? Can we untangle it from the (short-lived) web of homoeroticism? I think we can and should do so—to set the historical record straight and to reclaim androgyny for contemporary general consumption. As I shall attempt to argue, this concept may have been the brainchild of Woolf's lifelong struggle—not just with her sexuality (whether of the bi- or homo- or [most likely] repressed variety) but rather with her tangled relationship to her double "superego," the towering representations of *both* her parents in her highly impressionable psyche. (The two issues are not unrelated, of course, but shifting the emphasis between them does lead to different interpretations.) Whereas her oedipal struggle with her father was in a way resolved—I will argue—by writing Orlando's so-called biography, she was still haunted by her conflictual attitudes to (her) mother/hood. Androgyny may have been engendered in this breach, functioning as an antidote to the anxiety of the m/other—that anxiety I detected earlier in contemporary gender theory. It is in this capacity that the challenge of Woolf's androgyny is still so relevant. But, in order to expose this relevance, we need first to disengage the warp of Vita from the woo[l]f of Orlando; that is, to deconstruct the genesis and meaning of the dual composition of *Orlando* and *A Room of One's Own*.

Since recent scholarship has plumbed Woolf's life writing, a preliminary sketch of this history is readily available: *Orlando* was conceived in the aftermath of the deeply autobiographical novel *To the Lighthouse* (1927). According to Woolf's diary, it presented a change of pace, fun and games, the book being a joke, a hybrid, the end of the novel. It was to be a biography of Sackville-West, of her short-lived love affair with Woolf, while she (S-W) was, at the time, already "gallivanting" with her next female conquest. In a well-researched chapter of her *Vita and Virginia* Suzanne Raitt cogently argues two intriguing points. The first is that the text (and the surrounding correspondence) of necessity expresses the ambivalence of the writer, a spurned lover, who used her artistic superiority to mourn the loss but also to master and control the object of her frustrated affection. This means that the farce can be read not only as a social critique but also as a personal vendetta (as evidenced by Vita's less than enthusiastic response, quoted by Raitt: "I feel like one of those wax figures in a shop window, on which you have hung a robe stitched with jewels," 40).

The second point explores the generic conventions trespassed by this antinovel, placing it in the context of the historical poetics of biography.[22] Woolf, herself a sometimes "serious" biographer, was allegedly responding to the contemporary trends, helping to revolutionize—to a much greater extent than any of her peers, it would seem—Georgian biography. (The "new biography" by Lytton Strachey allowed for identification rather than objective distance between the autobiographer and his subject, thereby opening new options for women biographers and for women as subjects of biography.) That by doing so Woolf was in fact resolving unfinished business with her father is a psychological insight that lies beyond the interests of Raitt's study. It is crucial, however, for understanding the function of androgyny in its creator's psychology.

2. *Who's Afraid of Father and Mother(hood)?*
Back To the Lighthouse

But let us first rehearse the evidence. *To the Lighthouse*, written only two years before *Orlando*, was meant to be

> fairly short: to have father's character done complete in it; & mother's; & St. Ives; & childhood; . . . But the centre is father's character, sitting in a boat, reciting We perished, each alone, while he crushes a dying mackerel.[23]

The result is well known: the novel is not that short; Mr. Ramsay is indeed sitting in a boat, etc., but whether or not his character does in fact occupy the narrative center is an issue that still divides contemporary scholars.[24] Most feminist critics seem to take their cue not from this early diary entry but rather from the later "Sketch of the Past" (1939) in which Woolf foregrounds her mother, admitting to be obsessed by her presence until she was in her forties:

> She was one of the invisible presences who after all play so important a part in every life. . . . It is perfectly true that she obsessed me, in spite of the fact that she died when I was thirteen, until I was forty-four. Then

one day . . . I made up, as I sometimes make up my books, *To the Light-house*, in a great, apparently involuntary rush. . . . I wrote the book very quickly; and when it was written, I ceased to be obsessed by my mother. I no longer hear her voice; I do not see her.

I suppose I did for myself what psychoanalysts do for their patients. I expressed some very long felt and deeply felt emotions. And in express-ing it I explained it and then laid it to rest.[25]

When taken out of its context, this passage seems to convey a clear-cut message. Twelve years after the original diary entry, father, the intended center of the novel, has altogether dropped from memory. Mother takes over, only to be exorcised and put to rest. One can almost hear a (com-pletely understandable) sigh of relief.[26]

Yet one should also watch out for this passage's double-layeredness, a risk typical of autobiographical recollection: it shifts from the language of Proust (the "*involuntary* rush of memory"), Woolf's lifelong admired author, whose "dual vision" she identified and adopted,[27] to a rational-ization via Freud, whom she had recently (January 1939) met in his new home in London (and with whose *Collected Papers,* the first English edi-tion, she must have been familiar since the 1920s, when they were pub-lished by the Woolfs' Hogarth Press).[28] Clearly, the distant past is filtered and interpreted through a more recent consciousness. But is this interpre-tation trustworthy?

It may seem to be, for this is how Vanessa Bell, Woolf's sister, responded to the novel upon publication (May 1927):

It seems to me that in the first part of the book you have given a por-trait of mother which is more like her to me than anything I could ever have conceived of as possible. It is almost painful to have her so raised from the dead. . . . You have given father too I think as clearly but per-haps, I may be wrong, that isn't quite so difficult. There is more to catch hold of.[29]

Vanessa Bell's uneven syntax (compare the assurance of the first part to the awkwardness of the second) reveals what she perhaps would not like to admit to her sister: that in the portrait of their mother she accomplished more than in that of their father—and not necessarily for the reason she adduces.

We do not have to search very far for more convincing reasons, of which Vanessa Bell may have been aware but unwilling to explore. *To the Lighthouse* was conceived and written when Woolf was in her forties. Her diary documents her earlier struggles to come to terms with the childlessness imposed upon her (because of her mental frailty). It also documents, however, her awareness of her own dependence on the maternal presences of both her beloved Vanessa and adored Vita (each of them a mother and a creative artist in her own right), and even on her husband's: "the maternal protection which, for some reason, is what I have always most wished from everyone. What L. [Leonard Woolf] gives me, & Nessa [Vanessa] gives me, & Vita in her more clumsy external way, tries to give me." The "child" speaking in this diary entry (December 21, 1925) is a forty-three-year-old novelist embarking on a reconstruction of childhood.[30] Would it be wrong to read here a preconscious recognition of an infantile fixation in which childlessness is perhaps a choice rather than an imposition? One can only imagine the guilt feelings evoked in a woman with this predilection by her internalized mother representations, whose high standards she felt she had failed to achieve. A painful demonstration of these feelings is recorded in her diary the following year (September 15, 1926, 3:110): "I'm unhappy, unhappy! Down—God, I wish I were dead. Pause. But why am I feeling this? Let me watch the wave rise. I watch. Vanessa. Children. Failure. Yes; I detect that. Failure failure. (The wave rises)." Woolf's inordinately long weaning process, her inability to part with the memory of her mother should therefore be read not only as her mourning of her mother but also as a working through of the mixed feelings she had about her own never-to-be motherhood. That this conflict must have been exacerbated by her intimate closeness with her two mother substitutes (and, in the case of her sister, her children as well) is no doubt true. It is also probably true that through Lily Briscoe's ambivalent transactions with Mrs. Ramsay cum "mother" she played out her own conflicts with a superego composite of all three women.[31]

From this perspective the older Mrs. Woolf may have been right in her self-analysis; the compounded problem of mother/hood, reinforced by its (same-sex) identificatory power, was apparently paramount in her mind when working on *To the Lighthouse*. Except that the problem was not entirely put to rest.

Almost a year later, when working on the third chapter of *Orlando*, her diary registers the following (December 20, 1927):

> This flashed to my mind at Nessa's children's party last night. The little creatures acting moved my infinitely sentimental throat. Angelika so mature and composed. . . . And oddly enough I scarcely want children of my own now. This insatiable desire to write something before I die, this ravaging sense of the shortness and feverishness of life, make

me cling, like a man on a rock, to my one anchor. I don't like the phys-
icalness of having *children of one's own*. This occurred to me at Rod-
mell; but I never wrote it down. I can dramatise myself a parent, it is
true. And perhaps I have killed the feeling instinctively; or perhaps
nature does.   *(emphasis added)*[32]

This is the first entry in which the issue of motherhood takes the form of
a negative statement, with all the ambivalence attributed by Freud (among
others) to the negative ("I scarcely want . . . now"; "I don't like"). The
issue is apparently not yet settled, but a resolution of the conflict is almost
reached. Woolf is slowly coming to terms with her childlessness, exploring
its flip side—the freedom to create. The scale seems to tip in this direction,
giving up the option of "children of one's own" for what will crystallize
within the following year as "a room of one's own"—a guarantee that
women's artistic fulfillment will take the exact syntactic shape of the motherly fulfillment it replaces.

A Room of One's Own emerges, then, as the final stage in a long and tor-
tuous process of separation from mother/hood. But before we ask how it
brings this process to a close, another question is in order: What about the
father? We have left him, we may recall, in a boat, where he was originally
meant to occupy the narrative center. Yet recent interpretations, apparently following Woolf's late-life foregrounding of her mother's obsessive
power over her, seem to have moved him to a secondary position. But not
for long. For a close look at Woolf's artistic career may offer different readings not only of *To the Lighthouse* but of her filial position as well. Unlike
contemporary wisdom (following Chodorow's elaboration of Freudian
female psychology; see chapter 2), Woolf needed to separate not only from
her inner mother representation but from her father representation as
well. Her unusual biography dictated this double bond, which, moreover,
turned out to be a double bind. This comes through quite clearly in a diary
entry (1928) that accords her parents an equal obsessive power:

> I used to think about him and Mother daily; but writing The Light-
> house laid them in my mind. And now he comes back sometimes, but
> differently. (I believe this to be true—that I was obsessed by them both,
> unhealthily; & writing of them was a necessary act.)[33]

This equality may be misleading, however. While "mother" controlled
her by being absent (even before her death, apparently), "father" controlled her by his overbearing presence. Yet it is to his presence in her education (not to mention his genes), as problematically biased and tyranni-

cally directed as it was, that we owe the great intellectual curiosity that nourished his daughter's creative talents. Indeed, perhaps one of the greatest ironies of feminist history is the fact that its most famous slogan, "thinking back through our mothers,"[34] was coined by a woman whose creativity was clearly engendered by thinking back through her father . . . which may have indeed saved her from what Domna Stanton sees as the risks of the ubiquitous maternal metaphor of contemporary gender theory (see the epigraph to this chapter).

However, this towering intellectual, singly shaping young Woolf's superego (no college education in her résumé, per his decision—and to her own lifelong regret), turned out to be an emotionally dependent parent (especially after his wife's death), the most damaging and draining presence in his daughters' youth. One can only imagine the conflicted reaction he aroused in the impressionable mind of Virginia, his youngest daughter. Nevertheless, Leslie Stephen was the one parent with whom Woolf the artist would readily identify, believing it was from him that she had inherited her critical mind and her drive for intellectual pursuit. And although she regularly revisited this issue throughout her life,[35] feminist scholars widely ignore the fact that it was this fatherly inheritance that provided Woolf with a substitute for the motherly function missing in her life. This is true for psychoanalytically inclined interpretations, such as Francoise Defromont's study of Woolf's life and art:

> To bring together these various elements, we could say that because of the absence of the maternal figure, the ego does not succeed in organizing itself into a coherent whole, or in constituting for itself a satisfactorily narcissistic image. This ultimately provokes *an uncertainty as to sexual identity.* The biography, once again, enables us to elucidate these phenomena: we had picked up from the text an echo of the trauma provoked by the death of the mother; it is as though her absence had deprived the writer of a female figure to identify with. *There remained the father figure; and the father was committed to literature and dedicated to books.*[36]

I have quoted from this study at length (emphasis is mine, of course) since it represents a fashionable dismissal of the father's role in Woolf's "uncertainty" about her sexual identity (which she certainly experienced). Although he was no doubt committed to literature and books, he did not exclude his young daughter from his world; at least, he did not succeed in doing so—not even in imposing on her his own way with literature and books. I argue therefore that Woolf's strong identification with her father

אורלנדו

Deganit Berest, "Orlando" (1975), 20"x 14", color print and letraset.

is crucial to an understanding of her life and art: her confused or repressed (female) sexuality may be the result not only of the absent mother figure but of an oedipal struggle with her father. Such a struggle is fictionally dramatized in the famous father-and-daughter scene in *To The Lighthouse,* where "wicked" Cam measures herself up against her father's (Mr. Ramsay's) erudition.[37] A similar psychological fixation in a filial position may have rendered Woolf unfit to grow into the gender role of her sex, thereby exacerbating her maternal conflict.

At the same time, however, it also unduly prolonged her paternal conflict. For along with Cam's struggle with her father, Woolf allows Lily Briscoe, the (childless) artist, to get out of her creative impasse with the help (!) of Mr. Ramsay. Together, Cam and Lily dramatize Woolf's paternal conflict. The depth of this conflict is rarely expressed openly, but when it does force its way out, it has a shocking effect:

> Father's birthday. He would have been 96, 96, yes, today; and could have been 96, like other people one has known: but mercifully was not. His life would have entirely ended mine. What would have happened? No writing, no books;—inconceivable.[38]

This is no "daughterly" sentiment, not even an Electra complex, but the expression of a daughter's ("male") oedipal struggle, plain and simple. Nor could such expression come forth from a position of weakness. Predictably, it takes place on November 28, 1928, just a few months *after* the completion of *Orlando* and the famous Girton lectures ("Women and Fiction"), then in the process of being turned into *A Room of One's Own,* Woolf's apparent substitute for "children of one's own." I would therefore suggest that the writing of Orlando's antibiography right after *To the Lighthouse* was a logical step, an oedipal wrestling with the art of her admired and feared father. By shaping Sir Leslie's legacy in her own fashion, Woolf may have deconstructed not only generic conventions (see Raitt) but psychological constructs as well. She, in fact, "invented" *gender* as a social role unrelated to one's biological sex—about half a century before the term itself was deployed by contemporary feminists.

By so doing Woolf may have resolved a deep conflict between the expected role that was unrealizable for her (maternity) and her clearly preferred calling, the professional role inherited from her father. At the same time, the special twist she put on this inheritance makes *Orlando* a total departure from Sir Leslie's art (history), a final separation from the specific creative bent of her father representation. This separation enabled her to accept her cross-gendered sameness (being a woman who undertakes a fatherly rather than a motherly role) with impunity.

This conscious blurring of gender boundaries, the play of difference within sameness and of sameness within difference, strongly suggests that we may read *Orlando* as *an autobiography masquerading as biography.* Simply consider its conclusion: a marriage of the most unconventional kind, one that resolves the conflict between matrimony and creativity in a manner that mirrors the compromise reached by its creator, Mrs. Woolf.[39]

The problem was, however, that this "brazen" crossing over, in which professionality rather than sexuality was the major force, lacked a proper name. Although it is true that throughout her life Woolf was surrounded by strong single women who counterbalanced, in their "chaste maternal friendship" (Marcus), the biological maternity about which she may have been so conflicted, most of them could not provide her with an artistic model. Jane Marcus's ironic observation that Woolf "chose her mothers and nurses carefully," ostensibly guided by their virginal chastity,[40] illuminates the major model available in Woolf's environment as a stand-in for traditional gender roles: the semimonastic existence cultivated by Quakerism. As amply documented by Marcus, this tradition seems to have had deep roots in the Stephen family, the most obvious case being Carolyn Emily, the aunt who in 1908 bequeathed to her talented young niece the money that would later become her symbol for women's economic, and therefore artistic, freedom. Quakerism was also practiced by her earliest best friend, Violet Dickinson, who had an enduring role in Woolf's premarital life, both emotionally and pragmatically.

In a way, the spinster Quaker, devoting her life to the community (e.g., caring for ailing elderly parents), is a modern, almost secularized version of a tradition always available to women within the orbit of Christianity— the monastic order. Monasticism seems to have provided earlier on an alternative to motherhood unavailable in Judaism. The following impassioned rationalization, put in the mouth of St. Lioba by nineteenth-century Greek author Emmanuel Royidis (1835–1904) in his satiric masterpiece *Pope Joan* (1886!), superbly translated and adapted from the Greek by Lawrence Durrell (1974), offers a curious insight into the self-conscious choices he imagined present in the monastic tradition:

> They were neither fanatics nor fools those early virgins who rejected the world and chose quietness in the shelter of some nunnery. For they knew that marriage was full of grievance when they first heard a woman in childbed or being beaten by her husband. . . . It was [this] that drove

us into the nunneries. It was not a vision of angels and a taste for dry bread, as related by those fools who wrote of the early saints. In the shade of the cell we found independence and rest, uninterrupted by the cries of children or the claims of a master or any other care.[41]

Indeed, this encomium of female monasticism is the preamble to the story—half-legendary, half-chronicled—of a ninth-century nun turned pope, Joanna, who "made such progress in learning under the professors there [Athens], and coming to Rome, met with few that could equal, much less go beyond her, even in the knowledge of the scriptures" (10). The learned Joanna could not have accomplished this feat, however, except for her successful disguise as a monk. (Luckily, all this took place with the help of her young lover, so she was saved the complications that befell a later descendant, Isaac Bashevis Singer's "Yentl the Yeshiva Boy"!).[42] The life of another Joanna, the seventeenth-century Mexican Sor Juana Inés de la Cruz, obviously tells a different story. As an *un*disguised sister, creating and writing against the interdiction of the Church, her life (celebrated by the Mexican poet and writer and Nobel laureate Octavio Paz), may remind us that it is still questionable to what extent the Church encouraged—at least at that time and place—women's creativity and artistic expression.[43]

Woolf, at any rate, may have similarly adopted an updated, twentieth-century version of the monastic alternative. Her kind of marriage, and perhaps mostly celibate life, is a compromise formation between the monastic (Quaker) option and Bloomsbury reality. In the final analysis, the only way for her to fulfill a maternal role was to be both mother *and* father by exercising the productivity of her mind—an option she not only practiced but also rationalized. Ironically, and perhaps unconsciously to the point, androgyny—this emblem of *biological infertility*—was turned by her into a symbol of fecundity, of artistic creativity, enabling her to assume (creative) maternity without relinquishing her emotionally child-like dependence on the maternal presences surrounding her. Before post-modernism she in fact deconstructed any boundaries between sex and gender roles, unhinging essentialism's firm grasp on the Victorian imagination.

3. Jewish Mothers and Israeli Androgyny

Whereas Christianity has offered its women some options—limited as they were—of crossing traditional gender roles, historical Judaism has had little to offer. Despite the androgynous vision suggested by Genesis 1 and some strong female characters throughout the Hebrew Bible, Jewish tradition foregrounded sexual inequality, basing itself on a reading of Genesis 2. As a rule, Jewish women did not have any access to men's realm of spirituality. This is true even in the famous case of the Maid of Ludmir (1815–c. 1892/95), a woman who chose to follow a spiritual calling rather than the expected course of matrimony and maternity. Although she had been used earlier in this century to demonstrate the supposedly "liberating" tendencies of Hasidic Judaism, her story has recently been portrayed as that of "a deviant, whose ultimate failure serves precisely to reinforce the boundaries which she attempts to cross, not to undermine them."[44] In other words, in Judaism, even more than in Christianity, women were defined by their social role of motherhood. In practice they could be the family's breadwinners, of course, supporting their husbands' career as life-long students of the (Jewish) Law; but in the eyes of the Law, and society, their major obligation was to procreate rather than create. The recent award-winning documentary film, *A Life Apart: Hasidism in America* (1996; Menachem Daum and Oren Rudavsky, directors), which records contemporary life among the Hasidic communities in Brooklyn, New York, illustrates that this tradition is still alive and well in twentieth-century America.

In another guise, however, this tradition is also alive in modern Israel, even in its Zionist secularist population. And no wonder. As recent research has made clear, the liberatory impulse of Zionism has never "overcome" the traditional Jewish valorization of motherhood. Diaries, letters, and other documents from the early decades of this century bear witness to this conflict, "the curious combination of female liberation and the return of women to their traditional roles as wives and mothers."[45] Lesley Hazleton's critique of the Israeli "cult of fertility," written two decades ago (see chapter 3 of her 1977 book), is still valid, as attested by a 1992 *Intimate Report on Women in Israel.*[46] All the writers discussed in this study, for example, are mothers—as are most of the others only mentioned in passing. In general, although most claim to have "always" been writers, they also ascribe their late entry into the writing scene to marital and maternal pressures; others see child rearing as the cause, partially at least, for generic choices (from poetry to short fiction and only later to the novelistic form, as in the case of Shulamith Hareven; see the introduction). (Staying married is another matter—although a high percentage of women writers fall under this rubric, too.)

I believe that this is one of the reasons for the Israeli late acknowledgment of Woolf, the feminist, as recorded in the introduction. Israeli women, who mostly entered the writers' market when their children had already grown up—and without an Israeli equivalent of "500 pounds[!] a year"—found it difficult to identify with what they perceived as an elitist conception of the female artist. The idea of "a room of one's own" was, in particular, ridiculed in a country where such an option used to be beyond the realm of reality (and still is, for some). Although the experience of younger writers is probably different, for the "pioneering" generation, the women who began to write in the 1960s, this was clearly the case. As late as 1988—in a triple interview entitled "A Room of Your Own"—they registered their dismay, telling of moving their typewriters from kitchen table to balcony and back, or writing in pen on a large atlas that stretched across their knees.[47] Coupled with this is the perennial lack of time and privacy, continually interrupted by children, spouse, and household chores. However, in the final analysis, the "problem is not the room," as Yehudit Hendel concluded in that interview,

> because external conditions are changeable. The problem is the essential, internal difficulties. To be a mother is much more difficult than to be a father. It is a great commitment that totally preoccupies you and dwindles your resources; a lot of energy, constantly invested; a life always centered around children.

In view of this high prize on maternity and motherhood, it is curious to note that, until recently, mothers and motherhood played a limited role in Israeli prose fiction. This is indeed a paradoxical observation for a culture "known" for its *Yiddishe mame* (Jewish mother) legacy (so brutally exploited on this side of the Atlantic by Philip Roth in *Portnoy's Complaint*).[48] One could even contend that, despite all its (mostly ritualistic) exclusions, Judaism (and especially biblical narrative) has accorded (real-life) mothers a relatively autonomous space, one much more viable than the divine/demonic split of the Catholic tradition.[49] So the fact that this aspect of the Judaic tradition has not left its mark on modern Hebrew literature calls for an interpretation. Possibly it should be attributed to the influence of "Westernized" assimilation. The Zionist oedipal rebellion against Jewish culture, which is at the heart of the revival of Hebrew letters, has apparently absorbed the European oedipal-Freudian narrative that has, by and large, marginalized the mother.[50]

Curiously, however, the marginalization of motherhood in Israeli literature has not significantly changed even with women's admission into this writing scene, formerly dominated by male novelists. Yehudit Hendel, for example—whom I quoted above about the inherent (essentialist?) difficulties of motherhood—had most of the characters of her first novel (1958) lose their mothers at a young age, thereby foregrounding their oedipal struggle with their fathers.[51] The same holds true for Naomi Frenkel's autobiographical trilogy, *Shaul and Yohanna,* or Hedda Boshes's autobiographical collection of stories, *The Third Hill.* As I have demonstrated, the early feminist rewriting of traditional gender roles—as late as the 1980s—followed the Beauvoirian perception that motherhood and liberatory feminism are mutually exclusive (Kahana-Carmon's *Up in Montifer* and the contemporary single detectives of the later Lapid); at best, the maternal was assimilated into a liberation narrative without any questioning of the validity or feasibility of this act of inclusion (*Gei Oni*). In a way, the decentering of the Zionist metanarrative that begins in *Gei Oni* takes place—as in some recent fiction by male writers[52]—*within* the oedipal masterplot whose confluence with Zionist ideology has been often argued.[53]

In the following chapters, however, this psychonational masterplot wears thin. Gender binarisms associated with the Zionist and/or oedipal plot are deconstructed—by different means and to different ends, to be sure—by Shulamith Hareven, Netiva Ben Yehuda, and Ruth Almog. The strategies of subjectivity adopted by these novelists—albeit at different levels of sophistication and awareness—fall into the general category of androgyny. Refusing to acknowledge the objectifying male gaze, "skipping over" (Hareven's expression) the underpull of motherhood, they construct female protagonists who idealistically carry forth a hero(ine)'s quest, defined in terms of agency and autonomous subjectivity; up to a point, of course. For the national narrative has its say as well (especially dramatized in Netiva Ben Yehuda's Palmach trilogy). For now let it suffice to say that in the next chapter the narrative perspective entertains the option of *un*essentialism: the male/female dichotomy is viewed not as "pure otherness" (Beauvoir) but as a negotiable difference, one that allows the new Hebrew/Israeli woman not only "to work and love" but also to include (rather than exclude) the maternal.

Chapter 5

Israeli Androgyny Under Siege: Shulamith Hareven

I live on the top floors now, she summed it up to herself, where there is a constant commotion, workrooms, children's rooms, the kitchen, the living room, everyday things. The cellar's locked for good, and I don't even know where the key is. Perhaps one should not know.

—Shulamith Hareven, *City of Many Days*

The first attempt by an Israeli novelist to endorse androgyny as an option for the New Hebrew Woman—thereby going beyond the feminist romance—belongs, paradoxically enough, to the veteran writer Shulamith Hareven (b. 1931). "Paradoxically," because Hareven's first novel, *'Ir yamim rabim* (City of Many Days), was published in 1972, precisely a decade before the word *feminist* first appeared on the *jacket* of an Israeli novel (Shulamit Lapid's *Gei Oni*; see chapter 1).[1] As we have seen, prose fiction "by women" was epitomized at that time by the work of Amalia Kahana-Carmon, then at the height of her first phase of "feminism" (chapter 3). She had used her innovative style to foreground, throughout the 1960s, the frustrated housewife type and similar "others." Moreover, in her first novel (*And Moon in the Valley of Ayalon*, 1971) yesteryear's romantic idealists (of both sexes) were bending under the yoke of their disillusionment with the present, exhibiting a variety of female maladies, from the physical to the emotional. The feminine condition, magnified by Kahana-Carmon's superb literary lens, was *not*—essentially speaking—a state of grace.

It was precisely this literary representation of the feminine condition, popularly identified as the embodiment of women's—or even feminist—writing, that Shulamith Hareven set out to reject. Not immediately, however. Curiously, many of her own early protagonists—often single or childless women—fall into the category of the feminine condition as well. Nevertheless, it is not their gendered subjectivity that is at the focus of the narration. Since many of them are also Holocaust survivors or other recent immigrants, the interest they hold for the author is more as social outsiders than as gendered subjects.[2] In her first novel, on the other hand, she forthrightly challenged gender essentialism, fashioning an Israeli or even Jewish-specific version of Virginia Woolf's androgyny.

The early seventies were, it may be recalled, the heyday of the feminist discovery of Woolf (see chapter 4), including the early valorization of androgyny, as suggested by Carolyn Heilbrun's *Toward the Recognition of Androgyny*. Translations of Woolf's work into Hebrew began at the same time, except for *Orlando* which had already appeared in 1964.[3] Nonetheless, androgyny as a consciously cross-gendered position did not show up in Israeli literature before the 1990s (while inadvertent androgyny shows up in the work of Netiva Ben Yehuda [1980s], as I discuss in chapter 7). Even *City of Many Days* tacitly subverts stereotyped gender dichotomies, through otherwise realistically conceived plot and characterization. In a way, it turns into a realistic literary convention the idealistic options of cross-gender position choices recommended not only by Woolf but also by the contemporary French "nonfeminist" Julia Kristeva (chapter 2), long before her work became known in Israel.[4]

No wonder, then, that not unlike Kristeva (and the early Beauvoir, one may add), Hareven declared herself a "selective" feminist (her terminology).[5] Adhering to the view that a writer is a writer, gender notwithstanding ("Readers are unable to tell which is which"), she argued that "feminist writing is a political and sociological definition, not an artistic one."[6] Moreover, she is notorious for her refusal to participate in any forum dedicated to women's literature and for her emphatic rejection—repeated later by Shulamit Lapid—of the category of women writers.

The logic of this extreme position surfaces when we place it within its propagator's larger system of belief, a version of the old modernist attempt to keep art "pure" and separate from topical issues. Thus, although Hareven is politically very active, voicing her ideological positions in oral pronouncements and in her numerous pointed essays and press columns (which I revisit in chapter 6), she vehemently protests any attempt to read her political convictions into her fictional work: art is art and should not be confused with one's extraliterary positions.[7]

Hareven's staunch belief in the complete separation between "biography and bibliography," as she has humorously labeled it, resulted in the shortest biographical sketch to be featured in the *General Directory of Hebrew Writers*, published in 1993: "Shulamith Hareven is a novelist, poet, and essayist who lives in Jerusalem. She chooses not to publish further biographical information."[8] In contrast to Kahana-Carmon, who shared with her readers the anguished question of what enters into the creative process (see chapter 3.1), reexamining the modernist (Woolfian, in her case) position on the separation between art and life, Hareven refuses to deal with the question altogether. Taking an absolute formalist position, she puts the lid of repression over her life, asking us—as did Woolf in an essay that was brought to public attention as recently as 1966[9]—to read her oeuvre as an aesthetic artifact, divorced from the extratextual.[10]

Needless to say, as impressive as this rhetorical gesture is, it is not a fool-proof strategy. While we would not expect a writer of such convictions to embrace personal genres like fictional autobiography or autobiographical fiction (at least not until we discover otherwise!), and while we may sympathize with her protest against critical trends that blur (sometimes with grievous results, as I argue in chapter 4) the boundaries between the creator and her creation, we cannot avoid enriching our reading with the author's own extrafictional pronouncements. These would qualify—as I shall demonstrate in this chapter—several of the positions formally adhered to by our author. They also assist in clarifying Hareven's peculiar relationship not only with feminism but with other popular isms as well.

1. Gendered Subjects in City of Many Days: *Same, Different, or Repressed?*

In view of Shulamith Hareven's position of willed difference, we should perhaps expect that the New Hebrew Woman of her first novel would be refreshingly different. And, indeed, she is, carrying this difference through her romantic, marital, and maternal relationships. In this "feminist romance" work, love, and even motherhood seem to commingle with relative tranquillity in the life of its protagonist, Sara Amarillo. A scion of a veteran Sephardi family in Jerusalem (the "city of many days" of the book title), Sara seems to epitomize—at least for a while—the unconventional freedoms espoused earlier in this century by new women like the French writer Collette: "immodesty, brutality, realism, rapacity, and a spirit of decision, all of them qualities traditionally ascribed to men."[11]

Yet within this narrative Sara's freedom (expressed early on in terms of adolescent sexuality and later in terms of personal autonomy and agency) is realistically "motivated," understood in retrospect to be a sublimated family trait. With all their differences, Sara has apparently inherited at least some of her moral "freedom" from her father. For who can forget the irony of the novel's opening statement? "Sara's father, never having met Morality, had perhaps been exempted from it." Good-hearted, but also faint-hearted (especially when it comes to female charm), Sara's father exercised a freedom of sorts, the kind that in "better company" would simply be labeled "irresponsibility." This freedom drives him away from home and, finally, "down," as the text would have it, into the depth of insanity (187; 186).

But all this is, of course, retrospective knowledge, not available to readers at the opening of the novel. What does hit us head on with that first sentence is the inversion of roles insinuated here: it is the father who is identified by the narrative voice in relation to his daughter ("Sara's father") and not vice versa, as may be expected (Sara being her "father's daughter," second in status because of gender and age). In retrospect, we perceive this inversion as a foreshadowing of the father's infantile position at the end of the novel. But, for now, what seems like a playful breach of our expectations is reinforced by the next sentence, where we find out that Sara's father's name is . . . Isaac ! What is inverted here is the maternal and filial positions, respectively, of these characters' eponymous predecessors in Genesis (the biblical Sara being Isaac's *mother*, of course).

As the plot unravels, however, we find out that despite this reversal, Sara Amarillo is not denied the experience of motherhood. In fact, she realizes her "maternal instinct" far more fully than both her mother and sister, the seemingly feminine characters of her family. In the world of Gracia Amarillo, the mother who coquettishly plays the role of an abandoned, yet romantically unattainable, princess, there is obviously no room for motherhood in the true sense of the word. "My daughters are *brujas*, witches," is her constant complaint (105; 104). Ofra, her younger daughter, follows in her mother's footsteps by having an abortion ("No one's going to make a mother and a grandmother out of me," 108) and getting a divorce, finally disappearing in the mists of the European continent as the wife of the Prussian von Kluck.

Hareven has created, then, in the image of Sara an antitype, one diametrically opposed to Sara's own family feminine tradition. That tradition is traced through the narrative back to the paternal grandmother, "a mean woman who spent all her days bedridden in her tiny alcove, from where she issued orders to the household" (8; 5). Growing in the shadow of this tradition, coupled with the absence of a philandering father (who disappeared with a Lebanese fake "princess" when Sara was seven years old), in a household run by a stern but benevolent grandfather, the elder Amarillo, Sara and Ofra dramatize, in their divergent developments, choices and options available for contemporary female subjectivities.

To fully appreciate the meaning of Sara's choice (her bildungsroman, we might call it), the larger setting that both enables and circumscribes it must first be understood. For hers is not a Cinderella story. In typical Israeli fashion, history intervenes in this "novel of education." Its power is symbolized by Jerusalem, the city that pressures its inhabitants with the weight "of stones and infinite time" (121). This oppressive power is a prominent theme in Hareven's poems, as the title of her first collection, *Yerushalayim dorsanit* (Predatory Jerusalem) clearly attests.[12] Here, however, it signifies the brute forces that cause the breakdown of the multicultural equilibrium in mandatory Jerusalem between the two world wars.

As the tension heightens, the narrative is permeated by a sense of momentous change. "This is all for the last time," muses Sara in the midst of a pivotal scene, the novel's greatest celebration of cross-cultural friendship (chapter 4), "this city is full of tensions" (74; 72). As indeed it is. The oriental tapestry that had been Jerusalem—and that the novel recapitulates in its intimate-impressionistic mosaic—is doomed to oblivion, except in the nostalgic reconstructions of its literary mourners (e.g., David Shahar, Amos Oz, and Haim Be'er).[13]

The core of this nostalgia—which predictably gained momentum with the reunification of Jerusalem after the Six Day War in 1967—is the lost mosaic of the past, vividly dramatized in the first portion of the novel. Cutting across divisions of religious, national, and ethnic identities, interwar Jerusalem is depicted here as alive with the voices of Jews, Arabs, British, Greek Orthodox, and Germans, indeed with a literal Bakhtinian dialogue between Judaism, Christianity, and Islam. The Hebrew text resonates with the multilingual ambience of high-society soirees (chapter 4), as well as with the linguistic mélange of the alleyways of veteran Sephardi neighborhoods or the courtyards of Rehavia—the recently settled neighborhood that had become the address of "European" (mostly German-born) Jewish academics and intellectuals. With a superb ear for the vernacular, Hareven reconstructs her characters' direct speech, replete with Judeo-Spanish (Ladino) and French, Arabic, German, and English. While marking their social and cultural standing, these linguistic traces also bring to life a world of great fluidity, a polyphonic macrocosm in which cultural differences are mutually worked out and individual idiosyncrasies are tolerantly accepted:

The patient city gathers in people with the strangest ideas, philosophers, freaks, madmen, all of whom add to her a measure of themselves and disappear. Sometimes she seems to be built as much out of obsessions as of stones.   (*100; 99*)

At the center of this internationally mixed social setting are two Jewish "clans" that interact with each other (as well as with everybody else): the Sephardi Amarillos and the extended family of the German-born pioneer Dr. Heinz Barzel, who has recently married into a local family. Through these two families Hareven presciently explores issues of difference versus sameness—the very questions raised by gender theories throughout this century—as they play out in the private and the public domains, across gender and ethnic lines.

Most intriguing is the question of the "optimal distance" between self and other in cross-gender relations. While Dr. Barzel's young wife, Hulda (née Friedmann), is relatively other (being a native of Jerusalem, unlike the newcomer Barzel), Sara Amarillo ends up—after many sexual escapades (which include a brief relationship with Husni, an Arab co-worker, 79; 77), marrying another Amarillo, Elias. Although not so uncommon in the historical universe described here, this "endogamy" is more than a realistic reconstruction. It clearly functions semiotically, allowing for questions that a normative (exogamous) marriage would not have. Thus, when asked by Hulda if their being (second) cousins made a difference in the marriage, Sara admits to "a kind of tribal confidence," but quickly adds that it "has no justification. I am from the bad Amarillos, the ones who are always quarreling with life. He is from the good Amarillos" (113; 112). Not only are stereotypic gender expectations reversed here (that is, if we identify "good" and "bad" with "weak" and "strong" [= quarrelsome]), but difference is created within the same tribe, subverting the perceived sameness of "common ancestry."

A similar issue motivates another authorial choice that may have seemed arbitrary otherwise. Barzel's young wife, Hulda, comes equipped with a twin brother—an ideal setup for the exploration of cross-gender sameness and difference. In a startling passage the narrative voice introduces the twins' intimate chat about Amatsia's romantic conquests as an attempt "to rid their systems of an ancient desire" (43; 41). Anchored in "their common past" in the same amniotic fluid (43, unfortunately translated as "They had grown up together," 41), this incestuous attraction is nevertheless what foregrounds their gender "difference": "Next to her, his mirror image, but a woman, he [Amatsia] feels his own blustering masculinity even more strongly, the difference, inescapable, between his twin-ness and hers" (ibid). Again, difference is created within sameness; yet the apparent analogy to the case of the Amarillos is misleading. For here the divergence follows stereotypic patterns of masculine/ feminine behavior, articulated in terms of sexual freedom that is available to one but not to the other: "I am not permitted to sow my wild oats for the sake of my Organismus," avers Hulda without any resentment, "All I could do was get legally married" (44; 42). Hulda's acceptance of sociosexual mores is obviously meant to be contrasted with Sara's independence from them, but it is made all the more blatant alongside the behavior of her twin, her male mirror image. When war actually intervenes, this difference takes on a darker color, with Amatsia (among other men) going off to fight and Hulda left to worry at the home front.

With this we are back to the commonplace problem of normative gender roles and may ask in what way we benefit from its literary representation through the particular case of twins. Indeed, it seems that Hareven has inadvertently offered up a critique of one of the most ancient symbols of gender relations, twins of the opposite sex. Interestingly, it was precisely this symbol that was put forward by Carolyn Heilbrun as an emblem of androgyny in her 1973 book on the subject: "Unique among all androgynous symbols for its persistence through the ages is the 'identity' of opposite-sex twins," says Heilbrun. "Complementary, they seem to encompass between them complete human possibility" (34). Perhaps, but not in the manner Hareven endorses. Stripping twinship of its abstract idealization in the hands of the poets and playwrights of old (Shakespeare's not least among them, e.g., Viola and Sebastian in *The Twelfth Night*), she deconstructs its sameness as too circumscribed by biology (sex) and therefore unfit to subvert gender roles. Androgyny will have to be created elsewhere—more in the shape of Woolf's model.

Before we find it, however, another issue is at hand—the playing out of sameness and difference on a larger canvas, the social mosaic of Jerusalem. It is to the members of the Barzel and Amarillo clans that the premonition about the impending change is entrusted. "Something was ending, and something was about to begin: a dim understanding of this flickers through Hulda's mind, but it isn't enough to cast any light" (136). A light of sorts shines forth toward the end of the story, when Barzel (now Professor Barzel, his promotion being one of the markers of the passage of time in the novel) articulates his fear that the war will put an end to the Jerusalemite polyphony they have so far taken for granted:

"All the men will be coming home from wars now," said Professor Barzel. "They'll all have learned to fight. The country will change again. Everything will become more professional, the fighting too. The individual won't count any more, only the stupid plural. The plural is always stupid." . . .

"And what will be then, Elias?" Asked Hulda worriedly.

"We will be then," said Elias, so quietly they couldn't be sure they had heard him right. "For better or for worse, we."   *(182; 182–183)*

The "we" so ruefully reiterated by the male protagonists (Professor Barzel and Elias Amarillo, Sara's husband) is the notorious "we" of the Palmach, the 1948 generation (discussed in more detail in chapter 7) . Mythicized already in its time, the Palmach (and everything it stands for) has been the object of nostalgia since the 1950s—and the subject of debunking since the mid-eighties.[14] Hareven, herself a member of this generation and a participant in the War of Independence, is caught in the transition between the two. Walking the middle way, she has her characters grieve the loss of the first-person singular while understanding this loss as the inevitable result of the political situation.

A similar ambivalence is demonstrated by Hareven's treatment of her protagonist's interior monologue (quoted in the epigraph to this chapter). On the one hand, she allows Sara Amarillo a measure of self-awareness, the admission that she lives "on the top floors." But then she has her state flatly, without any change of tone, that "the cellar's locked for ever, and I don't even know where the key is" (184). Moreover, the attentive reader may note not only what is marked as "locked" but also what is marked by its absence: the curious omission of a bedroom from the list of rooms on the top floor, which is passed over unnoticed.

The imagery underlying this self-examination is well-known, almost a stock metaphor—the house as the image of its tenant and vice versa. Yet it is the implied vertical division of the human house that gives this particular metaphor an added twist, a specific psychological edge: the upper floors, full of movement and light, in contrast to the locked cellar—a clear analogue to Freud's topographic model of the human psyche. Although the impulse for self-knowledge is quite palpable here, it clearly stops short of breaking into the locked "cellar" of the psyche. The female voice using this metaphor seems to question, however, the very foundation of the Freudian quest: Does one *have to* unlock the inaccessible, unconscious, if you will, underground room?

Introspection is displaced, then, to the externally observable facts, and a potentially psychological exploration turns into a sociocultural inquiry. Within the parameters of this narrative this move is rationalized by Sara's need to join the war effort. For that purpose she must—like Professor Barzel before her—"skip over her own self" (184; cf. " 'You're committing workicide,' said Hulda sadly. But he wasn't really. He had just stopped thinking of himself, had skipped right over himself," 122; 121). Professor Barzel, the idealist physician who had willfully made this hot city his home (his strong will clearly implied by the Hebrew meaning of his name, "iron"), and who had trained Sara as a nurse in her youth, now insists that she help him prepare paramedics for the insecure threatening future. What is implied in his insistence is that in this society under siege male and female do share the same lot. Yet as the plot of our story thickens this ideal sameness wears thin. Though equally sharing in the burden, female and male protagonists experience it in different gender-specific ways.

It is Sara and not Professor Barzel who registers the loss in psychological rather than social or intellectual terms. While he is reported to "have lost the key" to his intellectual pursuits (122; 121), Sara is aware that what she misses is nothing less than the key to her own "underground room," to the cellar of her *psychic* apparatus (184).

The metaphoric language barely camouflages a psychological insight for which we might use the term *repression*. Yet, as a Freudian concept, this term is definitely unnameable in the discourse of this narrative. Indeed, an ambivalence (perhaps even antipathy) toward Freudian psychology is most palpable in the language and plot of this novel; its source, however, is not readily determined. It may derive from the historical materials themselves—the notorious stiff upper lip of the sabra (native) culture and the concomitant negative attitude to any preoccupation with "soft" emotional issues. As we have seen in chapter 1 (and see also chapter 7), these were typical of the *yishuv* (and of the Palmach in particular) in the thirties and forties, so they don't feel out of character in this interwar narrative.[15] Yet this attitude may also reflect the author's personal position as well. We will later return to Hareven's critique of the "cult" of Freudianism, especially of the oedipal metanarrative (see chapter 6). Although the public expression of this vehement critique gained momentum only in the 1990s, it is interesting to note that it had its origins in essays published in the Israeli press throughout the 1970s, following the publication of the novel under discussion here.[16]

It should come as no surprise, then, that this camouflaged Freudian insight does not lead to any action. Neither the protagonist nor the authorial voice shows any signs of rebellion. Sara seems reconciled to the loss of her key, ending her introspection with the rather surprising conclusion "Perhaps one should not know." Moreover, despite this great loss, the novel demonstratively closes on a lyrical note of mystical transcendence:

> A silent presence, the whole city spread at her feet, and [she] looked at the lambswool light out over the mountains, over the houses drowning in radiance, as if once this city, long, long ago, soon after Creation, had burst from some great rock and its truth flown molten and shiny over the hills. She could feel the moment to the quick. . . . And always, forever, this fleecy pile of light, that rock tumbled halfway down the hill to a lonely stop, a terraced alley, a dripping cypress tree, a caper plant in a wall. A place to walk slowly. A place to touch the sky: now it is close. To breathe in mountain and light. Now.   (189)

This is a magical moment, a blend of intense presentness, strong local color, and high-minded transcendence. We may label this unique blend, following the author's own clues, Levantine existentialism. Levantine, because of Hareven's conscious rejection of the European existentialism that has unquestionably been the preferred worldview of most Israelis of her generation. In a fascinating essay, unique in its personal, autobiographic exposure, Hareven introduced herself as European by birth but Levantine by love and choice. In a move that may be viewed as reverse *Orientalism*, she declares: "I am a Levantine, because life in the claustrophobia of the present bores me, and I yawn in the thin air of European existentialism" (172; 85).[17] Her description of what attracted her to the Levant clearly echoes the lyrical cadences of our novel's closure, written over a decade earlier:

> Born in Europe, all my days there passed in an obscure impatience, as if it were all a mistake, a confinement, like a wretched marriage—until I first saw strong light on rocky hedges on a mountain, a stooping summer olive tree, a well carved in stone—and I knew that was it. I had arrived at some deep palpable ancientness, the womb of the world, where virtually everything was and will be created. Here were the right light, the right smells, the right touch.   (168; 81)

Mountain and rocks, the light of Creation—here they are again, this time found not only in the city of many days but rather generalized as a Levantine substitute for the European "darkness" (this is the literal translation of the Hebrew *hoshekh*, rendered euphemistically as "obscure" in the English translation).

Light versus darkness is, of course, one of the most universal dichotomies in our culture. But here it has an additional semiotic edge, supported intertextually by one of Hareven's signature stories, "Twilight": "Last night I spent a year in the city where I was born. . . . The city of my birth was very dark, extinguished, because the sun had left it and gone away a long, long time ago."[18]

While the gloom and doom of her European birthplace metaphorically represents the Holocaust, which the author barely escaped unscathed as a child, Levantine sunlight holds—by the logic of this dichotomy—a promise for peace, for the triumph of common sense. "I am a Levantine," the essay concludes, "because I see war as the total failure of common sense, an execrable last resort" (173; 86). Published originally in 1985, just following the turmoil of the Lebanon War (1982), the anguish of this hope shines through. The closure of *City of Many Days*, though written much earlier and in a different context, holds a similar promise: the comfort of the (Levantine) light, the (domestic) calm that comes after the (public, historical) storm. At the same time, this confessional essay reveals something else: the reference to the Holocaust may betray the repressed matrix of this author's strong ideological commitment and political involvement (see chapter 6).

Unlike the essay, however, the novel has its own internal history. We may take the essayist at her word; it is more difficult to take Sara Amarillo at her parting words. Indeed, it is hard to exaggerate the contrast between this mature reconciled woman and the spunky girl she once was. Described by herself and by others as a tomboy (45; 43), as a chip off the old block, the strong and feisty Amarillos ("You, Sara, you're too big. Like Victoria. *Como todos los* Amarillos," 36; 34), those who "are always quarreling with life" (113; 112), this "phallic," emancipated woman suddenly takes a turn toward submission, "lying low, a wick trimmed all the way down" (179; 180). The woman who prided herself on her sharp tongue and unabashed "meanness" all of a sudden begins to wax emotional over her motherly duties ("Sara began to be over-concerned for the children, to give them too many sweaters and too much unsolicited love," ibid.). And the daughter who as a young girl vented her rage against her absent father by screaming, "No father! No mother! No grandfather! No grandmother! No anyone!" (16; 13), later processes her discovery of his helpless insanity (during the war he is found in an asylum in Egypt) through the distance of a poetic allusion: "I went down into a garden of nuts to see the fruits of the valley. Down down down. To the rock bottom beauty of madness" (187).

As with the loss of "her key," the anguish is camouflaged by the indirection of metaphor. And what a metaphor! As unsuspecting readers, we may indeed be astonished to recognize here the love poetry of the Song of Songs. What is especially startling is that the verse cited (Song of Songs 6:11) alludes to one of the most familiar tropes for (virginal) female sexuality, the locked garden (in classical rhetoric, the figure of *hortus conclusus,* which is based on Song of Songs 4:12).[19] So how does this erotic citation illuminate our scene, we may ponder, noticing along the way the reversal of the male-female perspective of our source (Sara observing her father in contrast to the male lover "figuring" his beloved in the biblical reference)? Well, this intertext apparently demands another hermeneutic step, for it gains its meaning only via its *mystical* interpretation. In thirteenth-century Kabbalah the nut (cited precisely from this verse) stands for the hard "shells" (*klippot*) that cover the spiritual core of any created being, which the Zohar actually calls the brain.[20] A modern awareness of the unfathomed enigma of the human psyche, of the impenetrability and undecipherability of the brain, is mediated here then through a secularized Kabbalistic image. But, again, both protagonist and narrator stop on the brink of the abyss: "Sarah looked at him for a long while, the great question that had haunted her for so long now lay before her, a mindless, spent little answer" (ibid.). This is all Hareven grants her protagonist by way of self-scrutiny. The haunting question is admitted entrance into language only when it has lost its power, when it turns into a "spent little answer."

Staged as it is two pages before the end of the novel, this encounter loses its potential force as a retrospective, all-embracing, psychological explanation. For, despite the intimation of Freudian depths, this is no novel of psychological motivation. In its laconic, pointillistic style, its spare descriptions and quick change in centers of consciousness ("a fugue for twenty-five voices," the author herself suggested),[21] the narration hovers above and around the characters, empathically engaging them and ironically disengaging itself but never aiming at rendering fully rounded psychological portraits.

Even Sara, whose education is at the core of the plot, is painted by brief surface strokes. Moreover, she does not occupy center stage by herself; as the lyrical fusion of her last narrated interior monologue makes clear, she shares it with another female, the city of the title of the book. Jerusalem is actually the strongest presence in this novel, because, ironically, it is "she" (city as well as land, country, state—are conveniently gendered as feminine in Hebrew) who embodies the powers of history: "This city abides no one's decision about who they are. It [she] decides for them, it [she] makes them, with the pressure of stones and infinite time. It teaches humility" (121). In the final analysis it is history rather than psychology that circumscribes human action in this novel, subsuming both anguish and pleasure, sameness and difference under its impersonal workings.

2. Androgynous "Jewish Parents"? Not in a War Zone!

We can finally come back now to the question posed earlier in our analysis: What place is there for a female subject in this kind of narrative "under siege?" How would she be affected by the powers of repression—whether it be historical, cultural, or psychological? Will she have "learned humility"?

The first part of our answer involves the lyrical coda of the closure of the novel. Despite the constant effort of the narrative voice to decentralize its focalization throughout the novel, to multiply its points of view, Sara emerges as the central consciousness of the narration. The more the rich mosaic of the past disintegrates, the more her introspective voice usurps that of the ironic narrator, culminating in the final monologue we have read. But what sort of consciousness is this?

The question is, in other words, how does a self-declared selective feminist like Hareven imagine the female subject of her choice? How different would she be from the feminist protagonists we have seen in earlier chapters?

To facilitate our probe we begin with a look at the only essay of this prolific essayist (three collections between 1981 and 1991) that directly addresses the issue of feminism. Published in 1971 (*Ma'ariv*, September 24), this early essay, tellingly named "Different and Equal," may help us understand the complex twist on feminism that *City of Many Days* (apparently conceived precisely at that time) dramatizes.

The essay opens with a question, rehearsing a concern heard then in some quarters of Israeli society: Why isn't there a women's lib movement in Israel like there is in the United States? Anticipating Homi Bhabha's critique of colonialist discourse, Hareven sees this question as an act of cultural mimicry, stemming from lack of understanding of cultural difference.[22] In her opinion, American women's liberation is a response to a process of objectivization typical of American culture but irrelevant to Israel. Furthermore, in America it is detrimental to men no less than it is to women. Since in Israel this process is much less severe, there is no need for a "corrective" in the form of feminism. Moreover, she asserts, in Israel there is no confusion of gender roles (as there is in America) because of the constant state of war and men's military service.[23]

We may no doubt raise a brow at this rationalization. The woman behind our novel is obviously an engaged person of clearly drawn convictions and priorities, yet "feminism" is not among them.

But instead of critiquing her assumptions, let us see how they are both supported and subverted by *City of Many Days*.

On the one hand, cross-gender equality as a realistic possibility is—as we have seen—an unquestioned premise of this novel, a premise that may be compared with Virginia Woolf's androgyny. However, the differences between the two androgynous paradigms are just as intriguing as the similarities. Hareven's is no doubt an interesting version, quite far from Woolf's original use of the concept, as dramatized by *Orlando* and theorized in *A Room of One's Own*. It has nothing to do with artistic creativity (except the author's), and it does not replace maternity. It does share with its model, however, the freedom to shuttle between gender roles, to cross the boundaries between them. Indeed, without this freedom the characterization of Sara would be totally spurious. In fact, in her independence of spirit, intolerance of weakness, and provocative sexual freedom she is almost a parody of the typical *male* adolescent. What is especially striking, moreover, is the fact that she seems to have been naturally born to all these "privileges," never having to fight for them. Sara *is* truly autonomous, easily brushing aside—with no separation anxiety, it would seem—the "weak" maternal tradition of her Sephardi stock (mother, paternal grandmother, and sister).

On the other hand, one of the claims of this story is that masculinity does not make one immune from weakness either: let us not forget that, just like his biblical eponym, Don Isaac Amarillo, Sara's father, is weak—both morally and mentally.[24] Finally, by providing a "strong" aunt (the colorful, single but happy "Tia Victoria: big, rumpled, laughing. No one knew exactly what she did. She liked best just to sit at home. Victoria's home was an oasis in the great family desert," 17; 14), Hareven seems to give the lie to the feminist cliché of "transcending" gender roles.

Orlando-like (though not for the same "reasons"), Sara has no need of transcending. She *starts* from a nongendered dichotomy, unproblematically rejecting one model and adopting another. The weak/strong (or passive/active) dichotomy available to her is free of gender connotations, as she is surrounded by strong (grandfather, Victoria) and weak (father, mother, sister) subjectivities on both sides of the gender fault line.

Shulamith Hareven

As such, the psychological dynamics imagined here seem to sidestep the Freudian oedipal script altogether. Unlike Kahana-Carmon's heroine Clara, for example, who labors to liberate herself by adopting the Beauvoirian ideal of "being like a man" (chapters 2, 3), Sara's androgynous development is blatantly nonoedipal and cross-gendered. In fact, the absence of a strong father image in her childhood (with the exception of grandfather, who keeps mostly to himself) makes her function somewhat like Jo Marsh in *Little Women*—a single strong presence in a female household.[25] Yet, unlike Louisa May Alcott, Hareven accompanies her heroine into matrimony. And with that arrives the moment of truth, the real test of this "new female" (the aunt, it may be recalled, has never married): How does this strong, androgynous woman function as a wife and mother?

Superbly, of course; but at a "cost." Giving birth to her first son, Sara for the first time allows weakness to penetrate her hitherto armored psyche. The self-centered, formerly *un*relational ego restructures itself, adjusting to a maternal position. Predictably, it reacts with a sense of loss and fear: "Help me, Grandpa," Sara prays from her maternity bed, "because a frightening vulnerability has opened up in me today" (111). Although the contemporary connotation of the word used in Hebrew for "vulnerability," *turpah*, is generalized, on the order of "Achilles' heel," the context no doubt activates the word's original denotation (in Rabbinic Hebrew) of "nakedness," "private parts," and we need not elaborate the sexual connotation of the use of the verb "open" in this connection (all of which is missing from the bland English translation, "I've never felt so defenseless before," 110).

Does motherhood put an end to "androgyny," then? Not so fast—at least not as far as this novel is concerned. For it is the father, not the mother, who is entrusted to articulate the effect of parenthood on one's subjectivity:

> "The first child forces you to define yourself," he told Sara. "When the second comes you're already defined. Not just as a parent. Whatever you are and aren't, you can be sure that's what your child will learn to demand from you."   *(112; 111)*

Furthermore, it is Elias who, "unknown to Sara, kept a diary in which he recorded all the stages of their development" (ibid). This father demonstrates—quite *un*characteristically—that one does not need to be a (biological) "mother" in order to be maternal. In other words, this rare version of androgynous parenthood seems to deconstruct precisely the polarity of (motherly) nurturance versus (manly) independence so criticized and bemoaned by gender theorists a decade later (see chapter 2). Add to this the emphasis on Elias's "fine, spare, impeccably Sephardi good looks" (92; 91; cf. "He had the lanky good looks of a cypress tree," 73; 71), his principled rejection of political aggression ("I hate the fanaticism of it, the blind passion," 86; 84), and his patient belief in peaceful solutions (joining Martin Buber's pacifist Brit Shalom, 117; 116), and the gender reversal is complete. (To understand this "reversal," we need to refer to the gendered link between women and pacifism that was originated by Woolf in World War II but would soon be theorized by feminists in Israel and elsewhere, as I discuss in chapter 6).

We are, at this point of the narrative, just past the midpoint of the story, and the myth of androgyny (as defined here) still holds. Unlike the Woolfian model, however, it does not exclude maternity. On the contrary, the flight from motherhood belongs here, as we mentioned above, to the weak women, Sara's mother and sister. Aunt Victoria rationalizes her avoidance of marriage by her fear of repeating the familial havoc to which she was a witness (both her mother and brother, in a sense, deserted their families: the first by retreating into her "matrimonial bed," the other by abandoning the family altogether; 95; 93). So it is left to Sara to complete her androgynous transformation by including rather than excluding maternity on her agenda.

In a typical Jewish way, then, progeny is not easily abandoned, not even replaced by "children of the mind" (à la Woolf). Nor does the maternal subvert androgyny; both parents share in "mothering," equally experiencing its blessings as well as its worries.[26] Significantly, Hareven's image of motherhood (= parenthood) is as far from Kristeva's apotheosis of the Maternal, the semiotic locus of creativity, as it is from Beauvoir's demonization of it!

What does finally undermine androgyny is the state of siege, the impact of war. Soon after the scene of shared parenthood, we witness the deterioration of Arab-Jewish relations and the palpable echoes of World War II. Life is disrupted; individual destinies get farcically and hopelessly entangled in plots they do not comprehend (Miracolo Orientale, for instance, caught climbing the neighborhood roofs, is apprehended by the police on suspicion of spying and then released as a peeping tom, unable to convince anyone that he was only trying to trace the source of mysterious flashlights he suspected as "signals to the enemy," 139–142). The dichotomy of weak/strong, so hopefully deconstructed in the sphere of gender roles, ominously sneaks back into people's discourse. Professor Barzel, one of the first victims of Arab atrocities (severely injured by a knife in his lung), constantly repeats his warning, refrainlike: "We are weak, friends, so weak" (84); "We shouldn't be so weak, Hulda" (89), only to be echoed by Sara: "We are weak, Eli. And we had no idea how weak" (85).

Against this background Sara slowly emerges to herself in her "difference"—only to realize that under the circumstances she cannot take this difference anywhere. The motive power behind this emergence is, predictably, a chance rekindling of her youthful love. The renewal of this romance is conducted—from beginning to end—in the shadow of the "events." By lucky chance Matti Zakai (and a friend) pass by when Sara is threatened by a group of Arabs who come to reclaim the house Sara and Elias live in, refusing to accept the fact that it is not theirs (the Arabs') anymore, as it had been legally sold years ago (148–151). While Elias, loyal to his politics of nonconfrontation, sends Sara "through the back door to the neighbors" (150), she cannot control her rage: seeing "the five of them treading deliberately, maliciously," on her freshly planted flower beds, she runs out the front door to confront them. With only a "little paring knife" to defend her, this confrontation really had no chance, but for Matti's miraculous appearance as a "knight in a 'khaki shirt.' " Yet this promising romance does not last long. Exhilarating (indeed, life-giving, stereotypically symbolized by Sara's volunteering to supply the underground fighters with milk . . .) as this emotional reawakening is for both Sara and Matti, it is painfully cut off, undermined by the historical moment—the underground military activities and national voluntarism that send Matti off to sea.

With this Matti drops out of sight, back to the oblivion that engulfed him for two decades of our plot. Sara, on the other hand, sinks into an emotional crisis, the first ever. Robbed of her "strength," "she lived from one day to the next and not a step outside it, lying low. A wick trimmed all the way down" (179; 180). All that she has left now is acceptance of her "locked cellar," *amor fati*. The metaphor is apt. Under the pressures of external forces, Hareven sees no other option but to put the lid on one's internal (repressed) seething cauldron. This is the only defense against losing human sanity, she claimed in an interview, sanity that we can preserve at only a very high cost: "In order to preserve this sanity, one often has to give up what is most cherished in his life. This is a terrible price. . . . But 'giving up' does not mean 'forgetting,' it is the opposite of forgetting; it is a full and conscious recognition of the past."[27]

Hareven gives expression here to the notorious "control" and discipline that any pioneering movement expects of its adherents—and that any era of political turmoil exacerbates. Zionism is no exception, of course, and Israel's history has obviously intensified this need of personal repression for the sake of preserving one's sanity (a process revisited in chapter 7). Such is precisely the moment at which Sara finds herself now, preserving her sanity by giving up (not/forgetting). Both Hareven and Sara seem to accept this verdict as a necessary evil. However, although Hareven's explanation is couched in the most general terms, gender does make a difference: "It dawned on him that in order to go on living he would have to give up most of himself," we are told earlier on about Professor Barzel (121). What he gives up is a European self-image he has cast in Frankfurt and in Heidelberg, that of the Renaissance man, the savior of mankind. Struggling with what he perceives to be the loss of his (existential) authenticity, he acknowledges Jerusalem as "the city that abides no one's decision about who they are" (ibid). Sara, on the other hand, is compelled to take a second step, to acknowledge that her subjectivity is finally to be defined in terms of *others*: "They recognize me: I have three sons and so little time" (189). The irony could not be any greater: Sara Amarillo, the paradigm of the new, Jerusalem-born, Jewish woman, falls back on the most traditional and often maligned Jewish definition of womanhood. Like her biblical eponym, she gains status through motherhood, giving up, it would seem, the androgynous privileges with which Hareven has originally equipped her. More significantly, she seems to experience her subjectivity only through the recognition of others. In the Hebrew phrase *makirim 'oti*, the protagonist is clearly the passive receptor of the action. Inadvertently, the text offers here a Lacanian insight: reflected in the gaze of others—the very gaze that has been the nemesis of gender theory, as we have seen in chapter 2—the subject of necessity perceives herself as an object ("me," *le moi*), in complete contrast to her narrative role throughout the plot.[28]

Does this mean that the subject is, *in principle*, alienated from her/his own selfhood, as Lacan would have it? Not quite. For unlike Lacan (and unlike the Judaic [postbiblical] tradition, one may add!),[29] Hareven optimistically harbors a contextual rather than essentialist explanation of the structure she has created. In her script maternity does not exclusively define the female subject, nor does it disrupt the myth of androgyny. Rather, the celebration of the subject—any subject—is *temporarily* compromised when the cannons are roaring. The very same sociopolitical conditions that have given rise to the ideology of "we," the "stupid [national] first-person plural," have also dictated the suppression of the Freudian quest, the throwing away of the key to the psychic underground room.

But all this is historically, not universally or essentially determined. "Gender Equality? Not in a War Zone!" unambiguously declared Israeli political scientist (and politician) Naomi Chazan.[30] Nor can the female subject of our narrative hold onto her androgynous status. Instead, she is finally allowed the empowerment of existential (be it of the Levantine variety) transcendence: stretching from Genesis to eternity, it is the big *female* Other, Jerusalem, that offers a moment of ecstasy, of metonymic submersion:

> Now this is me, she told herself, now this is me, here on this hill, with this feeling of great reconciliation [peace] . . . . Now this is me in this moment of hers. . . . A place to touch the sky: now it is close. To breathe in mountain and light. Now.

The uniqueness (among Israeli writers) of Shulamith Hareven's position on feminism is paralleled by the splendid isolation of her new Hebrew woman among Israeli female protagonists. Although in its ambivalent preoccupation with the gap between lofty ideals (both authorial and national) and the limitations of reality this novel has its analogue in Amalia Kahana-Carmon's contemporaneous novel *And the Moon in the Valley of Ayalon* (1971), *City of Many Days* goes much farther in dramatizing its own ideal— perhaps too far. Indeed, in some sense, this novel was ahead of its time. In the early seventies the horizon of expectations in Israel was not yet ready for a literary discussion of feminism, not even in this moderate selective form. Female victimization was convincingly evoked by the early work of Kahana-Carmon, but it would take her, as we have seen (chapter 3), more than a decade to get to a stage of protest and action, and even then she would stop on the brink of masculinist autonomy. In poetry one could hear revolutionary tones—some of them of the androgynous sort—in Yona Wallach's verse, but not too many were willing to listen. It is not surprising, then, that *City of Many Days* was perceived as another nostalgic tale about Jerusalem, "lacking highly significant themes and conceptual contents" and marked by "inadequate motivation," as a leading Israeli scholar, Gershon Shaked, has put it.[31] That issues of gender and female subjectivity, as well as their conflict with historical constraints, are central to the novel—this passed totally unnoticed. It goes without saying that the potential conflict with national ideologies implied by this material was not even surmised.[32]

This conflict is the subject of the following chapters; for now, another question is in order. How would this novel fit into the category of "masked autobiography" I argued for in chapter 1? Indeed, not a simple question to answer for a writer who, with the exception of a couple of early stories, never adopted an autobiographical modality in her writing.[33] I would nevertheless submit that in the image of Sara the author created a vicarious self, one that released her from the risk of personal exposure while giving her the liberty to explore both her ideals and her ambivalence about them. When I add the fact that Hareven herself served as a combat medic in the besieged Jerusalem of 1947–48, and that, despite her Polish birthplace (Warsaw), she does trace her maternal lineage to the sixteenth-century exiles from Spain, the parallels (as well as the disguises) become transparent.[34] Finally, the gender codes that govern the construction of Sara are much more representative of the new Hebrew woman adumbrated, at least *theoretically*,[35] by the Palmach generation—to which Hareven in fact belonged—than to those evident within the Sephardi community in interwar Jerusalem. While this displacement creates autobiographical distance, perhaps in the service of the separation between art and life prescribed by our author, it also reduces historical verisimilitude—a fascinating paradox for the otherwise politically engaged citizen Shulamith Hareven.

3. Trauma and Homoeroticism: "Loneliness," an Israeli Story

Any attempt to draw a straight line from Hareven's first novel to the next stages of her writing career will leave us somewhat at a loss. And no wonder. The publication of *City of Many Days* virtually coincided with the most traumatic moment in the history of modern Israel, the Yom Kippur War (1973). That momentous war, and its political aftermath, no doubt marked a seismographic fault line in the Israeli psyche. As a politically involved citizen, Hareven found herself in a predicament not unlike the one she had fashioned for the heroine of her first novel, whose personal choices were constricted by the maelstrom of World War II. It is not surprising, then, that the concerns of this novel seem to have been engulfed by the political upheavals of the decade. Both its lyrical nostalgia and its antiessentialist androgyny were irrelevant to the harsh realities of the time.

Indeed, Hareven's androgyny would be all but forgotten until the 1990s, when it did make some inroads into Israeli fiction.[36] As for the author herself, she let the historical momentum take over her creative production. While she never tried her hand again at writing a novel, her short fiction (*Bedidut* [Loneliness], 1980) was almost overshadowed by her masterful essays (1981, 1987, 1991) and biblical novellas (1983, 1988, 1994).

Throughout the 1970s the division of labor in Hareven's creative "economy" is quite clear-cut. In her short fiction she managed mostly to ignore the times, ostensibly maintaining a separation between art and life. This separation is clearly signaled by the two collections published by the end of the decade: a slim volume of short stories, *Bedidut* (Loneliness, 1980), and her first collection of essays, *The Dulcinea Syndrome* (1981). The latter will concern us below (chapter 6); here we will take a close look at the title story of *Loneliness*, searching for more clues for Hareven's feminism under siege.

Though its title signals a preoccupation with a universally defined human condition, *Loneliness*[37] is in fact an examination of the female condition. With one exception its stories feature women protagonists; most of them, however, are light years away from the spunky autonomy vested upon the Sara of *City of Many Days*. Ranging from metarealistic psychologism ("My Straw Chairs") to subversive realism ("Loneliness"), and from social commentary ("The Witness")[38] to a surrealistic Holocaust revery ("Twilight"), these spare narratives show no trace of the selective feminism of their direct precursor, *City of Many Days*, nor of the public issues that preoccupied their author in the essays written during the same years. They are mostly concerned with the power relationship between the sexes (both within and without the family structure), more often than not portraying women at the losing end of the struggle.

"Loneliness," the title story, is an instructive case in point.[39] The story covers two days in the life of "Mrs. Dolly Jacobus," a wealthy housewife, whose major problem is a lack of interest or passion that might fill her life with meaning. What nonetheless distinguishes her from most characters in "frustrated wife" stories is her childlessness. She shares this feature with Hareven's earlier heroines (see above) as well as with other protagonists in this volume. Interestingly, however, this is not a Beauvoirian or Woolfian refusal of motherhood in the name of feminist protest or artistic aspiration (respectively). Except for one early protagonist who claims that "the thought of an alien body growing inside me can make me hysterical,"[40] Hareven's protagonists do not choose to be childless. In a typically Jewish way, for most of them this is an unwelcome reality. Yet their struggle with this imposition functions variously in different stories. While in "My Straw Chairs," for example, barrenness is openly thematized, presented as a psychological cause of Lotta Stein's severe neurotic and physical dis- function, in "Loneliness" it is kept in check, at least at first blush. Dolly Jacobus's irritation over her "four consecutive miscarriages of indeter- minable cause" (11; 15) is mentioned obliquely, as a fact of the past that has recently "begun to wane" (ibid). In the narrative present we follow her routine "rounds" through the "stations" of her familiar turf—writing desk, lectures, parking lot, office (the husband's, of course), shopping, post office, Grandma Ḥaya. (If this rings a familiar bell, *Mrs. Dalloway*'s, for instance, it is probably no accident, as I argue below.)[41]

The opening of the narrative finds Mrs. Dolly Jacobus "pondering how to finish a letter" to her husband, who is out of the country on business. With a few crisp pen strokes (both the protagonist's, in her letter, as well as the narrator's), finely tuned at conveying an ironic point of view, Hareven manages to conjure up a marriage of means and convenience that is devoid of passion and intimacy.

This impression is created, however, not through an ironic style alone. For the Hebrew reader, at least, it is further bolstered by two intertexts that frame the opening paragraph, squarely placing it within the theme of female alienation and marital strife.[42] The first is the protagonist's first name, Dolly. Though not improbable as an Israeli name, its foreignness in Hebrew is quite noticeable. It thus calls attention to itself, foregrounding its bilingual semantics over its signifying function. The former quite read- ily leads to the English word *doll*, which the average Hebrew reader would not fail to recognize. (If the English reader entertains any jolly associations with *Hello, Dolly!* this story would soon compel her or him to abandon them.) From here it is but a short step to a classic Israeli text, Dahlia Ravikovitch's much-read and anthologized signature poem, "Buba memukenet" ("Clockwork Doll").[43] Written in the 1950s, this poem still lives in the Israeli imagination as *the* literary proof text of the female con- dition. Invoking Olympia, E. T. A. Hoffman's dancing doll (*The Tales of Hoffman*), this poem portrays and protests woman's objectified existence as a mechanical doll, "shattered to bits" but fixed again so that she can do "what they told me, poised and polite." But to no avail: "And then I went to dance at the ball, / but they left me alone with the dogs and cats / though my steps were measured and rhythmical."

The second intertext reaches further back, to Hebrew Nobel laureate author S. Y. Agnon. The title of his acclaimed story "Panim 'aḥerot" ("A Different Face," 1933) is actually grafted into the end of the opening paragraph of our story: "She could never imagine her husband once she was no longer by his side. Perhaps he had a different existence then, a different face."[44] The subject of Agnon's story is the aftermath of a divorce, acquiring its name from the "different" face the protagonist discovers in the woman from whom he has just separated. After years of shutting her off from his business concerns, consequently growing apart to the point of a divorce, he suddenly finds her attentive and understanding, minutes after leaving the court room. "A love story," the poet-scholar Leah Goldberg called it, in a well-known essay.[45] It describes, she argued, how two loving people can grow apart while living under the same roof but also how "their love, this futile postdivorce love, takes on 'a different face' " (219; 212).

Is this what our protagonist is about to discover, we may ponder—a different face? By means of divorce? At this early point in the story we cannot really be sure. But we may be wondering if this is one more story of the frustrated wife syndrome, made familiar in Hebrew by Kahana-Carmon's writings (chapter 3). A closer look unveils a variation, however. Unlike a typical Kahana-Carmon protagonist, Dolly is not aware of the emotional barrenness of her marriage. When we meet her she "had arrived at a sure sedate self-love"; she thinks she has learned to be in control of her life, which mainly means the adoption of her husband's view of their "station": "In the station that you have reached, Dolly, you can afford to be impractical" (10; 14).

The source of Me'ir Jacobus's privileged "elitism" is not only his material and professional success but also his inherent sense of "home" in Israel. Having deep roots in the country (he is a ninth-generation [!] Jerusalemite), his sense of self is naturally at odds with Dolly's own experience as a survivor who "had been twice-born, and her first, perhaps truer, life had ended abruptly at the age of fourteen" (30; 35; cf. "Twenty five years ago Dolly Jacobus had been a refugee"; 11; 16). "Butterflylike," she "had often wondered about the meaning of home" (24; 29). "To this day she was astonished by such things as central heating, which kept on burning warmly, really burning, while the rain remained outside. Truly outside; it wasn't just an optical illusion" (12; 16).

The power imbalance between Dolly and Me'ir hinges, then, on two stereotypical axes: one gendered, perhaps essentially so (in this narrative), the other experiential (historically or sociologically based). Dolly had apparently begun on the losing end of both. But soon we learn that she does have a secret weapon; she prides herself on her "insight" and "keen eye," considering herself to be "an astute observer" (15; 19). However, while this power is demonstrated in several small incidents that are fundamentally tangential to Dolly's life, the main action of the story questions the validity of precisely this power, perhaps even undermining it altogether.

Beautifully structured like a classic novella, in which restraint seems to control unmeasured depths, "Loneliness" unravels its heroine's inward journey toward a pointed moment of self-revelation. It moves from Dolly's trusting (though not overly intimate) letter to her husband, to a (surprisingly quiescent) halt—when she accidentally discovers her husband's infidelity (with the stereotypically ugly, good-for-nothing secretary, of course).

There is obviously nothing new about this script; but, in contrast to many other retellings of the theme (the wife is the last to know motif), this version manages to startle us with its closure. Despite the shock (for the protagonist, though less so for the reader) and the implicit pain, one can almost hear Dolly's sigh of relief. The charade is over, the mask of false bourgeois respectability can finally be taken off: "So that's how it is, said Dolly out loud in the empty apartment. That's how it has been all the time. I've really always known. But what actors we all are" (37; 42).

With this final admission the text in fact challenges both Dolly's and our understanding of her "keen eye," of her power of observation. How "astute" is it, a reader might ask. Indeed, how should one "judge" Dolly's consistent misreading of the clues she encountered on her way to the moment of truth? Was this misreading a willed blindness, a necessary defense (as implied by her last statement)? Or has she deluded herself about being "an astute observer," never really having a "keen eye"?

These questions are not meant to be an academic exercise. For our answer to this quandary would compel us to reconsider a pivotal scene, the one detail that makes this little story different, even subversive.[46]

I am talking about a "scandalous," unexpected scene of female homoerotic desire that the author has woven into an otherwise conventional plot. While waiting in line at the post office (to buy a stamp for the letter to her husband) Dolly notices, "directly in front of her," "a very small teenage girl with the emaciated, almost monkeylike appearance of a stunted child" (21; 26). The place is naturally congested ("the clerk at the window was slow and incompetent"), and Dolly Jacobus seeks to free herself by moving forward a bit, when she suddenly realized to her astonishment that the dark-skinned waif of a girl not only failed to move too, but deliberately seemed to press backward and turn her head, so that her dark mouth unmistakably delved like an inquisitive kitten's against the soft silk bodice covering Mrs. Dolly Jacobus's right breast.   *(22; 27)*

After another failed attempt to remove herself, followed by the girl's pressing "against Dolly Jacobus's stomach as though in an open and explicit invitation," the narrative voice zeroes in on Dolly's sensuous and visceral response:

> A hot wave, heavy, tropical, and damp, passed over Dolly Jacobus. She jerked back her hand so as not to touch the girl's waist and offendedly clamped her mouth shut. Yet she knew, with a weak, sinking feeling, that she could no longer resist the wave of desire rising, illimitably shameless, within her. . . . Compared to her, I am an amateur, Dolly Jacobus thought to herself, a rank amateur. She shut her eyes, conscious that in another moment she would move closer to the knowing little body of her own accord.   *(23; 28)*

She would not, of course. Just then, "the line melted away," and soon the girl disappeared "without looking at Mrs. Jacobus." It seems that Mrs. Jacobus's moment of rebellion is over, that she failed to act out "her new passion," "her need to trample, to violate [the norm]" (23; 28).[47] But the episode is not over yet. The next scene takes us to Grandma Ḥaya's home. There, helping the old lady to slice string beans while discussing the extent of her control over Me'ir's going away with or without "her permission" (which obviously scandalizes the old lady), Dolly is suddenly emboldened enough to comment, "Don't you think it might be better if women didn't marry men at all? Perhaps what a woman really needs is another woman" (29; 34).

To Grandma Ḥaya this is "nonsense," associated only with "Tel Aviv"—in her world the site and sign of moral depravity, of the erosion of the "good old times" (26; 31). This response is not unique to her generation, however. In the 1970s it was no doubt representative of the putative Hebrew reader. The only analogue I can think of shows up in a 1980 novel by Ruth Almog, *The Stranger and the Foe.*[48] There, however, female homoerotism is brought up merely as an option—only to be totally rejected by the protagonist, who refuses to give up heterosexuality despite her basic inability to partake in it. Even today the lesbian scene of "Loneliness" stands out as a sore thumb in a literature that has scarcely treated female homoeroticism. Readers have been especially wary about the jarring conflict they perceived between this theme and its immediate narrative context. The question is, then, to quote some of my baffled students, "What is this anecdote doing in this story?"

Hedda Boshes, in the only (cursory) reference to this issue at the time of publication that I could find, empathically interprets Dolly's suggestion as a "heresy," triggered by women's "fatigue and disappointment with the endlessly frustrating need to cope with men's world."[49] This is probably true, but not the whole truth. Too much passion and too much bodily sensation—clearly orgasmic, in fact—is invested in Mrs. Dolly Jacobus's "stormy" reaction (23; 28) for it to be merely a cerebral heresy, just a feminist response to the failing dream of equality. Nor does the storm subside as Dolly believes. To the contrary. Back home from her visit to Me'ir's grandmother, "a sharp burst of energy ran through her; now, at once, this evening, she must understand everything about herself once and for all. It was time she knew" (30; 35). This quest leads to a frenzied search for childhood, for childhood pictures. But none exist. Her (pre-Holocaust) childhood seems to have been erased without a trace. All that is left is a wrenching pathos, a pathos rendered all the more powerful through Hareven's circumspect style.

It is this pathos that is the key, I believe, to the meaning of Dolly's supposedly sensational lesbian episode. The need to reconstruct a lost childhood leads to a quasi-sadistic homoerotic fantasy. Interestingly, this fantasy centers on images of childhood, perhaps of deprived childhood. The girl from the post office is "cast up inside her again," arousing a "great wave of sadistic compassion, a feeling not unlike that of a little child who plays lovingly with a doll [!] and a minute later punishingly tears out its hair" (ibid.). As in a (day)dream, Dolly is both the child and the doll, working through her rage and self-pity, simultaneously inflicting on the other and enduring herself the pain of loss and dislocation. What was perceived earlier on as the intimation of a steamy sexual encounter has been transformed here willy-nilly into a healing fantasy, one that would perhaps repair a trauma beyond reach.

But there is more. Imperceptibly, the fantasy takes on a "different face"; the doll grows (in fantasy) into the real-life girl, performing still another healing miracle: "Already she was planning how the two of them would sit here, at this table, studying English together" (30; 36). Lover or daughter? The lines seem to blur. For a woman who suffered four miscarriages (exacerbating the loss of her own childhood), the roles may overlap and interchange. Homoeroticism seems to be sublimated and absorbed into an overdetermined post-Holocaust emotional hunger.

The fact that the attempt to translate this fantasy into reality fails (after much cajoling and preparation the girl does not show up) seems at first to be beside the point. What is meaningful, after all, is Dolly's psychological growth, her coming to terms with long buried emotions. Which is precisely what she achieves, of course. When reread, however, bearing in mind the evidence against the validity of Dolly's "keen eye" provided by the closure, the whole post office episode takes on a different face. Is it possible, we may wonder, that Dolly's eye betrayed her there too? Could the homoerotic temptation scene be a misreading on her part? Could this have been a projection, her own dreamlike way of removing the censor and acting out forbidden wishes?

Whatever the case, one thing is clear. Subversive as the story may be in its Israeli context, Mrs. Dolly Jacobus is not Mrs. Dalloway or, rather, she is a Jewish/Israeli Mrs. Dalloway. For despite obvious differences of genre and scope, the two share not merely their similar-sounding names (Dolly/Dalloway) and the structure of their respective plots (the daily routine of the present narrative, frequently interrupted by flashbacks and visions of the past) but also their midlife, "dead" marriages—and their turn to female homoeroticism for help.

Mrs. Clarissa Dalloway spent her nights, "like a nun withdrawn," in an attic bedroom, white and narrow like a coffin ("There was an emptiness about the heart of life; an attic room. Women must put off their rich apparel. At midday they must disrobe. . . . Narrower and narrower would her bed be. The candle was half burnt down" [33–34]). Although, unlike Dolly, she had given birth to a child, "she could not dispel a virginity preserved through childbirth which clung to her like a sheet" (34). She is also affected by a war, its impact alive all around her in post–World War I London. But, unlike Dolly, she experiences the trauma only vicariously. The heavy price is finally paid by her "double," the shell-shocked, raving, and suicidal Septimus Smith (see note 4, this chapter). Hence the differences between the function of homoeroticism in the two plots, both psychologically and narratively. For Mrs. Dalloway it is a nostalgic dream of an edenic adolescent love, remembered—while undressing in her attic room—for its precious purity and integrity and starkly contrasted to heterosexual "interest." Its same-sex, same-age nature is perceived as "protective, on her side; it sprang from a sense of being in league together" (37), a stage that will inevitably give in to the proper order of things—the "catastrophe" of marriage that "was bound to part them." Even "the most exquisite moment of her whole life," kissing Sally Seton (38), is an infinitely cherished gift, a diamond that keeps sparkling forever in the depth of her memory—but hardly impacts on the present. (When Sally does show up again she is a plump homebody, all adolescent spunk and glamour gone.) It certainly does not constitute any serious (ideological?) threat for the existing (heterosexual, patriarchal) order, which Mrs. Dalloway will obediently continue to observe despite her unhappiness.[50]

Mrs. Dolly Jacobus's homoerotic "fling" is quite a different matter. On the one hand, she is fully aware of its subversiveness, of its potential violation of the existing order.[51] Hers is not a naive adolescent experiment, idealized nostalgically as a distant memory, but a mature acknowledgment of her deviance in the here and now of her life. Recognizing the harsh repulsive reality of her situation, she soberly waits "for my poor ugly love with her smell of sweat and synthetic violets" (35; 39). On the other hand, by associating mature female homoeroticism with arrested developmental stages of the mother-daughter relationship, Hareven has endowed it with a deeper psychological edge, unwittingly anticipating recent, post-Chodorow (1978) feminist theories of women's psychology (see chapter 2).[52] At the same time, however, by anchoring this universal complex within a specifically Jewish trauma, the Holocaust, Hareven has contextualized it historically, thereby domesticating it, adding yet another chapter to her Israeli selective feminism.

Although in her public pronouncements Hareven continued to deny the legitimacy of women's literature as late as the 1990s,[53] her own late work belies this denial. Since the roots of this transformation were anchored in the political strain that began in the 1970s and has still not abated, we turn our gaze to this sensitive subject. Our next chapters probe the different faces of the feminist critique of national ideologies. We begin with the paradigmatic example of the late Virginia Woolf, using her "feminism under siege" in World War II as a comparative test case for the politically torn (and psychologically besieged) Israel of the last three decades.

Chapter 6

The Leaning Ivory Tower:
Feminist Politics

> The leaning tower not only leant in the thirties, but it leant more and more to the left. . . . In 1930 it was impossible—if you were young, sensitive, imaginative—not to be interested in politics; not to find public causes of much more pressing interest than philosophy.
>
> In 1930 young men at college . . . could not go on discussing aesthetic emotions and personal relations. They could not confine their reading to the poets; they had to read the politicians.
> —Virginia Woolf, "The Leaning Tower"

The leaning tower, Virginia Woolf's effective metaphor for the crumbling of old demarcation lines at a time of political upheaval, may be useful for characterizing the changing climate in Israel of the seventies. In this case it was the impact of the Yom Kippur War (which had taken Israel by surprise) that caused a similar shake-up of the existing order. The rippling effects of its aftermath have lingered throughout the following decades, manifested in the downfall of the Labor government in 1977, the Lebanon War in 1982, and the Palestinian *intifada* (civil uprising) in 1988. And although the major issue throughout this turmoil has been purely political—the still-unresolved Palestinian demand for self-definition and the perceived threat it constitutes to Israel's existence—its divisive ramifications have been tearing apart Israeli public opinion, affecting all aspects of Israeli life to this day.

One of the first cultural casualties of this politicized climate was—as may be expected—the modernist poetics of "pure art." What is less expected, of course, is that modernism would still be an issue as late as the 1970s. But in Israel, where Anglo-American and French modernist poetics (of the T. S. Eliot/Ezra Pound and *le roman nouveau* varieties) made their appearance only in the late 1950s and 1960s, literary modernism was still in evidence, at least in the separation between art and life held to by some writers (such as Kahana-Carmon or Hareven, chapters 3 and 5).[1]

Modernism was also furthered in another guise by the then young Department for the Theory [or Science] of Literature (*torat hasifrut*), established at Tel Aviv University in 1966 and presently bolstered by *HaSifrut*, a *Quarterly for the Science of Literature* (1968–1986). As I have argued elsewhere, the Tel Aviv practitioners so tenaciously adhered to the scientific paradigm precisely because of their fear of the overpowering presence of political issues in the Israeli experience. It seems that the delusion of rationality and objectivity is a greatly needed defense against the turbulent reality of Israeli life. That protective function of "scientific" research was painfully evoked by the founder of the department, Professor B. Hrushovsky (Harshav), when eulogizing the death of a disciple turned colleague, Dr. Yosef Ha'efrati (who fell in the Golan Heights in 1974 while on reserve duty):

> Our weaknesses are many. Our squabbles are petty. The circumstances of our lives are difficult. . . . We cannot escape into a camp of merely defensive cossacks. In the exact sciences, as well as in the humanistic sciences, we have to aspire daringly, realistically and uncompromisingly— to create via the highest standards available today in the world. . . .
>
> Of course, we have to be "engaged," but we must not give everything up for such engagement.
>
> And I believe that this was Yossi's will. Yossi was engaged in politics, he knew what our [political] situation was, but nevertheless he was building a research institute with the illusion that when we are in the house we do research. If our existence goes on, we need this research with all its strictures, without concessions.[2]

This anguished cry for disciplined research, delivered in 1974, adumbrated a position that was becoming harder and harder to defend. Before the decade was over most writers who had previously subscribed to the poetics of pure art (or science) found themselves in a predicament. For women writers, especially of the feminist persuasion, this dilemma was further exacerbated. The double bind in which they found themselves may have been summarily captured in the rhetorical question (and answer) we encountered in chapter 5: "Gender equality? Not in a war zone!" Apparently, there is hardly a place—psychological, legal, or practical—for the woman question under a state of siege; the existential concerns of the collective, as a rule, take over.

Yet this truism does not encompass the whole story. In a paradoxical way Israeli feminism came into being precisely in those decades that might be considered the most politicized in Israeli history, despite and perhaps because of its infamous "double bind" (the title of the first Israeli book by a team led by a bona fide feminist scholar; see section 2 below). For literary feminists this double bind was not unlike the one faced by Virginia Woolf when the roar of World War II airplanes impacted on her modernist aesthetics and feminist politics. It should therefore come as no surprise that, though distant in time and place, Israeli women writers solved their predicament in ways that were analogous to those devised by Virginia Woolf a few decades earlier. Yet, given inevitable divergences in historical circumstance and personal temper, this analogy is not without its distinctions. To better appreciate them we will first take a close look at that part of Woolf's late work that I label psychopolitics. It is the circumstances and particular terms of her psychopolitical analysis that make the Israeli analogues intriguing in their divergences as much as their convergences.

1. Oedipal Tyrannies: Woolf's Psychopolitics in Three Guineas

Censured by the younger writers of the 1930s for her Bloomsbury modernist aesthetics, which allegedly locked her in an ivory tower, Woolf turned the tables and, with her usual dexterity, attributed to her critics precisely that for which they blamed her—an inability to get out of the (ivory) tower. In her last public lecture, given at the Workers' Educational Association in Brighton in May 1940, she recast the ivory tower of old in a new metaphor, "The Leaning Tower," inspired no doubt by the Tower of Pisa.[3] This leaning (to the left) was the result, she said, of the political changes that had shaken Europe since World War I:

> In Germany, in Russia, in Italy, in Spain, all the old hedges were being rooted up; all the old towers were being thrown to the ground. . . . But even in England towers that were built of gold and stucco were no longer steady towers. They were leaning towers. The books were written under the influence of change, *under the threat of war.*
>
> *(139–140; emphasis added)*

This literature under influence, says Woolf, is suffused with "anger; pity; scapegoat beating; excuse finding" (141); it is a literature "full of discord and bitterness, full of confusion and of compromise" (142). The cause of all this turmoil, in her opinion, is the unavoidable conflict between the younger generation's recognition that their class privilege imposes certain limits on the view they have from the top of the tower and their inability to do without it: "Trapped by their education, pinned down by their capital, they remained on top of the leaning tower" (142). Woolf, on the other hand—as a woman who never enjoyed the privileges of capital and college education—sees herself free to get on and off the tower at will, exempt from its limiting class impositions. The dubious reader, for whom class barriers seem stronger than gender differences, may recall at this juncture that Woolf had already done away with her own "class" privilege in *Three Guineas* (1938). There she argued (not very convincingly, to judge by the reactions of her peers) that "economically, the educated man's daughter is much on the same level with the farm laborers. . . . Fear is a powerful reason; those who are economically dependent have strong reasons for fear" (137).

We may obviously question Woolf's democratic class consciousness, reading it rather as a confusion of identity, as some of her peers have done; but we must admit that she was on target when pointing to the political upheavals of the twentieth century as the cause of the downfall of the ivory tower—that metaphor for the tradition of nineteenth-century symbolism and aestheticism, which was still alive early in this century in the modernist ideal of separation between art and life. And although her "diagnosis" of the ills of the younger generation is directed outside, at "them," at least some of her insights can be applied to her own work in the same years. Indeed, in contrast to the image of the dainty Bloomsbury aesthete fostered by her own peers (as well as by later readers), recent research has unearthed Woolf's involvement in the burning issues of her time.[4] As she sharply observed, in the 1930s it was impossible to be sensitive and imaginative (at any age or of any gender, apparently), without getting involved in "politics." And Woolf herself was no exception. As early as 1936 (the outbreak of the Spanish Civil War), she qualified her own Bloomsbury-acquired abhorrence of "art and propaganda," allowing that "when society is in chaos" the artist cannot "still remain in peace in his studio. . . . He is forced to take part in politics."[5] Soon she would do just that, taking on fascism both directly, in her pacifist manifesto *Three Guineas* and in her 1940 essay "Thoughts on Peace in an Air Raid,"[6] and implicitly, in her last work of fiction, *Between the Acts* (1940).

Three Guineas is of special interest for our discussion of Israeli literary feminism because it weaves together different strains of Woolf's intellectual and artistic makeup, the very strains that jostle each other in the work of the Israeli writers under discussion here: modernism, feminism, and politics. As her diary amply documents, *Three Guineas* represents the angry (and bold) analysis that Woolf the modernist could not conceive as harmoniously inhabiting the fictional world of her historical (and to some degree autobiographical) novel, *The Years*.[7] The writing of that novel turned out to be an unusually arduous process (1932–1937) in which the planned essay-novel *The Pargiters* (only one of the provisional titles she had given the work in process) was transformed and split into two—an almost traditionally realistic novel, *The Years*, and a pugnacious long essay, *Three Guineas*. The latter was a sequel of sorts to *A Room of One's Own*, with two differences: it was angrier—and it was heavily documented and footnoted in the tradition of academic scholarship. The novel, on the other hand, was cleansed of "propaganda" (unfortunately, also of simple dialogue, resulting in almost mute characters) and was free to treat precisely those "aesthetic emotions and personal relationships" that Woolf thought the "young men" of the 1930s "could not go on discussing" (see the epigraph to this chapter). The "vulgar passions," to use Quentin Bell's locution—those very sentiments that had been excluded from the civilized thin air of Bloomsbury—were given unbridled expression in the essay, unnerving many a reader then as now. "Like the truths that Septimus Smith [in *Mrs. Dalloway*] so much wanted to communicate, the truths in *Three Guineas* belonged to an order of speech that was inadmissible at the time," says Roger Poole in his comprehensive review of the issue of Woolf and war.[8]

This bifurcation is apparently paradigmatic, as we have seen it also in operation in the post-1973 work of the politically involved Israeli Shulamith Hareven (chapter 5), to whom we shall presently return. What would have been unthinkable for Hareven and her peers, however (at least not until much later), is the impression that *Three Guineas* first gives of discouraging women from participating in the war effort. For, on the face of it, this is Woolf's response to the question that occupied center stage during the 1930s, namely, How is the free world ("civilization" in Bloomsbury parlance) to protect liberty and prevent war?—more specifically, How can "the daughters of educated men" help in this venture? Woolf's resolutely pacifist answer reveals that, like the tower of her younger peers, her own tower of pure art was also "leaning to the left," perhaps even more so. As is well known, this political bent has repeated itself in the Israeli scene, although not without modifications, as I shall argue in this chapter. In the case of Woolf, however, it did so with an additional twist; although she was concerned, as was everyone else, with the threat to civilization that was hatching on the continent, she had something else on her mind: the battle of the sexes. Never giving up her feminist perspective, she boldly analyzed fascism as a sex-based phenomenon, as the public face of masculinist aggression. In other words, she may indeed have been "forced to take part in politics," but her politics reached beyond the battle front; it encompassed the home front as well, that is, the status of women (in war *and peace*). With her, the personal was not only political, it was gendered, too.[9]

With the rage and courage that women generally dare to master only in middle age, as suggested by Carolyn Heilbrun,[10] Woolf took the "bull" of gender essentialism and sexual difference by the horns:

> For though many instincts are held more or less in common by both sexes, to fight has always been the man's *habit*, not the woman's. *Law and practice have developed that difference, whether innate or accidental.* Scarcely a human being in the course of history has fallen to a woman's rifle; the vast majority of birds and beasts have been killed by you, not by us.　　　　　　　　　　*Three Guineas, 9; emphasis added)*

Woolf's struggle with the question of gender essentialism takes an intriguing route. At the focus of her attention is the burning question of the time—aggression. Though confident that the sexes differ in their propensity toward it, she is hesitant when it comes down to putting her finger on the "source" of this difference. "Innate" (that is, essential) or "accidental" (that is, historically or culturally determined ["habit"])? This quandary has bogged down any discussion of sexual difference, as I have argued in chapter 2. By positing this question as unanswerable but going beyond it, to historical proof texts, Woolf in fact anticipated some of the sociocultural solutions with which contemporary gender theory has countered the fear of essentialism that automatically attaches itself to any conceptualization of sexual difference. At the same time, however, the very use of the concept "instinct" puts her dangerously near the biologist camp—thereby bringing her into the orbit of the Freudian analysis of civilization and its discontents, at the unavoidable cost of unsettling the validity of her own historical evidence.

But there is more here. Woolf also anticipated—in what may seem a rather reckless exaggeration—the feminist principle of "inclusion," the one later suggested by Beauvoir and recently adopted by contemporary feminists, in Israel and at large. In contrast to Beauvoir (and Kahana-Carmon; see chapter 3), however, who equated the subjugation of women to that of two universally "acknowledged" marginalized others, blacks and Jews (see chapter 2), Woolf dared to compare the plight of women to that of the liberal world at large. Maintaining a Cato-like campaign against the deprivation of women in education and in the "professions" (the two causes for which she figuratively donated the first two guineas of the title of this essay), she went on to equate male dominance over the fair sex with the would-be fascist dominance over the human race. This move may seem today totally disproportionate and tactless, especially from a post–World War II perspective (as was predictably the case with the Israeli negative reception of the book).[11] We should not let this hindsight cloud our judgment, however. Woolf worked on this essay between 1932 and 1937, when even her wildly imaginative mind could not yet foresee the horrors that the future had in store. In fact, the "sample" atrocities she collected while working on the projected essay-novel were those of the Spanish Civil War, in which her nephew, Julian Bell, was killed—a trauma she shared intimately with her sister Vanessa, and which probably exacerbated the "vulgar emotions" she experienced while writing.[12]

Bearing this timing in mind, we may be able perhaps to assimilate her analogy between the homespun (yet universal) patriarchal oppression of women and the danger posed by dictatorships abroad:

> There, in those quotations [advocating separate worlds for men and women], is the egg of the very same worm that we know under other names in other countries. There we have in embryo the creature, Dictator we call him when he is Italian or German, who believes that he has the right, whether given by God, Nature, sex or race is immaterial, to dictate to other human beings how they shall live; what they shall do.   *(61)*

> The daughters of educated men who were called, to their resentment [*sic*], "feminists" were in fact the advance guard of your own movement. They were fighting the same enemy that you [i.e., men] were fighting and for the same reasons. They were fighting the tyranny of the patriarchal state as you are fighting the tyranny of the Fascist state.   *(117)*

A startling conclusion indeed. Overtly, she arrives at this conclusion through close readings—literal and metaphorical—of cultural representations of women. But there is more to her analysis than the epiphenomena of culture. She boldly enlists the "help" of Freudian psychology, thereby inventing psychopolitics—an analytic modus I have elsewhere detected in Israeli fiction at large.[13]

My quotation marks around the word *help* are meant as an (ironic?) qualification. On the one hand, Bloomsbury's "major role in bringing Freud to the English" has been established early on, as well as the Woolfs' close association with several psychoanalysts—notably, Virginia's brother

Adrian, his wife Karin, and James and Alix Strachey.[14] Strachey was also instrumental (together with Ernest Jones) in the Woolfs' Hogarth Press becoming Freud's publishers in English (the first edition of Freud's *Collected Papers*, vols. 1–4, appeared in 1924–1925). On the other hand, there is no substantial evidence of the effect his writing may have had on Woolf during those years. We may even suspect a certain cautiousness on her part, perhaps a defensiveness that broke down only in her last years. In 1921 she is still very guarded: "James puny and languid—such is the effect of 10 months psychoanalysis," she wryly comments upon the return of James Strachey, Freud's translator, from a sojourn in Vienna.[15] The causes of this defensiveness are not too difficult to surmise, particularly in view of her wretched history with mental health specialists, so painstakingly described in Hermione Lee's recent autobiography. Add to this Woolf's notorious squeamishness about sexuality (cf. Goldsmith), and the popular perception that psychotherapy may damage one's artistic genius, and her wariness is perfectly understandable. Yet an additional reason emerges from what she confided to her diary in the besieged years of World War II. On December 2, 1939, almost a whole year after the Woolfs' acclaimed visit to the elderly master in his new home in Hampstead (January 1939),[16] she refers to his work in a brief diary entry: "Began reading Freud last night; to enlarge the circumference: to give my brain a wider scope. . . . Thus defeat the shrinkage of age. *Always take on new things.*"

The emphasis is mine, meant to highlight the impression this entry gives of never reading Freud before. Although scholars (with the exception of Abel) generally accept this "fact" without reservation, I believe this must be a false impression.[17] Nor would I take at face value her claim, cited by Goldstein, that she was acquainted with psychoanalysis "only in the ordinary way of conversation" (240). As Goldstein correctly observes, she neglected to say how close she was to some potential participants in such [maybe not so ordinary] conversations. At any rate, by 1929 Woolf's familiarity with the theory leaves a mark on *A Room of One's Own*, although in a typically mocking tone: "Had he been laughed at, to adopt the Freudian theory, in his cradle by a pretty girl? . . . A very elementary exercise in psychology, not to be dignified by the name of psycho-analysis, showed me . . . " (28). Still further on she soberly finds that she can adopt "a new attitude to the other half of the human race," almost "forgive" them, in fact, because "they are driven by instincts which are not within their control" (33). As we have seen above, the "instincts"—a fundamental psychoanalytic concept—serve her as well in the opening argument of *Three Guineas*. So what was the "new" Freud she was reading at the late date of December 1939?

As suggested by critics (Abel, Mepham, Lee), Woolf may have been reading Freud's nontechnical papers (possibly John Rickman's 1939 *Civilization, War, and Death: Selections from Three Works by Sigmund Freud*). She was also apparently reading another of Freud's "anthropological" essays, "Group Psychology and the Analysis of the Ego" (1921), which the Hogarth Press would publish in 1940. Her registered reaction to these readings (on December 9) may explain her earlier distance from (and reticence about) psychoanalysis. As Mepham correctly indicates, Freud's ideas must have upset her, as they totally undermined her Bloomsbury-inspired understanding of the nature of civilization and personal freedom, and of the source of artistic inspiration: "Freud is upsetting; reducing one to whirlpool; & I daresay truly, if we are all instinct and unconscious, what's all this about civilization, the whole man, freedom etc.?"

Disturbed as she sounds here, 1939 was still just the right time for her to absorb these ideas. They clearly informed what she wrote in the last year of her life, both personally and publicly. I have already noted (in chapter 4) her awareness that she was performing "psychoanalytic therapy" while working on her late autobiographical "Sketch of the Past." There is also no doubt, as noted by Abel, that in her 1940 essay, "Thoughts on Peace in an Air Raid," she consciously inverted the title of Freud's 1915 (!) "Thoughts for the Times on War and Death" (one of Rickman's selections).[18] A direct mention of Freud's influence on the younger writers of the 1930s shows up in "The Leaning Tower":

> The leaning-tower writer has had the courage . . . to tell the truth, the unpleasant truth, about himself. That is the first step towards telling the truth about other people. By analyzing themselves honestly, with the help of Dr. Freud, these writers have done a great deal to free us from nineteen-century suppressions. *(149)*

Although she goes on to call this Freudian introspection "creative and honest egotism," I am not sure that this is as much a "backhanded" Freudian manifesto as Goldstein believes it to be.[19] At any rate, the most significant Freudian traces in Woolf's work of that year are undoubtedly those manifested by the presence of Freud's *Civilization and Its Discontents* (1929; the major selection in Rickman's collection) in her last novel, *Between the Acts*. Here, for the first time in her fiction, humankind is perceived as part of the animal world, and the primal instincts play a major—

even if parodic—role. *Civilization* was, of course, Freud's most extensive analysis of the primordial struggle between Eros and Thanatos, the notorious "dual instinct theory" suggested first in 1920 in "Beyond the Pleasure Principle." In *Civilization* he elaborated his pessimistic view concerning the constancy of the aggressive ("animalistic") instincts and their unavoidable conflict (i.e., war) with mankind's hard-won civilization. It was however also his apotheosis of Eros and sublimation as the only protective wall against the aggressive instincts. This psychosexual double helix is translated by Woolf into the poetic closure of her last novel:

> Alone, enmity was bared; also love. Before they slept, they must fight; after they had fought, they would embrace. From that embrace another life might be born. But first they must fight, as the dog fox fights with the vixen, in the heart of darkness, in the fields of night.   *(219)*

This is Freudian ambivalence at its most poetic formulation, a fitting coda for Woolf's artistic oeuvre.

Yet this is not the last stop in our inquiry. For I strongly believe that Freud's *Civilization* left its mark not only on *Between the Acts*, with its wistful ending, but on *Three Guineas* as well. In contrast to the commonly accepted perception that she "anticipated Freud" (as both Mepham and Lee believe—just because she had not mentioned him before in her diary?!), it stands to reason that Woolf must have read *Civilization* already in Joan Rivière's translation, which the Hogarth Press and the Institute for Psycho-Analysis published in 1930.[20] Her Freudianly inspired writings in 1940 only reinforced the use she had made of psychoanalysis in *Three Guineas*, published two years earlier. To ignore the strong Freudian traces in *Three Guineas* is to miss, in my opinion, precisely the thrust of this " 'unreadable' work of genius,"[21] namely, that part of its analysis that is still alive today—in subversions of masculinism and militarism—despite and beyond the essay's sensationally disturbing analogies, unchecked rage, and even its "wrong-headed historical understanding."[22]

For there was clearly one staggering difference—so far hardly noticed by scholars—between what Woolf had read (in Freud's work) and what she wrote. The object of Freud's anthropo-psychological narrative is "Man," which for him (and for Western philosophy at large, as discussed in chapter 2) was a conventional stand-in for "humankind." Without articulating her discomfort at this identification, as later feminists have done, Woolf simply read Freud literally. Making the object of *her* Freudian narrative man, as in the male sex, she performed a sleight of hand that changed the whole burden of guilt and culpability. If humankind does not have any chance of eliminating Thanatos, the aggressive instinct (it can only be modified or channeled by an enhanced Eros, human erotic bonds, says Freud), Woolf would strike out *human* and replace it with *man* instead. In her narrative the culprit is "male-kind," even masculinity per se, while the female sex is taken out of the equation. Reading Freud against the grain, she is in fact not that far from contemporary critiques (feminist and others) that "blame" psychoanalysis for the valorization and dissemination of masculinist values.

So how does Woolf make use of Freudian psychology in her analysis? In part 3 of *Three Guineas* the instincts are joined by yet another quintessentially psychoanalytic concept, the Oedipus complex. After what may seem a tortuously circuitous line of argumentation (a veritable antithesis of Beauvoir's, and others', logocentric discourse), this concept finally emerges as the cornerstone of Woolf's outrageous psychopolitics, as the scientific proof that clinches her reasoning. Since similar analyses will curiously reemerge, almost half a century later, in the feminist-political discourse of Israel, we should take a closer look at this part of the manifesto.

On the face of it, the thrust of Woolf's argument is patently antipatriotic. She begins by inciting women to resist volunteering for the war effort, encouraging them instead to join what "could be called the Outsiders Society" (122–123). She explains her startling position by a no less shocking declaration: "As a woman, I have no country" (125). The puzzled reader is treated to a deconstruction (*avant la lettre*) of the idiom "our country," the country that "throughout the greater part of its history has treated me as a slave." Yet the deconstruction of national history does not go deep enough. The next to be put under the scalpel is the Church. Mercilessly exposing its double standards, Woolf takes her probe all the way back to the sources, protesting her inability to "altogether reconcile the ruling of St. Paul, or another, with the ruling of Christ himself who 'regarded men and women alike as members of the same spiritual kingdom . . . and as possessors of the same spiritual capacities' " (141).[23] Is this what she meant when, early in 1932, she gleefully reported in her diary (February 16): "I have collected enough powder to blow up St. Pauls"? Indeed.

The excavation does not stop there, however. In order "to blow up St. Pauls," she would dig further, with the help of the science of depth psychology. Admittedly, she does not enlist Freud himself, but rather one Prof. Grensted, whose "Report of the Archbishops' Commission on *The*

Ministry of Women" she documents (accompanying it with full scholarly apparatus, as is the essay throughout). The honorable professor of religion explains why the practice of the Church has so much diverged from its "democratic" origins. He seems incredibly well versed in Freudian jargon; in the space of one page we are treated to "infantile fixation," the "Oedipus complex," the "castration complex," "nonrational sex-taboo," male dominance, and female inferiority—all apparently at the root of "a powerful and widespread subconscious motive" (144).

For a moment the contemporary reader (myself) may suspect a parody; but apparently none is meant. In grave seriousness, and in a move that anticipates recent feminist revisions of psychoanalysis, Woolf turns the Freudian rationalization "against itself." In this deconstruction of Freud (as we might call it today), "infantile fixation" (148) is the root that lies at the bottom of men's need to dominate and of women's 'basic fear' (a surprise reversal of Erik Erikson's future [1950] "basic trust").[24] The oedipal complex is not the boy's rite of passage into morality and civilization; it is not the spring of the (specifically masculine!) superego, which holds infantile drives in check, allowing the subject to enter a Lacanian Symbolic Order. Rather, man (m.!) is held hostage at this infantile stage even in maturity, never outgrowing his subconscious need to control, dominate, possess, conquer. The transition from individual to collective psychology (politics) is imperceptible. Family relations, professional (male) achievements, personal and national greed, and even military tyrannies and imperialistic conquests—all are motivated by the same "strong force," which was "all the stronger because it was a concealed force" (156).

King Creon of Greek mythology is the classic example, of course, of oedipally driven tyranny—sowing death and destruction all around, both politically and personally, as king and as father of his son and his bride, Antigone (148; 161). Closer to home, Victorian biographies provide ample cases of oedipally fixated fathers who tyrannized their daughters (and sons, too, in the well-known case of Elizabeth Barrett-Browning's father; 149). Finally, "another picture has imposed itself on the foreground. It is the figure of a man; some say, others deny, that he is Man himself, the quintessence of virility" (162).

A contemporary reader may expect another fatherly tyrant in this sequence, not necessarily the führer or the duce, whom Woolf goes on to inscribe into her closure. Yet hers is not an exercise in therapeutic free association, so we must leave the ghost of Sir Leslie where she left him, in the shadows of her own unconscious.[25] After all, my focus here is not on

Woolf's psychic pain but rather on how she transformed it into a powerful social critique. At a time when the free world was bending under the most vicious adaptations of Otto Weininger's racial-sexual essentialisms, Woolf was calling for an overall reevaluation of the nexus of nationalism and masculinism, again anticipating recent scholarly interest.[26] Whatever she thought of Freudian psychology as individual therapy (not much, to judge from her circumspection in the matter and from Quentin Bell's testimony), she obviously learned from it one important lesson—that normalcy differs from the pathological margins only in measure, not in substance. Equipped with this tool, she was able to unmask masculinity per se, asking her readers to see "a very important connection": that "the public and the private worlds are inseparably connected; that the tyrannies and servilities of the one are the tyrannies and servilities of the other" (162).

With this conclusion in mind, her plea to women to join the Outsiders Society takes on a new meaning. What seemed at first a politically subversive act, inciting women to undermine the war effort, turns out to be a psychologically defensive move. Her pacifist position is motivated by her concern that women will be contaminated by the "male malaise"—unconscious Hitlerism, as she will soon name it (in "Thoughts on Peace"). What motivates her concern is a very progressive *un*essentialist intuition. For despite her reliance on a biological concept, "instincts," she is not at all sure that the female/maternal instinct, supposedly sex-specific (123), will withstand the pressure of socialization in the world of masculine aggression. This is in keeping, of course, with her careful historical contextualization of the "aggressive instinct" at the opening of the essay. Her practical conclusion makes her, however, the "mother" not merely of culturalist gender theory but of separatist feminism as well, advocating gender (rather than sexual) difference (see chapter 2). In the final analysis, the freedom from tyranny for which she yearns is not conceived by her as an "equal rights" ticket of entry but as permission to differ, as the liberty to keep one's own (cultural rather than essentialist) difference, so that women should not "merge [their] identity in yours" (121).

Whatever we might think—psychoanalytically—about Woolf's fear of loss of boundaries, which comes through clearly in this last statement, she herself perceived it as the result of the present political state of siege, an era of "the bark of the guns and the bray of the gramophones" (163), which she was at the time absorbing into the fictional universe of *Between the Acts*. Moreover, she was fully aware of the contradiction between the need to preserve intact one's gendered identity *under duress* and her old dream of androgyny, of "the capacity of the human spirit to overflow boundaries and make unity out of multiplicity." However, in contrast to Roger Poole's contention that in *Three Guineas* Woolf vindicated his doubts "about the possibility of 'the androgynous mind,' "[27] she wistfully avers that the capacity to overflow boundaries is a dream for the poets in times of peace. For now she must maintain her freedom by staying on the outside, and she must drive her point home by contributing *equally* to women's causes as to war-prevention efforts (to which she finally gave her third guinea): "The aim is the same for us both. It is to assert 'the rights of all—all men and women . . . to the great principles of Justice and equality and liberty' " (164).

"Gender equality? Why not in a war zone?" Woolf seems to be reiterating, paradigmatically weaving together feminism and politics, at the obvious expense of modernist ivory towers and . . . androgynous dreams. At the same time, however, the crux of her psychopolitical analysis, the gender base of aggression, results in a logically analogous inference that pacifism is female based. While recent feminist scholarship has found this conclusion problematic, to say the least, because of its essentialist connotations,[28] Israeli feminists have found it difficult to resist—as we shall presently see—because of its galvanizing pragmatic power.

2. The Leaning Israeli Tower: Feminism Reinvented

The response of Israeli women to the political turmoil of the 1970s, and to the even stronger pressures of the 1980s, took a slightly more winding path, although not without some intriguing analogues to Woolf's. In contrast to the England of the 1930s, where the memory of the suffragist movement was still alive (the vote was gained, in stages, after World War I), Israeli feminism had to be reinvented in the 1970s. About half a century had passed since the suffragettes of Jewish Palestine won the vote in 1920;[29] by the 1970s intervening events—primarily the Holocaust, the establishment of the state, and its prolonged state of siege—had turned the struggle and achievements of those new Hebrew women into a dim memory. The familiar images of female soldiers and even a female prime minister (who was *not* a feminist!) did little to change the life and status of the woman in the street. "From the time of Independence until the Six-Day War (1948–1967) the status of women was, for the most part, a non-issue," is the succinct summary of sociologist Dafna Izraeli, in her 1987 *Encyclopaedia Judaica* feature essay on "The Status of Women in Israel."

"The issue reappears," she continues, "between the wars—1968 and 1973—when an anticipated labor shortage and the emergence of the feminist movement stimulated public interest and debate."[30]

The feminist movement was generated then in the 1970s, precisely in the years Israel was led by the nonfeminist prime minister, Golda Meir (1969–1973). It first shook up the Israeli public arena during the aftermath of the Yom Kippur War, with the election, in November 1973, of the recent American immigrant Marcia Freedman to a seat in the Knesset (parliament). The trials and tribulations of Freedman's short-lived parliamentary career (she refused to run again after one term) are extensively documented in her memoir, *Exile in the Promised Land* (1990). Yet although her unsuccessful attempt to import American feminism into Israel (and into the Knesset) would come to fruition only in the late eighties, her Israeli sojourn in the 1970s illustrates two fundamental aspects of Israeli feminism: first, its American (or Anglo-Saxon, as all English-speaking immigrants are called in Israel) component (which was crucial in the 1920s as well)[31] and, second, the "marriage"—not always a happy one—between feminist and left-wing politics.

Before Freedman's "rise" to parliamentarism (on the ticket of the newly formed Citizen's Rights Movement, spearheaded by lawyer and civil rights activist Shulamit Aloni), she had, in Haifa, organized consciousness-raising groups, which originated in seminars on feminism that she and Marilyn Safir taught in 1970 at Haifa University.[32] This (mostly) "Anglo-Saxon" feminist enclave thrived throughout the 1970s, peaked with Freedman's election, and dissolved toward the end of the decade, shortly before Freedman herself returned to the States (1981). Several English books on Israeli women originated with this group, most notoriously, Lesley Hazleton's *Israeli Women: The Reality Behind the Myth* (1977), which I discussed in chapter 1, and Natalie Rein's *Daughters of Rachel: Women in Israel* (1979). Both clearly illustrate the gulf between the Israeli female self-image and the way it was perceived by Anglo-Saxon feminist eyes.

An "indigenous" feminist activity was simultaneously brewing, however, within the politically radical left-wing cells of Jerusalem (led by Leah Zemel and Michal Tzofen).[33] Its political anti-Zionist positions prevented it, though, from reaching wider circles or successfully cooperating with the women's movement that was slowly emerging in Haifa and Tel Aviv. The dichotomy between a broadly based women's movement and the left-wing radicalism of some of its forerunners was, in the final analysis, also one of the reasons for the "exile" (both in Israel and out of it) of Marcia Freedman, who was "too left wing" for many women activists in Israel.[34]

Still, Israeli feminism and left-wing politics were fated to dwell together, although not always amicably. This is a common enough phenomenon, as evidenced by the politization of many (and especially third world) feminist movements.[35] The Israeli case was, however, focused on one issue—the termination of war and bloodshed. The high point of Israeli women's involvement in the "politics of peace" (not an uncontested feminist proposition, as mentioned above) would come in the 1980s, when women on both sides of the Israeli-Palestinian conflict (not all of them self-acknowledged feminists!) initiated or joined the protest movements.[36] Women's active role in the peace movement—especially during the Lebanon War (1982) and the intifada (1988), but also as recently as 1997[37]—has obviously had great appeal for both media and academia, as the abundant documentation of this topic may attest.[38] But what is of a greater interest for our inquiry is the less publicized gendered analysis of war and aggression initiated by professional feminists soon after the 1973 war, which continued under different guises in the literary output of subsequent decades.

In 1974 the recently formed Israeli Feminist Movement named its newsletter (issue no. 4) *Women for a Renewed Society.* Barely a year had passed since the Yom Kippur trauma; predictably, this issue raised questions about the effect the war had on Israeli women. In a modest article, entitled "Women and War," Esther Eilam, the organizer of the Tel Aviv feminist group who became the leader of the Feminist Movement of Israel, analyzed the gender implications of Israel's prolonged state of siege.[39] Her major point, clearly reminiscent of Virginia Woolf's psychopolitics, was a critique of the mythicization and idealization of heroism and patriotism, which she saw as a crucial component in the sociopsychological construction of masculinity. In the spirit of the feminist-pacifist politics of *Three Guineas,* and in a sociocultural context that was just as inimical to her analysis as Woolf's was to hers, she argued for an equal valuation of feminist and political struggles against oppression and privilege.

Eilam's proposition was no doubt ahead of its time. It would take another decade—and a heavily burdened one, the 1980s—for a psychopolitical critique of masculinist values to filter through Israeli culture. First, another kind of groundwork had to be lain: the analysis of the "status of women" in Israeli law and society. This was the work of the 1970s, carried forth both publicly, through the parliamentary ventures of Marcia Freedman, and in camera, by the first Knesset Commission on the Status of Women, established in 1975 by Israel's prime minister "in keeping with the UN Declaration of 1975–1985 as the Decade of Women."[40] As argued by political scientist Dafna Sharfman, the commission report, published in 1978, "publicly revealed and described in detail the real situation of the women in Israel, and the discrimination to which they are subject."[41] It further exposed the persistence of the view that women's "contribution to society was marginal and supportive by nature . . . a reflection of their political status and the inclination of the Labor Movement elite to view them as voters but not as decision makers."[42] A similar condemnation was voiced in 1976 by Knesset member Shulamit Aloni, whose book, *Women as Human Beings*, analyzed the deplorable status of women within the Israeli legal system. In 1982 a team of five women scholars, headed by sociologist Dafna Izraeli, another Anglo-Saxon, expanded the canvas in *Nashim bemilkud* (*The Double Bind*), their analysis of the sociopolitical and psychological catch-22 of Israeli women.

On another front, the same years also saw the republication of Sara Azaryahu's 1947 *The Association of Hebrew Women for Equal Rights in Eretz Israel: Chapters in the History of Women in the Land, 1900–1947*, prefaced by Marcia Freedman (1977), as well as the establishment of a feminist press (the Second Sex) and the publication of the first "women lib" books in Hebrew.[43]

By the mid-1980s the missing new Hebrew woman began to show hesitant signs of coming back to life. *Nogah* (Venus), the first Israeli feminist journal, was established in 1980. Toward the end of the decade both the Hebrew University and Haifa University instituted programs for women's studies. Gender-related courses were offered in other universities as well. Israel Women's Network (IWN), spearheaded by Professor Alice Shalvi, was organized in 1984, "combating a climate of opinion in which feminism was considered irrelevant because Israel was perceived as having already achieved equality between the sexes."[44]

In her retrospective view (1994), Shalvi has put her finger on the very paradox we are trying to capture here. For this "climate" did not control public opinion alone, it penetrated the literary arena as well. It was this tension that we detected in the work of Lapid (1982), Kahana-Carmon (1984), and (earlier) Hareven, all of whom struggled—in their various ways—with the allure of the feminist romance and with the psychosocial powers that resisted it. A feminist turning point in the careers of both Lapid and Kahana-Carmon took place precisely within that 1980s climate of opinion. This climate may explicate their engagement not merely with women's liberation but with a critique of masculinist nationalism as well (extended by Kahana-Carmon to the deconstruction of any essentialist identity). As we shall see in the following chapters, they were preceded in this double venture by the writer Netiva Ben Yehuda, the veteran Palmach fighter who had waited for more than three decades before exposing—in 1981—her own experience in (and scathing feminist critique of) the heroic epic of 1948 (chapter 7). By the end of the decade they were also joined by writer Ruth Almog, who, without any modernist compunctions, used the feminist romance to unmask masculinism with all its deficiencies (chapter 8).[45] But before we turn to these authors we need to complete our probe into Shulamit Hareven's selective feminism; her pronounced ambivalence in this matter makes her recent work a fascinating test case of the leaning tower of Israeli literature.

Because of her earlier, feminist start (1972), qualified as that may have been, in the 1980s Hareven was more than ready to abandon (her version of) the feminist romance. As we have seen in chapter 5, her work had already in the 1970s developed on two parallel tracks—the fictional and the essayistic. In her short fiction she managed mostly to ignore the times, discussing precisely those "aesthetic emotions and personal relationship[s]" that Woolf excluded from literature written "under the threat of war" (see this chapter's epigraph). At the same time, she applied her sharp essayistic pen to the political and social fabric of Israeli culture, blatantly addressing its changing political realities.[46] A comparison between these essays and the fiction written in the same years confirms that the generic division governing her work reflects not merely a thematic bifurcation but an emotional one as well. There is a world of difference between the controlled ironic distance of her narrative tone and the impassioned admonitions of her essays. Like Woolf, she endeavored (though not always successfully) to maintain her artistic universe clean of "propaganda" and exempt from the "vulgar passions."[47]

The passions—not necessarily vulgar, of course—found their way into her essays and press columns. Predictably, her sociopolitical critique gained momentum in the aftermath of the 1973 war and the 1977 fall of the Labor government. Throughout the 1980s, no controversial topic escaped her pen: Palestinian refugees (with whom she spent time at the height of the intifada), "enlightened occupation" (which she claimed was a meaningless locution), internal religious and ethnic divisions, violence and the peace movement, the academization of literature (when she was a writer-in-residence at the Hebrew University in 1990), slang and linguistic norms (reflecting her work at the Israeli Academy of the Hebrew Language), charisma and its discontents, the dark side of myths (to which I shall return), and finally, "Eyeless is Gaza," the 1988 essay that gave its title to her third collection of essays (1991).[48]

Except for one early essay (1971), discussed in chapter 5, feminism is glaringly absent from these three volumes of essays. Nor are women at the center of the two "biblical" novellas published in the eighties, *Sone' hanissim* (*The Miracle Hater*, 1983) and *Navi'* (*Prophet*, 1989).[49] In fact, after the publication of *Loneliness* (1980) the author seemed to have made good on her principled objection to gender-specific thematics and style. In her later work the woman question was subsumed—in a typical Israeli fashion—by the concerns of the collective. Nevertheless, although she did not thematize gender, she continued to champion the position of the outsider and the marginal. In fact, her statement, "My position is that of the minority—almost in principle,"[50] sounds suspiciously close to Woolf's preferred Outsiders Society. It is also reminiscent of the "brotherhood of outsiders" we detected in the work produced in the 1980s by arch-Israeli feminist Kahana-Carmon (chapter 3). As argued below, Hareven and Kahana-Carmon share some of their narrative techniques, too. It should therefore come as no surprise that the last sequel in the biblical trilogy, *'Aharei hayaldut* (*After Childhood*, 1994),[51] inscribed into the desert narrative a heroine who is in conflict with the "patriarchal" order—a resurgence of the autonomous female protagonist of *City of Many Days*. This similarity notwithstanding, the gender roles imagined in *After Childhood* differ significantly from those of its precursor. The decoding of this difference is the challenge that preoccupies us in the following analysis.

3. Monotheistic Tyrannies: Israeli Psychopolitics

Without so much as even a hint of propaganda (in Woolfian terms), and with stylistic control and narrative economy that she had no doubt learned from both the Hebrew Bible and modern masters of the genre,[52] Hareven has crafted in *Tzima'on: Shlishiyat hamidbar* (*Thirst: The Desert Trilogy*) a well-wrought fictional universe that speaks of different times, different places, yet is wholly ours. She does this not allegorically, as many Israeli readers believed, but symbolically. Accordingly, the interpretation suggested below is not carved in stone; it is rather an attempt to shadow the author through the desert of her own making.

As implied by the title of the first novella in the trilogy, *The Miracle Hater*, these lean, poetic miniatures are nothing less than counterhistories.[53] By adopting the perspective of the other, the marginalized, or the outsider, they present a familiar (biblical) terrain from a totally unfamiliar angle. A similar technique of defamiliarization marks the opening scene of Kahana-Carmon's *Up in Montifer*, published around the same time (chapter 3). In that work this technique, I argued, unsettles readers' sense of Self and Other. It conditions them to empathize with the heroine's enchantment with the other (the "enemy") and thereby engages them in a philosophical questioning of otherness. Here, by contrast, a comparable technique is applied to a much more popular and familiar object: biblical history; it is also used much more vigorously, becoming the governing norm (the *dominanta*, in Russian formalist terminology) of the narration. As such, this trilogy has indirectly entered the conversation over the "rewriting of history," which was begun in Israel that decade by both historians and novelists.[54]

The novellas' revisionist aspect was not immediately transparent, however. The genre was evidently too foreign on the horizon of expectations of Israeli literature at the time. Only with the publication of the third sequel (more than a decade after the first) did the overall effect of its historical defamiliarization began to "make sense." By that time Hareven had also published her direct intervention in the Israeli historians' debate: in her 1994 article, "No One Asked the Medics," she made good her claim to view things—"almost in principle"—from the margins, thereby shedding light on her fictional strategies as well.[55]

This strategy is further reinforced by two stylistic hallmarks of the trilogy. One is Hareven's creative use of the biblical intertext: She borrows both narrative "type scenes"[56] and linguistic idioms, shifting them around from one context or character to another with impunity, consequently fashioning exhilaratingly new realities. Although she repeatedly insisted that this method was not new, since the Jewish midrashic tradition had always enjoyed "creative freedom" of this sort, her claim seems to have sunk in only with the publication of the trilogy as a whole.[57] The second stylistic hallmark is the author's unique presentation of nature through characters' *first* encounter with its manifold faces. The "mountains of the gods" (*The Miracle Hater*, 33), first snow (*Prophet*, 51; 63), a desert whirl storm (*After Childhood*, 28; 151)—all are rendered as first impressions of one astonished character or another. It is the arresting, awe-inspiring primacy of these impressions that deautomatizes our own habitual perception, powerfully revitalizing them as fresh subjective experiences.

This gift of rejuvenation does have its price tag, however. Readers are expected to constantly shift perspectives if they want to "get into" the narrative. This is especially true of the second novella. While in the first we are still within the Israelite camp, following the gaze of an internal other, in the second we are asked to step into the shoes of an utterly other, a Gibeonite prophet—a task that apparently caused more confusion than comprehension.

The Miracle Hater offers a subversive view of the Exodus, especially of Moses (and his elders, among others) through the eyes of another Hebrew, Eshkhar. Eshkhar is in fact a sort of a socially demoted double, almost a parody of Moses himself: he was saved at birth by a five-year-old Hebrew girl, Baita—obviously the author's pun on Bithia, the midrashic name for the Egyptian princess who saved Moses—a fact that naturally determines the different course his life would take. Like Moses, Eshkhar is motivated by a quest for justice, except that in his case it is individual rather than national. His "case" revolves around his deep (incestual) love for Baita, his mother/sister, who is given away to another, as was the custom. The newly established social (legal?) "system," however, is not equipped to take care of personal problems such as this. Eshkhar finds himself on his own, searching for his private interpretation of justice, god, and identity.

In its general lines the plot follows the biblical journey in the wilderness; unlike the latter, however, this narrative fills it with breathing individuals. The grand national epic is permeated with men and women "in the desert paths" (i.e., "in the street"), with personal emotions and conflicts, hopes and disillusionments. As they move on, and after Eshkhar and Baita have consummated their forbidden love (for which she is the only one to pay with her life—a surprisingly "patriarchal" verisimilitude in this otherwise revisionist midrash!), Eshkhar and his fellow "proletarians" form a parallel universe on the outskirts of the main camp, complete with a popular leadership (a kind of a mock shadow government) headed by Eshkhar and his friend Aviel, and accompanied by Aviel's sister Yona (a plebeian mirror image of the Moses-Aharon-Miriam trio, of course). Since their guiding principle is the avoidance of miracles, a subject highly relevant to the Israel of the 1980s, it is only logical that readers could not resist a political-allegorical reading.[58]

In their later attempt to decode *The Miracle Hater* Israeli reviewers (and mainly interviewers) often associated it with one of Hareven's early essays, "Fraternal or Filial Society?"[59] In this essay the author expressed her worry—as early as 1974—about the paternalistic norm of contemporary political leaders, from Ben Gurion to Moshe Dayan. Their "big daddy" image conditions the sons, she argued, to be dependent and to shirk personal responsibility. She nostalgically hankered after the yishuv (the prestate Jewish community and the 1940s Palmach generation), which exemplified her ideal fraternal community—an alliance of personally responsible individuals.[60]

Does Eshkhar illustrate the politically responsible "brother" by his rejection of a filial position prescribed by Moses's monotheism? Perhaps; the fiction is no doubt richer than any one narrow interpretation would allow. But the essay itself is of interest, as it offers us a glimpse into the genesis of an ideational thread that Hareven will continue to weave in her essays throughout the decades (and almost up to the present). This thread is her own contribution to what I label Israeli psychopolitics.

As I argued elsewhere, "never had Zionist ideology been placed on the analyst's couch as it has been in recent Israeli fiction."[61] Since the 1970s Freudianism had been put to the task of analyzing "the Israeli situation." The mouthpiece of this venture has been the author A. B. Yehoshua, whose affinity with Hareven we noted above.[62] Although they greatly differ in their evaluation of Freudianism (not to mention in their writing styles!), they share a fascination with Freudian mythologies. They also share a liberal-secularist belief in the necessity to preserve political "sanity." What they (and others) mean by this is a denigration of any kind of extremism, of religious fanaticism or political obduracy. But the metaphor is nevertheless psychological. Sanity is first and foremost a mental state—hence the propensity of both for psychopolitics.[63]

Accordingly, Hareven's critique of the political complacency of the average Israeli is analyzed through a Freudian grid. Resonating with Freud's anthropological narrative in *Totem and Taboo*, she reads the primeval herd's "primal sin" as a progressive step toward a fraternal democracy, which she equates with maturity. Within this logic a social formation governed by a strong leader is viewed as a worrisome regression into infantile dependence . . . hence her concern. Bracketing for a moment the practical implications of Hareven's analysis, this essay is intriguing in its unconscious (I think) subversion of the Freudian narrative. It unwittingly eats away at the basic oedipal structure postulated by Freud. If the parricide of the (all powerful) Father is a step toward progress and maturity, where would Freud's myth of oedipal castration, sublimation, and superego formation find its place? More important, what would it mean?

Since the essay is not concerned with the follow-up of the story, we will leave it hanging in the air too. But we will make a note to ourselves that strong paternal images are not Hareven's favorites—at least not in myth and in politics. Does this apply to individual psychology too, as it does in Woolf's *Three Guineas*? Right now we cannot be sure. But we can wait and see.

The second novella, *Prophet*, confronts readers (at least Israeli readers, who are deeply familiar and, to some degree, identify with the Hebrew Bible) with a more intense feeling of dislocation than *The Miracle Hater* does. Here the ratio between the biblical source and its fictional remaking is quite different. Hareven focuses on one chapter (Joshua 9; the historical record of Joshua 10 holds no interest for her) and lets her imagination soar. This is a modern midrash at its best—but not an easy one to digest.[64] It is also the longest and most complex of the three miniatures, consisting of four distinct chapters. In the first (which covers about a third of the text), we are enclosed in the walled city of Gibeon, where the events are focalized mostly through the mind of Hivai, the Gibeonite seer (prophet, in his eyes).

With quick, precise pen strokes Hareven evokes a polytheistic culture where incest and ritual infanticide are the norm, and soothsaying is considered to be prophecy. Hivai suffers from a "prophet's block" at the very moment his divination is most needed—when the Hebrews "are at the gate."[65] In desperation, he resorts to forcing a vision by the cruelest method ("reading" the bowels ripped out of a slave), yet he fails. He will eventually pay for his misreading by the loss of his beloved daughter (the object of his sexual needs), Sahali, the very person he was trying to save by forcing the future out.

For the Hebrew (or any biblically literate) reader, the reversal of narrative perspective is immediately signaled by the phrase "It was from the east, from the desert, that evil would come" (4). This inversion of Jeremiah's famous prophetic dictum, "From north evil shall come" (1:14, with many repetitions throughout), puts us on the alert from the very start. Along with the Gibeonites, we experience the fear, panic, and despair of a city that had been so powerful for ages that "it had forgotten what fear was like" (7). Although the cause of all this agitation has not been seen in the city yet, the Gibeonites "know"—"Ask the shepherds; they had seen them with their own eyes" (4)—that their unseen enemy is the young and strong "invaders"—the Hebrews.

Clearly, it was not just any identification with the other that Hareven expected of her Israeli readers; she also put them in the uncomfortable position of reading about *themselves* (at least in the generic sense—biblical ancestry being an integral part of Israeli identity) as the *Other*, and as the menacing other to boot. Alternatively, they could also read it, as some did, as a reverse allegory—identifying Israel with the besieged Gibeon, a suggestion that promptly aroused the ire of the author.[66]

I can think of only one precedent for such a reversal in Israeli fiction— Amos Oz's medieval novella *'Ad mavet* (Unto Death). Narrated from the perspective of the first crusaders, with "the accursed Jews" as their object of contempt and murderous intentions, that novella makes for a tough read, too, but in a completely different way. There it is the disturbing associations of the Holocaust, and especially the contrast between active and passive patterns of Jewish behavior—and the futility of both—that makes Oz's narrative difficult to absorb. In *Prophet* a different set of self-images make their appearance: the Hebrews as the conquerors, the devastators of the mighty Ai and the dread of all the peoples of "the land," or, conversely, a mighty people losing its cool over the "glint in the distant dust" (4), a threat that has no basis in sane reality. That by the end of the 1980s (a year or so into the intifada) these images would arouse conflicting reactions in different (Israeli) readers is only natural. That the variance would follow readers' political convictions is also quite predictable. It only follows that critics jumped to the conclusion that Hareven "translated" her own political positions into biblical allegories—to the great dismay of the author.

I suspect, however, that such readings are possible only if one stops short after the first chapter of the novella—or does not read the rest of it attentively. For, in this case, reading appropriately would mean rigorously shifting perspectives and angles of vision, having the facts deliberately confuse one's received presuppositions. While reading chapters 2–4, the reader is compelled to go, along with the protagonist, through the demanding process of distinguishing fact from fiction, reality from myth, one contrastive reality from another. There is really no escaping this constant unmasking, since it is required of the reader even on the most basic level of narrated events.

First, the Gibeonite elders are amazed when they encounter the "mighty Hebrews" in all their nomadic squalor and total ignorance of elementary ways of subsistence "in the land." Surely, the elders would bring home the tidings of a myth (mighty Hebrews) coming undone. Then Hivai, who chooses to stay on as a handyman but in fact teaches the

Hebrews the practical crafts they desperately need (Hareven obviously entertains here a different rationale for the biblical punishment the Gibeonites get for their ruse), goes through one cultural shock after another. He slowly discovers—which does not mean he comprehends—the intruders' absolute otherness: in law (Do not kill ever?), in attitudes to the alien (too receptive), in raising children (too much attention), in gender relations (tall, bold, strong-minded women), in social organization (much "democratic dissension" and no strong leadership), and, finally, in divine worship. It is the last that eventually causes his utter disappointment and final expulsion: in his desperate quest to regain contact with the gods, he is caught searching at night for the idols that he believes the Hebrews hide from him. To his astonishment, rather than paying for his "crime" with the fingers of his right hand, "as was the custom of the land," he goes free with a puny financial settlement. Nevertheless, at the demand of his master's wife, who never liked him and his ways, he is sent off—but amicably. The covenant they made seven years earlier is annulled by mutual agreement, and Hivai is paid, as decreed by the Hebrews' law, "his full wage and even more" (65; 78).

Hivai's share of surprises is not over yet, however. Bewildered as he is by the conflict of realities he suffered while living with the Hebrews, his education—since this is, in a way, a Bildungs novella—calls for still another test: a first-hand experience of the making of myth—more specifically, a myth about might and heroism. When an excited Canaanite youth tells him about the brave warriors of mighty Gibeon, who seven years ago "fought well and prevailed" over the great enemy that had laid siege to the city—Hivai, and the reader with him, has once more to compare notes with the truth he knows. Because his own "mythicized" image is part of the new myth ("There had been a prophet too, a great traitor," whom the king put to death "along with the treacherous elders," 72; 85), Hivai is keenly aware of its falsity; yet at the same time, he is powerless to deconstruct it.

Myths, and especially the damaging potential of myth, had preoccupied Hareven since the 1970s. She was particularly drawn to myths of "primary violence" in their different guises, probing once and again their cultural significance and their effect on contemporary life.[67] But none of these early inquiries had the force and the impact of the lecture-essay she published now, less than a year after the publication of *Prophet*. "What Should We Do About Myth?"[68], she asked her audience at a festive Hanukkah lecture in Jerusalem (December 1989). The puzzled listeners, who probably were, at that moment, enjoying the Hanukkah lights in the lecture hall (I imagine), perhaps recalling the mythical memory they symbolize, might have been silently responding with a counterquestion: "What's wrong with myth?"

Soon enough they would learn, however, that the lecturer is not concerned with myth per se but rather with the use of myth "to manipulate political power" (18). Nor is she worried about the "deep, primordial myth, but [about] new myth that has just now been made up" (20). Examples are myriad, of course, from Nazi Germany (Horst Wessel) to Stalinist Russia (the mummified Lenin) or Maoist China (the huge picture); in short, "every totalitarian regime."

But what makes these potboilers, these "deadly," "kitsch" myths, as Hareven calls them, so powerful? What is their secret? The answer takes us back to basic psychology:

> Every totalitarian regime knows how to confront our preadult persona with the mythic world, so that we will feel like children with a great savior, a redeeming father: he decides, he is the strong man, we have no responsibility for our actions whatsoever. *(21)*

We are back to the image of the strong father then. A negative image, we should add. The fact that our inborn constitutional "talent for myth" is rooted in the psychological dynamics of our infancy, when mother [*sic!*] and father are "all-powerful mythological creatures" (16–17), is what makes the modern political myth so powerful—and dangerous. Its mortal danger derives from its inevitable need "to guard it, jealously, through punishment and incarceration" (21). Hareven has no reference to Foucault, but his succinct title, *Discipline and Punish,* summarizes well the causes of her fear.

Her own frame of reference is, however, manifestly Freudian—again. The link between personal and political big daddy images is finally made here. As is the political implication of adult regression into infantile dependence. We have seen a similar psychopolitical continuum in Woolf's analysis of (Nazi) aggression, a similar reliance on Freudian psychoanalysis (which at this end of the century is taken for granted, of course), a similar scapegoating of the Father with a capital *F*, yet their conclusions are wholly different.

For one thing, despite the fear of the father figure, Hareven's concern is not gendered (at least not yet). Nor is it purely political. For, after a cursory discussion of some homespun "abominable" "instant myths," she returns to her original question, now focusing on "the deep myth that determines patterns over time" (23). The Oedipus myth is—once more—a natural example of deep myth. Its Jewish analogue is the myth that by that time had already become the acknowledged hallmark of Jewish/Israeli psychopolitics—the *akedah* (the binding of Isaac). But rather than falling into the trap of politics again (as we will presently do), Hareven's discussion leads, in a rather ingenious maneuver, into the realm of language and midrash: "Even the most ancient myth is nothing more than a midrash. . . . All art is a type of midrash" (25).

The conclusion? Cultural relativism is the only way to diffuse the power of deep myth and to prevent it from ossifying and generating violence. Thus Hareven recommends a comparative reading of the manifold versions of myth (aborted infanticide being one of her prime examples), so that its cross-cultural analogues may surface (e.g., Isaac and Iphigeneia). The strongest remedy however is that of artistic recreation and retelling. In a way, Hareven counters the danger of political instant myth by offering the antidote of "instant" remaking of old myth. The only way to "open up" (as Hareven calls it; do we dare substitute "deconstruct"?) entrenched myths is by "adding another midrash and another interpretation and some more knowledge." (28)

In 1990, in another lecture she gave (as a writer-in-residence at the Hebrew University), Hareven noted, in passing, that most good writers become fully aware of what they have done (written) about a year *after* a book is *published*.[69] This casual comment speaks for itself, I believe. But we would do well to remember it when Hareven's next postpublication essay(s) come our way.

Unlike its two precursors, *After Childhood*, the third installment of *The Desert Trilogy*, aroused a barrage of responses, most of them enthusiastic.[70] Readers and reviewers alike immediately responded to this direct and streamlined version of an ancient boy meets girl story. There are no jarring shifts of perspective here, and historical verisimilitude is reduced to a minimum: only at the very end of the story is the name of the current judge, Ben Anat, casually mentioned. (Naturally, Hareven has chosen the only judge that has a single verse to his name; see Judges 3:31.) History is replaced by geography in an attempt to create a sense of local "presentness." The cover design of the Hebrew edition cleverly hints at a post-mythical orientation. The recognizable silhouettes of Adam and Eve, holding fingers but half backing away from each other, covertly interpret the title: after the Garden of Eden, after the romantic myths of human, tribal, or national beginnings.

This is the story of the "morning after" then. The great adventures—the journey and the conquest—are over; the nomads are not the "mighty intruders" anymore, they (at least the marginal Hebrews we meet in this story) eke out a meager living in a nameless village on the outskirts of the civilized world, "not far from the Valley of Zin" (7; 131). Preferring the dry but relatively nonviolent wilderness to the discord that rules the mountains, they live now in a constant state of thirst—for water and for God. But neither is forthcoming. A pathetic attempt to force both down (Is there a difference?) is a golden opportunity, which the author does not forego, to recreate an exotic ritual, executed with a verve and precision rarely accomplished in fiction. (The curious reader, however, may find some intriguing clues in the author's riveting record of her visit to "Strange Siwa," an oasis in the far wilderness of Western Egypt.)[71]

Into this tough reality, delineated in spare, elliptical prose, Hareven introduces the no less tough Moran, the first female protagonist of the trilogy. Strong, big, and independent, Moran is clearly an ancestress (in historical terms, not in chronology of artistic creation) of Sara from *City of Many Days*. Within the trilogy she is clearly a descendant of the Hebrew women from *Prophet* who disoriented Hivai in their physical and social autonomy (46; 55, 54; 65). But her most significant forerunner is the biblical Rebecca—a strong matriarch in her own right. Like her, Moran is brought over from afar (the mountains) to be a wife to the Isaac of our story, Salu. Like her, too (though for different reasons), she is autonomous, choosing to go of her own free will.

Salu, on the other hand, is the victim of an attempted ritual infanticide. Like Isaac, he has lost his mother in his youth. Unlike Isaac, however, Salu is "modernly" conceived as a psychologically motivated character. Since infanticide has long been ruled out by the Hebrews (this is not Genesis, despite the analogies, a point to which we later return), Salu's biography makes him an outsider. He is painfully aware of this status, as his psychosomatic symptoms testify: "Ever since then his eyes blinked rapidly" (7; 131). Estranged from his father (who dies soon after anyway), he yearns after his absent mother and seeks to dissolve the obscurity engulfing her death. It is this quest, presumably, that is responsible for his darker side: his Esau-like attraction to the other, to the neighboring Hittites (cf. Gen 26:34).

The palimpsest nature of Salu's character ushers in the story's major personal conflict, in which, ironically, he recapitulates his father's primal sin. The conflict involves a classical gender issue—progeny. In a reversal of Genesis, here it is the Hebrew, Moran, who is fertile (shades of the matriarch Leah, whose praises Hareven has sung in an early essay),[72] while a nameless Hittite (with whom Salu is "involved") is "unable to conceive." Thus the familiar biblical pathos of barrenness is shifted outside, whereas Moran gains stature on account of her gendered subjectivity—motherhood. Salu has no visible part in this venture. After his failed attempt to redeem the Hittite woman by giving her his own first-born child, relations with Moran sour. The intimate body language that they continue to share barely makes up for Moran's suspicion and Salu's embarrassed inadequacy. Thus, while she is focused on raising children and olive trees, he continues with his quest, not knowing "what he was looking for" (54; 177): perhaps his dead mother, perhaps leadership, or God, or an escape from a demanding agrarian existence, plagued by drought and fatigue—the archetypically mixed motivation of the (male) hero's quest since the dawn of mythology.[73]

There is a world of difference between the optimistic reversal of gender roles we uncovered in *City of Many Days* (chapter 5) and the traditional, essentialist division between the sexes in *After Childhood*. Androgyny is definitely in evidence *in* childhood, in the spunky tomboy behavior of the young Moran (pointedly illustrated in her exhilarating discovery of the allures of the desert). It still lingers on *after* childhood, in her equal sharing in the stubborn effort to master a reluctant mother nature (the portrayal of which unavoidably evokes literary representations of Zionist pioneers "conquering the motherland"; cf. Lapid's *Gei Oni* in chapter 1). Salu, however, does not partake in this androgynous script. Unlike the mostly *un*aggressive males of *City* (or Yehiel, the male protagonist of *Gei Oni*), Salu is lured by the world of (masculinist) power and military prowess, compactly represented here by a neighboring Egyptian fort.

It is there that Salu loses his life, when an adventurous occupation of the deceptively deserted fort turns deadly. The meaninglessness of his action is anticipated by Moran, whose respectful but resolute refusal to join him in his (and practically everyone else's) adventure is emblematic: "If her master wished, she said, he could visit her at home. She had four small children. The trip was too much for her" (55–56; 178). This is the last time Moran would hear from Salu. The demarcation lines are tightly drawn. Maternity and male escapades do not mix. For the rest of the spare narrative Moran will only "fight with Salu in her dreams, shouting as loud as she could until her anger melted away in hot, sorrowful tears" (57; 181). Yet she would go on living and preserving life, playing Eros (Freud's life instinct) to his Thanatos. Her matronly portrait signs off the trilogy (and Hareven's fiction so far) in a mythicized, larger than life version of the motherly Sara that we observed at the closure of *City of Many Days*:

> She sat, her hands in her lap, the warm air stroking her face as if the whole strong wilderness were breathing close to her, quiet and warm.
> And when the wind grew very strong, she shut her eyes.

A mother alone, making peace with the loss of a beloved husband (whom we may think undeserving, but . . .)—this is the wistful image that the closure of *The Desert Trilogy* imprints on our memory. It retroactively foregrounds the closure of *Prophet* (and that of *City* too): family and nature are the only solace left at the close of day. Hivai's education ends, we may recall, on a similar note: he serenely watches the sunset, together with the boy he "adopts" at the close of the story.

The universal familiarity of this solace should not detract from its suggestiveness. However, behind and beyond this closure, another question presents itself: Why would Hareven violate her self-imposed "ban" on gender-specific fiction only to give up her androgynous dream? Why did she, like Woolf in *Three Guineas*, shift to a sexual difference reality?

There is probably more than one answer to this loaded question: the intensification of the political situation in the 1990s, a stronger reality principle that comes with age, and, perhaps, a slowly growing consciousness of a "vulgar passion," anger, which Hareven still found difficult to express, but which has imperceptibly found its way into *After Childhood*. The clue for the latter is the presence of the akedah in this last story.

In retrospect, this presence demands an explanation on two counts: First, why graft this emblematically patriarchal trauma, which transparently signals the distant mythical era of Genesis, into this postmythic story of settlement, ostensibly taking place around the time of Judges? Second, why does the akedah make its first fictional appearance in Hareven's work at this late date? What I mean by late here is double-edged: late in Hareven's career and late in the Israeli conversation about the akedah, which had already passed its peak by the time this novella was published. By the mid-1990s the akedah had long become a code word for a certain political position—and was therefore immediately recognized as such by most readers.[74] Yet I believe that, for Hareven, this breakthrough encodes something slightly different, a personal reassessment of some deep structures of her thinking. And it is this difference that I shall attempt to decode in the concluding segment of this chapter.

The akedah—that Jewish story of aborted infanticide—is one of the myths that has repeatedly preoccupied Hareven in her essays. In an early essay named "Violence"[75] Hareven introduces the akedah as the Jewish "myth of primal violence." This reading was not her own invention, of course. At the time, however (1976), it was a relatively new understanding of the famous biblical chapter (Genesis 22). For although the presence of the akedah in postbiblical Hebrew literature is about two thousand years old, it had rarely been read in this fashion before. This is true even for its ubiquitous presence in Israeli culture—up to the moment in time under scrutiny here, the 1970s. To argue this point in detail (as I have done elsewhere recently) will take us too far afield.[76] I will therefore limit my discussion to one aspect of this vast topic, the one that underlines Hareven's use of it too: the special oedipal coloring that the akedah took on in the 1970s.

As I argue in my recent essay, "Isaac or Oedipus?" it was in this period that the akedah became—after a rather long historical process—the Israeli equivalent of the Oedipus complex, the primal scene (and sin) of Jewish tradition. A major enhancer of this transformation was one of Israel's bêtes noires—controversial writer, mythologist, criminologist, and social critic Shlomo Giora Shoham—who in 1975 fixed the akedah as a universal psychological complex in his article, "The Isaac Syndrome."[77] Since it is this "penetrating and merciless probing into the appalling conflict of Abraham's guilt"[78] that serves as Hareven's point of departure in her discussion of violence, we need to take a closer look at Shoham's analysis.

Briefly, Shoham revitalized the Israeli discourse on the akedah by linking it with recent psychoanalytic interpretations (begun in Erich Wellisch's 1954 study of Isaac and Oedipus, which is not, however, available in Hebrew).[79] Shoham correctly compared the akedah not with the Oedipus complex itself (which Israeli literary critics have often erroneously done) but with that oft-neglected preamble to the oedipal myth, what psychoanalysts call the Laius complex. Shifting emphasis from the son's oedipalism to the father's "negativistic deprivational attitude toward the son" as "a prime archetypal dynamism of the human family" (302), Shoham chose nevertheless to name it not after the father of his Hebraic (biblical) test case, namely, Abraham, but rather after—and here is the paradox— the *son* of the biblical story, Isaac.

The unconscious motivation for this intriguing renaming is a delicate matter, which we had better leave unexposed here. Shoham's conscious motivation, on the other hand, is not too difficult to peruse. Couched in psychoanalytic idiom, this guilt-ridden essay by a bereft father of the Yom Kippur War was an outright indictment of "the fathers" as the perpetrators of aggression in the name of various sites of power, whether religious, national, or statist. Indictments of this kind were sounded by Israeli authors as early as 1970.[80] But these were couched in the language of metaphoric and fictional representations, not in the garb of "scientific" terminology. In Shoham's essay a personal trauma and a painful self-examination were translated into a psychopolitical analysis, endowed with the authority of psychoanalytic truth. Plumbing the depths of the retellings of the akedah in Genesis Rabbah, the author did not hesitate to diverge from their (by now classic) interpretation by Shalom Spiegel (1950),[81] and to hear in the words of the midrashic devil "the voice of subconscious dynamism, which identifies the absolute command of God with the covert infanticide wishes of the father" (313). Yet it is not with the biblical God that Shoham has a quarrel, nor even, apparently, with the fathers' murderous "subconscious wishes" (precisely what Woolf labeled "subconscious Hitlerism"). His major nemesis is the modern state, the paradigm of which is Israel, sacrificing its young to the Moloch of (ideological) wars (311).

We may now understand Hareven's admiration for and deviation from Shoham's watershed essay. Impressed as she is with the window he has daringly opened into the "yet unterminated, and perhaps interminable, Jewish self-reckoning concerning our primal violence" ("Violence"), she shifts the terms of the argument to a *contrastive* analysis between the Jewish tradition and its alleged Greek/Christian analogue, the Oedipus myth. After covering the familiar comparative terrain, she ends up with a conclusion that is reminiscent of Wellisch's (in his psychoanalytic study of Isaac and Oedipus) but diametrically opposed to Shoham's: "Apparently, we would not be mistaken in stating that what makes us different is our refusal to make peace with our own myth of primary violence" (230). The Jewish tradition, defined here on the basis of the biblical narrative, offers, then, a way of transforming Jewish subconscious primal violence. In contrast to Shoham, who explored the postbiblical tradition for its analogues with the Greek/Freudian myths of primary violence, Hareven is happy to rely on the ethical promise suggested by the biblical *closure* of the story. That closure safeguards the transition from denial (of primary violence) to a conscious and conscientious wrestling with it—a process she considers a positive Jewish value that she hopes to see nurtured in Israeli culture at large.[82]

Paradoxically, it is not difficult to identify Freud's script—in its general lines—behind Hareven's. Except that here it is applied to a specifically Jewish context. While her critique of violence is reserved for the Western tradition, she reads the akedah as a guide book, leading us to civilization out of primary instinctual chaos. Violence prevails only if one denies it, not if one's faces up to it and learns to sublimate it ethically (via the superego).

A similarly mainstream analysis shows up in another essay, "A Secret Ancient Guilt."[83] Here the focus is not on myths of primal violence but on the universal practice of infanticide, ancient and modern. Christian dogma is again placed within this context, as are the historical blood libels. Significantly, the interpretation of the akedah is less self-congratulatory: the story registers Abraham's failure, says Hareven, "to say NO of his own initiative" (163).

Over a decade passed before Hareven would acknowledge the darker side of the Jewish myth of primary violence. The occasion was that Hannukah lecture we described above, whose title was the anguished question, "What Should We Do about Myth?" Buried among the myriad examples of instant and deep myths, in an almost parenthetical passage, is the midrashic "truth" that Shoham had made public (and psychopoliticized) fifteen years earlier:

> And *most of us don't even know* that in Hebrew thought there is much doubt as to whether Isaac was indeed saved from the sacrificial knife. . . . Many *midrashim* tell us . . . that Isaac was indeed slaughtered and sent heavenward so the angels could treat his wounds, or his trauma. . . . In the popular consciousness Isaac is indeed slaughtered, the psychological truth of the akedah is that Isaac was slaughtered.[84]   *(emphasis added)*

Interestingly, Hareven does not link the akedah—even in its dark midrashic garb—with the oedipal myth in any of its phases. But not long after her lecture this linkage was startlingly fictionalized in A. B. Yehoshua's novel *Mar Mani* (*Mr. Mani*). In this novel the akedah is "acted out so it can be undone," as the author proclaimed (in response to the furor this counternovel had aroused). Indeed, *Mr. Mani* is perhaps the most extreme novelistic translation of Shoham's oedipalization—be it in reverse—of the akedah.[85] Yet, for Hareven, despite her consistent critique of powerful fathers and of "charismatic" leaders (a negative adjective in her vocabulary),[86] Oedipus and Isaac still did not meet. It would seem, if

I am allowed the freedom of speculation, that to identify Isaac with Oedipus, especially with the young Oedipus, the victim of Laius's infanticidal wishes, would be a blow to her initial belief in the extra value of the Jewish tradition (see "Violence"). In other words, to identify Abraham with Laius would mean to give up the perceived difference that Jewish tradition had carved for itself over the generations, and which Hareven—flaming secularist though she is—totally accepted.

The biblical story supports this difference; at least as long as we stick to its surface meaning—which of course is precisely what psychoanalysis loves to undermine, as did Shoham in his essay (not without the help of post-biblical tradition). Hareven fought long and hard to defend the edge she believed Judaism had over other old-modern mythological systems. Her impassioned Hanukkah lecture in praise of a comparative view of myth may have been addressed to herself as much as to her audience. Perhaps she was finally ready to relativize her cherished inheritance.

It is here that I would place the story of Moran and Salu. It is in *After Childhood* that the psychological implications of the akedah, even if aborted, are acknowledged by Hareven for the first time. The impact of a (castration?) threat, carried out by an all-powerful father, is detrimental not only in myth—but in daily life. What's worse, it is translated into a system of control beyond the individual—into political violence, into the search for nondemocratic, nonfraternal power structures. And—Hareven seems finally to admit—this *is* an all-male scenario. Mothers *are* out of the picture. So they are exempt. They can preserve life. And this is perhaps why androgyny has no chance. Because, after all, this is what the "deep myths" tell us: in the beginning there was a father against his son.

Hareven's rejection of patriarchy does not stop here, however. In a startling move she has her heroine exercise total independence—even of her heavenly father. Moran's response to a habitual farewell blessing, "God be always with you," by the elder Hiram, whose hand in marriage she has just refused, is a sarcastic closure of the search for divine revelation conducted by (mostly male) protagonists throughout the trilogy:

> She was not worth Father Hiram's anger, but she would rather God stayed away from her. Let him ignore her in his heaven, because the gods burned all when they came. They brought death and sickness and madness and drought. . . . Spare us both their honey and their sting. We're no match for them. *(60; 183)*

Virginia Woolf was ready, we may recall, to give up the social privileges of patriarchy in order to escape the damaging impact that its aggression—

whether instinctual or habitual—may have had on women. Hareven has her heroine take this protective rejection a step further, into the heart of theology. Applying to God a rather disparaging popular Hebrew saying (Not of your honey nor of your sting), Moran in fact makes up for Abraham's lack of initiative to say No to God. She thus carries on a dialogue with the existentialist drama of subjectivity theorized by the philosophers (see chapter 2) and fictionalized by Kahana-Carmon ("the day I said NO"; see chapter 3). Although her husband's childhood trauma is not counted among the evils she blames on the gods,[87] this is at least one possibility implied by the psychological perspective of the story. Whether this causal link was indeed a deliberate step by the author, we have no way of knowing. Perhaps she herself did not know it then. She may have known better, however, by the time her post-book essay was published.

In December 1994, shortly after the publication of *After Childhood*, Hareven published an attack on Freud and Freudian therapists (apparently she didn't need to wait a whole year this time). As is her wont, the article is a mix of theoretical musings and practical criticisms. Titled "Laius, the Father Repressed by Freud,"[88] it starts by acknowledging the late date of her reckoning with Freud. Fully aware of recent (mostly American) anti-Freud publications, and their various scholarly angles, she goes on to count the damages of his theories and "most of all: the consistent and systematic concealment of the original violent persona, the root of all evil—usually the father or the father figure—as if he does not exist and one is not allowed to think about him and about his part in whatever was taking place." The predictable example of the repressed Laius (in Freud's narrative) is accompanied by three counternarratives that Freud ignored, and chief among them is, interestingly enough, the akedah: "the murder of Isaac by Abraham (prevented last minute), the murder of Jephtah's daughter by her father (which did take place), and . . . the murder of Jesus by his father—God." Moreover, although her ultimate aim is to offer a general corrective to therapeutic practices that cause a confusion of roles between the victim and the victimizer, between objective reality and psychic reality, she does single out women as special victims of both Freud (the case of Dora) and contemporary Freudian therapists, who treat battered wives, for example, for masochism rather than getting them out of home and into a shelter.[89]

Hareven's scale of preferences seems to begin tipping here. The balance between her different loyalties must have been shifting—at least somewhat. Like Virginia Woolf before her, she probed the issue of violence via Freud; unlike her, however, she had not identified violence as a masculinist problem—at least not until the "Israeli situation" swept her out of the national consensus, consequently attenuating her distance from the cause of feminism.

Hareven's literary career exemplifies to the most extreme degree the conflict between gender and nation. A resolution of this conflict is perhaps signaled in her most recent lecture, entitled "The Sane Talent of Women" (or, Woman's Talent for Sanity).[90] The thrust of this lecture is double: first, in a move reminiscent of Woolf's initial search for "Women and Fiction" (later renamed *A Room of One's Own*; cf. *Women and Writing*),[91] Hareven seeks to establish the antiquity of the link between women and writing—thereby retracting her veteran refusal of the category. She traces this link much further back than Woolf—all the way back to the dawn of civilization, to Akkadian lullabies (originally composed by a Sumerian priestess and recently translated into Hebrew). Second, she confirms the existence of a slightly younger counterforce, a detrimental myth "which was not the invention of woman" but is, "amazingly, the basic myth of all three monotheistic religions: the father sacrificing his son." It is this deep structure of Western culture, which "most of us prefer to ignore or repress, that has warped even Freud's memory in his retelling of the ancient myth." Unfortunately, she argues, we do not have one image of protest against this repressed myth—not even by women. It is time that woman's talent for sanity transform all the entrenched roles of this myth—stop the father from sacrificing and the son from being sacrificed.

Hareven has come a long way from her total faith in the values of the akedah—as a metonymy of national Jewish ethics—on one hand, and from her refusal to identify with gender difference, on the other. Moran may have been her creative response to precisely the lack she pointed out—a woman's protest against the core myth of monotheism, paternal aggression. By so doing she has joined by default the camp of feminist pacifism that was initiated half a century earlier by Virginia Woolf and has recently been resurrected by women on both sides of the Palestinian-Israeli conflict.

In chapters 7 and 8 the conflict between gender and nation takes a different route. Differences notwithstanding, our next two authors confront this conflict head on, each situating it within a crucial point on the continuum of the Israeli national narrative: the 1948 War of Independence and the 1982 Lebanon War, refracted through the dilemmas of the Zionist pioneer settlers at the turn of the century.

Chapter 7

1948—Hebrew "Gender" and Zionist Ideology: Netiva Ben Yehuda

> I was never ever a suffragette. But as I was anyway stuck deep in this business [the Palmach]—I was ambitious, very ambitious, to prove my worth; especially since I knew that from that particular aspect which pre-occupied us at the time—the war—I was surrounded by many males who were much worse than me. Much more "feminine" than me. I used to call such a male "a *feminus*."
>
> —Netiva Ben Yehuda, *1948—Between Calendars*

Netiva Ben Yehuda's language, no less than her ideas and convictions, poses a great challenge to the translator and interpreter. She is unique among the authors studied here not only by her late entry into the Israeli writing scene (1981) but also because of her lifelong devotion to the cause of spoken Hebrew. Her uniqueness does not stem from these factors alone, however. Though she has become somewhat of a media figure since the 1980s, she had hardly been recognized before as a professional writer. Rather, Netiva Ben Yehuda (b. 1928), Tiva to her (many) friends, had long been identified as a living emblem of the myth of the Palmach, those legendary elite units that spearheaded the struggle for Israel's inde-pendence in 1947–1948. Indeed, Ben Yehuda had for many years embod-ied precisely that heroic voluntarism and utter loyalty to the "Jewish national rebirth in its homeland" that had been the hallmark of the Pal-mach since 1948. She was also known for her sharp tongue and scathing humor—qualities that stood her in good stead when she finally came into her own as a writer.

Simultaneously, however, Ben Yehuda was ahead of her time: her bold sexual permissiveness stood out like a sore thumb in a period marked by sexual puritanism. In a way, she brazenly carried out her own private sex-ual revolution, "living (rather than writing) through the body" in an age that locked up both body and emotions "in the cellar," to use Hareven's useful metaphor once again; we may even conjecture that Ben Yehuda's sexual freedom might have served as the model for Hareven's characterization of Sara (see chapter 5).

Less familiar, but crucial to her story, is the fact that the "nickname" by which she had become known early on, "the yellow devil," was actually given to her by the neighboring Arabs. This nickname came along with the high price that had been put on her head after she single-handedly commandeered the first successful Jewish ambush of an Arab bus early in 1948. That ambush was meant to retaliate for the growing frequency of Arab attacks on civilian transportation in the Galilee following the November 1947 UN vote for the division of Palestine. It turned out to be, as will be seen below, the first step in Ben Yehuda's "voyage in."

Even less known is her premilitary history: this "model" sabra, the daughter of a leading pioneer and educator (Baruch Ben Yehuda, later the first director general of the Israeli ministry of education), was an outstanding athlete. Her achievements as a discus thrower had in fact made her a serious candidate for the Olympics—a projected career that was cut short in 1948 by a bullet that damaged her arm muscles.

Fearlessness, physical prowess, and total devotion were thus some of the features that distinguished this young officer, whose military specialties included topography, reconnaissance, and demolition. Yet, for later generations, it was mainly Ben Yehuda's "fearlessness" that captured the imagination, expressed now not in military pursuits but in the battle for the soul of the Hebrew language. A few years past independence, after studying at home and abroad (art, language, and philosophy), Ben Yehuda became a freelance editor, openly "fighting" the chasm between the spoken Hebrew developed in the Palmach, marked by humorous slang and linguistic inventiveness, and the elevated, highly stylized standards "required" then by Hebrew belles lettres. Her devotion to this matter resulted in the publication, in 1972, of *The World Dictionary of Hebrew Slang*.[1] Indeed, this hilariously irreverent book, coauthored with another palmachnik, the late writer and satirist Dahn Ben Amotz (1924–1990), added another layer to the cultural idiosyncrasy of that legendary generation.

Still, all that in no way prepared the Israeli public for Ben Yehuda's dramatic entry into the scene of Hebrew writing between 1981 and 1991.[2] True, the title of her first book, *1948—Bein hasfirot*, should have alerted her readers that this was not one more run-of-the-mill "recollection in tranquility," to use William Wordsworth's famous phrase. Rather, despite the intervening three decades, Ben Yehuda's title signaled that she still experienced 1948 as a momentous breach in history, a transition of tremendous magnitude. Unfortunately, the English translation of the title, *Between the Calendars,* fails to convey this sense; for the Hebrew *sfirah* (*sfirot,* pl.) does not really mean "calendar" (*lu'aḥ*) but rather "counting" or "era." It is used to denote the distinction in the Gregorian calendar between B.C. (*lifnei hasfirah,* "before the counting") and A.D. (*'aḥarei hasfirah,* "after the counting"). The title then invests 1948 or, more exactly, "the months between the 29th of November 1947 to March 1948," with a potential to transform contemporary Jewish history that is analogous to the Christian transformation of Western (and Jewish) history two thousand years ago. In a way, it resonates with the title of Virginia Woolf's last will and testament, *Between the Acts,* which was published in Hebrew as well in 1981, under the title *Bein hama'arakhot.* Written under the threat of Nazi invasion (1940), Woolf's book title was characterized by one commentator as implying "the time between history as we have known it and the future," a future that will be "a violent break from history."[3]

Yet, even with this warning, many readers were not really ready for *1948—Bein hasfirot.* Some rejected Ben Yehuda's idiosyncratic language, colloquially repetitious and associative, at times preserving slang and idiomatic Hebrew of days gone by. Others felt uneasy with her generic hybridity: this book is not history, she said in the brief preface, not fiction, not even memoir—and some readers believed her.[4] The rhetorical disclaimer (it is "just me talking" about "what was stuck in my head since 'then'; always, all the time, everywhere . . . living with me; growing old with me") intensified in her next book, *Miba'ad la'avotot* (Through the Binding Ropes, 1985), where she defended her kind of writing by denying any literary aspirations. Like its predecessor, she said, this book is "a report from the field, a 'worm's eye view' of a low ranking soldier. And I *speak* this report. . . . Perhaps it can be best named *divrut* [= "speakature", coined to sound like *sifrut,* "literature"], if such a name existed." Well, it exists now, perfectly capturing Ben Yehuda's special "genre."

Those readers who were willing, however, to ignore the author's disclaimers (and many other "masks" woven into the narration itself), found themselves not only in the presence of a garrulous but consummate storyteller but in the current of a gripping narrative; one that has moved this reader, at least, to both laughter and tears as few other narratives have ever done. Moreover, those readers would slowly realize that this was a subversive telling of a major chapter in the Israeli national narrative—the "collective memory" of the 1948 War of Independence.[5] In fact, the Palmach trilogy as a whole, published between 1981 and 1991, contributed to the process of demythicization of the past that has been taking place in Israel since the early 1980s. Recognition of this contribution gained momentum with the publication of the second volume of the trilogy, which directly challenged—as its title transparently implied—the Israeli public conversation over the akedah (cf. chapter 6).[6] Ben Yehuda's unique contribution to this discourse was the foregrounding, perhaps for the first time in Israeli culture, of the *Titzḥaks*: in her language, the female Isaacs of Israel's wars.[7] Apparently, it was no accident that Ben Yehuda's confessional memoirs coincided with the revisionist feminist research that gained momentum in the 1980s as well as with the work of the Israeli new historians. Her books functioned as a courageous corrective by a first-hand witness, reducing the myth of a glorious past to human, and at times petty, proportions. In the words of one young contemporary (a high school teacher who had been wounded in the 1973 Yom Kippur War): "My God, how the myth has been shattered. I have thought that with you (pl.) everything was so beautiful, so spotless, with no problems, and only now the truth has come out."[8]

Whether or not the trilogy has also somewhat discolored the *gender* binoculars of its readers (as it should have . . .) is one of the questions I address below; how it fits into our history of the literary representation of the New Hebrew Woman and her conflict with the "national narrative" is another. First, however, a different question is in order: Why had Netiva Ben Yehuda waited for so long—over three decades—before publishing her story? And why did she qualify and hedge each of its installments, apologetically masking and disclaiming her meticulously structured autobiographic narration?

The Palmach Trilogy

Ben Yehuda herself has addressed this question in an extensive interview, conducted after the publication of the third volume (1991), which coincided with the fiftieth anniversary of the establishment of the Palmach.[9] As she tells it, she had not meant to wait at all, but had in fact already begun to write her memoirs in 1949. But those early chapters, actually commissioned by Ma'arakhot (the publishing house of the Israeli Defense Forces) as part of its planned official history of the 1948 war, were rejected because of their *style*—and no wonder. Even today her Hebrew style stands out, as we have noted, in its striking colloquial immediacy and vivid plasticity. Five decades ago, such speakature was unthinkable "on the printed page." In those days the gap between the refined literary style of her comrades (from Moshe Shamir to S. Yizhar, and everyone else in between) and her own audacious street Hebrew was utterly unbridgeable. And the truth is that if this gap has been narrowed since then, it is in no small measure due to the efforts of Ben Yehuda herself.

Since Ben Yehuda had been widely known as a champion of spoken Hebrew, the reading public readily accepted the stylistic explanation for her belated breakthrough. Much ink has been spilled on this issue in the critical reviews of her work, but both supporters and objectors accepted it as a legitimate factor. Add to this another of the author's explanations, saying that she started to write again when her daughter's classmates began returning "burnt and dead" from the Yom Kippur War (1973), and the question seems to be satisfactorily settled: "My daughter drew at that time a certain painting, which later became the cover of *Between Calendars*, so I looked the painting in the eye and talked into the tape," as she tells it in that interview.[10] Yet I would argue that a closer look at the process of reception of her trilogy reveals that other, perhaps darker, factors were at work as well.

To identify these factors we need some historical perspective. An interesting insight (and some explanatory statistics) is suggested by an anthology that was published about a decade ago, apparently in celebration of Israel's fortieth anniversary. *Written in 1948: Poetry and Prose Written During Israel's War of Independence*[11] includes works by about fifty writers, all published between 1947 and 1951 in the Israeli press, literary journals, and various anthologies. Of the fifty authors—only six (!) are women. Of the six, four belong to the Palmach generation; three of them participated actively in the war and one fell while on duty (Bat-Sheva Altshuler, 1928–1948). Of the four, three write poetry and only one writes fiction. Of the three that survived the war, two have entered the Israeli canon—Shulamith Hareven and Yehudit Hendel—but they are hardly identified with the literature of the Palmach. (The third is Zafrira Ger [Gerber], b. 1926.)[12]

These statistics are doubly surprising, since women accounted for about *half* the members of the Palmach. Still, despite their numbers, they had hardly left their mark on the literary legacy of their generation. Nor has the situation changed since. As I mentioned earlier, a critical change of taste has greatly eroded the artistic status of the literary corpus of the

Palmach. By the 1960s it had already fallen into disrepute. As we have seen in earlier chapters, both Kahana-Carmon and Hareven—each of them a Palmach fighter in her own right—distanced themselves from this experience as soon as their early literary apprenticeship was over. There is hardly a trace of this momentous experience in their later oeuvre. Nor is this reticence ever directly addressed, except indirectly, in Kahana-Carmon's condemnation of the national double standard that—secularized and modernized as it was—has continued to enclose women in a "women's gallery" of Israeli culture (*'ezrat hanashim*).

We should not forget, however, that Kahana-Carmon voiced this charge for the first time in the late 1980s, that is, a few years *after* Ben Yehuda's first book had already shaken up the Israeli readership. Ben Yehuda may be considered, then, one of the pioneers of the phenomenon we have been following throughout this study—the belated literary "debut" of the New Hebrew Woman. Surprisingly, she was hardly given credit for this breakthrough. Most of her reviewers (the women as well) have ignored what I consider central to her writing—her analysis of the ideological roots of what she perceived as the Palmach's betrayal of its promise for sexual equality, which was inscribed on its flag (see the epigraph to the introduction). Since these roots were anchored in the Zionist national narrative to which she enthusiastically subscribed, her discovery resulted in a conflict that was not easy to settle. To my mind it was this ideological wound, so to speak, that had silenced her for three decades; as we have seen, sexual equality was not a topic of discussion in the Israel of the 1950s through the 1970s. By the late seventies things began to change, however. Ben Yehuda's impediment turned into the motivating power behind her writing; her private trauma became the hidden center around which her dramatic narrative was structured and in which it would culminate.

This trauma is, nevertheless, well camouflaged by what may seem to be narrative and rhetorical repetition. Paradoxically, however, it is this apparent redundancy that directly reflects the trauma, albeit by way of denial. In fact, we may have here a different version of the masked autobiography; this time not in the form of a historical displacement but rather in the shape of the most straightforward tell-all autobiographic narration, which manages to bury its most painful moment under mountains of relevant and less relevant details, circuitous argumentation and tangential evidence. Time and again, to almost comic effect, Ben Yehuda repeats her disclaimer of any commitment to "suffragism." Speaking in the name of her female comrades as well, she keeps protesting and denying:

Netiva Ben Yehuda

> It was not me who invented the suffragism that is inscribed on the flag
> of the Palmach, and [on the flag] of its shitty Russian socialism.[13]
>
> We were not suffragettes. I said this a thousand times and I will say this
> another thousand times. The Palmach was suffragist—self-declared suf-
> fragist. . . . But I was never ever a suffragette.
>
> *(296; see the epigraph to the introduction)*
>
> And since I was not a suffragette, and am not one even now, and since
> my private social status did not interest me, I was very miserable.   *(297)*

Paradoxically, in between the last two vehement denials of suffragism is
sandwiched a pertinent feminist analysis of typical Palmach songs, showing that the "new Hebrew female fighter," Tiva and her like, was nowhere
to be seen. In songs (and in paintings as well) Shoshana or Dunia or Tzipp
is always waiting (often at the window), saying goodbye, or happens to be
in the kitchen. "I don't think that there has ever been any other underground movement in the world in which 'male chauvinism' triumphed so
powerfully; and so proudly," charges Ben Yehuda, with justified grievance.[14]

The rhetorical contradiction speaks for itself, raising questions about
the narrator's reliability. For how are we to understand the constant denial
of suffragism that comes paired with a heavy condemnation of an all-powerful male chauvinism? And why should this fearless fighter "be afraid" to
acknowledge suffragism, whereas, in fact, she "has undertaken to realize
its principles" (296) by doing her best to excel among the rather small
group of elite fighters (of both sexes)? Doth the lady protest too much?

Indeed she does. For it is not suffragism per se that she rejects but
rather the ambivalence it engenders. The truth is that by the end of *1948—
Between Calendars* this skillful, brave officer, who had already proven the
success of her training as a demolition specialist on the front line, experiences firsthand the familiar conflict that neither *A Room of One's Own* nor
The Second Sex (let alone contemporary gender theories on both sides of
the Atlantic) had managed to settle satisfactorily: the wish to overstep
boundaries of any kind, including sexual boundaries (as epitomized by
Woolf's *Orlando*), vis-à-vis the fear of losing one's personal identity as a
result of this overstepping; alternately, the need to define woman's subjectivity on its own merits, separate from the "other sex" (sexual difference, in contemporary parlance), and, at the same time, the fear of the
essentialist limitation of that very subjectivity (see chapter 2).

This familiar conflict is doubly poignant here, because it takes place in an arena most identified with masculinism—military aggression. If we recall that it was precisely the aggressive instinct that was the object of Woolf's critique of masculinism in *Three Guineas* (the Hebrew translation of which appeared in 1985! and see chapter 6), we should not be surprised at Ben Yehuda's impasse. The sexual equality that she tries to achieve pertains to a sphere about which Woolf had not even dreamt—the battlefield. In Woolf's earlier script, we may recall, military experience was only part of Orlando's *past*, practiced by the ancestors of her early (should we say primitive?) masculine self (see chapter 4). A decade later, on the brink of World War II, she saw aggression and militarism as the inevitable exception to her dream of androgyny, as the one area from which she wished to exclude women (see chapter 6). The Palmach fighter, on the other hand, has unwittingly tried to transpose Woolf's androgynous vision from the field of artistic creation to the field of military prowess—with rather dire consequences.

This difference notwithstanding, Ben Yehuda's "Orlando" asks questions about gender that are not so different from those asked by Woolf (via *Orlando*) about half a century ago (and that gender theorists have been asking ever since): By what is our sexual identity determined? By biology ("Who's got or hasn't got balls," in the slang of the Palmach)? By our clothes, gait, body language? Or by the other's gaze, by the role imposed on us by society, culture, the system into which we are born and in which we have to function? In other words, is "sex" destiny, our unescapable essentialist portion on this earth, or is it a cultural construct, a performance that varies with time and place and is, therefore, given to change and modification?

The theoretical solution to this problem is well known by now—the modern reinvention of *gender*. We reviewed in chapter 2 the various definitions of the term and how they relate to the definition of *sex* (culture/nature). We might do well now to add another aspect of its meaning, one that may be lost on the average English speaker.

In most European languages nouns (any noun, including those that have no biological/sexual function) are gendered (m., f., or n.). As these gender attributions differ from one language to another (e.g., *la table* [Fr.]—f.; *der Tisch* [Ger.]—m.), the grammatical origin of the concept is a reminder of the arbitrary and relative nature of linguistic classification into "masculine" and "feminine." As such, gender is *un*essentialist, by definition, and helpful in constructing a dichotomy between nature (sex) and culture (gender).[15]

In Hebrew, however, such a dichotomy does not exist. There is no equivalent of "gender" in Hebrew grammar books; there is only "sex." The word *min* covers both "sex" and "gender," with the result that Hebrew speakers are not "naturally" aware of the difference. When the reinvestment of gender with its contemporary feminist sense did reach Israel, a few years ago, a frantic search for a new word began. *Minaniyut* soon gave way to *migdar*, which has been recently (in the last year or two) accepted as a translation of *gender*. The problem is, however, that the root base of this neologism, *g.d.r.* (fence, boundary, definition) covers just one aspect of the newly invented "gender"—its description of the division of gender roles between the sexes. This meaning, often used by historians, anthropologists, and sociologists, paradoxically makes *migdar* sound as if it were almost the opposite of "gender" in the grammatical sense: it tends to convey the meaning of a division of roles that is defined and fenced in by sex, losing in the process the cultural relativity implied by grammatical gender classifications.

The solution? Here is where Ben Yehuda's linguistic acumen comes to our aid. Let us listen again to one of her disclaimers, especially the one quoted in the epigraph to this chapter: "I was surrounded by many males (*zekharim*) who were much worse than me. Much more "feminine" (*nekevot*) than me. I used to call them *hanekevim ha'eleh*."

In the epigraph I have translated the final noun of this passage, *nekevim*, by an equally made up word, *feminus*, attempting to convey, even partially, the poignancy of Ben Yehuda's Hebrew neologism. The original word is an untranslatable play on two gender-related issues that are specific to Hebrew vocabulary and grammar: on the one hand, a lack of lexical distinction between "female" and "feminine," which are both represented by the word *nekevah* (whereas both "male" and "masculine" are represented by *zakhar*), and, on the other hand, the consistent morphological distinction between the sexes by means of a transparent marking, especially in the plural cases. As a rule, plural feminine nouns end with the suffix *ot*, while plural masculine nouns end with the suffix *im*. Since *every* Hebrew noun is gendered as m. or f. (there is no neuter in Hebrew, a "sex maniac" language, as poet Yona Wallach labeled it), this morphological sexual difference is quite ingrained in the mind of the native Hebrew speaker. The subversiveness of Ben Yehuda's neologism, *nekevim*, is therefore quite in evidence. By appending the opposite-sex suffix to the noun that means female/feminine, she signals a disjunction between one's biological sex (in this case masculine, as implied by the ending *im*) and one's "feminine" non- or weak functioning in "that particular aspect that pre-occupied us at the time—the war."

That this linguistic analysis may open up, rather than seal, an essentialist can of worms is no doubt clear. Yet before we get into this complex problem, a word about my translation choices is in order: as the reader of this study is probably aware, English does not offer any morphological equivalent to Hebrew gendered suffixes. Hence I have no choice but to fall back on Latin suffixes, which I append to Latin root bases common in English (*femina* and *homo*). In order to reproduce the neologist effect of the original, I crisscross the respective Latin suffixes of these words. Since in Latin the singular suffix is much more manifest than the plural (*a* for feminine and *us* for masculine), I have substituted a singular hybrid formation for Ben Yehuda's plural forms. Hence, her *nekevim* is represented by *feminus*, while her *zekharot* (which we encounter below) is represented by the singular *homina*.

With this technical difficulty behind us, we may now turn to the larger picture. In her Palmach trilogy Ben Yehuda has made a curious lexical choice, one that made many readers wince. Of all the pairs of nouns applicable to humans (men/women, guys/dolls, boys/girls, *hayalim/hayalot* [m. soldiers/f. soldiers], etc.), she has chosen by and large to refer to her fellow palmakhniks by the pair of terms *zakhar/nekevah*. For the English speaker, this pair is the equivalent of both male/female and masculine/feminine. But for the Hebrew reader, the immediate association of this pair is that of the grammar book or the dictionary (that is, masculine/feminine), often in the abbreviated form Z/N (= m./f.). As such, the use of this grammatical terminology may be seen as the least "humane" and most sexist way to relate to one's fellow comrades, essentialistically reducing their identity to sexual difference. This possible connotation is exacerbated by the derogatory use of *nekevah* in Yiddish (*nekeve*)—a usage that may be alive for many contemporary readers but was apparently less so for the young members of the Palmach. Bracketing this last objection, I would suggest another interpretation of Ben Yehuda's use of Z/N. This is, of course, the only pair of terms that can be applied to any noun, including nouns with no biological sex. In other words, Z/N is the closest that Hebrew can come to the connotations of arbitrariness, relativity, and fluidity implied by grammatical gender . . .

Add to this the androgynous resonance of the first biblical human pair (*zakhar unekevah bara' 'otam*, Genesis 1:27, discussed in chapters 4 and 5), and the further use to which Ben Yehuda puts her Hebrew "gender" is quite clear. By manipulating its form, as we have seen above, she throws a monkey wrench into the sex/gender unity of the Hebrew lexicon. Moreover, she inadvertently deconstructs the sexual dichotomy, exposing the lack of fit between the linguistic sign and its sexual signifieds, between the connotation of a given appellation and the functioning of its bearer in the real world. If in her first book she undermined the masculinity of her male peers, creating the neologism *nekevim* (s. *feminus*), in her second, *Through the Binding Ropes*, she took a further step—she counted the many different ways by which female fighters, the *zekharot* (s. *homina*), mimicked the soldierly trimmings of their male peers, adopting a manlike (L. *homo*) gender performance.[16]

This process of emptying out the gender content of linguistic signs reaches its climax when the narrator of *Through the Binding Ropes*, now serving in headquarters rather than on the front line, is asked to organize—"the first time in the history of the Palmach"—the registry of its membership:

> Suddenly we found ourselves in a bind, the first time in the history of the Palmach: we needed to go over name by name and decide: Is he a fighter or not. Is he "girls" or not. . . . This was how we discovered that [the category] "fighters" has some girls in it; that [the category] "girls" (services) has too many [persons] in general; and, most important, that many of them [the "girls"] are boys.   *(89)*

The irony speaks for itself; as does the author's intuitive use of quotations marks as a signal of disjunction between the linguistic sign and reality: "girls" (*banot*), which—in a blatant sexist manner—stands for "services" (the explanatory parenthesis appears in the original), turns out to have too many "boys." The final implication of this discovery is troublesome, and definitely deals a blow to the Palmach myth: "In general, it turned out that "fighters" had the least people, and they were much too few in the face of the challenges that lay ahead of us" (ibid).

To call this "a woman's charge sheet" (*ktav 'ashmah nashi*), as did one reviewer (apparently, with the best of intentions),[17] is to miss the mark. This is rather a sweeping revision, a deconstruction of a generational myth that is shown to be more rhetoric than fact.

In truth, however, this is just the beginning of the revision, the tip of the iceberg. For the linguistic games that capture our imagination (or threaten us—all in the eye of the beholder), only camouflage Ben Yehuda's deeper revisionism. The latter is located elsewhere—in her exceptional ability both to observe and articulate the changes that took place in her own mind while the fighting was still going on. It was this gift (or curse) that turned her early on into an "observer," even as she was fully participating in the notorious "collectivity," the first-person plural of her peer group.

The first step in this process takes place immediately after the success of the ambush described in this chapter's opening paragraphs. The target of this ambush was, we should mention, "the bus of the *najjada*—the Arab Defense Forces, which used to go every morning from their base in the Ḥula Valley . . . to their bases up in the Galilee" (144). To her surprise,

> It became clear to me that I do not at all feel like taking pride in this business. All my life I was confident that I would be very proud, but I am not. Never mind what took place. Human beings died—so I do not want to be proud of this. The whole story is totally different. It is totally different when someone really gets killed. *(161)*

It is this sober correction of the romantic myth of military heroism that was applauded by Dan Miron, a first-rate commentator on Israeli culture, who has devoted scholarly attention to the literature of the Palmach.[18] His approval of Ben Yehuda's revisionist view of what has become an integral part of the Israeli national narrative was hedged by a qualification, how-ever: "Had It Been Written Then [*bizmano*]" is the title of his 1983 essay, in which he justly questions the three decades of silence that Ben Yehuda imposed upon herself. He rightly points out how much more effective her story would have been "then."

Ben Yehuda's narrative had countered this charge, however, even before it was made. As she clearly describes it, her dissension was promptly suppressed:

> I decided one thing: not to get it out of my mouth. This is no time for "critical discussions" (*yemei 'iyun*). I need to swallow them. I can't erase them, but at least I can put them aside, so that they don't interrupt. . . . When everything is over, I can come back to them; can deal with them then. *(163)*

On first blush, we may think of this process of repression as a universal reaction, typical during any time of pressure—as a necessary defense under duress that is in no way related to the "tip of the iceberg," to the "enter-taining" deconstruction of Hebrew gender signifiers proffered above. But this is not the case. The narrator's decision to suppress her feelings does not come naturally. It is the result of a Zionist "sermon" delivered to her by one of her father figures, a friend of her parents, who happens to be around at her moment of weakness. His rebuke, as she relates it, is rather extreme. It recapitulates the familiar Zionist dogma, structuring the image of a New Hebrew Man around the dichotomy of a strong, liberated, healthy, "normal" man (*'adam* = human being?) vis-à-vis the weak, cowardly, dependent diaspora Jew (162–163). It tiresomely invokes the long history of Jewish passivity, of the diasporic inability to use weapons effectively, as the anathema of the New Zionist Man, whose credo is "hakam lehorgekha hashkem lehorgo," namely, 'preempt the aggressor.'

In Hebrew the gender of the "subjects" of his sermon, the good Jew as well as the bad Jew, is masculine, of course. It is the "generalized" masculine, the one that is said to cover both genders (e.g., *'adam*). His final censure, however, falls back on gender distinction, thereby exposing one of the oldest antisemitic slurs that is no doubt hiding behind its better-known cousin, the Zionist dichotomy outlined above: "If you cannot be like that [the New Hebrew Man], either you are a woman or you are a diaspora-kike (f.)" (162).[19]

Who in her right mind would want to be a woman under such heavy accusations? Who would want to express feelings? To tell anything? "I need to be strong. And stronger. But strong people do not talk. Strong people keep silent," is the immediate conclusion.

So Netiva Ben Yehuda continued to keep her silence. Keeping her strength intact for over thirty years. Or so she thought. For she really needed to be much stronger to relate her full story. Because we have not yet reached the end of this story. We still have not touched its hidden trauma.

About midway into this very "talky" book there are two pages with three drawings, delicate pencil sketches of the topographic variety (220–221). The first two represent the "event" of the bus (ambush); the third, double in size (221), tells the story of the "event" that immediately followed, an event that seems not to want to be told. When finally pieced together, it tells about a young training commander who did not have the courage of her convictions in the face of her superiors and thus took her trainees to an area that in her judgment was topographically indefensible. She was right. They were soon surrounded on all sides. With great difficulty she managed to get her unit out—but one of her braver soldiers paid with his life.

Back in headquarters her commander refused to acknowledge any responsibility. She was censured for her actions—and suffered a breakdown. After ten days in a stupor with no medical help, she fled the scene, vowing never to return to the line of fire again. The rest of the narrative, spanning three books and hundreds of pages, painstakingly describes not only how she coped with her "shell shock" (Miron) but how she in fact violated her vow—once and again risking her life in activities that were barely distinguishable from what is narrowly defined as the front line.

What is missing, however, from this brief ouline of the story, is the *reason* for that tragic experience. Why didn't the young officer, fully trained and ready to fight, have the courage to fight for her own opinions? The painful answer, which the author herself recognizes retrospectively, is that her gender was in the way of reasonable argumentation. It was the (justified) fear that her commanders would not "distinguish between her opinions and her genitals" that prevented her from airing her objections—the fear that she would be perceived as weak, "feminine," like a diaspora Jew. In other words, despite the almost caricatured presentation of the "Zionist sermon" she describes, Ben Yehuda admits that she had internalized its very terms (236 et passim). We can only imagine how—throughout all those silent years—this self-destructive internalization was eating away not only at her gender identity but at her Zionist conscience as well.[20]

Could Netiva Ben Yehuda have told her version of the New Hebrew Woman "then," as suggested by Dan Miron? She no doubt could not. Even when she did tell it, three decades later, very few were willing to listen. Perhaps today, after two more decades of feminist-political consciousness-raising, Israeli culture is ready to reevaluate her subversive *divrut*/speakature.

Chapter 8

Beyond the Feminist Romance: Ruth Almog

> The woman novelist must be an hysteric. Hysteria is . . . simultaneously
> what a woman can do to be feminine and refuse femininity, within patri-
> archal discourses.   —Juliet Mitchell, *Women, the Longest Revolution*

> Female hysteria seemed to be on the wane, as feminism was on the rise.
> . . . The despised hysterics of yesteryear have been replaced by the fem-
> inist radicals of today.   —Elaine Showalter, *Hysteria Beyond Freud*

With the publication, in 1987, of the prize-winning novel *Shorshei 'Avir*
(Roots of Air), Ruth Almog (b. 1936) has revitalized not only her own
two-decade-long career as a "woman writer" but the Israeli feminist
romance in general.[1] While it would take Shulamith Hareven another
decade to resolve—perhaps only tentatively and by implication—her personal conflict between gender and nation, while the gender implications
of Ben Yehuda's demythologizing of the Palmach had barely reached the
consciousness of its readers, and whereas Kahana-Carmon and Lapid had
by then (1984 and 1982, respectively) merely touched on the issue, still hiding behind the mask of historical displacement, Almog has confidently
planted this conflict in the here and now of her ambitious novel. She
openly challenged, in her own extratextual words, "the need for superiority, power, and control, which expresses itself in trampling the Other—in
our case, the Palestinian neighbors, or the Arabs at large."[2] That she does
this through a female protagonist who arrives, at the end of her journey,
at a deconstruction of any ideology of "freedom," embeds her juxtaposition of gender and nation in a critique of masculinist aggression that
brings her very close to Virginia Woolf's *Three Guineas* (published in
Hebrew, we may recall, in 1985); at the same time, however, her critique
also challenges feminist liberation to the extent that it relies on the very
same male-modeled ideologies of freedom.

Needless to say, it was not this demanding message alone that won the hearts of both critics and readers. All seem to have been charmed by the rich fictional web Almog has woven, couched as it is in a delightfully poetic style and dotted with some of the most evocative descriptions of the Israeli landscape ever written. Few, however, fathomed the full effect of the intricate journey—both narratorial and ideational—on which Almog has embarked in this complex novel. And no wonder. In a surprisingly postmodernist move Almog has prevented any unambiguous reading of *Roots of Air*. In this she in fact anticipated A. B. Yehoshua, who was busy structuring his own counternovel, *Mr. Mani* (1990) in the same decade. As we shall see, both novels challenge the linearity of historical reconstruction while seeking to subvert readers' expectations and shake up any of their preconceived idées fixes or essentialist notions. Like Yehoshua, and to some extent also like Anton Shammas in his contemporaneously published novel *Arabesques* (1986), Almog has done that both structurally and thematically.[3] She complicated and interlaced several plot lines and narratorial perspectives (the latter shifting even within a single narrative strand) and, in so doing, juxtaposed and undercut familiar referential fields as diverse as botany and history, psychology and philosophy, political creeds and theories of gender. As can be expected, this *embarrassment de riches* has not always worked for the novel; as some readers commented, it definitely calls for more than one reading—and for some perspective.

"The appearance of *Roots of Air* on our bookshelves, more than six months ago, was quiet," says Ariel Hirschfeld in the most penetrating review of the novel. "Now," he continues, "when the short-lived plants [*gidulei hakikayon*] around it have died, it suddenly looks like an oak sapling, knotty and dense, expecting many years of presence and growth." I wholly agree.[4] Except that, from my perspective, even Hirschfeld's astute analysis misses one aspect of the novel that is important for the present study, its feminist implications. Other reviewers seem to have been equally blind. My contention is, however, that while orchestrating—not necessarily harmoniously—several of the female-feminist paradigms we traced in earlier chapters, *Roots of Air* constitutes a bold departure from the feminist romance in Israeli literature. Moreover, while it offers a critique of the liberatory feminism of its Israeli precursors it also problematizes some of the master narratives of Enlightenment-based feminism in general. To my surprise, however, this was barely noticed in the myriad of reviews and interviews following the book's publication.

In view of this unanimous denial, our first task is to justify our appropriation of *Roots of Air* as a novel underlined by feminist concerns. For it is precisely these concerns that make the other interests of the novel that much more poignant—as I hope to show in this chapter.

1. From the Madwoman in the Attic to The Women's Room

The "misunderstanding" we uncovered in the critical reception of *Roots of Air* is actually not that difficult to fathom. For, in keeping with her attempt to complicate rather than simplify matters, Almog's critique is implicit rather than explicit. On the surface *Roots of Air* is a typically "virile (*gavri*), political novel" as the author herself suggested in an interview: "I was trying to engage large, important themes. . . . I was inspired by a woman who impressed me with her courage—a feisty woman, diametrically opposed to the passive women I have treated so far."[5] This "transition" rings a familiar bell. As we have seen in chapter 3, a few years earlier Israel's foremost (feminist) writer, Amalia Kahana-Carmon, declared a similar turning away from passive characters to active ones. Following in her footsteps, Almog was determined to counteract what she saw as the Israeli marginalization of women's experience: "In Israel, if you do not write about national issues and you do not have a sociopolitical message— you (f.) do not exist!"[6] But here the resemblance ends. For, in contrast to any of her predecessors, Almog has woven together two novelistic modalities hitherto employed mostly by *male* Israeli writers: fictional autobiography and the historical novel. In so doing she was able to enter the mainstream of Israeli fiction and subvert it from within.

Roots of Air is structured in two dissimilar parts, ranging from turn-of-the-century Palestine to 1960s Europe. Book 1 of the novel, "Madness Is the Wisdom of the Individuum" (7–160), is a dialogic narrative in which two modalities alternate antiphonally chapter by chapter, demanding an analogical reading of the reader. In one, Mira Gutman, as a rather conventionally autobiographic narrator, recounts her atypical childhood in a typical moshavah (= small town, established at the beginning of the century) in the early years of the state. (Notice the here and now of this strand of the story line.) In the other she attempts to piece together (in a manner that may seem somewhat frantic and chaotic but is not, as I show below) the life story of her maternal great-grandfather, *Lavdovi* (or perhaps *Levadovi*, "Mr. Alonely"?), an eccentric Zionist of the First Aliyah. Her involvement with this father figure is not historical in the strict sense of the word. It is psychological and ideological, displacing contemporary concerns that reached their peak in the wake of the 1982 Lebanon War

(Jewish-Arab relations and general attitudes toward power) to historical events. Yet, as a period piece, this is an impressively convincing historical construction, the fictional liberties taken by the author notwithstanding. And since it is this narrative that opens the book (constituting all the following odd-numbered chapters), it successfully plunges the reader into the illusion of a third-person historical narrative. (The name of the first-person voice of the narrator is withheld until the end of this chapter; we therefore identify it as Mira's only in the second chapter, where her auto-biographic narration begins.) Indeed, it is this strand of the narrative that contains the seeds of the "virile, political" novel that will come to fruition in book 2 of the novel, "Anatomy of Freedom" (161–359). Here the mature Mira finds herself in the Europe of the 1960s, totally involved in "work and love," as well as in the 1968 student revolts in the invaded and violated "free" Prague.

Almog allowed her heroine, then, both the closed intimacy of stereotypic female Bildung and the ostensibly open horizons of the male hero's quest—repeating Hareven's androgynous compromise formation (in *City of Many Days*, chapter 5), but on a much larger scale. Furthermore, unlike any Israeli woman writer before her, and more than Hareven, she fully developed both the psychological and the sociopolitical matrices of her protagonist, making her the first Israeli heroine to narrate a complete lifespan—from childhood in a small town (modeled on Zikhron Ya'akov, as Almog has recounted), through urban adolescence in Jerusalem (significantly, the least developed of the "chapters" of her life), to an allegedly autonomous adulthood abroad. Thematically and generically, *Roots of Air* seems to have come as close as possible to the "malestream" of the Hebrew literary canon; a fact that has no doubt contributed to the warm reception it received from the literary establishment and reading public alike. (In the wake of this book Almog was invited to inaugurate, in 1988–1989, a new writer-in-residence program at the Hebrew University.)

At the same time, however, the novel sports some highly "feminine" features. Most significantly, Mira is the first Israeli female protagonist to be endowed with a mother, Ruhama, who cuts an impressive figure, crucial to the shaping of her daughter's life.[7] In this she is fundamentally different from Almog's own earlier (and later!) heroines, who as a rule suffer from a "father fixation," without the benefit of a viable maternal role model (more about this below). She is also different from our earlier protagonists ("Virginia Woolf" not excluded), whose mothers were generally absent—either textually or psychologically. When maternity is represented, as in Lapid's or Hareven's work, it often functions symbolically rather than realistically (*Gei Oni* or *After Childhood*) and rarely fully represents the psychological burden of the mother-daughter axis (Sara, we may recall [*City of Many Days*], simply ignores her mother's legacy, conveniently escaping it in her own turn by having only sons . . . as does Moran in *After Childhood*).

This shift to mother-daughter relations deserves our attention not only because of its novelty at the time but because it makes Almog's take on feminism so complex and, in the final analysis, also subversive. If we recall that precisely this psychological nexus has been unearthed from Freudian unknowability by feminists on both sides of the Atlantic (to different ends, to be sure; see chapter 2), the significance of its belated entry into the discourse of Hebrew feminism may surface.[8] Almog's candid foregrounding of the mother-daughter continuum (in her interviews as well—she is the only writer who refers to her own daughters, "the most significant bond in my life," openly talking about their problematic attitude toward her writing and the ensuing competitiveness)[9] may be credited with ushering a new element into feminist literary discourse in Israel, as the spate of recent writing about this topic attests.[10]

This is no idealized portrayal of "Jewish" motherhood, however. For Ruhama is a frustrated artist and a hysteric, often on the verge of suicide. Indeed, in contrast to Hareven's fascination with sanity, Almog is dangerously attracted to insanity; and while for our earlier authors the thin line between the two functions mostly as a threat hidden in the margins, (e.g., the would-be scholar-writer Tehilah in Kahana-Carmon's first novel, *And Moon in the Valley of Ayalon*, Sara's father in Hareven's *City of Many Days* [as well as the brilliant sociopath Nahman in her early story "Winter of the King of Cards"], and Fania's deranged brother in Lapid's *Gei Oni*), Almog has made insanity—and especially its feminine connection—a major focus of her *Roots of Air*. In fact, by making the mother both a frustrated artist and hysteric she has anchored her narrative at the heart of one of the major debates in recent feminist discourse—the relationship between the infamous female malady, women's creativity, and feminist survival (see the epigraph to this chapter).

In a way Almog has written another contemporary revision of *Jane Eyre*, apparently learning her trade not from the rich crop of academic rereadings of it but from Jean Rhys, the West Indian writer who "well before any of these women [scholars]," says Elizabeth R. Baer, "had spent ten years 're-vising' *Jane Eyre* for twentieth-century readers. The revision is a novel, *Wide Sargasso Sea*."[11] In *Wide Sargasso Sea* (1966) Rhys has constructed the evolution of female madness via a "prequel," as Baer calls it, to *Jane Eyre*. In her novel she imagines the early life of Rochester's first wife, Berta, the one we get to know in Charlotte Brontë's novel only as the "madwoman in the attic." At the same time, her heroine Antoinette, presumably the young Berta, also anticipates the biography of Jane herself (orphaned, educated in a convent, etc.), so that her fate can serve as a sisterly warning to Jane not to repeat her own (Berta-Antoinette's) mistake by surrendering herself to *in*equality in her love relationship. "A re-vision which is an act of survival," says Baer, quoting Adrienne Rich's "When We Dead Awaken: Writing as Re-Vision."[12]

It is small wonder that this novel (published in Hebrew in 1981) caught the imagination of Ruth Almog.[13] At the time, she had just published a novel of sorts, *'Et hazar veha'oyev* (The Stranger and the Foe), that was in fact a fictional probe—chilling in its medical-scientific accuracy—into the unfolding of depression (an antecedent of William Styron's notorious 1990 *Darkness Visible?*). Although the subtitle of the novel, *A Report on a (Writer's) Block*, as well as the author's extraliterary comments have presented this book as a "working through" of a personal ten-year hiatus in her creativity ("not only because of the pressures of motherhood," she insisted),[14] in the fiction the heroine's depression is rationalized by her fixation precisely on that kind of unequal, dependent love affair that Rhys is said to have set out to prevent in *Wide Sargasso Sea*, her rewriting of *Jane Eyre*. Because of that psychological (oedipal, as we argue below) complex, Almog's book is in fact torn between two foci, the intersection of which is not clear, or at least not sufficiently motivated. Possibly, the theme that was paramount on her mind was the age-old identification of creativity with madness. Quoting in her epigraph the positive appreciation of madness in Plato's Phaedrus ("Madness is the gift of the gods"), she has her *heroine* voice the familiar fear that artists have of psychiatric help, worrying lest their creativity be "cured" along with their depression (cf. Woolf's guarded attitude toward Freud, chapter 6.1). Concurrently, however, Almog does not shy away from outlining the devastating effect that such a depression would have on the woman's emotional and mental life, virtually to the point of suicide. The *narrative voice*, whose position in this work is unfortunately rather fuzzy, actually undercuts the protagonist's (and perhaps the author's own) valorization of "artistic madness."

However, to judge from the impassioned responses that this slim, unusual book aroused, this undercutting must have drowned out the other facet of the protagonist's madness—her fixation in an oedipal dependence that renders her passive and totally helpless to escape from her vicious circle. Significantly, Mordekhai Geldman (writer and psychotherapist) and Nurit Zarhi (writer and analysand, I presume), respectively, "argued with the author" over her thesis on "the connection between creativity on one hand and suffering and love on the other" (Geldman) or challenged her "platonic understanding of disease as artistic uniqueness" (Zarhi).[15] Whereas the first at least acknowledged the validity of Almog's feud with the psychiatric establishment (cf. Woolf) and concluded by lauding her Promethean (!) courage in provoking the complacency of "sane" human existence, Zarhi, in reminding us that "mental diseases disfigure the soul in their limiting, monochrome repetition of the same symptoms," seems to have missed precisely that second voice, the narrator's, through which Almog's voiced her own ambivalence about this difficult issue.[16]

She would revisit this complex in the collection *Nashim* (Women), which appeared shortly before *Roots of Air*, in 1986. However, brief mention should be made, before we turn our attention to this collection, of the novel that came out in 1982, *Mavet bageshem* (*Death in the Rain*), the only one of Almog's works available in English translation.[17] The complex structure of this fascinating novel is quite beyond the limits of our discussion.[18] It is enough to point out that this novel contains the seeds of several thematic and structural innovations that were further developed in *Roots of Air*.

First of all, the complication of first- versus third-person narrative by a Rashomon-style aggregation of different voices that "report" on the same missing protagonist, Henrietta; then, the blurred distinction between the fictional and the documentary (in the tradition of the Hebrew writer Y. H. Brenner, 1882–1921, as Shaked has pointed out), by making a story "out of" letters, diaries, and the like; third, sending her protagonists off to Europe, in this case, Greece (and Italy), an issue to which we will later return; fourth, the opening up of her protagonists' subjective inner world to social issues, in this case, ecology; fifth, and most significant, piercing the bubble of her "female" world by introducing three viable male characters, fully convincing in their psychological differentiation. While Dr. Likht (= light!), the author who ostensibly assembles the story out of the various documents, attests to Almog's inability (yet!) to entrust so creative an endeavor to a female character, two other males, Alexander and Yanis, represent important steps in her journey out. Into these two men Almog

deflected the complex of insanity/love attachment that debilitated Elisheva Green, the heroine of her recent *The Stranger and the Foe* (who has
curiously "bequeathed" her name to the most active "voice" in *Death in
the Rain*). Alexander is medically insane (schizophrenic?), and his accidental (?) killing, "in the rain," of his beloved wife Henrietta, the platonic
love object of all three protagonists (Elisheva not excluded), is the actual
prime mover of this novel. Yanis, on the other hand, is the forlorn Romantic lover whose love for Henrietta in fact kills his life instinct—almost,
although not as devastatingly, as it did in the case of Elisheva in *The
Stranger and the Foe*. With this transfer of the complex to the "stronger
sex," Almog for the first time transcended the gender limits of her own
making—a move toward an androgynous awareness that she will redo in
Roots of Air. The extent to which she was conscious of this move comes
through clearly in an in-depth interview conducted by Anat Levitt a few
months after the publication of *Women* (and shortly before the publication of *Roots of Air*). Asked why she writes mostly about women, she first
says that she knows the "inner worlds" of women better than those of
men, but then she adds:

> Nevertheless, I find that men too have the same sensitivities that I con-
> sider exclusively "feminine." Not all of them. Just as there are women
> who do not have them. Perhaps we need to coin a new concept that
> would define an inclusive sex/gender [*min*] for men and women who
> share similar identity problems.[19]

When we add to the above the preoccupation of *Death in the Rain* with
European culture (Yanis being of Greek descent), which is crucial for
Roots of Air as well (though in some significantly diverging ways), it is
tempting to see the latter as a direct outgrowth of the former. Yet we cannot ignore the collection *Women*, apparently incubated in the same years.
Indeed, *Women* and *Roots of Air*, following each other in such proximity
(1986, 1987), form a kind of twin product, an opposite-sex pair, if you like,
because of their diametrically opposite psychological impulses.

While in *Women* Almog further magnified and metaphorized the oedipal complex or fixation (or artist's block) she addressed in *The Stranger
and the Foe*, in *Roots of Air* she devised for her protagonist a way out of
this dead end. Indeed, all seven stories of *Women* are variations on this single theme, with one difference: mental instability encompasses here an
array of psychosomatic diseases (including cancer [!])—all marking womanhood as a general state of "unfinished femininity," as Almog admitted

in an interview.[20] Apparently, Almog came to the sad realization that not every frustrated loveless woman has the ability to redeem her fragile, painfully exposed femininity through the therapeutic sublimatory power of "insane" creativity; the less fortunate may "simply" get sick, go mad, or become suicidal. In short, rather than creative artists, they might very well become the "madwomen on the balcony" (see the cover design of *The Stranger and the Foe*, a woman sitting alone in an armchair on the balcony), incarcerated not by an authoritarian husband but rather by their own unsurmountable psychological handicaps.

With this we are back to *Roots of Air* as an Israeli rewriting of *Jane Eyre*. Like Rhys in *Wide Sargasso Sea*, Almog has equipped her "Jane" (Mira) with a predecessor that would serve as her warning sign and thereby warranty her (Mira's) survival. Except that in this case it is not a former wife of a future husband that fulfills this "sisterly" function (see the title of Baer's essay); here it is the mother, Ruhama, whose madness and suicide are the signals heeded by her daughter, Mira.

Before we enter this complex relationship, it is perhaps time to pause and ponder the source of Almog's preoccupation with mental malfunctioning and "its environs." Going beyond a possible personal involvement in psychoanalysis and therapy (for reasons that will be clarified in the next section), it is clear that her treatment of the subject transcends the particular nexus of art and madness that presumably stimulated *The Stranger and the Foe*. In one of her interviews she credited her hometown, Petah Tikva, with inducing such a proclivity. Because the heroic myth of this veteran town had been found (by her generation) to be merely an empty shell, a facade, she said, its writers were made conscious of the dark side of things, of decay and stagnation: "The same madmen and the same traumas circulate in Yehoshua Kenaz's stories and mine."[21] This is probably true, yet there is obviously more to the story than childhood traumas, be they personal or collective. As readers of *Women* were quick to detect, this book smacks of the existentialist questioning of the meaning of human freedom.[22] Within this Dostoyevskian questioning suicide epitomizes the outer limit of free choice (as developed in Camus's *The Rebel*). Almog's fascination with this question attests to a deeper involvement with existentialism than that of the average Israeli (see the introduction). A student of philosophy in her youth, she is thoroughly immersed in the subject (her 1987 interview with Levitt sounds, in fact, like a lecture in existentialist philosophy) and has reworked it more than once into her fiction. It is interesting, however, that reviewers never questioned the fact that the "existentialist condition" is represented in her work mostly (or only) through the female sex. In other words, although Almog has been preoccupied with gender-specific issues most of her (creative) life, these were not necessarily identified as such. The shift to the "mother-daughter continuum" (in *Roots of Air*), doubly problematized by the mother's mental instability as it is, may have been Almog's signal, calling attention to the gender specificity of her probing into the question of personal freedom, of the existentialist choice between life and death.

The idea for this shift may have occurred to her while reading Marie Cardinal's groundbreaking autobiographical novel, *The Words to Say It*, published in Hebrew in 1985. She reviewed this book in her weekly column in *Ha'aretz*, where she has been the assistant literary editor for many years. In general, this column is a trove of information about books received and reviewed, charting a broad picture of world literature to which Almog has been exposed and which she has introduced to Israeli readers. The share of her preferred topics is obviously very high, including women writers, from Erica Jong (*Fear of Flying*) and Sylvia Plath (*The Bell Jar*) to Virginia Woolf (numerous reviews) and, more recently, Julia Kristeva; "madness"—in most of the above, plus Paul Celan ("Art and Madness") and Pirandello ("The Theatre of Madness"); philosophy—from Heidegger and Sartre (plus Beauvoir) to Levinas and Derrida; and Greek culture—the poet Elitis, who is quoted lavishly in her fiction. Her critique of Marie Cardinal's book, titled "To Play Without Cards," is exemplary in its broad sweep:

> One of the important results of the feminist movement is the option it has given woman to relate to herself as to a separate being that has her own problematics and interests which are uniquely her own. This does not contradict, nor does it negate equality. . . .
> One of the issues that rose to the surface in this process of woman's differentiation as an object for self-observation, as an object that is both separate and different, just like the child or the teenager,[23] is the unique complexity of the relations between mothers and daughters.

Although Almog is critical of Cardinal's attempt to tell a "true" life story while shooting for literary effects (stream of consciousness, fragmented narration, etc.), she still finds that the baring of a pathological maternal relationship, in which a daughter regains her own sane self by escaping her mother's "madness," does address some deep problems, common to all women.

We are very close here to the fabric of *Roots of Air*. Through the mother's hysteria and the daughter's struggle to escape her pathology Almog seems to question the valorization of the "mother-daughter continuum" that had revolutionized feminist discourse ever since Nancy Chodorow's reevaluation of the Oedipus complex made its appearance. Moreover, in Almog's construction, the "daughter of a hysteric" would transverse the distance between the two different positions on female hysteria adumbrated by Juliet Mitchell and Elaine Showalter (see this chapter's epigraphs). However, as if anticipating the latter, she has her "Jane" escape the lot of the "despised hysterics of yesteryear" by becoming a radical of the 1960s. And although she sends her close to home, to Europe, her name clearly aligns her with the staple fictional representation of American feminist radicalism of the same period, Marilyn French's *The Women's Room*. This novel, published in Hebrew in 1980, is perhaps the most famous contemporary feminist bildungsroman. The name of its heroine is Mira (!). Her story is told by her and about her simultaneously (through changes in narratorial perspective like the ones we find in Almog's novel). She narrates a whole life span in retrospect (different from Almog's in its emphases, in keeping with other generational and cultural differences), tracing the evolution of Mira from middle-class wife and mother to divorced woman, now a successful Harvard student who strives to "work and love" through the political and ideological maelstrom of the 1960s. The high point of her transformation is naturally 1968, but it goes downhill from there on. In the wistful narrative present, Mira—the accomplished Ph.D.—is a college teacher in a small town in Maine (this is the 1970s and academic positions are hard to come by). Pacing alone on the wintry shores of Maine, trying to escape her nightmares and loneliness (often by mentally challenging Virginia Woolf, evidently perceived as a foremother) and wondering if she is losing her mind, Mira decides to put the shadows of the past to rest by writing down the story we have just been reading.

How will Almog's Mira emerge from her stormy 1968? We have to wait and see. Before we get there, however, there is some more unfinished business we need to bring to a close. Now that we have established, with the help of three strong foremothers, the feminist pedigree of *Roots of Air*, we can look beyond them. Indeed, while piecing together the madwomen of yesteryear with the radicals of the present (of the 1960s) via the mother-daughter "discovery" of the 1980s, Almog exploded the gynocentric intimacy of this triple-decker narrative. Her Mira gets out of her women's room to explore two androcentric ideologies of freedom: those of twentieth-century philosophies, from existentialism to Laingian psychoanalysis (more about this in section 3), and those of nineteenth-century national-ism, especially in the guise of the early Zionist pioneers in the Land of Israel. We will later see how her "Anatomy of Freedom" turns into an ironic critique of self-centered aggression, recalling, apparently not by chance, Robin Morgan's *The Anatomy of Freedom* (1982), itself an analysis of "Feminism, Physics, and Global Politics." For now, suffice it to point out that she achieves this by tracing the mother's age-old female malady to a *male* predecessor—Ruhama's grandfather, Lavdovi. In so doing, Almog has crossed over the gender boundaries of the feminist discussion, expanding its parameters to the question of madness at large.[24] Moreover, by juxtaposing "the mad Lavdovi" with his co"believers," the early settlers who were impervious to their own masculinist aggression, she puts into question the possibility and efficacy of madness as a willed social critique, thereby adding another Woolfian theme to our repertory (i.e., Septimus Smith's "anti-militarist hysteria" in *Mrs. Dalloway*, to whom we return in section 3).

In view of this plethora of feminist intertexts—most of them available in Hebrew—the silence of Israeli reviews on this matter is curious, to say the least. Apparently, Almog succeeded in her ploy: her novel was perused for all the "serious," namely, politically relevant issues it explored, as well as for the psychological implications of the symbiotic codependency of its two heroines, but not, so far as I know, for its questioning of the nexus of madness, creativity, and liberal feminism.[25] That she does this by means of a bicultural pun on the ostensible root of female hysteria, the "womb" (in Hebrew, *reḥem*), passed totally unnoticed.

In what follows I will reverse this procedure, focusing on the semantic distance traveled by Ruhama's daughter from the Greek to the Hebraic connotations of her mother's name and on the implications for both gen-der and nation that this transformation harbors.

Before this can be done, however, we need to briefly answer a covert question. How (and why) has Ruth Almog reached the unprecedented choices, generic as well as ideological, that her novel espouses?

2. The Sins of the Father(s); or, A Portrait of the Artist as a Young Girl

This is not an easy query to answer in view of Almog's earlier literary out-put. Her early short stories, published in the late 1960s, made her feel guilty, as she later related, about the contradiction between the private fantasy world in which she indulged and the "big" issues on the national agenda (in the wake of the Six Day War).[26] What made these early stories (1969 and 1979) different from the corpus of her female predecessors, was their transparently autobiographical nature. In opposition to the "modernist" separation between life and art attempted by both Kahana-Carmon and Hareven, Almog has kept close to her roots from the very beginning—and unproblematically shared them with her readers, who reciprocated accordingly. With a special ear and eye for the fauna and flora of her birthplace, Petaḥ Tikva, she lovingly brought to life the sights and smells of its landscape, the personalities of her extended Orthodox (!) family (grandparents, uncle, cousins, let alone parents), as well as neighbors and friends.[27] With these Proustian miniatures, often narrated in the first-person voice, she in fact anticipated the wave of Israeli fictional autobiographies that gained momentum in the 1970s (see chapter 1). Her nostalgic style, juxtaposing past and present ("What once was does not exist any more") betrays the influence of the Israeli prototype of the genre, Benjamin Tammuz's *Holot hazahav* (Sands of Gold, 1950!). It also resonates—like David Shahar's cycle of novels (begun in the 1960s)—with the Proustian effort to remember, to salvage scraps of a lost time ("I remember a lost, different time, a transparent time").

As I argued in chapter 1, few Israeli women indulged in this genre. To the best of my knowledge, Almog was, and to some degree still is, the only woman writer who has given us a tangible picture of childhood, of growing up within the structure of a very particular family.[28] For Kahana-Carmon's typical heroine, for example, life—biographically speaking—seems to have begun with the experience of her first great romantic love—not as an adolescent, as we might expect, but when she was a student and a soldier (in Israel's 1948 War of Independence). This is the climactic moment (*ha-siʾ*) from which life seems to have gone downhill, and this is also as far back as her retrospection would go. Any representation of earlier stages of life are well masqueraded either historically (*Up in Montifer*) or socially ("Neʿima Sasson Writes Poetry," "The Veil"). For reasons that we can only surmise, authentic childhood experiences (Kahana-Carmon was born on a kibbutz) are utterly absent from her artistic universe. The same is true for Hareven, whose single childhood story, which is in effect a social critique rather than a personal recollection, revolves around her "great-aunts" on the eve of the Holocaust.[29] Her only other first-person story also involves the experience of first love while serving in a Palmach unit in 1947–1948.[30] Even in Ben Yehuda's "confessional" narratives the balance

is tipped away from childhood, although she does indulge in some insightful glimpses into the psychological dynamics of her family.

Almog is unique then in her unmasked Freudian exposition of the
"portrait of an artist as a young girl." It is this paradigm that has been
recently identified as typical of the (oedipal) male bildungsroman.[31]
According to this view, few women writers have chosen this model,
because it does not fit the developmental experience of women; most follow the "mid-life awakening" model, precisely the one that may be
vaguely glimpsed behind our reluctantly (un)autobiographical Israeli
authors. In this model a woman sets on her journey out (or in) only after
her marital and maternal obligations have been met. Woolf's *Mrs. Dalloway* is held up as a paradigmatic example, supplementing epiphanies of
the past for a linear progression from childhood to maturity (see chapter
5.3). Kahana-Carmon's protagonists obviously follow this paradigm.
Hareven's Sara follows the traditional "male" model with some emenda-
tions, and—as I argued above—at a hefty distance from her creator's biography. Almog, on the other hand, seems to feel comfortable within the
confines of the "linear" plot of male development, unrestrainedly going
back once and again to her "origins," fictionalizing the same scenes of primal sin in early childhood.

A rare glimpse into her unique perception (and admission) of the
deeply personal nature of her art takes place in a late interview in which
she goes back to the objections she had encountered in her youth: "People found my desire to write objectionable. I'm not sure why. Perhaps it
is because writing involves a revealing of one's soul, a sharing of pain
which people find embarrassing. My peers simply could not suffer *my
desire to write stories about myself.*"[32] The emphasis is mine, of course,
meant to highlight the difference between this utterly transparent authorial self and the modernist separation between art and life practiced by her
precursors.

It is not easy to determine the reasons for this uniqueness. Possibly an
age difference, though not that great (a decade or less), is decisive here.
Perhaps not being part of the Palmach generation allowed for a different
ethos and a different attitude to psychology and personal matters. Perhaps
the traumatic loss of her father at age fourteen, and her subsequent adolescent rebellion against "his" oppressive Orthodox education (the
mother was not so observant) made the young Almog more self-intro-
spective and self-conscious. Whatever the case, a retrospective reading of
her early work uncovers clearly defined psychological structures that have

Ruth Almog

their roots in the autobiographical materials but are present in the other, third-person stories as well. Apparently, these structures have accompanied her throughout life—and entered into the fiction. Their prime feature is an obsessional oedipal attachment, one that expresses itself in a fear of an authoritarian lawgiver, a strict and forbidding father (a veritable Lacanian *nom/n du père*), and an insatiable yearning for the same figure—not only for the warmth and protection he can give yet withholds, but—and this is significant—for the stories, especially of Greek mythology, that he bequeathed to his daughter. The mother, on the other hand, is mostly overshadowed; rarely is she a meaningful presence, notably in one early story (where she is quite antagonistic).[33]

This childhood trauma is astutely "translated" into a constant, manifestly frustrated, search for father substitutes in the narrative present of the grown-up daughter, the "author" of these early childhood recollections. That these substitutes are mostly older men (her father's age cohort) is quite predictable. In fact, Almog charted out here a "psychology of orphans," unwittingly anticipating the treatment of this subject in A. B. Yehoshua's *Mr. Mani*.[34] In contrast to Yehoshua, however, who will interpret orphanhood as a grand-scale national symptom, as is his wont, Almog is preoccupied with the individual aspect of this psychological complex. This was made apparent in one of her literary columns written during that period, titled "Libraries of (in) My Life."[35] She recalls several works by Hebrew male authors (Burla, Berdichevsky, Agnon), whose female protagonists had affected her. Most significant among them was Agnon's notorious story "Bidmi yameiha" (In the Prime of Her Life), "which not only fashioned one aspect of my [literary] taste, but also has determined several issues in my own life" (*kava' kamah kevi'ot behayay*). Agnon's young heroine, it may be recalled, sets out "to get" her late mother's true love—the one the mother had been prevented from marrying by her own father—finally marrying him, though not necessarily living happily ever after. This early self-realization on the part of Almog will bear fictional fruits in *Roots of Air*, as we shall see below.

Almog seems to indulge with impunity, then, in a rather amazing conflation of Freudian and Lacanian interpretations of the oedipal complex. Her "collective" fictional daughter figure definitely "thinks back through her father"; which is precisely what I argue in the case of Virginia Woolf. Indeed, one of Almog's recent interviews concludes with a revealing insight, clearly reminiscent of Woolf's notorious note on her late father's ninety-sixth birthday (cited in chapter 4):

One of the problems that bothered me upon my father's death was the fact that his death, as traumatic as it was, brought me freedom. Mom was not as [religiously] strict as he had been, so only after his death could I go out in the evenings for all sorts of activities, formerly forbidden. Who knows how much guilt I carried with me; no wonder I erased what I could.[36]

The similarity between Woolf's and Almog's belated self-analysis is astounding. For both, the father was the first guide into the Symbolic Order, into the world of letters.[37] Both, however, see the father also as an impediment to a full participation in this order (and probably to mature sexuality as well) and therefore remember his death as a (guilt-producing) moment of liberation.

Almog, who admits to having done "auto-analysis" since young adulthood, has reworked this ambivalence in her fiction in various ways, having her heroines experience freedom at the cost of constant guilt, on the one hand, and frustration with the patriarchal cultural codes—inherited through myth and history—on the other. They also indulge in daydreaming, paradoxically using the mythological legacy of the father to fulfill unrequited erotic desires—in complete agreement with Freud's infamous distinction between the contents of daydreams by young male and female dreamers (the wishful achievement of self-centered—worldly—ambition versus erotic goals, respectively).[38]

Indeed, Freud is everywhere present in this early fiction, even parodied. Thus the protagonist of Almog's first novel, *Be'eretz gzera* (The Exile, 1970),[39] surrounds herself with African trophies and penis-shaped ivory artifacts—seeking to partake in that male power that successfully keeps her at arm's length. . . . Predictably, her first act of rebellion is an act of rewriting: Marguerita Rosenbaum is a failed academic, whose dissertation on "The Law of Minos, King of Crete" is judged—by the male academic establishment, of course—"not very scientifically accurate; an overdeveloped imagination and a penchant for literature undermine the research, despite the hard work invested in it." In response, she determines to write a historical novel, "The Life and Death of Ariadne, Princess of Crete."

The impulse is familiar. Nineteenth-century women novelists sought to subvert fairy tales—the Symbolic Order that had structured their roles as passive objects of desire and victimized others; Almog's protagonist has progressed to mythology. And the first thing her (first-person) narrator does with "her" father's heritage is to shift the balance—replace science with fiction, the king with the princess. Marguerita Rosenbaum seems to be well on her way to thinking back through her father, as did Fania in *Gei Oni* and Clara in *Up in Montifer* (chapters 1 and 3). Moreover, she seems to be on her way to an artistic career—the first among our new Hebrew women—revolutionizing her "father's mythology" from within, using her imagination to recast it, as did Woolf to her father's "trade" when writing *Orlando*'s fantastic biography. Yet all this founders on the rocks of unrequited love, to which we are introduced in the first ten pages of the book. The rest of the story is Marguerita Rosenbaum's struggle with her own obsessional needs, as with a line of father figures who try to put her "in her place" as "a Jewish wife and mother" (*'isha ve'em be'israel*) with the authority of all the Hebrew scriptural sources they can marshal. Her struggling takes the shape of a hero's quest—a journey to her German (!) birthplace, to her "father's house," to use the metaphoric language of recent scholarship.[40] We may rightly expect her to emerge from this journey rejuvenated, leaving behind "her father's house" to become "her father's daughter," able to speak "in the name of the daughter" rather than "in the name of the father." But this is not what happens. Marguerita's is a mock quest—a surrealistic journey that lands her en route in an asylum and ends in a "voluntary" death in her German hometown, textually evoking the horrific story that signs off the book of Judges, the (ritual?) murder of the "concubine" from Gibe'a.

Rather than allowing its protagonist a liberating feminist revision of Greek mythology, *The Exile* takes her on a regressive journey from Crete to its darker biblical/"Germanic" analogue in the book of Judges.[41] Although this is an early reworking of an oedipal fixation and its corollary "death in life," the outcome in the later work is not much more satisfactory (as we have seen in the last section). Even more than Kahana-Carmon's protagonists, Almog's early and middle heroines, including the seven main characters of her 1986 *Women*, are all doomed to the same vicious circle: they are arrested in an unattainable oedipal love, a fixation that prevents the free flow of sexuality, creativity, or a life of love and work. Their only consolation is the circulation of patriarchal mythology, "stories I tell myself," stories that never have closure (which paradoxically leaves room for hope, in Hebrew *petaḥ tikva*, the last words of Almog's first collection of stories, and the name of her hometown).

This same basic deep structure is ingeniously retold in many different ways. Almog devised formal innovations—a novel that verges on a scientific psychological report (1980), a Rashomon-style novel of diaries and letters (1982), seven variations on a theme (1986). This last experiment must have exhausted the potency of her "story," however. In a heroic act that is comparable to cutting one's own umbilical cord (which in *The Exile* the protagonist imagines as being attached to her male lover [!] rather than to her mother), Almog has severed the patriarchal lineage of her storytelling, revived the missing mother (endowing her—rather than the father—with the gift of storytelling), and proceeded to invent a new narrative . . . at which we are now ready to take a closer look.

3. *Work and Love? Embracing the M/Other in* Roots of Air

We begin with the novelty: the image of the mother, who seems to come from nowhere. Ruhama, Mira's mother, is portrayed as a stereotypically feminine charmer, exemplifying almost every cliché: she is attractive, sensuous, artistic, imaginative, in tune with nature (and with her own sexuality), communicative when she feels like it and enigmatically distant when she does not, and, most important, an expert inventor of stories. At the same time, however, she is a woman alone, an outsider living on the outskirts of a small town. Independent by default—she was left by her estranged husband to run the estate by herself—she is hopelessly self-centered and capricious, hysterical and suicidal, as her name may unobtrusively imply.

For the Hebrew reader the first connotation of this name is, of course, that of compassion and mercy, *rahamim*. A more semantically inclined reader may recall that it is ethymologically related to *rehem*, womb. A biblically oriented reader would no doubt conjure up the full matrix of its appearance in the Bible: Hosea 1:6, where *lo'-ruhamah* ("the unloved one"), the allegorical daughter of the prophet's wanton wife, is promised redemption by being renamed *ruhama* (2:2; "the loved one," but literally, "the object of compassion, mercy"). A feminist reader, however, cannot help but recalling the significant (should we say pregnant?) divergence between the semantic fields associated with the female womb in the Hebraic and Greek traditions: that between compassion, even love (in Hebrew), and malady or even pathology ("hysteria") in Greek (from *hystera*, "womb").[42] The bilingual semantic field of this name thus conflates several themes developed in the personality of the mother: female sexuality and hysteria, compassion and "redemption." Being *"lo'-Ruhamah,"* rather than Ruhama, she in actuality lives up to the Greek/European connotations of the Hebrew etymology of her name.

Living in a fantasy world and always on the brink of emotional breakdown, (lo') Ruhama is heavily dependent on Mira, who, in a reversal of roles, loyally mothers her with all the ambivalence that such family dynamics of necessity entail. This unhappy woman, in short, could have readily been another "madwoman in the attic,"[43] had this not been a 1980s novel, whose first part carries the enigmatic title "Madness Is *the Wisdom* of the Individuum" (emphasis mine).

That the "exoneration" of madness is at least one of the psychological questions with which this book grapples is no doubt clear.[44] The title of book 1, and several of its major themes, clearly smack of R. D. Laing's idealization of schizophrenic madness, from *The Divided Self* (1960) through *The Politics of the Family* (1969) and *The Politics of Experience* (1970). We may recall that these psycho-existentialist theories enjoyed quite a vogue among left-wing ideologues of the 1960s—precisely the time frame of book 2 of our novel and the ostensible "moment of writing" of its autobiographic narrator. There is even a trace of this vogue in the plot itself, when Mira is sent to cover a meeting of psychiatrists in Bonn, where Laing is expected "to cause a scandal" (326). We have already seen Almog's general fascination (both textual and extratextual) with the thin line between sanity and insanity. Following the publication of *Roots of Air*, when asked if she thought one could choose insanity, she candidly equivocated over the question: "I don't know. I once thought it was possible, but today I do not know. I once even thought one can consciously choose insanity. But new scientific findings undermine this supposition."[45] In fact, the question whether an escape into madness is a matter of free *choice*, and whether it can function as a conscious rebellion against the social order, constitutes the deep structure of this novel. The legacy of madness, woven into the two narrative strands of book 1 (both Mira's mother and her great-grandfather), may have been inspired by Laing and Esterson's *Families of Schizophrenics*. Although not schizophrenic in the clinical sense, Mira's family bears some features typical of Laing's case histories: the centrality of mother-daughter relations (accompanied by an "absent father") as well as "the feminine predicament" of "leaving home and letting go."[46] Yet Almog's treatment of this paradigm takes another route. While book 1 both foregrounds and problematizes a Laingian idealization of individual madness (namely, the wisdom of this alleged personal freedom), book 2 offers a merciless analysis of the other side of the coin—the use and (aggressive) misuse, both personal and political, of the philosophies of freedom and existential choice.

Bearing in mind this nexus of madness and freedom under question, we may better understand the significance of Mira's tolerance of her mother's deviances, the playful as well as the grievous (the latter include Ruhama's symbolic castration of her daughter, furiously and uncontrollably cutting Mira's beautiful long hair, as well as her attempted suicides). Still, one is hard put to swallow Mira's total acceptance of her mother's rationalization for her symptomatic flights into fantasy:

> Mom told me once, and I have never forgotten it: "What did God give humans imagination for, if not to invent things. I am telling you, to invent stories is the most marvelous thing there is. Fantasy knows no limit. One can even invent a life for oneself."
>
> . . .
>
> And when Dr. Shapira would reprimand her for fibbing, she would say: "This is no fib. It is fanciful and amusing. After all, life is so gray. Nothing interesting ever happens here. Ever. So I tell stories and make life more exciting. And you know what? Sometimes such a story even becomes true." (75)

"Nothing interesting ever happens here"—could this description be out of an Israeli novel? Is this a valid assessment of life in a country as volatile as Israel? Doesn't it require a greater measure of the suspension of disbelief normally expected of readers? I suspect that it does, particularly if the reader is preconditioned by the androcentric canon of Hebrew literature, notorious for its preoccupation with the always urgent issues of the public arena. But this is, of course, precisely Almog's point. In order to have her younger protagonist experience both the pleasure and the pain of the "real" world, she must make her break away from the "private sphere"—the prison house of female hysteria—in which, presumably, "life is so gray."

Yet breaking away is not that simple; and not only because of pragmatic obstacles or psychological inhibitions (major among the latter is Mira's inordinate sense of guilt and obligation, being, despite her young age, her mother's only caretaker—until Ruhama's remarriage). In the daughter's approval of her mother's strategy of self-invention, the age-old Scheherazade foible of spinning stories, we may hear echoes of one of Almog's own strategies of survival. Apparently, Almog herself feels the same way about her own life. When asked, "Why don't you write about your daily experience?" she responded with a rhetorical question: "To write about this? Never. This is what I want to escape from. My real life takes place elsewhere . . . when I begin to travel, in my imagination."[47] It is clear, therefore, that in having Mira appreciate the exercising of one's imagination as an act of personal freedom ("I did not care. Like Mom, I believed that anyone had the privilege to invent his or her life any way they wished"), Almog signals a possible common ground for the mother-daughter continuum, despite the pressures bearing on it. This common ground is embodied in Mira's own imaginary creation—the life story of her mother's grandfather, the eccentric Lavdovi.

In this life story, which constitutes the second strand of book 1 (the odd-numbered chapters, we may recall), Almog has ingeniously orchestrated a screen, a panoramic backdrop on which the psychological complexity of Mira's life is projected and magnified to the extent that it becomes "history." I put *history* in quotation marks for two reasons. First, history, or rather historiography, is precisely what is deconstructed in this story. History turns out to be a story, hewed from Ruhama's quite limited personal recollection and Mira's imagination and empathy rather than from the meager historical documents that she manages to find. One of the graphic signs of this undermining of historiography is the fact—never noticed by critics—that Lavdovi's life is narrated backward, in the opposite direction to our expectations. Readers of Israeli literature are familiar with this "trick," which was not only practiced but highly thematized in A. B. Yehoshua's *Mr. Mani* (1990), whose counterhistory has been the subject of much discussion. Almog had (once again) anticipated Yehoshua's move, utilizing a backward narration to foreground her own equivocation about the thin line dividing history from her story.

With this we are into the second reason for the quotes around *history*. Not only is this a story, it is "her" story. Although the protagonist is a male, he is clearly a *maternal* forefather—and the source of the female malady of this family. Lavdovi's act of self-mutilation, narrated accurately in parallel to Mira's mutilation by Ruhama, marks him as a male hysteric, uncomfortable with his sexuality, in complete agreement with Freud's theories (of female hysteria, of course) at the time. If we remember that this is the turn of the century, and that Lavdovi takes part in the greatest collective oedipal rebellion imaginable—the Zionist revolution—the role of his bisexual identity may emerge. Like Virginia Woolf's hero Septimus Smith (in *Mrs. Dalloway*), who registers his protest against the cult of masculinist militarism (as well as against its unquestioned heterosexuality) by "the dislocation of the mind from the reality it had inhabited,"[48] and by suicidal regression (viewed in recent scholarship as a much deeper psychological disturbance than the "shell shock" attributed to him by his fictional contemporary psychiatrists),[49] the hysterical Lavdovi registers a female protest against his co-settlers' blindness to the threat they constitute for their Arab neighbors. His pacifist ideas (precursors of Buber's Brit Shalom) put him, of course, on the side of the (1980s) feminist politics I describe in chapter 6. Yet despite this transparent anachronism, and notwithstanding the historical evidence Almog has or has not found in the annals of the First Aliyah,[50] she interestingly endowed his madness with several features that roughly mark him as a child of his fictional time.

The coupling of a religious or other moral fervor with a conflicted sexuality that underlies Lavdovi's personality (identified by one critic as a Christ figure)[51] was one of the hallmarks of two towering personalities, living on both sides of the turn of this century: the Russian writer L. N. Tolstoy (1828–1910) and the Hebrew writer Y. H. Brenner (1882–1921), the latter in many ways a disciple of the former. Tolstoy is also famous of course for the educational innovations he introduced on his estate, Yasnaya Polyana, as well as for the Christ-like pacifism and disregard for property he adopted by the end of his life (viewed as sheer madness by his wife and children).[52] The educational games devised by Lavdovi, his disdain for property and his nomadic life—all of which aroused the derision of his compatriots—these might be seen as Tolstoyan. Brenner, on the other hand, as the fictional mediator between the two, bequeathed Lavdovi his "desperate Zionism" (famously captured in the phrase *'af-'al-pi-khen*, "nonetheless") as well as his psychosexual inhibitions.[53]

In fashioning Lavdovi in this manner, Mira has "translated" into the past and into the collective her own personal conflicts. By inventing (rather then discovering) a twin soul, she was perhaps able to channel her anger and frustration with both her mother (projected onto Lavdovi with all the ambivalence his personality would arouse) and father (projected onto the Zionist forefathers whose nationalist ideals and sins alike parallel his, as we will soon see). The life she invented, though not hers literally, is hers metaphorically—a reflection of the strategy of masked autobiography we uncovered as the preferred genre of Israeli literary feminists. In the juxtaposition of the two strands of book 1 Almog has unwittingly constructed an opposition between two options of female self-invention, that of the past and that of the present: Ruhama's storytelling and Mira's story of Lavdovi represent a strategy that has already exhausted itself, leading nowhere; it may have been instrumental, though, in enabling Mira to face her autobiography squarely, in the here and now of her account, and to act upon it accordingly. For, in the final analysis, Almog does not let

Ruhama serve as Mira's role model. Despite the allure and conso!_:̲ ̲n of mythmaking, Mira is not going to stay at home and amuse the neighbors with potentially self-fulfilling stories; she will actively make one of these stories come true.

That the model she chooses is typically androcentric should come as no surprise: this may be one more link in a tradition we have been unearthing in recent Israeli literature—a feminist self-invention, modeled on Enlightenment-based masculine subjectivity. Like her predecessors—and despite her own Chodorow-styled mother attachment—Mira thinks back through several father figures. In addition to her own father, who dedicated his life to the implementation of the Zionist dream (about which she is particularly ambivalent), and Lavdovi, her half-imagined great-grandfather, her subjectivity is shaped by two father substitutes: Alexandroni, her mother's lifelong admirer, and, later, Jacques Berliavsky, her lover/husband. The age of the latter obviously make them good candidates for the pattern of psychology of orphans uncovered in section 2. For Mira is psychologically an orphan, perhaps even doubly so, smarting from her father's geographical and emotional distance as well as from her mother's complex blend of mental fragility and sexual competitiveness. Thus her marriage to Berliavsky, who is of the same generation as her parents, is an incestuous choice that eventually exacerbates her jealousy of her mother; on the other hand, her later attempt to sexually consummate Alexandroni's attachment to her mother (and his fatherly loyalty toward Mira herself), resonates with Agnon's "Bidmi yameiha" (At the Prime of Her Life), which we encountered in section 2 above. In both cases the older lover is the bearer of knowledge of the Symbolic Order (signified here by his name, which evokes Alexandria, the ancient library and museum of Greek wisdom) as well as a father manqué, which makes him a convenient object for an oedipal attachment.[54]

All this sounds very familiar. We have gone through this complex several times over with Almog's earlier protagonists. But the resemblance is only superficial. For what is surprising here is Mira's attitude to the model she chooses to follow. In contrast to her predecessors, she does not do this out of blind admiration. Mira is not going to surround herself with penis-shaped artifacts. If her penetrating critique of her own father is any measure, she is fully cognizant of the true dimensions of his masculinist world. Indeed, it is this insight that makes Mira's evolution so psychologically interesting.

On the face of it, Almog seems to offer a "feminist" corrective to the Laingian predicament, reinscribing the absent father into Mira's life. This psychoanalytic "missing third term"[55] is supposed to help her over the hurdle of the claustrophobic (if not schizophrenic) feminine symbiosis with her mother and move her into the world of political action and masculinist freedom. And so it does. But at what price?

> [Mira] told herself that her father was a man who looked into a small mirror all his life, but there was nothing one could do about this, because he was unable to be any different, he was simply not capable of looking into a bigger mirror, because such a mirror did not exist for him, at least not in his reality. There, in his world, only two options existed: either a tiny mirror, or a magnified picture, namely: national concerns. . . . But that was not all. . . . Not only was his mirror small, it was also always positioned at the same right angle, and it would never dawn on him that it was possible, really possible, and sometimes even greatly necessary, to position the mirror diagonally, for example, perhaps at a 45 degree angle, or a 135 degree, or even a 180. . . . True, the portrait reflected in the mirror might be slightly cut off, at the chin or the forehead, but instead some other views might be reflected in the free areas along it. Yes, yes, Mira told herself, Mira's dad is an onlooker, merely an onlooker, not an insightful observer. This is how his eyes are built, that's all. That is why, Mira thought, his opinions are so predetermined and unequivocal, and that is why he is only preoccupied with issues external to him. *(133–134)*

The apologetic tone of this inner monologue is unmistakable. Mira is clearly caught between an oedipal idealization of her father and a ruthless adolescent observation of his dogmatism and self-centeredness. Indeed, it is difficult to avoid the tragicomic effect of this passage, at least for a reader versed in contemporary psychoanalytic discourse. This paternal figure seems to be arrested forever in an unfinished infantile mirror stage, a travesty of Lacan's great symbol of the birth of the human "split" ego. Moreover, the association of this infantile fixation with the father's exclusive preoccupation with "national concerns" brings to mind the terms of Woolf's psychopolitics in *Three Guineas* (chapter 6.1).

Mira, however, uses the mirror metaphor defensively, protecting herself from fully comprehending the brunt of her own accusation. What is more, this is the first time that the "autobiographic" narrative voice splits into first and third persons, being itself conscious of the defensive function of this specific technique:[56]

> Yes, with all this turbulence of fear, rage, and insult also came elucidation. And I told myself that at times I stopped being me and that Mira

particularly stopped being me when she was thinking about her father, that father of Mira's. . . . Mira wanted to protect him for me, she wanted to protect him from me, because it was important to keep him away, safe from my harsh disappointment, from my hurt. It was important to keep him for herself in some way, because she did not want to lose him completely and she was afraid of me, because I exposed and befouled him.   *(133)*

Fettered by one of the oldest psychological taboos, Mira is unable to integrate her father's betrayal—his refusal to help her get rid of an unwanted pregnancy, thereby exacerbating his perennial denial of her blooming sexuality. Her solution to the conflict is ingenious: instead of splitting off the "bad" father, she externalizes her own forgiving, rationalizing self, while "internally regressing into her 'deviant' thinking," which she uses as "a dam against the rage he would arouse in me" (134). It is here, in this crucial event, that the protagonist of *Roots of Air* emerges as a postmodernist (Lacanian) split subject. Yet this split is doubly motivated. For Mira an integrated self is unrealizable not only because of the universally endemic gulf between one's authentic perceptions and the perceptions about self that are approved by the Symbolic Order but also because of her very personal impossible choice between the Scylla of Mom's rich but totally vicarious fantasy life and the Charybdis of Dad's active but narrow-minded public life.

It is this tragic conflict that is dramatized by the break in the hitherto smooth flow of Mira's first-person retrospection: from now until the end of Book 1 her strand of the narration shuttles between first and third persons, indecisively moving from the ostensibly authentic but private "I" to the other, more public "Mira," who is perhaps better socialized but also more repressed and alienated from her "true" self. That this splitting originates in the father's mock mirror stage, that is, in a paternal infantile fixation, is of course part of an inescapable irony—trying to escape one kind of vicarious life, Mira unwittingly undertakes another. And although the last word is given to the narrating "I," its actions speak louder than words: "I then crossed the street. There, on the other side, Dad was already waiting for me. Together we entered the port and boarded the ship" (160). The choice is made; the Rubicon crossed. The protagonist has left behind mother, home, hometown, and homeland. Now she is on her way to join the sound and fury of her father's world, that other world of which she used to be so critical. Unlike her mother, she is going to invent a life, not a story of a life. But will she escape the typical female lot, shared by her mother as well, of living vicariously? Will she emerge as the first new Hebrew woman to sidestep the trap of the feminist romance? Will she, in short, live up to the "work and love" agenda of feminist expectations?

Ruth Almog's answer seems ambiguous. Yes, she allows her protagonist freedom of choice (book 2 is entitled "Anatomy of Freedom") and sends her off to Italy to study medicine. True, she releases her from the prison of the female private sphere, where "nothing interesting ever happens," and plunges her into the "colorful" world of international journalism and left-wing politics. At the same time, she immerses her in the discourse on freedom, both personal and political, of that generation (behaviorism versus existentialism, freudianism versus marxism, Marcuse versus Fromm, possessiveness versus ego boundaries, authenticity versus power relations), only to find out their blind alleys (176, 182, 190–196 ff., 237 ff.). She also involves her in one of the most intriguing love affairs of Hebrew literature, enabling her to conduct a dialogic discourse on love and female desire while testing firsthand the practical in/validity of the rhetorics of freedom. The eccentric, unpredictable, and finally also unreliable Professor Jacques Berliavsky is one of the most exasperating, finely drawn character portraits in Israeli fiction. Yet one should not miss the irony implied by the title of part A of book 2, "Freedom According to Jacques" (pp. 163–266).[57]

This version of the new Hebrew woman definitely has its fair share of work and love. But they do not dwell happily ever after. Nor do the protagonists. In a twist that might be unexpected in the heroine's euphoric text (see chapter 1) but is quite predictable for the sober realism of this novel, Mira's "total, absolute love" (189 ff.) founders on the rocks of marriage (218ff.). And although the reason for this foundering is overdetermined (her dependency, the vacuousness of his "freedom"), it clearly takes Mira one step further in the deconstruction—which began with her critique of her father—of the masculine ideal. The hard lesson of her exercise in "freedom according to Jacques" is that love and work elude not only aspiring young females, they are rare in the male world as well. Other differences notwithstanding, Jacques' "balance sheet" turns out to be just as warped as her father's. From this perspective it is not Mira who has failed the test of the "masculine, political" plot, it is the ideal that has failed her.

Nevertheless, she is denied a continuous voice, an uninterrupted line of discourse. Although Mira remains the central consciousness through which book 2 is focalized, she loses her own voice. As we meet her again in book 2, she is presented to us mostly through third-person narration, with several exceptions: her brief homecomings (for her own wedding and for her mother's funeral, pp. 207–222, 298–317), her traumatic fantasy, evoking the "primary neurosis" of her childhood—her jealousy of her beautiful mother (258–259), and her final long letter to her father (333 ff.).

It is on the pages of this letter that the autobiographic quest for self-knowledge finally materializes. And it is here that the protagonist discovers the paradoxical truth about the otherness of her self. For, although successfully disengaged from her mother's vicarious life, Mira has not really come into her own. To her surprise and perhaps horror she learns that in all her love ("object") choices she has unconsciously recapitulated the structure of her relationship with her father, thereby "ensuring" their failure. Furthermore, her ideological positions are constantly referred to as "borrowed," "recited," "a cheap recipe," etc. In the final analysis, it is not her own life that Mira has invented. Although in a different fashion, her self turns out to be no less vicarious than her mother's, and her "freedom"—both political and psychological—seems nothing more than spurious. The road to freedom, Mira discovers, leads through a history of masculine violence and aggression, terror and rape (which she experiences firsthand).[58] Fraternity is overcome by fratricide, equality by oppression. It is therefore not surprising that the charming autobiographic "I" of book 1 has almost no place in the harsh world of book 2. Through the inner logic of this novel, autobiographic introspection and political or other malestream activism are mutually exclusive.

4. From Hysteria to HerStory: Artistic Mending

Roots of Air both continues and transcends two novelistic trends recently developed by Israeli women, the masked autobiography and the feminist romance. Without these antecedents the specific features of this novel in their particular combination would have been unthinkable. At the same time, however, Almog deserves credit for the steps she has taken to transform these models both structurally and thematically. Unlike her predecessors, she is far from idealizing a masculinist construction of the female subject; neither does she trust compromises of either Virginia Woolf's androgyny or Julia Kristeva's third generation women, to which some of her peers subscribe; nor does she find consolation in the apotheosis of sexual difference argued by Irigaray and Cixous and ambivalently practiced by Kahana-Carmon and the later Hareven.

Hers is the sober observation of the specific, intensely personal, psychological matrix of a female subject (filtered in this novel through the prism of various psychoanalytic models) and the no less intense and painful political contingencies imposed upon it. Her protagonist stands alone in Israeli fiction in her endeavor to actually carry out, here and now, "classical" feminist expectations. But, at the same time, the outcome of Mira's "education" undoes or deconstructs the very ideal it has set out to achieve. Almog's venture, the inscription of a female protagonist into "a virile, political novel" (her own wording) has turned out to be its own best refutation. That this endeavor takes place in exile, outside the borders of Israel, is of course part of the critique implied in the structure of this novel. Yet the critique is double-pronged, for this portrait of the feminist as a young woman crashes against the unyielding realities of both the protagonist's internal (psychological) and external (sociopolitical) worlds. In the final analysis, the source of discontent in this novel is not easily determined (perhaps overdetermined): Is the inhospitability of Israeli nationalistic culture to blame for the exile, if not disappearance of the New Hebrew Woman, as repeatedly argued—extratextually—by Ruth Almog herself (as by Kahana-Carmon before her)?[59] Or is Western feminism itself under scrutiny here, exposing the naïveté and risky optimism of some of its basic propositions?

Almog's answer to these questions is embedded in her narrative, of course, by means of plot, discourse, and closure.

Although at the end of her sad story Mira is still in exile, smarting from her psychological and ideological wounds, her final actions offer a glimpse of hope: lifting off the lid of repression from her childhood traumas, she is finally ready to embrace the "madness" of her maternal heritage, which she has attempted to suppress throughout book 2 (335 ff.). Replacing her mother's oral storytelling with the autobiographer's pen, she is about to find her authenticity in (creative?) writing, not in political action. Given the limitations of our condition, Almog seems to be saying, creativity is the only true freedom, one that transcends gender, class, and national divisions. "Artistic imagination fashions the unconscious memory of failed emancipation, of a betrayed promise," Mira finds in one of Jacques's books, followed by a quote from Adorno, that "Messiah" so "often quoted by her German friends": " 'In the absence of freedom, art can preserve the spirit of freedom only by negating non-freedom.' . . . Mira grimaces and closes the book. The words sound hollow. She, at least, does not understand them." (355)

Mira may not understand, but her imagination does. "Jacques hates disorder, she thinks, for him everything has to be in place. Only within order he feels free . . . only within order . . . only within order . . . How? How? . . . " (356). Needless to say, she does not find out how. Rather than decoding the secret of the obsessional scientist's Symbolic Order, she gives in to the rhythms, sounds, and fragrances of her near and distant memories. In a tapestry of free associations, her imagination shuttles back and forth between past and present, the real and the imaginary, finally replicating the very language that was earlier used to represent her mother's unique bond with nature. With this Ruhama's madness is not only internalized, it is also redeemed. The Freudian (Greek) connotation of her name (*reḥem*, womb, *hystera*) gives way to its biblical (Hebrew) meaning (*raḥamim*, compassion, love). Exhibiting the cadences of Freudian primary processes, of the Lacanian preoedipal Imaginary, or of Kristeva's maternal Semiotic, these final pages hold the promise for artistic sublimation. We are not sure whether Mira will return from her exile ("I do not want to walk in the footsteps of my maternal great-grandfather . . . and be called a madwoman," p. 358), or whether she will fare better in her future love choices, but we feel confident that she is able to "befriend" her legacy of madness and contain it within the "chaos" of artistic creativity.

About a decade ago, in an article that discussed some of the predecessors of *Roots of Air*, I asked why none of the Israeli women writers of the seventies and eighties could imagine a protagonist with the same artistic freedom they themselves enjoyed, why none of the masked autobiographies I analyzed were in fact a portrait of the artist as a young woman.[60] Ruth Almog's novel finally accomplishes precisely that. And, just like her male peers, she does not shy from baring some very personal wounds that have engendered (pun intended) her artistic mending.[61] She thus brings our search for literary constructions of the new Hebrew woman to an appropriate close. Having Mira go not only beyond "the despised hysterics of yesteryear," but even beyond their replacement, "the feminist radicals of today" (Showalter),[62] Almog still questions the claim that "the woman novelist must be an hysteric" (Juliet Mitchell, contra Kristeva; see the epigraphs to this chapter).[63] If her own actions are any measure, she would not let her Mira wallow in the hysterical self-pity of Marilyn French's Mira at the end of *The Women's Room*. Perhaps she would have her move from therapeutic autobiographical fiction—whether masked or not—to other genres and other interests. Significantly, this is precisely the direction

Almog has taken in her latest book. *Tikkun 'omanuti* (Invisible [lit. Artistic] Mending, or, in the language of the American sartorial industry, "reweaving") is a collection of heartrending stories, meticulously executed, in which she artistically mends the life stories of a variety of characters—mostly children—who are socially marginal without necessarily being "mad" and/or female. With this Almog seems to have completed a journey, begun about a decade earlier, from the option woman was given by the feminist movement, as she said, "to relate to herself as to a separate being that has her own problematics and interests" to another object of observation, mentioned parenthetically in the same comments, "an object that is both separate and different, just like the child or the teenager."[64] Overcoming both the oedipal fixation and the daughter-mother identification, Almog has now embraced the mother in herself ("A woman is her own mother," in Anne Sexton's famous words), to move from hysteria to her story, and from her story to the story of children, both male and female, whose only redemption is an artistic mending by a loving maternal heart.

This is an interesting Israeli twist on the "maternal metaphor" that has aroused both support and critique in recent feminist scholarship. This writing from the position of maternal care is perhaps a step toward that elusive narrative that is still mostly untold, in Hebrew as much as in other languages: the story of the mother herself, not as m/other, not from the perspective of the daughter (or the son), but from her own perspective, as her own subject.

Afterword: The Nineties—Prelude to a Postmodernist Millennium?

Somewhere around 1987–1988 an unseen gate seems to have opened and Israeli prose fiction was pervaded by an unprecedented number of women writers—most, though not all, of a younger generation. This timing, with hindsight, seems loaded with symbolic meanings. The one hundredth birthday of the first Hebrew woman writer, Dvora Baron, was celebrated in January 1988 by a symposium at Tel Aviv University. That salute followed, moreover, the first International Conference of Women Writers to be held in Israel (1987), organized by the recently established Israel Women's Network. The conference in Jerusalem functioned, Alice Shalvi argued, as a trigger for the "coming out" (as feminists) of several Israeli writers who had formerly equivocated about the advisability of categorizing themselves as "women writers."[1] Add to these public events the fact that by 1988 most of Virginia Woolf's oeuvre had been translated into Hebrew, culminating in Quentin Bell's biography (1988; see appendix A, this volume), and the picture seems complete.

But not quite. True, the trend of women writers gathered momentum in the following decade—reaching its zenith with the 1997 "feminization" of the Israeli best-seller lists described at the opening of this study. Women seem, then, not only to have acquired a room of their own but even a room at the top. What remains unclear, however, is to what extent this outburst of female creativity carries on or breaks away from the feminist legacy—precarious as it is—of the "foremothers" considered in the present study. Particularly curious is the apparent lack of interest exhibited by most writers of the 1990s in the struggles of their foremothers with the competing demands of gender and nation, namely, the conflict between their besieged feminisms and their no less troubled Zionist loyalty.

Indeed, the picture that emerges from the cultural output of the last decade exhibits a paradoxical movement both toward and away from feminist consciousness. Although Israel is still far from being a haven for feminism, both male and female writers share a new recognition of androgyny, one more in tune with contemporary versions of the concept.[2] While few young male writers declared themselves "feminists" (see Kobi Niv's 1990 *'Ani feminist* [I Am a Feminist (m.)]), veteran male writers announced their fascination with the literary construction of women, "the superior sex," but could not avoid killing off their female protagonists in so doing (A. B. Yehoshua in *Molkho* [Five Seasons], 1987 and *Massaʿ 'el tom he'elef* [A Journey to the End of the Millennium], 1997; Amos Oz in *Ladaʿat 'ishah* [To Know a Woman], 1989; and Meir Shalev in *Keyamim 'aḥadim* [As a Few Days], 1994). On the other hand, younger (and not so young) women writers who emerged toward the end of the 1980s have mostly bypassed the feminist romance (or any other model of feminist narrative).[3] It goes without saying that for this generation the masked autobiography has lost its raison d'être altogether.

So what is this new wave of women's fiction all about? While a few among these writers have distinguished themselves as unique voices that deserve (and receive) attention, we still lack the required distance and perspective to judge the phenomenon as a whole. In what follows I therefore draw merely a general outline of the broad picture, while pointing out some of its more prominent voices.

To begin with, along with the feminist romance, the oedipal masterplot in this literature is also put under scrutiny, giving way to other narratives. These often pursue traditional "female" themes, such as love and personal relationships, while fashioning a recognizable "feminine poetics." Some of these writers follow the thematics and poetics of the early Kahana-Carmon rather than those prominent in the novels of the 1980s. The most veteran among these is Savyon Liebrecht (b. 1948), who has carved out her own style in a series of short story collections, published since 1986 (see especially *Sinit 'ani medaberet 'eleicha* [It's All Greek to You, 1992] and the selection *Apples from the Desert*, recently released in English, 1998). Other variations of these feminine poetics include the foregrounding of female desire, often of the frustrated kind, or the "poetics of the body" (Yehudit Katzir, whose 1990 *Closing the Sea* is available in English, 1992; cf. Michal Govrin, Zeruya Shalev, Nitza Ken, Shifra Horn, Yael Hadaya, Dorit Rabinyan) or of mother-daughter relations (Repler-Zilberstein, Batya Gur, 1994, Eleonora Lev). Most of these new stories put a different spin on "old" motifs, as illustrated, for example, by the teasing title of a recent collection of women's short stories, *Nymphs in Jeans.*

Still another group of writers apply this thematic cluster—utilizing quite a broad range of different poetics, to be sure—to the newly discovered area of the religious sector of Israeli society. Some confront head on the constraints imposed on women in this community, especially in the areas of education (both general and sexual) and marriage—bitterly criticizing the objectivization of women as brides (in arranged marriages), wives, and mothers (Yehudit Rotem, Yocheved Brandeis). Others weave more sophisticated narratives about unrequited love and repressed sexual desire, which strike the reader as especially powerful precisely because they are set against an oppressive, "no-exit" Orthodox society (Hannah Bat Shahar) or because they walk the delicate line between the modern-observant (rural) community and the secular urban world, fully cognizant of the inadequacies of each (Mira Magen). The novelty of this thematics in Israeli literature—much more prominent among women authors than among men authors—has already attracted the attention of the media but still awaits full scholarly evaluation.[4]

Other expansions of women's creativity include fictional representations of the Holocaust, particularly from the perspective of the second generation—an experience the women share on the whole with their male peers (Nava Semel, Savyon Liebrecht, Dorit Peleg, Gila Almagor, Lily Perry, Rivka Keren)—or new genres, such as the thriller or detective story (see the introduction, note 17). Women have also made their presence felt as writers and directors for the screen and the stage (Michal Bat Adam, Gila Almagor, Shulamit Lapid, Michal Govrin, Miriam Kaini, Gail Hareven). While few authors construct fractured, postmodernist subjectivities (Dorit Peleg, Zippora Dolan, Lea Ayalon, Lea Aini), still fewer directly engage feminist issues (Gail Hareven), though not always in the most convincing manner.[5] Finally, special attention should go to the work of Ronit Matalon (b. 1960), whose 1995 outstanding novel, *Zeh 'im hapanim 'eleinu*, now in English translation (*The One Facing Us*, 1998), successfully imports postcolonial modalities, extending even further the boundaries of contemporary women's fiction in Israel.[6]

The fictional variety of female creativity has also been stretched by the appearance of another genre that was formerly available in Hebrew only in translation—the popular romance (Irit Linor, Geffi Amir). This non-canonic Hebrew genre has been bolstered by the revival of some "dead areas" in the history of women writing in Hebrew. Literary scholars have recently brought to light prose fiction that thrived on the margins of the literary canon earlier in this century (Shoshana Shababu, Pnina Kaspi). With this they have restored balance to a cultural polysystem that had been totally dominated by a strong canonic center.

As the reader may recall, this multifaceted, burgeoning phenomenon took the Israeli readership by surprise. It naturally caused many eyebrows to be raised, in both admiration and panic (i.e., the temporary "male backlash" cited in the introduction). Among these immediate responses, however, there was at least one serious attempt to gauge the meaning of the "inundation of Israeli fiction," as Amalia Kahana-Carmon called it in 1996, by women writers. Indeed, her latest statement may offer an initial insight into the issue at hand. Kahana-Carmon's perspective on the writers of the nineties concluded the interview titled "Women Who Run with She-Wolves" with which this study opens.[7] In her analysis this veteran feminist unflinchingly continued to weave the line of argument she developed in her essays throughout the 1980s. "The answer is rather simple," she avers.[8]

> We live in a time of change—the walls of the consensus have collapsed, at least for now. The pose of the outsider is "in." Attention is given, though fleetingly, only to the "margins," just because they are "margins." The more these margins are exceptional and extravagant, the more they are sought after. . . .
>
> In this picturesque chorus—why not—among all the rest, there is also room for the voice of a woman, although the existential experience about which she writes has been perceived until now as [an experience] outside the general repertoire. . . .
>
> For as long as we were a community that perceived itself to be under duress, and as long as the "collective I" occupied center stage . . . this was the picture:
>
> . . . While those [collective] experiences constituted the cornerstone of Hebrew fiction, which functioned as the spiritual synagogue of the secular Jew, woman's existential experience had to sit down silently, separately, ghettoized behind the partition, in the secular women's gallery of [Hebrew] fiction. . . .
>
> In fact, this is the norm today too. With one difference: Today, since to be marginal and minor is "in," woman's ways of experiencing her life and the world suddenly find an equal place. But where?
>
> —Within the lines of the riffraff that make up the camp of minorities, who are all bizarre in their own right. This riffraff today constitutes the "good guys." Now, in this newly topsy-turvy world, the "bad guys" are those who not long ago represented the normative "collective I," the canonic Israeli experience. This "collective I" has now lost its stature. And the rats are abandoning the sinking ship.

Cassandra-like, Kahana-Carmon does not let go of her familiar metaphors. Nor does she hesitate to throw a monkey wrench into the exhilarating sense of equality ostensibly illustrated by the current proliferation of women's creativity. Obviously, she does not trust the seismographic upheavals that have shaken Israel's normative system, shifting around center and periphery, mainstream and margins. While the younger generation of women seem to enjoy their moment of glory, their current center-stage position, the seasoned artist is worried that the change may prove transitory; that when order is restored woman will be returned to her seat behind the partition. In other words: as she sees it, the recent victory does not constitute a true metamorphosis in woman's place, only a temporary shift in the general social map. Ironically, this shift, the collapse of the Zionist metanarrative against the constraints of which Kahana-Carmon had inveighed throughout the 1980s, has apparently made feminism seem superfluous for the women of the 1990s. The fall of women's "other," the national consensus, has paradoxically preempted the urgency of feminist liberation.

Kahana-Carmon's argument is an intriguing exposition of the effect of postmodernism on Israeli culture. Although she does not use the *p* word, her metaphorical language vividly portrays the impact of this recently imported worldview on both the national narrative and the feminist project. Here, finally, we encounter an Israeli version of the infamous "postmodernist threat to the feminist subject" that has torn apart contemporary feminism (see the introduction, section 3). While it has affected most writers of the 1990s (male and female) unwittingly by and large, it has been employed with a vengeance by the writer Orly Castel-Bloom (b. 1960), by far the most audacious, innovative, and prolific among the group that has made its appearance since the late 1980s. Her unique voice—articulated in three collections of stories and four novels, published since 1987—has already left its mark on Israeli prose fiction. Predictably, her work has also bewildered the scholarly establishment, dividing critics precisely over the question of her position within the malestream of Hebrew literature (namely, the meta-Zionist narrative) on the one hand, and within the recent tradition of feminist protest on the other. Although all seem to agree on labeling her a *postmodernist*, there is little agreement on the precise meaning of this label, nor on its impact on the *feminism* some critics expect her to deliver.[9] Indeed, Castel-Bloom fully demonstrates that from the perspective of the post-Zionist, postmodernist 1990s, the New Hebrew Woman is one more *grand récit*, to recall Lyotard's useful formulation, whose time is over.[10]

I would argue, however, that despite the obvious postmodernity of Castel-Bloom's fictional world (e.g., its constant wavering between the literal and the metaphorical [see McHale] and its subversive debunking of essences and boundaries), it does not achieve the total dislocation and decentering characteristic of postmodern fiction at large. In a typically Israeli way, her fantasy world (see especially her 1992 novel, *Dolly City*, published in English in 1997), is deeply anchored in Zionist realities. The novel conducts a dialogue—albeit through parody—with foundational Zionist texts (Herzl's utopias, as shown by Ginor) as well as with a major Hebrew/Jewish (as well as Zionist) paradigm, the akedah (see chapters 6, 7 of this study). At the same time, it also takes feminism to task: to the extent that this unorthodox akedah is carried out by Dolly (a single mother of sorts), the plot may be read as a feminist appropriation of a traditionally patriarchal role. Yet the narrative perspective takes away what the plot may seem to imply, undercutting any delusion of a meaningful crossing over of gender boundaries within the Zionist metanarrative— itself an object of debunking and deconstruction. In the final analysis it is the belief in the bankruptcy of all metanarratives that Castel-Bloom shares with her postmodernist male peers (Etgar Kerett, Yitzhak Laor), all (generational?) differences between their poetics notwithstanding (cf. Yuval Shimoni, Yoel Hoffmann, Avram Heffner).[11]

This eclipse of the Enlightenment metanarrative (the foundation of both Zionist ideology and liberatory feminism, as I argued in chapter 8) is doubly palpable in various areas of academic scholarship, from art and literature to politics and history. A cursory look at several pioneering publications that had foregrounded the subject of women in the early 1990s will uncover a preference for postmodernist or continental models (primarily Lacanian and Kristevan). This is true for the July 1989 issue of the journal *Politika*, for *Feminine Presence*, a catalogue of a 1990 exhibit by Israeli women artists at the Tel Aviv Museum to which Deganit Berest, our frontispiece artist, is a major contributor, *Zman hanashim* [Women's Time, echoing Kristeva's essay by this name], a 1993 issue of the historical quarterly *Zemanim*, and the heated 1994 literary exchange carried out in the pages of the cutting-edge journal *Te'oria vebikoret* (Theory and Criticism), in which the participants pulled no punches in a manner that should discount any argument for sexual difference.[12]

Within this postmodernist climate the tension between gender and nation has naturally not abated. What has been lost in fictional visibility has been gained in scholarly interest and political activism. The first may be exemplified by a conference dedicated to "Feminine Identity and the National Narrative in Israel," held in 1993 at the Van Leer Institute (representing the gender component of *Te'oria vebikoret*'s postcolonial agenda; the aforementioned journal was founded by the same institute in 1992). The second is best illustrated by the women's peace and protest movement (still active today, calling for Israel's withdrawal from Lebanon), which took on the suggestive name Four Mothers (see chapter 6). Still a different area of conflict has recently surfaced in the Orthodox sector, where women's demand for a more liberal education is confronted by the growing conservatism of their community (see chapter 4). Nevertheless, notwithstanding Kahana-Carmon's conclusion that "only time will tell what is to remain from all these galloping batallions,"[13] it seems that a kaleidoscopic portrait of new Israeli women—artists, critics, political activists—is slowly emerging, no doubt fashioning new modalities of feminist consciousness for the coming century.

Appendixes

APPENDIX B   ISRAELI WOMEN'S FICTION IN ENGLISH

Almog, Ruth. *Death in the Rain*. Trans. Dalya Bilu. Santa Fe: Red Crane, 1993.

Baron, Dvora. *The Thorny Path*. Trans. Joseph Schachter. Jerusalem: Israel Universities Press, 1969.

Castel-Bloom, Orly. *Dolly City*. Trans. Dalya Bilu. London: Loki, 1997.

Dayan, Yael. *New Face in the Mirror*. Cleveland and New York: World, 1959.

Eytan, Rachel. *The Fifth Heaven*. Trans. Philip Stimpson. Philadelphia: Jewish Publication Society, 1985.

Govrin, Michal. *The Name*. Trans. Barbara Harshav. New York: Riverhead, 1998.

Gur, Batya. *Murder on Saturday Morning*. Trans. Dalya Bilu. New York: HarperCollins, 1992.

— *A Literary Murder*. Trans. Dalya Bilu. New York: HarperCollins, 1993.

— *Murder on A Kibbutz*. Trans. Dalya Bilu. New York: HarperCollins, 1994.

— *Murder Duel: A Musical Case*. Trans. Dalya Bilu. New York: Harper-Collins. 1999.

Hareven, Shulamit. *City of Many Days*. Trans. Hillel Halkin. San Francisco: Mercury House, 1993 [1977].

— *The Miracle Hater*. Trans. Hillel Halkin. Berkeley: North Point, 1988.

— *Prophet*. Trans. Hillel Halkin. Berkeley: North Point, 1990.

— *Twilight and Other Stories*. Trans. Hillel Halkin. San Francisco: Mercury House, 1992.

— *The Vocabulary of Peace*. Trans. Marsha Weinstein et al. San Francisco: Mercury House, 1995.

— *Thirst: The Desert Trilogy*. Trans. Hillel Halkin. San Francisco: Mercury House, 1996.

Hendel, Yehudit. *The Street of Steps*. Trans. Rachel Katz and David Segal. New York and London: Herzl and Thomas Yoseloff, 1963.

Horn, Shifra. *Four Mothers*. Trans. Dalya Bilu. New York: St. Martin's, 1999.

Katzir, Yehudit. *Closing the Sea* (Stories). Trans. Barbara Harshav. New York: Harcourt, Brace, Jovanovich, 1992.

Liebrecht, Savyon. *Apples from the Desert*. Trans. Marganit Weingerger-Rotman, et.al. New York: Feminist Press, 1998.

Matalon, Ronit. *The One Facing Us*. Trans. Marsha Weinstein. New York: Henry Holt, 1998.

Rabinyan, Dorit. *Persian Brides*. Trans. Yael Lotan. New York: Braziller, 1998.

Shalev, Zeruya. *Love Life*. Trans. Dalya Bilu. New York: Grove, 2000.

Notes

INTRODUCTION

1. Estés, *Women Who Run with the Wolves*, *Ratzot 'im ze'evim*, trans. Hirsh.
2. See Lazovski, "Running with She-Wolves." All translations from the Hebrew are mine, unless otherwise noted.
3. See Zevuloni (of Kibbutz Usha), "Hame'ah vehamakor."
4. Handelsaltz, "The Miraculous Revival of the Israeli Canon." Cf. an earlier press discussion by Yehuda Koren on the im/balance between canonic and popular ("airport") fiction in Israel, under the title "Is the Airport-Literature Landing?"
5. Baym, "Melodramas of Beset Manhood," p. 68.
6. Reported in Hemda Ben-Yehudah, *Ben-Yehudah*, p. 118. Quoted by Berlovitz, "The Literature of the Early Pioneer Women."
7. Baym, "Melodramas of Beset Manhood," p. 63.
8. On the English tradition, see Showalter's pioneering study, *A Literature of Their Own*.
9. Even as poets, women entered the mainstream only in the 1920s. On the problematics of this late entry see Miron, *'Imahot meyasdot*; for a partial English rendition, see his "Why Was There No Women's Poetry in Hebrew Before 1920?" in Sokoloff, Lerner, and Norich, *Gender and Text*, pp. 65–94. For a rejoinder see Gluzman, "The Exclusion of Women."
10. See Galchinsky, *The Origin of the Modern Jewish Woman Writer*.
11. For Woolf's original query about the literary output by women in the early nineteenth century, see *A Room of One's Own*, p. 55: "But why, I could not help asking, as I ran my eyes over them, were they, with few exceptions, all novels?" As for the Hebrew/Israeli "difference," it is addressed in chapters 1 and 5.
12. In English see Baron, *The Thorny Path*.
13. Cf., for example, the poeticizing effects indulged in by such epic or dramatic prose writers as Moshe Shamir (especially in his 1947 first novel *Hu halakh basadot*) and Igal Mossinshon (*'Aforim kasak*, 1946). Gershon Shaked, in his *Hebrew Narrative Prose*, vol. 4, rightly points to the dominance of poetry in the intellectual climate of the time (p. 46 et passim). These novelists' prose style was influenced by Avraham Shlonski and Natan Alterman, while their titles were borrowed from poems by the latter (pp. 242–245). Leah Goldberg was slightly more original in her choice of title, culling it from a

medieval poem by Moses Ibn Ezra, one of the luminaries of the Hebrew Golden Age in Spain.

14. Interest in this novel has grown in the 1990s, following a resurgence in the Israeli fascination with the "female malady" and its psycholiterary expressions, as illustrated in chapter 8. See Lieblich's psychobiography, *'El Lea*, pp. 37–40. Despite its autobiographical material, however, this novel cannot be considered a precursor of contemporary women's fictional autobiography, for the reasons I discuss in chapter 1, note 25.

15. Most notorious in this regard is Amalia Kahana-Carmon, whose "feminine" (namely, poetic) style—paramount in both her shorter and longer narratives—has been a major topic of discussion throughout her career (see chapter 3); but see also Shulamith Hareven (chapters 5, 6.3), Ruth Almog (chapter 8), and the later work of Yehudit Hendel (chapter 6, note 45). Hareven, as well as Shulamit Lapid (chapter 1), also published collections of poetry, while Almog published poems sporadically but never collected them.

Another stylistic aspect that has no doubt contributed to what has been perceived as feminine writing is the strong pictorial element present in the works of Kahana-Carmon and Almog, both of whom share an active interest in painting as well.

16. The major exception to this rule is Naomi Frenkel's historical trilogy, the autobiographically based saga *Shaul and Yohanna*, which was published in the 1950s and 60s (1956, 1962, 1969). Less epic in their scope were the social novels published by Yehudit Hendel (1956, 1969) and Rachel Eytan (1962, 1974). Finally, credit should be given to the wife-and-husband team, Yonat and Alexander Sened, for their early attempts at epic representation of the historical nexus of Zionism and Holocaust (1951, 1958–1964).

17. I have described this growing phenomenon in my articles "Historical Novels or Masked Autobiographies?" "Gender In/Difference in Contemporary Hebrew Fictional Autobiography," "Feminism Under Siege: The Vicarious Selves of Israeli Women Writers," and "Ideology and Self-Representation of Women in Israeli Literature."

In English the new territory covered by women writers is represented by the mystery novels of Batya Gur (b. 1947), published since the late 1980s, e.g., *Murder on Saturday Morning*, *A Literary Murder*, and *Murder on a Kibbutz*, translated by Dalya Bilu (1992, 1993, 1994). The pioneer of the genre was, however, Shulamith Hareven (see chapter 5), who published the thriller *The Link* under a male nom de plume. A different kind of thriller was introduced by Shulamit Lapid (discussed in chapter 1). The popularity of these detective novels has recently brought more female (as well as male) writers into the fold, e.g., Ruth Almog (chapter 8) and Esther Ettinger, *A Perfect Lover*, Adiva Geffen, *A Murder Upon First Reading*, with two more sequels, 1997, 1998.

Cf. Berg, "Oleh ḥadash," and Furstenberg, "Israeli Thrillers," who draws attention to possible gender differences within the genre as well as to the new fusions in the second (female) generation (e.g., Limor Nachmias, *Mother Used to Creep, Pinch me*).

18. See Aschkenasi, *Eve's Journey*, and Fuchs, *Israeli Mythogynies*.

19. The only exception is Bar Yosef's article on Bialik's poetry; see Sokoloff, Lerner, and Norich, *Gender and Text*, pp. 145–170.

20. Cf. Sokoloff's more extensive survey, "The Impact of Feminist Research."

21. An English version of this collection, *Ribcage* (edited by Diament and Rattok), includes a different selection, probably dictated by the availability of translations, plus a partial rendition of Rattok's postscript (pp. xvi–xxxiv). Both essays, however, conspicuously ignore feminist and gender-oriented studies of Israeli prose fiction written on this side of the Atlantic for the last decade.

A similar "repression" of antecedents unfortunately takes place in a new Israeli study of women writers, Shirav's *Ktivah lo' tamah*, which has reached me upon completion of my own manuscript. This otherwise well-researched and cogent book neglects to mention that one of its major parameters, "patterns of female *Bildung*," especially in novels that practice "historical displacement," was mapped out by myself in a series of articles, in Hebrew and English, between 1986 and 1991, as detailed in note 17 above (see also chapter 1). Especially disturbing is Shirav's use of the Hebrew concept *harḥakat ʿedut* in this connection (p. 130), without acknowledging that this was the key concept I had introduced in my pioneering Hebrew essay in 1986 (p. 208), which she cites in her endnote without any comment.

22. These anthologies, facilitated by the Israeli Institute for the Translation of Hebrew Literature, have appeared as far away as India. See *Stories from Women Writers of Israel*; Domb, *New Women's Writing from Israel*. An additional selection appears in Abramson, *The Oxford Book of Hebrew Short Stories*.

A breakthrough of sorts in the translation of women's novels is currently taking place, although it pertains mostly to the young generation of the 1990s, as I outline in the afterword to this volume.

23. Scholarship has not paid attention to this phenomenon yet. See Gurevitch's "Feminism and Postmodernism," whose heroines are Grace Paley, Cindy Sherman, and the late Israeli poet Yona Wallach. (For a somewhat extended version see chapter 5 of his recent book, *Postmodernism*). In his "Postmodernism in Israeli Literature," published in *Modern Hebrew Literature*, he treats, on the other hand, the young Orly Castel-Bloom as well without so much as mentioning her "gender trouble" (punning on Judith Butler's title; see the following note); the same holds true for the relevant chapters (10–12) in his *Postmodernism*, where Hebrew literature plays a small role. Con-

versely, the radio symposium on this theme, conducted by Avraham Balaban and published in the same issue of *Modern Hebrew Literature* (pp. 3–5), sorely misses central foci of recent postmodernist discourse, some of which are explored in the present study. Similarly, Balaban's recent book on postmodernism in Israeli fiction, *Hagal ha'aher* (The Other/Different Wave), treats male writers only.

24. Jardine's "Gynesis" was first presented in *Diacritics* and later published as *Gynesis: Configurations of Woman and Modernity*.

For a fuller history of feminism as a historically changing concept and movement see Offen, "Defining Feminism." The debate over the feminism/postmodernism nexus within the American camp is evident in the exchange between Daryl McGowan Tress and Jane Flax in the same issue of *Signs* (no. 14, 1988), pp. 196–203. Although criticized for siding with the postmodern deconstruction of subjectivity, Flax's later wide-ranging probing of this issue, *Thinking Fragments*, clearly spells out the "*un*usefulness" of this practice for "feminist emancipation" (see especially her "No Conclusion," pp. 225, 230 et passim). For a different perspective on this question see Butler, *Gender Trouble*, and *Bodies That Matter*.

More generally on this problem see Nicholson, *Feminism/Postmodernism*; Sherzer, "Postmodernism and Feminisms"; and Ferguson and Wicke, *Feminism and Postmodernism*.

25. Flax, *Thinking Fragments*, p. 220.

26. The definition of postmodernist poetics (especially in its relation with modernism) is a problem that requires a separate discussion. Of the vast literature on the subject, see, for example, Hutcheon, *A Poetics of Postmodernism*. See also note 49 below.

I address this issue in my "Postcolonial Memory, Postmodernist Intertextuality."

27. See Balaban, *Hagal ha'aher*.

28. The "New Hebrew Woman" is a conflation of the "New Hebrew Man" of Zionist ideology at the turn of the century and the "New Woman" propagated by Virginia Woolf and other early feminists. The former has been interpreted for the English reader in Harshav's *Language in Time of Revolution*; for the latter, see Showalter, *A Literature*, chapters 7, 8. Cf. Shilo, "The Double or Multiple Image of the New Hebrew Woman."

29. Findings on this issue have been published in Hebrew since the early 1980s (ironically, mostly by women of "Anglo-Saxon" background, as I argue in chapter 6). The "literary" expression of women's discontents at the beginning of the century (including Ben-Yehudah's wife Hemda mentioned above) is brought out in Berlovitz's collection, *Stories by Women of the First Aliya*.

In English see Izraeli, "The Zionist Women's Movement in Palestine, 1911–1927"; and Bernstein, "The Women Workers' Movement in Pre-State

Israel, 1919–1939"; for an overview see Bernstein, *Pioneers and Homemakers.* Of special interest to our topic are the essays by Yaffa Berlovitz, Sylvi Fogel-Bijoui, Dafna Izraeli, and the editor. Cf. Swirski and Safir, *Calling the Equality Bluff*, and Azmon and Izraeli, *Women in Israel*, which includes a valuable bibliography. See also chapter 8, "Zionism as an Erotic Revolution" in Biale, *Eros and the Jews*, whose major theme is the internal ideological contradictions within the Zionist movement on the issue of erotic liberation and gender equality. This chapter also makes clear that it was mostly the women who articulated their unease about this problem.

30. See Ben Yehuda's *1948—Between Calendars, Through the Binding Ropes, When the State Broke Out.* Not accidentally, Ben Yehuda's Palmach trilogy coincided with the revisionist historical and sociological feminist research that also gained momentum in the 1980s. Her idiosyncratic language, however, as well as her stylistic hybridity (not history, not fiction, just "her report" from the field) made her texts less transparent. While her general subversion of the Palmach's mythological aura was immediately grasped, causing great upheaval, most of the reviewers (even women) did not properly appreciate the extent to which gender *in*equality is the deep trauma that has both motivated and structured her "novels." See chapter 7, this volume, and my Hebrew article, "'Anu, 'anu hapalmach: A Subversive View from the Women's Gallery."

31. Schohat's biography, *Before Golda*, told by Rachel Yanait Ben-Zvi, is available in English. See also Reinharz, "Manya Wilbushewitz-Shohat and the Winding Road to Sejera." Rachel Katznelson-Shazar's lifelong diaries were published posthumously as *'Adam kemo shehu* (The Person as She Was), unveiling for the first time her conflicts between a twenty-five-year career as an editor of *Devar Hapo'elet* (from its establishment in 1934 to 1959), as a writer of literary essays (which she began writing in 1918, but ultimately gave up on; collections appeared in 1946 and 1966), and her other social commitments as an activist in the women's movement, a mother, and a wife of the future president of Israel, Zalman Shazar (1963–1972). Cf. Miron, *'Imahot meyasdot*, pp. 249–272, and Harshav, *Language in Time of Revolution*, pp. 183–194. On Dvora Baron in English, see Lieblich, *Conversations With Dvora*, trans. Naomi Seidman. For more about her, see below, chapter 1, note 21. The life and work of the poet Rachel has given rise to a whole industry that is outside the pale of our subject (i.e., women *prose* writers).

32. Dayan, *New Face in the Mirror.* For a cogent analysis of its "nonfeminism" see Ulman-Margalit, "A Different Face in the Mirror."

33. See on this point Shulamith Hareven's 1971 argument in "Shonim ve-shavim" (see chapter 5, this volume). Golda Meir, another link in the "false" Israeli equal rights' image, would have certainly share this sentiment. Cf. chapter 6, this volume.

Ironically, recent research has placed the ideological roots of Betty Friedan, whose *Feminine Mystique* had initially defined the "suburban" character of American feminism, in the communist politics of the labor movement in the 1940s and fifties. In a paradoxical way Friedan is now faulted for "suppressing" precisely that social consciousness she was criticized as lacking both in Israel and, later, in America. See Horowitz, *Betty Friedan and the Making of the "Feminine Mystique."*

34. Offen, "Defining Feminism," p. 149; see also Moi, *Sexual/Textual Politics*, p. 91; and Ferguson and Wicke, *Feminism and Postmodernism*, pp. 86–102. Cf. Nye, *Feminist Theory and the Philosophies of Man*, chapter 4, especially pp. 82 ff.

35. See Shapiro, *'Elit lelo' mamshikhim.*

36. E.g., Marcia Freedman, who finally gave up and returned to the United States in the early 1980s; see her *Exile in the Promised Land*. For more on this issue see chapter 6, this volume.

There is to date no "history" of this period, though to judge from the current ferment, some are probably in the works (as witnessed by papers and heated debates in a conference organized in Jerusalem by the Hebrew University Lafer Center for Women's Studies and the International Research Institute on Jewish Women of Hadassah/Brandeis, June 2–4, 1998).

37. See my "The 'Other Within.' " The emergence of women prose writers from the religious sector is one of the highlights of the 1990s abundance of "women's fiction."

38. See O'Brien, *The Politics of Reproduction*, p. 235 et passim.

39. See Kahana-Carmon, "The Song of the Bats," in Sokoloff, Lerner, and Norich, *Gender and Text*, p. 237 ff.

40. For a summary in English see Cohen, "Loosen the Fetters of Thy Tongue Woman." Cf. my "The Ability to Speak Entirely New Phrases"; Rattok, *An Angel of Fire*; Sarna, *Yona Wallach*; Kartun-Blum, "A Modern Mystical Experience."

A similar revival of interest in the work of an even earlier "feminist," the poet Ester Raab (1894–1981), has recently been taking place. Her *Collected Poems*, edited by Ehud ben Ezer, was reissued for the hundredth anniversary of her birth. Following Miron's lead (in *Founding Mothers*), several studies of her poems have been published as well as a biography: Ehud ben Ezer, *Days of Gall and Honey*; Bar-Yosef, "Trapped in the Equation"; Lerner, "A Woman's Song" and "The Naked Land;" Luz, *Esther Raab*.

41. Lyotard, *The Postmodern Condition*, pp. 32–37.

42. For a basic textbook (one among many), see Natoli and Hutcheon, *A Postmodern Reader*.

43. A representative of the rich literature on the subject is the comprehensive collection edited by Cadava, Connor, and Nancy, *Who Comes After*

the Subject. For a feminist rebuttal see, among others, Probyn, *Sexing the Self.*

44. Another door simultaneously opened by this decentering—that of homoerotic subjectivity; for a Jewish celebration of this opening see Boyarin, *Unheroic Conduct.*

45. Flax, *Thinking Fragments*, p. 232. In fact, Flax translates Luce Irigaray's continental (i.e., philosophical and metaphorical) indictment into the Anglo-American language of object relations theory and extends it to the texts of contemporary writers (Irigaray stops with Freud). See also her distinction between the notion of the "unitary" self and a "core" self, p. 210 ff.
The difficulty of giving up the notion of a core self is not unique to feminist theories. See Schwab, "The Insistence of the Subject," *Subjects Without Selves*, pp. 1–22.

46. Ostriker, *Stealing the Language*, p. 216.

47. Stimpson, "Woolf's Room, Our Project." Moi, Marcus, and Stimpson had been anticipated by Perry Meisel, however. Without any reference to her feminism, Meisel reads Woolf postmodernistically, highlighting her Derridean "difference from herself," especially in her deconstruction of "the Captain self, the Key self" in *Orlando* (*The Absent Father*, p. 159). For detailed studies see Marcus, Pinkney, and Caughie.

48. Kristeva, "Women's Time" (1979). For more about her essay, see chapter 2, this volume.

49. On postmodernism's constant oscillation and refusal to choose, and its defiance of the "logically necessary" either/or choices, see Hassan, *The Postmodern Turn*, p. 89. Brian McHale limits this oscillation to the choice between the literal and the metaphorical (*Postmodernist Fiction*); while Natoli and Hutcheon define it as "a commitment to doubleness" (*A Postmodern Reader*, p. xi).

50. See Benhabib and Cornell, *Feminism as Critique*, p. 15.

51. See especially a Kristevan interpretation of Amalia Kahana-Carmon by Feldhai, "Drash nashi" (A Feminine Midrash); and Orly Lubin's application of Patrocinio Schweickart's "feminist theory of [subversive] reading" to a story by Ruth Almog in "A Woman Reading a Woman." Both were critiqued by Rattok, "Two Responses," and both summarily rejected her critique in the same issue, pp. 178–181.

52. Translated from the Russian by Tzvetan Todorov in his *Mikhail Bakhtin*, p. 13.

53. Selections of *The Second Sex* were, however, published, appropriately, in the left-wing working women's journal *Devar Hapo'elet*, no. 28, 1962.

54. On the adoption of Western existentialism, especially by the literary journal *'Akhshav* (Now), as part of the revolt against the "social literature of the Palmach generation," see Gertz, *Hirbet hiz'a vehaboker shelemohorat*, p. 35.

55. Camus's *Letters to a German Friend* was translated from the French by Adina Kaplan and included a postscript by David Ohana. Reviewed by Nirad, "Nationalism and Humanism."

56. Keisari, "A Woman Recipient of the Prize."

57. Beauvoir, *Hamandarinim*, trans. Zvi Arad.

58. For a list see Moi, *Simone de Beauvoir*, p. 301.

59. Typically, these reviews were written by women—some of them writers we will meet later in this story (Leah Goldberg, Jacqueline Kahanoff, Shulamit Lapid), and often published in the "working woman's" journal, *Devar Hapo'elet*.

60. Personal communication, December 13, 1998. A tape of a meeting, which also included writers Amos Oz and Amos Kenan (invited "at her request," says Shalvi), is available at the Widener Library, Harvard University. For press coverage, see *Davar/Massa'*, April 25, 1975, p. 1, and May 9, 1975, p. 3.

61. Beauvoir, *Mavet kal me'od*, trans. Mira Frankel.

62. Ibid., *'Isha shvura*, trans. Miryam Tiv'on. For a representative critical review see the veteran journalist Heda Boshes, "Simone de Beauvoir—with No Delusions."

63. Beauvoir, *Damam shel 'aherim*, trans. Miryam Tiv'on.

64. See Paz, "The Observers of an Ethical Double Standard."

65. Especially Bair, *Simone de Beauvoir*. The essence of Bair's "exposé" was summed up in the title of her column in the *New York Times Magazine*: "Do as She Said, Not as She Did" (1990).

66. The title of Ariana Melamed's preview of a television program on Beauvoir, apparently inspired by Bair's biography. Cf. Adar's necrology, "Simone de Beauvoir"; Paz, "The Death of the Princess Beauvoir"; and a commemorative interview a decade after her death, Hazak, "The Woman Who Broke Frameworks."

67. For the contemporary revival of interest in *The Second Sex* see Butler "Variations on Sex and Gender: Beauvoir, Wittig and Foucault," in Benhabib and Cornell, *Feminism as Critique*, pp. 128–142; Nye, *Feminist Theories and the Philosophies of Man*, pp. 73–114; Moi, *Simone de Beauvoir*; Moi, "Ambiguity and Alienation in *The Second Sex*," in Ferguson and Wicke, *Feminism and Postmodernism*, pp. 86–102.

68. For a rare treat (and treatment) of *Flush* see Caughie, *Virginia Woolf and Postmodernism*, chapter 5: "*Flush* and the Literary Canon: The Value of Popular Appeal."

69. Woolf, *Orlando*, trans. Zvi Arad.

70. Renan, "Facts: On Virginia Woolf's *The Years*."

71. Oryan Ben-Herzl, "Clarissa's Adventures"; Luchtenstein, "The Form Hidden in the Chaos."

72. Oryan, "Boredom Has Many Faces"; Lubin, "The Forerunners of a Revolution."

73. Renan, "Virginia Woolf's Poetics and Ideology." Renan's Hebrew translation of Woolf's "The Narrow Bridge of Art" was also published in the same issue of *Hasifrut* (pp. 51–56). Cf. Renan's earlier essay, "On the Principles of Human Existence and their Artistic Embodiment in Virginia Woolf's *Mrs. Dalloway*."

74. E.g., Naomi Doudai, "Two Approaches to the Tragic: Tournier, Genet, and Virginia Woolf," and Rachel Feldhai Brenner, "D. H. Lawrence and Virginia Woolf: A Comparison of Their Concepts of the Novel"; both at Tel Aviv University, 1975. Shulamit Barzilay, "The Development of Narrative Techniques in Virginia Woolf's Fiction," Hebrew University, 1979; Brenda Oded, "The Symbolic Use of Parent-Child Relationships in Major Twentieth-Century English Novelists," Bar-Ilan University, 1981; Galia Porat, "The Function of the Conventional Direct Quotation in Virginia Woolf's *To the Lighthouse, The Waves*, and *Between the Acts*," Tel Aviv University, 1989. My thanks to Chanita Goodblatt for helping me compile a list of dissertations.

75. Ayelet Negev, interviews with Prof. Alice Shalvi and Dr. Shuli Barzilay, *Yediot Aharonot/Seven Days*, May 10, 1991, pp. 40–42, in a preview of a broadcast on Virginia Woolf, "Between the Lines." We revisit Alice Shalvi in chapter 6.2.

76. Ariana Melamed, "Who is Afraid of *Orlando?*"

77. E.g., Lindsey Hababu, "A Postmodern Reading of Virginia Woolf," 1993; Edna Kelman, "Bakhtinian Concepts and Virginia Woolf's Novels," 1997; both at Bar-Ilan University.

78. Woolf, *Between the Acts*; *Three Guineas*; "The Leaning Tower" and "The Artist and Politics" in *The Moment and Other Essays*, pp. 128–154 and 225–228, respectively. See chapter 6 for a detailed analysis.

79. On Woolf, see Joplin, "The Authority of Illusion"; Beer, "The Island and the Aeroplane"; Mepham, "Arts and Politics," in *Virginia Woolf*, pp. 159–180; Hussey, *Virginia Woolf and War*. For a different approach, see chapters 1 and 4 in Caughie, *Virginia Woolf and Postmodernism*. A representative bibliography is available in Wirth-Nesher's rejoinder, "Final Curtain on the War." My thanks to Hana Wirth-Nesher for sending me her helpful essay. See also Lee's biography, *Virginia Woolf*, and Pridmore-Brown, "1939–40."

80. See chapters 3 and 6, this volume. For a socialist interpretation of Woolf, based, first and foremost, on her notorious "call" to the working classes to join women in protesting war, see the "project" of Jane Marcus, from " 'No More Horses,' " to *Virginia Woolf and the Languages of Patriarchy*. See also Mepham, *Virginia Woolf*, pp. 148–171.

81. The literature on androgyny is too copious to be cited here. For a detailed discussion see chapters 4–8. A useful interim summary is available in Moi, *Sexual/Textual Politics*. Later additions to the debate are Weil, *Androgyny and the Denial of Difference*; and Schwartz, "The Strategy of Androgyny," chapter 5 of

her *Dead Fathers*. Most recently, two essays in the *Journal of Modern Literature*: Kennard, "Woolf, the *Dreadnought* Hoax, and Sexual Ambiguity," and Cervetti, "In the Breeches, Petticoats, and Laughter of *Orlando*." See also *The Lure of the Androgyne*, the September 1997 issue of *Mosaic* 30:3.

82. This argument, advanced to great acclaim in the 1960s by the psychiatrist H. D. Laing, was anticipated by Woolf in her diaries as well as in her novel *Mrs. Dalloway*. On the latter, see Showalter's introduction in the Penguin edition, 1991, as well as her *The Female Malady*, and "Hysteria, Feminism, and Gender." Cf. Caramagno, *The Flight of the Mind*, especially chapters 7, 9; and Kahane, *Passions of a Voice*, chapter 6.

For the application of this cluster of ideas to Hebrew literature, see chapter 8, this volume. This is perhaps the place to note that as these pages are being written a new Hebrew novel, 'Aharon Megged's *Mandrakes from the Holy Land*, features a protagonist who is an English pilgrim to Palestine in the early 1900s, a virgin ostensibly suffering from the "female malady." She is diagnosed by a psychiatrist despite the protestations of her best friend, who is, curiously enough. . . . Vanessa Stephen (V. W.'s sister)!

I. EMERGING SUBJECTS

1. Hareven, *'Ir Yamim Rabim*; *City of Many Days*, trans. Hillel Halkin. Page citations refer to the Hebrew and English editions, respectively. For a detailed analysis of this novel see chapter 5.

2. For the repatterning effects of closures and the potential rereading they may generate, see Herrenstein-Smith's classic *Poetic Closure*. On the suggested use of "interpreting signs," see Riffaterre, *Semiotics of Poetry*.

3. See Shaked, *Hebrew Narrative Prose*, vol. 4, pp. 33–37; Alter, "Fiction in a State of Siege," in his *Defenses of the Imagination*; Yudkin, *Escape Into Siege*; and my own "Feminism Under Siege." For a more critical analysis of this complex see Gertz, *Shvuya bahaloma*.

For earlier bibliography, see my "Poetics and Politics" and "Back to Vienna." The interest in the cultural nexus of literature and ideology, or the "national narrative," has grown, particularly since the 1980s, as discussed in the following chapters; for some of the titles of this scholarly orientation see Miron, *'Im lo' tihye yerushalayim*, and his *Noge'a badavar*; Shaked, *'Ein makom 'aher*; Gertz, *Sifrut ve'ideologya*; Ezer, *Sifrut ve'ideologya*.

4. See Yehoshua Sobol's 1977 play, *The Night of the Twenties*, and my analysis in "Zionism—Neurosis or Cure?" For a preliminary outline of the historical reception of psychoanalysis by Zionist culture see my "Back to Vienna."

A differently oriented exploration of the Freudian-Zionist nexus has recently been suggested by Boyarin, *Unheroic Conduct*.

5. See Feldman, "Gender In/Difference"; and " 'Living on the Top Floor.' "

6. Obvious examples of this genre are novels by David Shahar, Hanoch Bartov, and Amos Oz that are discussed in Feldman, "Gender In/Difference."

7. Ibid., p. 193.

8. In 1978, *Modern Language Notes* issue 93 was tellingly devoted to *Autobiography and the Problem of the Subject*. Rodolphe Gasche's introduction to this issue gives a good summary of the "metaphysics of the subject" typical of "classical autobiography." A more comprehensive overview of the state of the art was drawn in Olney's introduction to his edited volume, *Autobiography*. See also his edited collection *Studies in Autobiography*. Earlier theoretical milestones include Mehlman, *A Structural Study of Autobiography*; Bruss, *Autobiographical Acts*; Sturrock, "The New Model Autobiography"; cf. Spengemann, *The Forms of Autobiography*; and Lejeune, *On Autobiography*. See also note 9 below.

9. Gusdorf's seminal essay, "Conditions and Limits of Autobiography," appeared in translation in Olney, *Autobiography*, pp. 28–48; de Man's infamous essay, "Autobiography as Defacement," was published in *Modern Language Notes*; the full title of Eakin's book is *Fictions in Autobiography: Studies in the Art of Self-Invention*. However, Eakin later counterbalanced his exposition of autobiographical fictions by probing their referential aspects; see *Touching the World*.
See also Jay, *Being in the Text*.

10. See Mehlman and Sturrock, summarized in Feldman, "New Psychoanalytic Models."

11. Gunn, *Autobiography*, pp. 119–120.

12. See Rowbotham, *Woman's Consciousness, Man's World*; Chodorow, *The Reproduction of Mothering*; Gilligan, *In a Different Voice*; Person, "Sexuality as the Mainstay of Identity: Psychoanalytic Perspectives," in Stimpson and Person, *Women*, pp. 36–61.

13. See Blackburn, "In Search of the Black Female Self"; Mason, "The Other Voice"; Abel, "(E)merging Identities"; Friedman, "Women's Autobiographical Selves"; Watson, "Shadowed Presence"; Brodzki and Schenck, *Life/Lines*, especially part 2, "Colonized Subjects."

14. Ironically, in a collection of essays titled *What Does a Woman Want?* chapter 5. See Lapid's "response" to this question below.

15. Stanton, "Autogynography: Is the Subject Different?" in Stanton, *The Female Autograph*, pp. 3–20. For Brée's rejoinder, see "Autogynography."

16. Brée, "Autogynography."
If we add here Virginia Woolf's observation, in another context, that "Proust was wholly androgynous, if not perhaps a little too much of a woman" (*A Room of One's Own*, p. 85), we may uncover the unnamed basis of the cross-gender identity of these three authors—their homosexuality. In the absence of

this component in the Israeli authors discussed in this study, they present a much stronger argument for antiessentialist gender definitions.

17. See Cohen, "Personal Identity and Sexual Identity"; and Seidenberg, "Is Anatomy Destiny?"

18. See Berlovitz, "The Literature of the Early Pioneer Women"; and her collection, *Stories by Women of the First Aliya*. For the recent application of feminist reading to this early literature, see Lubin, "A Feminist Reading of Nehama Puhashevski's Stories."

19. See Jelinek, *Women's Autobiography*; Smith, *A Poetics of Women's Autobiography*; Benstock, *The Private Self*; Heilbrun, *Writing a Woman's Life*.

20. Gilbert and Gubar, *No Man's Land* 1:13.

21. Despite this divergence, however, we cannot avoid wistfully noting the sad biographic convergence between these two distant "sisters": a mysterious constitutional weakness (still undecoded to date) kept Baron in bed (Florence Nightingale-like) for most of her life, while Woolf finally paid with her life for her mental weakness.

See Govrin, *Dvora Baron*; Lieblich, *Rekamot*; *Conversations with Dvora*.

22. Personal communication, 1989.

23. Woolf, *A Room of One's Own*, pp. 55–56. Additional historical reasons adduced by Woolf are women's sensitivity to personal relations and feelings, which they developed while sitting "passively" in the family's single common sitting room, and the novelty of the novelistic genre, its lack of a rigid tradition, which allowed women to improvise more freely than in the more classical poetic genres.

24. Ibid., p. 65. Cf. Peggy Kamuf, who makes these interruptions a metaphor for female style of indirection and postponement of closure; "Penelope at Work," in her *Signature Pieces*, pp. 145–164. On the other hand, many of Woolf's disciples were troubled by the essentialist implications of her in/famous search for "a woman's sentence."

25. This is not to say that these narratives do not use autobiographical materials—e.g., Noami Frenkel, Rachel Eytan, Amalia Kahana-Carmon, Dalia Ravikovitch, Hedda Boshes, Yehudit Hendel—but rather that their writings do not take the *shape* of autobiographic retrospection. This applies also to Leah Goldberg's 1946 autobiographical novel (see introduction): Although *Vehu ha'or* may be clearly read as a belated "working through" of a deeply felt autobiographic trauma (only slightly disguised in its details), it takes the shape of a third-person narration (rather than a first-person retrospection). As such, it may have set the paradigm of the "*masked* autobiography" of women writers in Hebrew. For more on this novel, see chapter 8. On a rare development in the opposite direction, where in a direct autobiographic narration the feminist core of the story is still hedged and masked by different means, see Netiva Ben Yehuda's Palmach trilogy (chapter 7).

26. Gilbert and Gubar, *The Madwoman in The Attic*, p. 73.

27. Woolf's voluminous "autobiographical" scribbling, in notes, diaries, letters, and different fragments and sketches, was brought to light only posthumously. In her lifetime she shied away from any direct autobiographical representation. Critical editions of her novels show the tremendous effort she invested in camouflaging her "raw materials," eliminating from the final product more personally biographical material that found its way to the early draft(s). Most notoriously, *To the Lighthouse* (1927) is known as a novelistic reworking of her childhood, effectively exorcising the hold that the memory of her dead mother had on her mind for over thirty years. Recent scholarship, however, treats most of her writings as autobiographical, in different levels of disguise; see Stimpson, "The Female Sociograph"; Heilbrun, *Writing a Woman's Life*, chapter 5; Mepham, *Virginia Woolf*; and Felman, *What Does A Woman Want?*, chapter 5. For more details see chapter 4 below.

28. Although Offen traces the term to late nineteenth-century Europe, she does not find it in Russian, the historical background of *Gei Oni*, before 1898. In the Oxford Dictionary, on the other hand, which was composed between 1884 and 1928, *feminism* gets the briefest treatment of all female-related entries. It is defined as "the qualities of females," and is accompanied by the qualifier "Rare."

29. Heilbrun, *Reinventing Womanhood*, p. 134.

30. Ibid., p. 71.

31. See, for example, Gubar, "The Birth of the Artist as Heroine."

32. The literature on this issue is too vast to be cited here, stretching from Coltun, *The Jewish Woman*, and Heschel, *On Being a Jewish Feminist*, to Levitt, *Jews and Feminism*. For a recent overall review and bibliography see Azmon's introduction to her edited volume, "Judaism and the Exclusion of Women from the Public Arena," *A Window Onto Women's Lives in Jewish Communities* [Hebrew], pp. 13–43. On the Israeli scene, see Kahana-Carmon, "The Song of the Bats," in Sokoloff, Lerner, and Norich, *Gender and Text*. See also chapter 2 below, note 7, and chapter 4.3.

Attention should be called, however, to the growing literature that seeks to stress a diametrically opposite perspective—the tradition of Jewish women's activism and their recent adoption of feminist agendas, especially in America; see, for example, Pogrebin, *Deborah, Golda, and Me*; Sacks, *Active Voices*; Fishman, *A Breath of Life*.

33. I borrow the concept from Abel, Hirsch, and Langland, *The Voyage In*, which nicely puns on Virginia Woolf's first published novel of undevelopment (ending in the death of the aspiring heroine), *The Voyage Out* (1915).

34. For a recent analysis and a comprehensive bibliography of this much debated and studied topic, see Judith Buber Agassi, "Theories of Gender Equality: Lessons from the Israeli Kibbutz," in Azmon and Izraeli, *Women in*

Israel. Cf. Bernstein, "The Women Workers' Movement" and *Pioneers and Homemakers*, Izraeli,"The Zionist Women's Movement"; and Hazleton, *Israeli Women.*

35. Shulamit Lapid, personal communication, 1984.

Literature does not score much higher on this point, the few exceptions notwithstanding, for example, Alper, *Hamitnahalim bahar*, and Shamir, *Tahat hashemesh,* and *Rahok mipninim.* Israeli literature has done well in inscribing women's victimization, as shown by Fuchs, *Israeli Mythogynies,* but not their "equal sharing" in the pioneering project. As conteporary scholarship redresses this lacuna, perhaps literature will accordingly follow. See Shiloh, "The Woman—A 'Worker' or a 'Member.' "

36. See Oryan, "The Wild East"; and cf. Har'el, "Around the Settlement."

37. Miller, *The Heroine's Text.*

38. See Lapid, "Haroman haromanti."

39. Feldman "Inadvertent Feminism."

40. Feldman, "Historical Novels or Masked Autobiographies?" [Hebrew]; see note 17 of the introduction.

41. Hazleton, *Israeli Women,* p. 93. For the sociocultural context in which this book was written see chapter 6.2, this volume.

42. Neumann, *The Origins and History of Consciousness*; and *Amor and Psyche.*

43. Neumann, *The Great Mother.*

44. See Heilbrun, *Reinventing Womanhood,* pp. 140 ff.; Edwards, "The Labors of Psyche"; Mary Anne Ferguson, "The Female Novel of Development and the Myth of Psyche," in Abel, Hirsch, and Langland, *The Voyage In,* pp. 228–243.

45. For the place of this concept in Virginia Woolf's thought (and after) see below, chapters 4–8.

46. I explore this issue in "Zionism—Neurosis or Cure?" and "Back to Vienna"; see note 4 above.

47. Beauvoir, *The Second Sex,* p. 161; and see chapter 2 for my analysis.

48. See Offen, pp. 134ff. For an overview of the history of this received dichotomy in the deliberations of gender theory see next chapter. The debate over the complicity of philosophy and psychoanalysis in the valorization of gender stereotypes, opened by Irigaray's *Speculum of the Other Woman,* is still raging. Cf. Lloyd, *The Man of Reason.* Later writings emphasize the politics of gender identity, as in the works of Flax and Butler. Cf. Boyarin, *A Radical Jew.*

A helpful corrective to the binarism of male independence versus female dependence has been suggested by Johnson in her *Strong Mothers, Weak Wives.* Distinguishing between "dependency" and "interdependence," or between "dependent" and "relational" (or "expressive"), she argues that "whereas a woman's relational needs get defined as her 'dependency,' men may disguise their dependency needs because they are being met everyday by women. . . . Women are financially dependent on men, but this dependence must not be confused with psychological dependency" (p. 46).

49. Freud, *Civilization and its Discontents* (New York: Norton, 1969), p. 48.

50. Ibid.

51. Deleuze and Guattari, *Kafka*. For further discussions of the concept, see Lloyd, *Nationalism and Minor Literature*.

52. Bhabha, *Nation and Narration*.

53. See *Lilith* (Summer 1989), p. 20, where a translation of Lapid's story "The Bed" is also published (pp. 19–22).

54. Personal communication by Alice Shalvi, the organizer.

55. *Mekomon* [Local Paper], 1989; *Pitayon* [The Bait], 1991; *Hatakhshit* [The Jewel], 1992; *Ḥol ba'einaim* [Sand in the Eyes], 1997.

56. On the English tradition of female detectives see Klein, *The Woman Detective*. On the "spinster detective" in particular see Susan Katz, "Singleness of Heart," chapter 5: "The Intriguing Heroism of the Spinster-Sleuth."

On the intersection between this genre and feminist scholarship, see the life work of Carolyn Heilbrun, alias Amanda Cross, creator of amateur sleuth Kate Fansler, Ph.D.

57. Lapid has fictionalized here the popular "deconstruction" of Freud's myth of women's dependency, as suggested, for example, by Eichenbaum and Orbach, *What Do Women Want*. See also Johnson, note 48, this chapter.

58. Shulamit Lapid herself is a "happily married mother," as she said, and the former chair of the Israeli Writers Association.

59. After all, Lizzie's last name, Badiḥi, which reverberates with the Hebrew word for "joke," *bediḥa*, is perhaps meant as a warning against taking her characterization too seriously. See, for example, Miron's severe critique, "Lizzie Badiḥi's Innocence."

60. In the collection *Happy Spiders*, 1990; an English translation appeared in *Lilith* (Summer 1989). It should be noted that Lapid's earlier stories (1969, 1974, 1979) are rarely touched by feminist protest, the only exception being her story "The Order of the Garter" (1969).

61. As this manuscript goes to press, Lapid has taken another turn. Her novel *Chez Babou* gives voice to a new minority recently found on the margins of Israeli society—foreign laborers.

2. ALTERITY REVISITED: GENDER THEORY AND
ISRAELI LITERARY FEMINISM

1. I quote from the English version: Beauvoir, *The Second Sex*.

2. Flax, *Thinking Fragments*, p. 126; attributed to both Jacques Lacan and D. W. Winnicott.

3. On the Hegelian underpinning of *The Second Sex,* see Lloyd, *The Man of Reason,* chapters 5, 6. Cf. Moi, *Simone de Beauvoir,* part 2.

4. See Wittig, "One Is Not Born a Woman"; cf. Butler, in Benhabib and Cornell, *Feminism as Critique,* especially "Gender as Choice," p. 131 ff.

5. See Deleuze and Guattari, *Kafka,* and Lloyd, *Nationalism and Minor Literature;* Bhabha, *Nation and Narration; The Location of Culture.*

6. See, for example, Gilman, *Freud, Race, and Gender;* and "Hysteria, Race, and Gender."

7. E.g., Plaskow, *Standing Again at Sinai;* Boyarin, *Carnal Israel;* Davidman and Tenenbaum, *Feminist Perspectives on Jewish Studies;* T. M. Rudavsky, *Gender and Judaism;* Peskowitz and Levitt, *Judaism Since Gender.* And see my own " 'And Rebecca Loved Jacob.' "

8. On these issues see Sokoloff, Lerner, and Norich, *Gender and Text;* Baskin, *Women of the Word;* and Diament and Rattok, *Ribcage.*

9. Offen, "Defining Feminism." To judge by the reports of the "celebration" of the fiftieth anniversary party of *The Second Sex* in Paris, the French rejection of Beauvoir has not changed much. See Riding, "The World Reintroduces Beauvoir."

10. See Woolf, *Three Guineas* (1938), and her lecture "The Leaning Tower," at a meeting of the Worker's Education Association in 1940. See also chapter 6, this volume.

11. Rubin, "The Traffic in Women."

12. Ibid., p. 200.

13. Benhabib and Cornell, *Feminism as Critique,* p. 15.

14. See de Lauretis, *Technologies of Gender,* pp. 25 ff. Cf. Flax, p. 146.

15. E.g., Morgan, *Men Writing the Feminine,* p. 195.

16. Ibid., p. 196.

17. De Lauretis, *Technologies of Gender;* Butler, *Gender Trouble;* and *Bodies that Matter.*

18. See especially the critique of Young, "Is Male Gender Identity the Cause of Male Domination?"

19. Benjamin, *The Bonds of Love,* p. 221; Johnson, *Strong Mothers, Weak Wives,* p. 46.

20. Cf. Dinnerstein, *The Mermaid and the Minotaur.*

21. Gilligan, *In a Different Voice;* Ruddik, *Maternal Thinking.* These two books highlight not merely the embracing of female-specific features, but their foregrounding as superior to their male counterparts in both ethical and political terms; for Woolf's *Three Guineas* as a precedent, see chapter 6 below.

22. E.g., Mulvey, "Visual Pleasure and Narrative Cinema." For the application of this concept to Israeli cinema, see Lubin, "The Woman as Other in Israeli Cinema."

23. The reference is to Sandra Gilbert and Susan Gubar's critique of Harold

Bloom's "masculinist" conceptualization of the transmission of literary tradition. In their *The Madwoman in the Attic* (1979) they claim that his use of the "oedipal agon" as the paradigm for the relationship between literary generations is not applicable to women writers because they do not confront strong (female) precursors. They have qualified their position in *No Man's Land*, where they move to the twentieth century. My understanding of the short history of French feminism supports that later position.

24. Irigaray, *Speculum of the Other Woman*, p. 145. Cf. Lloyd, *The Man of Reason*.

25. Ibid., p. 133.

26. Ibid., p. 224.

27. Rich, *Of Woman Born*; "Compulsory Heterosexuality and Lesbian Existence."

28. Irigaray's later work, however, *The Ethics of Sexual Difference* and *Sexes and Genealogies*, points to still another direction, seeking to reevaluate heterosexuality. My thanks to Eve Tabor-Bannet and Susan Pensak, who called my attention to these books, respectively.

29. Cixous modeled this ideal after Freud's Dora (*The Portrait of Dora*, 1975).

30. See, for example, Spivak, *In Other Worlds*; and "Political Commitment and the Postmodern Critic"; de Lauretis, *Technologies of Gender*; Diamond and Quinby, *Feminism and Foucault*; Trinh Minh-ha, *Woman, Native, Other*; Suleiman, *Subversive Intent*; Mohanty, Russo, and Torres, *Third World Women*.

31. Contemporary Hebrew distinguishes between Sephardim, the presumable descendants of the fifteenth-century exiles from Spain, and Mizrahim, the recent twentieth-century immigrants from Middle East countries. See *Ha'aretz*, July 12, 1996, TV review. The leading theorist of the group is Henriette Dahan-Kalev, with whom I shared a panel at the conference "Women at the Yishuv and Early State," at the Hebrew University (June 2–4, 1998). Her consciousness-raising paper, "Mizrahi Women and the Roots of Their Political and Social Status," faithfully "translated" American gender separatist politics to the Israeli scene, without considering some of the cultural differences.

32. See note 2, this chapter.

33. For similar charges against Foucault, Lyotard et al., see de Lauretis, *Technologies of Gender*.

34. See Cornell and Thurschwell, "Feminism, Negativity, Intersubjectivity."

35. Flax, *Thinking Fragments*, p. 232.

36. Cf. Segal, *Straight Sex*.

37. In her *Gender Trouble* Butler revisits this concept in order to uncover

the repressive power of heterosexual binarism; needless to say, my questioning follows a diametrically opposite direction, one that had been sketched out in Luce Irigaray's later work, *The Ethics of Sexual Difference* and *Sexes and Genealogies*.

38. Cf. Cornell and Thurschwell's ("Feminism, Negativity, Intersubjectivity") use of Adorno's "self-difference," developed, they argue, in order to ward off the danger of "self-identity," of freezing into the Same.

39. Kristeva, *Revolution in Poetic Language*.

40. See Moi, *Sexual/Textual Politics*. For a critique, see Butler, *Gender Trouble*.

41. See *The Kristeva Reader*, pp. 187–213. See also Moi, *Sexual/Textual Politics*, p. 164 et passim; and Smith, "Julia Kristeva et al."

42. See Harcourt, "Feminism, Body, Self."

43. Other readings of this author discovered in her work aspects of Kristeva's Bakhtinian-derived concept of the "other"; see the introduction, note 51.

44. See Gilbert and Gubar's critique of this topos in their book by this name. For a fuller exploration of the conjunction of female creativity and madness/hysteria see chapter 8.

45. Kuykendall, "The Subjectivity of the Speaker."

46. Doane and Hodges, *From Klein to Kristeva*, p. 76.

47. Stanton, "Difference on Trial." See the epigraph for chapter 4, this volume.

48. Derrida, "The Law of Genre."

49. Kristeva, "Stabat Mater," in *The Kristeva Reader*, pp. 160–186.

50. On the Catholic tradition, see Warner's exhaustive survey, *Alone of All Her Sex*.

3. EMPOWERING THE OTHER: AMALIA KAHANA-CARMON

1. All translations in this chapter are mine, unless otherwise noted. In the absence of published translations, I have deliberately preserved the unconventional syntax of the original. Portions of the following analyses were presented in papers between 1988 and 1993 and published in "The 'Other Within' " and "From Feminist Romance to an Anatomy of Freedom."

2. Moi, *Sexual/Textual Politics*, p. 24.

3. Kahana-Carmon's fiction includes *Under One Roof*, stories; *And Moon in the Valley of Ayalon*; *A Piece for the Stage, in the Grand Manner*; *Magnetic Fields*; "High Stakes"; *Up in Montifer*; *With Her on Her Way Home*; *Here We'll Live*.

4. See note 36 for complete list of essays. For an annotated bibliography and a sample essay in English—which will be revisited below—see Sokoloff, Lerner, and Norich, *Gender and Text*, pp. 235–245.

5. Although she claims to have already discovered Woolf in her high school years (personal communication), the close association of Kahana-Carmon's work with Woolf's (to which some of her early stories allude) was no doubt encouraged by the publicly known fact that she spent several of her formative years as a writer in England.

On her earlier work see Shaked, *Gal ḥadash*, pp. 168–179; Balaban, *Hakadosh vehadrakon*; Herzig, *Israeli Fiction in the 1960s*; Rattok, *Amalia Kahana-Carmon*; Fuchs, *Israeli Mythogynies*; Fuchs, "Amalia Kahana-Carmon and Contemporary Hebrew Women's Fiction"; and "Amalia Kahana-Carmon's *And Moon in the Valley of Ajalon.*" On her Woolfian connection, see Shaked and Rattok, above; and Hazan-Rokem, "Like a Person Stumbling Over a Mirror."

6. See, for example, Woolf's argument with the writer Vita Sackwill-West: "As for the *mot juste*, you are quite wrong. Style is a very simple matter: it is all rhythm" (*The Letters of Virginia Woolf* 3:247), cited in Raitt, *Vita and Virginia*, p. 3.

7. On Woolf see Torgovnick, *The Visual Arts, Pictorialism, and the Novel*, especially chapter 3, "The Sisters' Art"; Gillespie, *The Sisters' Art*. On Kahana-Carmon see Gold, "To Reach the Source."

8. See Showalter, *A Literature of Their Own*, and her "Toward a Feminist Poetics." Cf. Jonathan Culler, "Reading as a Woman," in Culler, *On Deconstruction*, pp. 43–64.

9. See on this point Shaked, *Gal ḥadash*; Balaban, *Hakadosh vehadrakon*; Rattok, *Amalia Kahana-Carmon*.

10. See Woolf, *Moments of Being*.

11. Published in Kahana-Carmon, *Bikhfifah 'aḥat* (Under One Roof), pp. 136–151. See also Diament and Rattok, *Ribcage*, pp. 48–66.

12. Notice the irony of the name, particularly when contrasted with Agnon's famous heroine of that name, the symbol of piety and traditional Jewish gender roles. See Agnon, "Tehilah," in Agnon, *'Ad hena*, pp. 178–207.

13. Kahana-Carmon, *Veyare'aḥ be'emek 'ayalon*, pp. 135–142.

14. Ibid., pp. 149–151.

15. Ibid., p. 142.

16. Ibid., p. 199; emphasis added.

17. Quoted from Woolf's *Women and Writing*, in Mepham, *Virginia Woolf*, p. 137. In *A Room of One's Own* Woolf uses the ability to transcend one's emotions as THE criterion for the great artist, citing Shakespeare and Jane Austin as her prime examples.

18. See Zwerdling, *Virginia Woolf and the Real World*; and Hussey, *The Singing of the Real World*.

19. Woolf, "American Fiction," in Woolf, *The Moment and Other Essays*, p. 116; Woolf, *Collected Essays* 2:113.

20. Woolf's attraction to the Romantics is amply documented in her diary;

her modernist sublime is in fact a transformation of Wordsworth's moments of revelation, except that she found hers in the "singing of the real world" rather than in platonic visions; see also Warner, "Some Aspects of Romanticism in the Work of Virginia Woolf;" Tremper, "*Who Lived In Alfoxton?*"

For a general argument about the Romantic/Modernist continuum, in which Woolf's critical essays are established as a significant link, see Silva, *Modernism and Virginia Woolf.*

21. Kahana-Carmon, *Veyare'aḥ be'emek 'ayalon*, p. 203.

22. "Israeli" because, despite her central position in Israeli literature, Kahana-Carmon is unfortunately not familiar enough to English readers to arouse a similar stir. Although a few early stories are available in translation (for appropriate collections, see notes 21 and 22 of the introduction), none of the longer works are, a sorry situation that in this case cannot be blamed only on androcentric translation policies but also on the linguistic difficulties of the text, which—coupled with the perfectionist expectations of the author—make renditions into other languages a rather taxing task, to say the least.

23. Entry for October 23, 1929, in Woolf, *A Writer's Diary*, p. 148.

24. Entry for September 22, 1931, ibid., p. 176.

25. Kahana-Carmon, "The Song of the Bats in Flight," trans. Sokoloff, in Sokoloff, Lerner, and Norich, *Gender and Text*, p. 236 et passim.

26. See Irigaray, *Speculum of the Other Woman*; Lloyd, *The Man of Reason*; Fuss, *Essentially Speaking*; Butler, *Gender Trouble*; Boyarin, *A Radical Jew.*

27. Cf. to the disparity between A. B. Yehoshua's political polemics and his much more sophisticated novelistic representations of these issues. See on this point my "Back to Vienna" and "Back to Genesis."

28. See Jardine, *Gynesis*; Moi, *Sexual/Textual Politics*; Flax, *Thinking Fragments*; and chapter 2, this volume.

29. See Johnson's succinct summary, p. 16 ff. The overlapping of the tactical dichotomy (equal rights vs. sexual difference) with the geographical one (Anglo-American vs. French) is commonplace. Even constructions of *The Female Body in Western Culture* , (ed. by Susan Rubin Suleiman, Harvard, 1985) are neatly organized around this principle as evident in the 'prooftexts' used by the editor in her opening essay, "(Re)Writing the Body: The Politics and Poetics of Female Eroticism" (pp. 7–29).

30. Julia Kristeva, "Women's Time" (1979), in Kristeva, *The Kristeva Reader*, p. 209 et passim; and see chapter 2, this volume.

31. The pro and con arguments concerning "feminine writing" have been raised and summarized by Moi. See also Jardine and Jones, "Writing the Body."

Whether or not this concept, and especially the feminist ideology it implies, is applicable to Kahana-Carmon is in my opinion still an open question. Kahana-Carmon's style, though often cited as "feminine," is also clearly kin to the impressionism of U. N. Gnessin (1879–1913) and S. Yizhar (b. 1915), two major male writers of Hebrew prose. The question then is: Is there anything inherently (that is, essentially) feminine about this style, or is it identified as such because a woman has happened to fashion it? Another option is to adopt Julia Kristeva's notion of a supra-gender "feminine" (which she ironically applies mostly to male writers!). Although this concept would include all three writers, this position seems to me no less "essentialistic" despite (or perhaps because of) its "metaphysical" position (and see chapter 2 above).

32. Curiously, the subversive element in Kahana-Carmon's work may have similar consequences but not the same means or sources as those theorized by Kristeva. I am referring here to a debate among Israeli scholars over the applicability of Kristeva's "Semiotic" to Kahana-Carmon; see Rivka Feldhai, "Derash Nashi," *Te'oria vebikoret* 2, 1992, pp. 69–89, and Lily Rattok's response in a later issue (1994).

33. Aptly analyzed by Fuchs, *Israeli* (1987), p. 101 et passim, and in her "Amalia Kahana-Carmon's *And Moon in the Valley of Ajalon*," *Prooftexts* 8 (1988): 129–141.

As can be expected, stylistic analyses of Kahana-Carmon abound, not always, however, with an eye to its feminist function. This topic deserves a separate treatment; for best results, however, it should be done in Hebrew.

34. On the transformation of "The Whirling Sword" into "Beer-Sheba, the Capital of the Negev," in *Bikhfifah 'ahat*, pp. 52–59, see Gertz, *Hirbet hiz'ah*, p. 66. For the nostalgic representation of 1947–1948, see *Veyare'ah be'emek 'ayalon*, chapters 3–4. Cf. "The House with the Blue-Painted Stairs," *Bikhfifah 'ahat*, pp. 83–91. For a rather jaundiced view of the same era, see chapter 7 below.

35. See "Befahei nefesh" [Frustration], chapter 5 of *Veyare'ah be'emek 'ayalon*. Cf. Balaban, *Hakadosh vehadrakon*, p. 54 et passim.

36. "Lihyot 'ishah soferet" (To Be a Woman Writer), *Yediot Aharonot* (April 13, 1984): 20–21. Other programmatic essays followed: "To Be Wasted on the Peripheral," *Yediot Aharonot* (15.9.1985): 22–23; "Brenner's Wife Rides Again," *Moznaim* 59:4 (October, 1988): 13; "She Writes Rather Pleasingly, But About the Insignificant," *Yediot Aharonot* (4.2.1988): 20, 25; "The Song of the Bats in Flight," *Moznaim* (November-December, 1989): 3–7.

For her recent response to the burgeoning wave of women authors, described in my introduction, see "Why There Is a Flood of Women Writers," *Ha'aretz* (8.3.1996), and "Do You (f.) Want to Write a Book?," *Ma'ariv* (3.10.1997): 15.

37. Although far too complex for "young adults," Hebrew readers were quick to recognize echoes of the didactic "historical novels for young readers" (*Memoirs of the House of David*) that were popular in their (as well as the author's) youth; see Shamir, "And He Saw a Woman of Beauty" and Golan,

"Yearnings in Search of an Address." On the history of that didactic genre see, Nitza Ben-Ari, *Roman 'im he'avar.*

38. A third distancing technique is the special language used by the narrator, an amalgam of biblical and contemporary Hebrew that is meant to give the impression of an authentic voice from the distant 17th century. Its closest historical precedence, however, is the linguistic amalgam of the Hebrew Enlightenment novel, known for its mosaic technique and flowery idiom (*melitza*). Although this stylistic feature (and especially the beautifully-wrought purple passages it produces) has alienated as many readers as were enchanted by it, it deserves special attention as a major achievement of this text. This will be done elsewhere, however, as little justice can be rendered to this topic in translation.

39. Kahana-Carmon, *Lema'lah bemontifer*, pp. 59–192.

40. "Hasismah hanekhonah" [the correct password], an interview with Orly Lubin, *Ha'aretz* (March 9, 1984). As is her wont, the author accompanied the publication of the book with a detailed commentary, also published that year, "Hineh hasefer" (Here Is the Book). Although this essay contains fascinating clues to some structural problems in the narrative, it will take us too far afield to deal with it here. The same goes for the novel's rich allusive language and its intertextual ties with the Hebrew canon (e.g., Bialik, Agnon, Alterman, Rachel, Ravikovitch).

41. "Hasismah hanekhonah."

42. See especially Moked, "I-Thou Encounters," and Navot, "Up on Montifer." For the disagreement on the "meaning" of the novella between the author and her editor, Menahem Perry, see Yaglin, "Up by Amalia."

43. This topos caught the imagination of most readers, of both sexes; see Blatt, "The Fiction and the Captivity"; Golan, "Yearnings in Search of an Address"; Harnik, "More About Montifer"; Kubovi, "From Slavery to Freedom"; London, "Battered Women"; Oren, "*Up in Montifer*—Up!"; Shamir, "And He Saw a Woman of Beauty."

44. Although he is aware all along of her otherness as a Jew ("They are damned, the curse of the world, Jews"), he is nevertheless helpless to resist its charms: "This is what I want. And she will pay for this too," (p. 120).

45. Kahana-Carmon anticipated here one of the major effects activated by A. B. Yehoshua's unique narrative technique in *Mr. Mani* (1990), where it is also related to the theme of decentering the self and its boundaries; see my essay "Back to Genesis."

46. See Rattok, *Amalia Kahana-Carmon*; "Woman is the Jew of the World."

47. I place this probing in a wider socioliterary context in my "The 'Other Within.' "

48. The allusion is to Jeremiah 38:7–12 and 39:16, where *'eved-melekh*

hakushi saves the prophet from the pit (38) and then is rewarded by God (39). It is the only biblical reference in which a *kushi* ("Ethiopian" in the Bible, but used in modern Hebrew to signify "a black") is identified as a royal servant or slave (*'eved*). By omitting the "king" (*melekh*) from the title and using it as a proper name, the author not only invokes modern black slavery but also points to its allegorical function.

49. Davis, *Women on the Margins*, pp. 5–62.

50. Ibid., pp. 140–202.

51. "While [retroactively] checking whether it was plausible to have a seventeenth-century female merchant travel alone"; conversation with Kahana-Carmon, June 18, 1997.

52. Davis vividly describes and documents the Jewish connection of Surinam plantations, recorded as early as 1788 by David Nassi (see p. 336, note 5), and more recently by Robert Cohen (1991).

53. Davis, p. 174.

54. Ibid., p. 211.

55. The mother/daughter relationship will preoccupy us in chapter 8, where it emerges as a significant step beyond the feminist romance. The reason for its low profile in constructions of liberal feminism may be inferred from our present text: Clara's unconscious identification with her mother is controlled by a compulsion to repeat; she reenacts her mother's crippling state of otherness-producing captivity. This identification is prefigured also in naming the narrator's doll Clara (several chapters before her own name is revealed to the reader), a transparent allusion to a well-known Hebrew poem (Dalia Ravikovitch's "Mechanical Doll") that has recently gained the status of a Hebrew feminist "classic." Cf. chapter 5.3, this volume, where this feminist intertext is revisited.

56. After her last, liberating encounter with Peter, Clara states twice: *'Ish 'eino patron li 'od* ("No one is my master anymore"), Kahana-Carmon, *Lema'lah bemontifer*, pp. 154, 158.

57. The scar naturally symbolizes Clara's mark of captivity and servitude—even "castration," metaphorically speaking. However, it resonates also with the biblical law (Exodus 31:16) that marks a Hebrew serf who willingly remains in bondage even after the seventh year by piercing his ear. The scar is another symbol of Clara's ambivalent "captivity," an ambivalence that will soon replicate itself.

58. Which preceded a similar grafting of Shylock and the Arab Other in the Israeli movie *Avanti Popolo*, directed by Rafi Buka'i and released in 1986.

59. See Alter, *The Art of Biblical Narrative*.

60. This allusion is "tricky": In the midrash Moses does not really choose the coals; as an infant he naturally stretches his hand to the glittering gold; which was risky, of course, because the pharaoh would have interpreted this

as Moses coveting his crown (a little oedipal awareness). Hence it was the divine angel who pushed Moses's hand toward the coals, thereby safeguarding the future of the redeemer of the Hebrews.

61. Beauvoir, *The Second Sex,* pp. xxiv–xxv. See Lloyd's analysis in *The Man of Reason*, chapter 6.

62. See Rattok, "Woman Is the Jew of the World"; cf. Litvin, "The Tangle and the Way"; her description of Eved as "a fickle and deceitful character" aroused the ire and protest of the author; see Kahana-Carmon, "Response," *Yediot Aḥaronot,* June 15, 1984.

63. See Avrum Goldfaden's version of "Rozinkes mit mandlen" in his play *Shulames.* This "matrix" is acknowledged earlier on in the narrative: "With commerce in raisins it began. And, in time, to the commerce in figs and all kinds of dried fruit it evolved" (Kahana-Carmon, *Lema ʿlah bemontifer,* p. 111).

Another possible subtext for this "portrait of seventeenth-century Jewish merchant" is the diary of Glikl from Hamlin, that precious seventeenth-century Yiddish document of female autonomy and courage. See, most recently, Davis, *Women on the Margins,* discussed earlier in this chapter.

64. Like the repetition of so many shorter motifs and figurative expressions, this verbal duel is a stylized intensification of an earlier one, the parting duel between Clara and Peter (Kahana-Carmon, *Lema ʿlah bemontifer,* pp. 143–144).

65. In a postscript to the novel the author gives a more mundane explanation for the delay in its publication. Her "apology" supplies an intriguing clue to the position of this narrative among her other books. Apparently embarked upon in 1971, and then again in 1980, it seems to have been postponed in favor of more distant and displaced versions of her "masked autobiography."

The contemporary setting of this novel should be appreciated then for the courageous (though partial) lifting of the mask that it represents.

66. Without crossing the boundary from scholarship to gossip, let us just imply that, unlike the masked autobiographies of the present study, the biographical displacement of this novel is much "thinner," since it does not hide behind historical distancing and clearly uses undisguised materials from its author's life.

67. Me'ira derives from *'or,* the Hebrew word for "light" (n.), while *heller* is a Yiddish adjective meaning "bright(er)." Both are variations on the Latin root of Clara, which means "bright, clear, transparent."

68. As mentioned before, motherhood is not problematized in the earlier stages of the Israeli "feminist romance." For more about this topic see chapters 4, 5, 6.3, and especially 8.

69. "The second Israel," an Israeli euphemism referring to the underprivileged and underdeveloped segments of Israeli society, mostly the postwar (1948) immigrants from Arab countries.

70. For my use of this semiotic terminology in the production of meaning, see Riffaterre, *The Semiotics of Poetry*, and *Text Production*.

71. Literally, "counterhelper"; the complementarity implied by Genesis 2:18 is better rendered by "counterpart" than by "helpmeet." I elaborate on this point in my essay " 'And Rebecca Loved Jacob.' " See also Trible, *God and the Rhetoric of Sexuality*.

72. There seems to be a world of difference between this use of cross-gender brotherhood and the black/feminist uses of the English corresponding terms with their emphatic closure of otherness, whether racial or gendered.

73. The poets H. N. Bialik, Rachel, and Leah Goldberg are just a few that come to mind; they are joined by "citations" from the painters Malevitch (whose "black square" opens the novel), Vermeer, and Ensor. On the latter see Gold, "To Reach the Source;" "On *With Her on Her Way Home.*"

74. For the effect of marital "playfulness" and sibling (rather than oedipal) dynamics on the construction of gender that is at the heart of biblical "patriarchy," see my essay " 'And Rebecca Loved Jacob.' "

75. Amichai, *Yehuda Amichai*, p. 371. It is interesting to compare this perception to Diotima's speech in Plato's *Symposium*.

76. Goldberg, "'Aḥarei 'esrim shana," p. 184. The translation is mine.

77. See Kahana-Carmon, "How Does the Elephant Imagine Itself?"

78. Kristeva, *Revolution in Poetic Language*. For more on this subject, see chapter 2, this volume.

79. My reading obviously diverges from Robert Alter's review of this book, which rejects the suggestion that the reordering creates a new dynamic and meaningful relationship between the old stories.

4. WHO'S AFRAID OF ANDROGYNY? VIRGINIA WOOLF'S "GENDER" *AVANT LA LETTRE*

1. See Moi, *Sexual/Textual Politics*; Weil, *Androgyny and the Denial of Difference*; Nina Schwartz, "The Strategy of Androgyny in *A Room of One's Own*," in Schwartz, *Dead Fathers*, pp. 123–256; Jacobs, *First Things*; Scott, *Refiguring Modernism*, chapter 1; and *Mosaic* 30.3, *The Lure of the Androgyne* (September 1997). While these studies differ in their emphases, they share a preoccupation with theories of difference versus sameness that inform, as we have seen, postmodernist discussions of essentialism and the politics of gender identity. Building on these arguments, my own emphasis veers toward a biopsychological contextualization of Woolf's use and practice of the concept.

2. Some of the earliest studies include Daiches's *Virginia Woolf* and Bennet's *Virginia Woolf: Her Art as a Novelist*, both from 1945. A few more trickled down until 1972, the year that saw the publication of Bell's two-volume *Virginia Woolf: A Biography*.

3. For sales statistics culled from Leonard Woolf's autobiography, see Mepham, *Virginia Woolf*, p. 130.

4. Topping, *Virginia Wolf and the Androgynous Vision*; and Heilbrun, *Toward the Recognition of Androgyny*. For a counterview see Stimpson, "The Androgyne and the Homosexual."

Interestingly, Woolf is missing entirely from a book propagating androgyny as a New Age theory of sexuality published in 1977. Neither Woolf nor *Orlando* is mentioned in this book, which scours the length and breadth (and East and West) of mythical and psychological theories in its documentation of its subject. See Singer, *Androgyny*.

5. Showalter, *A Literature of Their Own*, p. 287.

6. Gordon, *Virginia Woolf*, p. 188.

7. Especially when compared to the chapter devoted to it in the later biography by Mepham, "1928–1931: Androgyny and the End of the Novel," pp. 119–144, *Virginia Woolf*.

8. See Weil's distinction between the androgyne and the hermaphrodite in part 1 of her study, *Androgyny and the Denial of Difference*.

9. See Sedgwick, *The Epistemology of the Closet*; Barrett and Cramer, *Virginia Woolf*.

10. See Raitt, *Vita and Virginia*.

11. See, for example, Caws, *Women of Bloomsbury*; Marsh, *Bloomsbury Women*.

12. To the writer-diplomat Harold Nicolson; this is the picture painted by their son, Nigel Nicolson, in his *Portrait of a Marriage* (1973), published in Hebrew in 1995.

13. Since the 1976 publication of Woolf's formerly unpublished autobiographical writings, *Moments of Being*, the psychological literature about her has multiplied by leaps and bounds. At the center of many of these studies is the attempt to define the nature of her "madness" and its relation to her extremely repressed sexuality. While classical Freudian "neurosis" figures in some interpretations, object relations theories inform others. Few follow Leonard Woolf's initial manic-depressive diagnosis (see especially, Caramagno, *The Flight of the Mind*, who also offers a succinct summary of recent psychoanalytic readings in his chapter 1, to which one should add Abel's exceptional study, *Virginia Woolf and the Fictions of Psychoanalysis*). Others follow Poole, *The Unknown Virginia Woolf*, who was the first to utilize Woolf's late admissions of sexual abuse in childhood and youth by her half-brothers. For these interpreters Woolf's "madness" was nothing but a "normal" reaction to an abnormal situation, a defense against a psychologically damaging experience. Cf. DeSalvo, *Virginia Woolf*.

My own reading of Woolf's psychology veers in another direction. While taking her repressed sexuality as a given, and her childhood abuse as a possible contributing factor, I have my doubts about their usefulness for the comprehension of Woolf's exceptional mind and superb artistic creativity. My reading is therefore geared toward understanding how she "overcame" some of her psychological conflicts by working through them in her writing. "Androgyny" is, I shall argue, the result of such a process of "working through," functioning as one of her defenses against the psychological and cultural pressures of her midlife crisis.

14. For the most extreme approaches see Gordon, *Virginia Woolf*; Raitt, *Vita and Virginia*; a middle-of-the-road approach is taken by Mepham, *Virginia Woolf*. Cf. Kennard, "Woolf, the *Dreadnought* Hoax, and Sexual Ambiguity."

15. Woolf's diary provides ample evidence of her reading in both the romantics and the classics (of which she was a student since early childhood).

16. For the debate over the biblical "androgynous" sources, see Trible, *God and the Rhetoric of Sexuality*, p. 89; Fox, *In the Beginning*, p. 13; and my " 'And Rebecca Loved Jacob,' " p. 20.

17. Jane Marcus, "Sapphistory," chapter 8 of Marcus, *Virginia Woolf and the Languages of Patriarchy*, pp. 163–187. It should be noted that in Woolf's diary (October 23, 1929) the term *sapphist* registers an anxiety of being "attacked for a feminist and hinted at for a Sapphist," which leads to the projected fear, "I will not be taken seriously."

18. The reference is to *A Writer's Diary* ("Being Extracts of the Diary of Virginia Woolf"), edited and published by Leonard Woolf in 1953. Predictably, the first analyses of the Vita-*Orlando* connection followed this publication, which unravels the process in which *Orlando* came to be the ostensible "biography" of Vita. See, for example, Frank Baldanza and David Green's exchange in *PMLA* (1955–1956).

With the publication of Woolf's letters and complete diaries (in the 1970s and 1980s) more refined insights into this issue became available, e.g., Stimpson, "The Female Sociograph"; Pinkney, *Virginia Woolf and the Problem of the Subject*, chapter 5; Gilbert, "Costumes of the Mind"; Weil, *Androgyny and the Denial of Difference*, chapter 6 ("The Third Generation, Where Orlando Comes of Age"). More recently, Raitt, *Vita and Virginia*, placed *Orlando* in the context of the falling out between Vita and Virginia (making Vita the object of a literary revenge rather than an idealized model) as well as in the context of Woolf's irreverent refashioning of Edwardian biography. For the oedipal overtones of the latter see below, chapter 4.

19. See, for example, Snider's Jungian interpretation, "A Single Self."

20. There is room to claim Woolf as the virgin-mother of science fiction androgynes; see Le Guin's 1969 story "Winter King," reprinted with "androgynous" revisions (and a telling preface) in her collection *The Wind's Twelve Quarters*, pp. 93–117, and her *The Left Hand of Darkness*. Cf. *Mosaic* 30:3.

21. See her comment, in a letter from December 26, 1924, "Why she writes, which she does with complete competency, and a pen of brass, is a puzzle to me"; cited in Raitt, *Vita and Virginia*, p. 3.

22. See on this point, Wilson, "Why is Orlando Difficult?"

23. Entry for May 14, 1925, *The Diary of Virginia Woolf* 3:18

24. For a succinct summary see Tremper, "In Her Father's House"; and her *"Who Lived in Alfoxton?"*

25. Virginia Woolf, "A Sketch of the Past," in Woolf, *Moments of Being*, pp. 80–81.

26. On the predictable ambivalence of Woolf's mother fixation see Lilienfeld, " 'The Deceptiveness of Beauty.' "

27. See Woolf, *Collected Essays* 2:85.

28. This edition was characterized by historian Peter Gay, in his monumental biography, as "the most vigorous translation into English, capturing Freud's virile and witty German speech better than any other." See Gay, *Freud*, p. 741–742. This issue will be revisited in chapter 6.

29. Letter of May 11, 1927, quoted in Gordon, *Virginia Woolf*, p. 39.

30. Woolf, *The Diary of Virginia Woolf* 3:52.

31. See Marianna Torgovnick, "The Sisters' Art," in Torgovnick, *The Visual Arts, Pictorialism, and the Novel*; Dunn, *A Very Close Conspiracy*. Cf. Rhoda's interior monologue in *The Waves*: "You . . . are committed, have an attitude, with children, authority, fame, love, society; where I have nothing. I have no face" (p. 158).

32. Woolf, *A Writer's Diary*, p. 119.

33. Woolf, *The Diary of Virginia Woolf* 3:208.

34. See Marcus's essay by this name in her edited volume, *New Feminist Essays on Virginia Woolf*, pp. 1–30. Cf. Jacobus's warning that "reading back through a dead mother may have been a problematic form of maternal identification"; Jacobus, *First Things*, p. 107.

35. For example, in 1928, 1939, and cf. diary entry on December 22, 1940: "I have been dipping into old letters and father's memoirs. He loved her: oh and was so candid and reasonable and transparent—and had such a fastidious delicate mind, educated and transparent"; Woolf, *The Diary of Virginia Woolf* 5:345; Cf. Meisel, *The Absent Father*.

36. Defromont, "Mirrors and Fragments," p. 66. For an exception to this view see Tremper, "In Her Father's House." My thanks to Ellen Tremper for her generous reading and for sharing with me her essay and book chapter, which confirmed many of the observations developed here. See also Brownstein, *Becoming a Heroine*, p. 275: "On the other hand, had Sir Leslie Stephen not been who he was . . . there would have been no such life, writing, or books, no such vision of a life of writing books."

37. See Abel, " 'Cam the Wicked' "; and her *Virginia Woolf and the Fic-*

tions of Psychoanalysis. For a different reading see Tremper, "In Her Father's House"; *"Who Lived in Alfoxton?"*

38. Woolf, *A Writer's Diary*, p. 138.

39. Upon the completion of *Orlando,* in a letter to Vita (March 20 [?], 1928), Woolf writes: "Did you feel a sort of tug, as if your neck was being broken on Saturday last on 5 minutes to one? This is when he died—or rather stopped talking, with three little dots." (L, iii. 474) Who is the HE in this teasing paragraph? Is it Orlando, "compensatory to Vita," according to Raitt, who reads it as part of Woolf's "biography of hate" (Raitt, *Vita and Virginia,* p. 38)? Or is "he" perhaps the author's own male half, her controlling father representation? If my suggestion is plausible, the figure of the father is finally "done with" not by being "done complete" in *To the Lighthouse* as planned (see her diary entry of 1925, note 23 above), but by being overcome, by her going beyond him in the very writing of *Orlando.*

40. Marcus, *Virginia Woolf and the Languages of Patriarchy,* p. 103.

41. Durrell, *Pope Joan,* p. 29.

42. Of course, Joanna did not escape the snares of her sex either, and in a much more severe manner; the "historical" record has her die in birth while serving as the pope, thereby uncovering her true sex for the first time; Durrell, *Pope Joan,* p. 148. Isaac Bashevis Singer, on the other hand, in a typically Jewish manner, rewards his heroine with a wedding rather than a "scholarly" career; see his *The Collected Stories,* pp. 149–169.

43. Paz, *Sor Juana.* See Bergmann, "Dreaming in a Double Voice."

44. See Rapoport-Albert, "On Women in Hasidism," p. 506. Interestingly, the Maid of Ludmir finally caught the imagination of Israeli popular culture when she made her first stage appearance in a play written by Yosepha Even-Shoshan and named after her, performed at the Khan Theater, Jerusalem, December 1997.

45. Biale, *Eros and the Jews,* p. 182. The studies recorded by Biale have been recently reinforced by feminist readings of foundational texts of the period, e.g., the writings of A. D. Gordon by Einat Ramon and the 1920 collection *Kehilyatenu* (Our Commune) by Yael Weiler and Tamar Hess, as presented in a recent feminist conference at the Hebrew University in Jerusalem, June 1998.

46. See Shemer, *An Intimate Report on Women in Israel,* pp. 197, 586 et passim for the contemporary picture. In the Orthodox communities, meanwhile, attempts to broaden the educational horizons of women resulted in what anthropologist El-Or calls "educated but ignorant" (see her book by that title).

47. Bokser, "A Room of Your Own," an interview with Ruth Almog, Yehudit Hendel, and Amalia Kahana-Carmon. For a similar argument by Shulamith Hareven see an interview in *Yediot Aharonot,* December 20, 1991.

48. See Fisch's thought-provoking analysis of this prototype (*A Remembered Future*, chapter 6). Intriguingly, his samples lack representatives of *Hebrew* fiction, though they are rich in examples from Jewish literature (Roths, both Henry and Philip). We could add to his list the mother in Agnon's *Simple Story* as well as a few protagonists of contemporary Israeli fiction (e.g., David Grossman's *The Book of Internal Grammar*).

49. On this point see my " 'And Rebecca Loved Jacob' "; and Pardes, *Countertraditions in the Bible.*

50. To a certain extent, this applies also to the representation of the fathers, who "stand in" for the Jewish tradition against which Zionism revolted. See Fisch for the nineteenth-century European roots of this topos. On the recent oedipalization of the Zionist narrative, see my "Isaac or Oedipus?" On the exclusion of the maternal from the European oedipal narrative, see Hirsch, *The Mother-Daughter Plot.*

51. Hendel, *Rehov hamadregot;* see also Shirav, *Ktivah lo' tamah,* chapter 1.

52. For the deconstruction of the oedipal masterplot by male writers see Hoffman, "Constructing Masculinity in Yaakov Shabtai's *Past Continuous*"; and "Oedipal Narrative and Its Discontents."

53. See my "Back to Vienna"; "Back to Genesis"; "Isaac or Oedipus?"; see also Boyarin, *Unheroic Conduct.*

5. ISRAELI ANDROGYNY UNDER SIEGE: SHULAMITH HAREVEN

1. Hareven, *'Ir yamim rabim; City of Many Days.* References are to the 1983 Hebrew and the 1993 English editions, respectively; when the page numbers are identical, only one reference is given.

In contrast to other Israeli women writers, most of Hareven's fiction is available in English. See *Twilight and Other Stories;* and *Thirst: The Desert Trilogy.* A selection of her essays appeared under the title *The Vocabulary of Peace.*

2. Hareven's early work includes *Yerushalayim dorsanit* (Predatory Jerusalem; poems); *Bahodesh ha'aharon* (In the Last Month; stories); *Mekomot nifradim* (Separate Places; poems); *Reshut netuna* (Freedom of Choice; stories). See her rationalization of this chronology in my introduction.

Some of those early stories are still unformed and do not always rise to the level of narrative control and nuance of voice Hareven developed later in her career. I therefore refer to them only to the extent they shed light on later issues in her writing. See note 33 below. Cf. Hagorni, "Reshut netunah"; Avishai, "Life in Crisis"; Shaked, *Hasipporet ha'ivrit 1880–1980* 4:128–130; Nash, "Character Portrayal and Cultural Critique."

3. *Orlando,* trans. Zvi Arad.

4. It should be pointed out that while Kristeva's work was not known in Israel until recently (1990s), Hareven did not have to rely on Hebrew transla-

tions to get to know Virginia Woolf. A lover of language and linguistics (and a member of the Israeli Academy of the Hebrew Language for many years), she is fluent in English and may have early on "discovered" Woolf, whose name is evoked in her *first* collection of stories (1966) as one of the nicknames the heroine is fondly given by her lover (see "Winter of the King of Cards," p. 128). Woolf's *A Room of One's Own* reverberates in the title of her piece "Wordsworth's Sister," which obviously puns on Woolf's "Shakespeare's sister" (*A Room of One's Own*, chapter 3). As this indirect reference to *Room* may indicate, Harveven seems to have been attracted mostly to Woolf's gender revisionism (in contrast to Amalia Kahana-Carmon, who was inspired by her poetics).

A later trace of Woolf in Hareven's work may be Theo Stein's bizarre idea to speak Latin with the ravens (see "My Straw Chairs," *Bedidut* [Loneliness], p. 62; p. 75 in the English collection *Twilight*). This is reminiscent of the Greek-speaking sparrows in Septimus Smith's mad ravings in *Mrs. Dalloway* (p. 28), which was published in Hebrew in 1975 (for more on the intertextual presence of this novel in *Loneliness*, see section 3 below). For the roots of the "Greek-speaking birds" fantasy in Woolf's personal breakdowns, and its association with her history of sexual abuse, see Poole, *The Unknown Virginia Woolf*, pp. 173–184.

5. Personal communication, August 16, 1989. See also Navot, "Not One Needless Word," an interview in *Yediot Aharonot*. " 'I am a selective feminist,' she says, and adds that she does not believe that in literature and the arts women are underprivileged."

A different kind of ambivalence about feminism—though under the term *suffragism*—is a major theme in Netiva Ben Yehuda's work, which we encounter in chapter 7.

6. Personal communication, June, 1998. Cf. Hareven's critique of "power-driven, political groups like those of 'women's literature,' " in "Professional Questions," an article published in *Al Hamishmar*.

7. See especially her latest biblical novellas (collected under the title *Thirst*), which many read as political allegories, to the great chagrin of their author. For more on this, see chapter 6, this volume.

8. Shaked, *Hebrew Writers*, p. 61. Cf. an interview with Orly Toren, Hareven, "Consensus with 3 S's": "She herself does not believe in the connection between biography and bibliography." When obliged to provide some kind of a "bio" to an interviewer, she has significantly chosen her service in the 1948 war as a starting point, refusing to volunteer any more information—a point to which we shall return; see Chertok, *We Are All Close*, pp. 77–91.

9. Virginia Woolf, "American Fiction," which was posthumously republished in *Collected Essays* 2:113. See also chapter 3, this volume.

10. See, for example, an interview with Shifra, "A Struggle for Sanity," in which Hareven responds to a question about the autobiographical background of *City of Many Days* by arguing that "literature is out of luck. A painter or a musician is never asked about the autobiographical background of his work. In developing a literary idea one grabs building blocks from whatever comes handy. . . . This will be a complete artistic truth, not a biographical truth."

11. Furbank, "Portrait of a Lady," p. 30. A corrective may be added to this generalization by limiting it to members of the "middle class," postulating greater "freedoms" in the conduct of women of both the higher and lower classes . . .

12. Cf. Kaniuk's enthusiastic approval of the role and representation of Jerusalem (and the Jerusalem stone) in this novel: "Mountain, Stone and Beauty." Hareven's fascination with the power of the "Jerusalem stone" can be traced to her predecessor, the poet Leah Goldberg, whose Jerusalem poems are replete with similar motifs. It is perhaps also worth noting that the author's last name, Hareven (though acquired by marriage, not choice, as she wryly commented), actually means "mountain of stone."

13. Gershon Shaked, "Suffused with the Love of Jerusalem,"in Shaked, *Gal 'ahar gal*, pp. 19–23; and see my essay, "Reconstructing the Past in Israeli Fiction."

14. This process of demythologizing, often attributed to the work of the Israeli "New Historians," had its fictional antecedents in the novels of Netiva Ben Yehuda (see chapter 7, this volume). For the first "revisionist" history of this era see Morris, *The Birth of the Palestinian Refugee Problem*. See also Sivan, *The 1948 Generation* [Hebrew].

15. *Yishuv* is the Hebrew term for the Jewish community in Palestine before 1948.

16. See chapter 6.3 for my discussion of the essays "Violence," "A Secret Ancient Guilt," and "A Society of Brothers or of Sons?" published in Hareven's first collection of essays, *The Dulcinea Syndrome*. Hareven repeated her dislike of classical Freudianism in her conversation with me, August 16, 1989.

17. Hareven, "'Ani levantinit." References are to the Hebrew collection, Hareven, *Messiah or Knesset*, pp. 168–174, and to the English version, "On Being a Levantine," in Hareven, *The Vocabulary of Peace*, pp. 80–87, respectively. Cf. Said, *Orientalism*.

It should be noted that this particular use of "levantinism" in the sense of a liberal, pluralistic, Mediterranean culture was introduced into Israeli discourse by the Egyptian-born writer Jacqueline Kahanoff (1917–1979), in the early issues of the liberal journal *Keshet* (1958–1976), founded and edited by the Canaanite writer Aharon Amir (b. 1923). Amir "revived" the expression *dor halevantinim* (the Levantine generation) in his preface to Kahanoff's collection of essays, *Mimizraḥ shemesh* (From the East). Kahanoff's cosmopolitanism was an exception in the Israel of the late fifties and sixties, and her essays served no doubt as a model for our author, whose early short stories appeared in the same journal, e.g., "A Question of Identity." On the Canaanite roots of *Keshet* (Rainbow) and its rivalry with the mouthpiece of Israeli existentialism, *Akhshav* (Now), see Gertz, *Ḥirbet ḥizʿa vehaboker shelemoḥorat*, pp. 36–40, and note 54 of my introduction.

This connection may also explain Hareven's choice of Amir as the Hebraized surname decided upon by the Amarillos to replace what was then considered an overly ethnic name (p. 117; p. 116).

18. Hareven, *Twilight and Other Stories*, p. 1. As Shaked, *Hebrew Narrative* 4:132, has indicated, this story stands out in its Agnonic surrealism (which American reviewers naturally identified as Kafkaesque . . .). The change in the position of this story in the English publication is a dramatic testimony of cultural shifts: what was used as the title story in Hareven's English collection in 1992 had originally been the last story in the 1980 Hebrew collection, *Bedidut*. For more on this see section 3 below. Cf. Brenner, "The Reception of Holocaust Testimonies."

19. See Frye, *Anatomy of Criticism*, p. 152.

20. See Scholem, *Zohar*, p. 28:

> When King Solomon "penetrated into the depths of the nut garden," as it is written, "I descended into the garden of nuts" [Song of Songs 6:11], he took up a nut shell and studying it, he saw an analogy in its layers with the spirits which motivate the sensual desires of humans . . .
> The whole world, upper and lower, is organized on this principle. . . .
> All are coverings, the one to the other, brain within brain, spirit inside of spirit, *shell within shell.*   (emphasis added)

For the Hebrew see Tishbie, *Pirkei Zohar*, p. 228.

21. Shifra, "A Struggle for Sanity." This musical metaphor notwithstanding, the impressionistic style of the novel, which to my mind constitutes a great advance over Hareven's earlier uneven "realistic" style, aroused some discontent among critics who had been conditioned to expect the "fullness of characterization" associated with psychological realism. Most pertinent in this regard is Shaked's deliberation upon whether to classify Hareven among the "realists" or the "impressionists" of Hebrew narrative prose. See Shaked, *Hebrew Narrative* 4:128, 133–134, and note 178, where he cites Heda Boshes and Yosef Oren as unreceptive to Hareven's impressionism.

22. Homi K. Bhabha, "Of Mimicry and Man," in Bhabha, *The Location of Culture*, pp. 85–92.

23. Hareven, "Shonim ve-shavim," in Shulamith Hareven, *The Dulcinea Syndrome*, pp. 179–189.

24. On the domesticity of the biblical Isaac, and my androgynous inter-

pretation of Jacob (and Rebecca), see Feldman, " 'And Rebecca Loved Jacob.' "

25. Feminist scholarship on *Little Women,* and especially on the meaning and function of its central character, Jo March, is too rich to be cited here. For a good summary of the controversy see Murphy, "The Borders of Ethical, Erotic and Artistic Possibilities in *Little Women.*" Of special interest to our story is her citation of Carolyn Heilbrun's assessment of Jo as "the single female model continuously available after 1868 to girls dreaming beyond the confines of a constricted family destiny to the possibility of autonomy," except, of course, for her marriage . . . (p. 565).

26. Both Daniel Boyarin and Elliott Wolfson argued (differences notwithstanding) for an appropriation of the maternal or the feminine by the Jewish male or masculine principle (in Talmudic and Kabbalistic texts, respectively). See Wolfson's interpretations of the "Divine Androgyne" in "Woman—the Feminine as Other in Theosophic Kabbalah"; and "Crossing Gender Boundaries in Kabbalistic Ritual and Myth," in Wolfson, *Circle in the Square,* pp. 79–122.

Especially relevant to the contemporay androgyne is Boyarin's distinction (in his "Jewish Masochism," first published in *American Imago,* later incorporated into his *Unheroic Conduct*) between the Christian and Jewish "maternal" male prototypes. Their difference hinges, he claims, precisely on the contrast between celibacy (namely, sexual renunciation, or "castration," in Freudian terms) and fecundity (namely, fatherhood, even maternal parenthood). His definition of Talmudic masculinity as penile but "nonphallic" (resisting "the myth of bodily coherence, power, singularity and unimpairability," p. 25) may indeed fit the characterization of the "maternal father" of our story. Unlike Boyarin's prooftexts, however, Hareven's text supplements her Jewish androgynous male with a Jewish androgynous female who is a true counterpart to his subversion of the "dominant fiction" of Greco-Roman/Freudian phallocentric masculinity described by Boyarin (who in turn relies on Silverman, *Male Subjectivity at the Margins*).

27. Shifra, "A Struggle for Sanity."

28. Lacan, *Ecrits,* pp. 1–7.

29. See Boyarin, *Carnal Israel;* and my " 'And Rebecca Loved Jacob.' "

30. Chazan, "Gender Equality?" Cf. Izraeli and Tabori, "The Political Context of Feminist Attitudes in Israel."

31. Shaked, "Suffused with the Love of Jerusalem," p. 23. Shaked does not repeat this critique, however, in his overview of Hareven's work in *Hebrew Narrative* 4:133–134.

32. In the only extended review of the book, Amnon Hadary interprets *City of Many Days* as a theological allegory (!) about an absent God (Don Isaac Amarillo) and the beloved/Zion/Jerusalem/Sara who mourns his absence.

See Hadary, "*City of Many Days*." The political implications of the novel, on the other hand, were hinted at by the author herself in the interview with Shifra, "A Struggle for Sanity." More on this below.

33. "In the Last Month," the title story that opens Hareven's first collection (1966), features an unnamed first-person female narrator. Its opening is couched in a descriptive style that too transparently (and inappropriately for the occasion, as Shaked rightly pointed out; *Hebrew Narrative Prose* 4:129) evokes the notorious rhapsodies to the Israeli landscape written by S. Yizhar, the eminent author of the 1948 generation. As the narrative unravels, however, it reconstructs, in an adequately realistic manner, the story of a Palmach unit (a group of youths, most of them seventeen years old, p. 10), on the eve of the 1948 war. The core of the plot is a love triangle that is cruelly ended when the other girl gets killed by an Arab sniper. A letter sent from Jerusalem by the narrator's mother (p. 17) resonates with the Arab-Jewish-British relationship as described in *City of Many Days*. The story ends with the War of Independence breaking out while the narrator is in Jerusalem, unable to return to her unit: "This is how I was trapped in Jerusalem under siege, enclosed and isolated; I was assigned a different task, and I never regretted it" (p. 30).

Another first-person narrative in the same collection, "The Great Aunts," reads as a memoir of a European childhood, dated before 1939. It is mostly a reconstruction of the sibling rivalry between the narrator's grandmother and her three sisters. "How many years had the aunts been coming to these tea parties? Probably all through my childhood," she summarizes (p. 56), holding her bitter irony for the conclusion:

> In September 1939 the aunts stopped coming for tea, but they were firm on the phone: "We are lucky to be conquered by the Germans and not by the Russians. . . . A cultured nation, they have respect for cultured people." The aunts brushed up their good German, and the gold frames of the paintings . . . made tea and waited for the worst to be over with, and for the conquerors to come in. The colonels, they have agreed, could be appropriately invited for tea.   (*p. 57; my translation*)

It should also be noted that many of Hareven's other stories feature Holocaust survivors and other dislocated newcomers, perhaps unwittingly disclosing a topic too painful to be represented directly. One of these characters is a *daughter* of survivors, apparently the first such protagonist in Israeli literature, over a decade before "the second generation" captured center stage in Israeli letters (see the last story in *Freedom of Choice*, 1970). On the latter see my "Whose Story Is It, Anyway?"

34. A skeptic representation of a similar legacy is offered in the early story "Margalit Ezer's Kingdom" (*Freedom of Choice*, 1970, 16–67). Margalit's father arouses the excitement (and envy) of his son-in-law when he tells him that his own grandfather used to keep in his document cabinet the key to the

family house in Toledo; but "Margalit blushes like a tomato. . . . She is absolutely certain that the key has never seen Toledo, nor crossed the Mediterranean" (40).

35. For more about this problematic perception, see the introduction and chapter 7, this volume, and especially Netiva Ben Yehuda's curt statements in the epigraphs.

36. Androgyny is explored, interestingly enough, by several veteran writers, both male and female, whose earlier concerns lay elsewhere: the writer of children stories, Nurit Zarḥi ("She is Joseph," 1993), mystery writer Batya Gur (*Afterbirth*, 1994), scriptwriter and postmodern novelist Avram Heffner (*Alelim*, 1993); they are joined by the younger writers Eyal Megged (*Barbarossa*, 1993) and Dorit Abbush (*Hayored*, 1995). For an earlier experiment, rather unnoticed, see Ruth Blumert, *Hatzariah* (The Tower, 1984).

37. In English this volume is named after the story "Twilight"—Hareven's phantasmagoric treatment of the Holocaust—which also opens the collection. See my comment in note 18.

38. In the English collection this story is replaced by two stories from earlier volumes, "The Emissary" (1966), and "A Matter of Identity" (1970).

39. "The subtlest and the deepest of Hareven's realistic stories" is the evaluation of Shaked (*Hebrew Narrative Prose 4:131*). I agree; though my close reading veers in a different direction. Cf. Ben-Ezer, "Stories of Loneliness"; Bartana, "A Gray Reality."

40. Said by Dalya, the first-person narrator of "Days of Frost in the Impenetrable Mirror," *Freedom of Choice* (1970), p. 131; and see note 51 below for the later psychosexual vicissitudes of this complex . . . Aside from this neurotically conceived fear of motherhood, the only other critique of "motherhood" in Hareven's fiction belongs to the sphere of political (feminist?) protest (rather than feminism proper); see her use of historical allegory in the stark early story "A Great Hunger in Samaria," *In the Last Month* (1966), pp. 87–91.

41. *Mrs. Dalloway* (1925) was Virginia Woolf's female "answer" to James Joyce's *Ulysses* (1922), which rather annoyed her on first reading; after the first two hundred pages she felt "puzzled, bored, irritated and disillusioned by a queasy undergraduate scratching his pimples." August 16, 1922, *A Writer's Diary*. The sibling rivalry she felt for this peer who was "about a fortnight younger than I am," as she put it in her diary upon his death on January 15, 1941 (she took her own life about ten weeks later), was instrumental in the structuring of her heroine's peregrinations in London on a single day, June 13, 1923, as both parallel to and divergent from Leopold Bloom's adventures in Dublin on a day in 1904. See Church, "Joycean Structure in *Jacob's Room* and *Mrs. Dalloway*"; Showalter, "Introduction."

Woolf's and Hareven's heroines, on the other hand, share what Showalter called an "eponymous title" ("Introduction," p. xii). In both cases the "emphatic use of 'Mrs.' . . . draws attention to the way in which the central woman character is socially defined by her marriage and masked by her marital status" (ibid). As mentioned above, the Hebrew translation of *Mrs. Dalloway* appeared in 1975 (see my introduction, section 4).

42. My use of intertextual decoding generally follows Riffaterre's classic *Semiotics of Poetry.*

43. Published in Ravikovitch, *'Ahavat tapu'aḥ hazahav* (The Love of an Orange), 1959. In English see Ravikovitch, *The Window,* p. 7.

44. First published in 1933; collected in Agnon, *'Al kapot haman'ul* 3:449–468. Other typical Agnon themes, especially from his short stories in *The Book of Deeds* (e.g., the "home" and the "post office"), further enrich this intertext, as does the finely tuned irony.

45. Goldberg, *'Omanut hasippur,* pp. 204–221.

46. See Smith, *Poetic Closure,* for "retrospective patterning."

47. I prefer this translation to Halkin's "assail," which misses the connotation of *lifro'a ḥok,* "to violate [or break] the law (or the norm, the behavioral codes)."

48. See chapter 8, note 16.

49. Boshes, "Moments of Still Silence."

50. Cf. Abel, "Narrative Structure(s) and Female Development," from which my own reading takes off in another direction.

51. This is a far cry from the perception of lesbianism offhandedly suggested in Hareven's earlier story, "Days of Frost in the Impenetrable Mirror" (1970; see also note 40 above). There the narrator (f.) drifts into a homoerotic relationship as a last resort, after a long succession of failed heterosexual relations. In contrast to Mrs Dalloway's insistence on the *difference* between heterosexual and homosexual relationships, here the narrator places lesbianism within the range of "normalcy," arguing that "we are absolutely normal, but at times it is more convenient this way. Less complicated." She felt the same (she said) with her female lover as with her past male lovers, playing in both cases the role of the "feminine" partner, "as if I am a nimble vine climbing over the trunk of a big oak tree" (p. 158). Obviously this resigned bisexual has nothing of the subversive drives that play themselves out in Dolly's "sadistic" lesbian outburst.

52. See Adrienne Rich's transition from the psychology of mother-daughter relations (*Of Woman Born,* 1976) to her 1980 concept of the "lesbian continuum" ("Compulsory Heterosexuality and Lesbian Existence"). Cf. Luce Irigaray's similar conceptualization, also the product of the 1970s (details in chapter 2 above); and Abel ("Narrative Structure(s) and Female Development") who sees the same orientation budding already in Woolf's "Minoan" female psychology. My argument, however, is that in Hareven's plot the ramifications of an absent maternal link is much more direct, in keeping with the

historical moment. As Abel says about Woolf's construction of "matriarchy" in Mrs. Dalloway's past, "These are radical claims, and Woolf suggests them indirectly" (175).

53. She still held to this view in a debate carried on in the pages of *Devar Hashavu'a*, conducted by Yehudit Rotem, "Dvora Baron is Not Alone Anymore." It features the pictures of three of our writers—Almog, Kahana-Carmon, and Hareven—as well as the latter's daughter, Gail Hareven, a writer in her own right, who shares her mother's view (apparently, no oedipal conflict in this family).

6. THE LEANING IVORY TOWER: FEMINIST POLITICS

1. For a historical outline and bibliography in English, see my study *Modernism and Cultural Transfer*; cf. Kronfeld, *On the Margins of Modernism*. In Hebrew see Shaked, *Gal ḥadash*; Gertz, *Ḥirbet ḥiz'a*.

2. Harshav [Hrushovsky], "About Yosef Ha'efrati's Contribution to Literary Research"; and see my "Poetics and Politics."

3. Virginia Woolf, "The Leaning Tower," published posthumously in Woolf, *The Moment and Other Essays*, pp. 128–154.

4. See Beer, "The Island and the Aeroplane"; Hussey, *Virginia Woolf and War*; Joplin, "The Authority of Illusion"; Wirth-Nesher, "Final Curtain on the War"; Lee, *Virginia Woolf*; Pridmore-Brown, "1939–40."

5. Woolf, "The Artist and Politics," *The Moment and Other Essays*, pp. 225–228. Cf. her diary entry a year earlier, where she is concerned that "this novel [*The Years*] is dangerously near propaganda" (April 14, 1935, *The Diary of Virginia Woolf* 4). See on this issue Marcus, " 'No More Horses' "; John Mepham, "Art and Politics," in Mepham, *Virginia Woolf*, pp. 159–180.

6. Virginia Woolf, "Thoughts on Peace in an Air Raid," in Woolf, *Collected Essays* 4:173.

7. See Marcus, " 'No More Horses' "; John Mepham, "The Outsider: 1932–37," in Mepham, *Virginia Woolf*; Hussey, *Virginia Woolf and War*, particularly Poole, " 'We all put up with you Virginia' "; Caughie, *Virginia Woolf and Postmodernism*, chapters 3, 4.

8. Poole, " 'We all put up with you Virginia.' "

9. For the flourishing of the slogan "The personal is political" in the American women's movement, see Morgan, *Sisterhood Is Powerful*. For the later backlash see Kaminer, *A Fearful Freedom*.

10. Heilbrun, *Writing a Woman's Life*, chapter 7. A similar argument has been recently heard on public television, disseminated by the plucky Dr. Christiane Winthrup, author of *Women's Bodies, Women's Wisdom*.

11. See Ginossar, "A Delicate Hand," a very angry critical review of the Hebrew translation, calling *Three Guineas* a "limited book" and arguing that

Woolf did not understand the "concrete historical situation." Perlis's similar approach is summarized in the (amazing) title of her review, "One Woman's Problem."

12. See Lawrence, "The Facts and Fugue of War" in Hussey, *Virginia Woolf and War*, pp. 225–245.

13. See my "Back to Vienna"; "Whose Story Is It Anyway?"; and my forthcoming "The Psychopolitical Narrative," unpublished manuscript.

14. See Goldstein, "The Woolfs' Response to Freud," p. 235.

15. Woolf, *The Letters of Virginia Woolf* 2:482.

16. See Gay, *Freud*, pp. 639–640.

17. See Goldstein, "The Woolfs' Response to Freud," p. 239; Abel, *Virginia Woolf and the Fictions*, p. 103; Mepham, *Virginia Woolf*, p. 198: "In April 1938, before she had read Freud."; Lee, *Virginia Woolf*, p. 722, repeats the same assertion: "She began reading Freud after the outbreak of war." Not much has apparently changed since Quentin Bell's account that "in her last years" his aunt showed almost no interest in, and definitely no enthusiasm for, Freud's discoveries (while Leonard was reading and reviewing *The Interpretations of Dreams* as early as 1914); see Bell, *Virginia Woolf: Biography*, vol. 2, chapter 1; Goldstein, "The Woolfs' Response to Freud," p. 248. The only scholar to be aware of the "unreality" of this assumption is Abel, who, after quoting the 1939 famous diary entry also quotes Woolf's 1936 enthusiastic diary response to a "psychoanalytic" discussion at a dinner party at her brother Adrian's (and wife Karin's, both psychoanalysts). Abel's subsequent analysis of *Three Guineas*'s "dialogue with psychoanalysis" seems to have been ignored by later scholarship. My own reading, though taking a different tack, supports her insight that "near its end" *Three Guineas* "initiates the explicitly psychoanalytic moment in the text" (ibid).

18. Cf. Abel, *Virginia Woolf and the Fictions of Psychoanalysis*, p. 165, note 44.

19. Goldstein, "The Woolfs' Response to Freud," p. 246.

20. See the history of publication in Freud, *Civilization and Its Discontents* (New York: Norton), p. 5. See also Gay's enthusiastic appreciation of Reviere's translation, *Freud*, pp. 741–742.

21. Poole, " 'We all put up with you Virginia,' " p. 99.

22. See note 11 this chapter.

23. Woolf is wrong, of course, attributing to Christ the "democratic" principles suggested by Paul. On the latter see Boyarin, *A Radical Jew*.

24. See Erikson, "The Eight Ages of Man," p. 247.

25. Had she been writing today, in these times of personal exposure, she might have perhaps adduced Sylvia Plath's infamous poem "Daddy"; see Plath, *The Collected Poems*, pp. 222–224. Written in 1962, the poem does seem to be inspired by Woolf's basic metaphor of the father-tyrant, with one differ-

ence: in contrast to Woolf's monochrome dark coloring of the private-public
father figure, Plath is Freudianly aware of the ambivalence. While, like Woolf,
she fears the "father" ("I have always been afraid of *you*, / With your Luft-
waffe, your gobbledygoo. / And your neat moustache / And your Aryan eye,
bright blue."), she is also masochistically attracted to "the brute." Her notorious lines, "Every woman adores a Fascist, / The boot in the face, the brute /
Brute heart of a brute like you," would have been categorically rejected by
Woolf, who bitterly ridiculed the commonly held assumption about female
masochism, passivity, and "endurance" (*Three Guineas*, p. 160).

26. Weininger, *Sex and Character*. Though recent scholarship has focused
on Weininger's *self*-hatred (e.g., Sander Gilman's work from *Jewish Self-
Hatred* on), Weininger's impact on Nazism is no doubt clear. In the words of
David Abrahamsen, the author of *The Mind and Death of A Genius*: "As late
as 1939 [!] I heard in Norway a radio broadcast beamed from Nazi Germany,
which used some of Weininger's attacks upon the Jews" (122). For a contemporary analysis of the nexus of nationalism and masculinism see Mosse, *The
Image of Man*; and Boyarin's recent *Unheroic Conduct*.

27. Poole, " 'We all put up with you Virginia,' " p. 100, note 8.

28. See Ruddik's *Maternal Thinking*, and the debate surrounding it. It is
concisely summarized in Carroll, "Women and Peace Politics." For earlier
deliberations see her edited volume, Carrol and Mohraz *In a Great Company
of Women*; and Pierson, *Women and Peace*.

29. Not without some later setbacks, however; see Azaryahu, *Hit'aḥdut
nashim 'ivriyot leshivuy zekhuyot*.

30. Izraeli, "The Status of Women in Israel Today," pp. 37–52.

31. In a paper given in Jerusalem, June 1988, Hana Safran described the contribution of Dr. Rose Wald-Strauss, a leader of American suffragism, to the
suffragist movement in Jewish Palestine, which she had chaired since 1919. See
also Azaryahu, *Hit'aḥdut nashim 'ivriyot leshivuy zekhuyot*, pp. 53, 94–95.

32. See Swirski, "Israeli Feminism New and Old," pp. 285–302.

33. See "Mashehu feministi zaz"; cf. Swirski, "Israeli Feminism New and
Old."

34. The dynamics of Freedman's story may retroactively explain why Betty
Friedan had to "suppress" her left-wing roots, as recent scholarship has
argued. See the introduction, note 33.

35. See Davies, *Third World—Second Sex*; Kumari Jayawardena, *Feminism
and Nationalism in the Third World*; Trinh Minh-ha, *Woman, Native, Other*;
Mohanty, Russo, and Torres, *Third World Women*; Butler and Scott, *Feminists Theorize the Political*.

36. For earlier conceptualizations and international precursors see note 28
above; and Harris and King, *Rocking the Ship of State*; Swerdlow, *Women
Strike for Peace*; Alonso, *Peace as a Woman's Issue*.

37. On the Four Mothers movement, which in January 1997 began to call for the army's "peaceful exit from Lebanon," see press coverage by Ariela Ringel-Hoffman, "The Four Mothers Movement."

38. Studies of women's role in the peace movement in Israel and in Muslim countries have proliferated since the late 1980s; for a good historical overview and bibliography in English see Sharoni, *Gender and the Israeli-Palestinian Conflict*; cf. the anthropological, perhaps more optimistic study by Emmett, *Our Sisters' Promised Land*. For a sobering sociological analysis see Azmon, "War, Mothers, and a Girl with Braids."

39. Eilam, "Women and War."

40. Izraeli, "The Status of Women in Israel Today," p. 50.

41. Dafna Sharfman, "The Status of Women in Israel," p. 14

42. Ibid.

43. Bat Oren, *Shiḥrur ha'isha—le'an?* (Women's Liberation—Where To?) "imported" Friedan's feminism to Israel; translations of American feminist staples filled the slate of the Second Sex Press.

44. Shalvi, *Networking for Women*; cf. Swirski and Safir, *Calling the Equality Bluff*.

45. A glaring exception to this feminist "awakening" was the publication, also in 1984, of *Hako'aḥ ha'aḥer* [The different/other power], by veteran writer Yehudit Hendel (b. 1926). Hendel's early books (1950, 1956, and 1969) are marked by a strong social consciousness, of which women are an integral part but not exclusively so (cf. her "suppression" of the mother, chapter 4.3). After a long hiatus she reclaimed her writing career with this paean to her deceased husband, the artist Zvi Meirovitz. This complex narrative weaving of female self and her [male] "significant other" is a precious illustration of the difficult emergence of the female subject, of the difficulty of a talented woman artist to tell her own story as distinct from her "other half's" story. Although the argument, voiced by one commentator, "I don't understand how Hendel succeeded in writing a whole book about her husband without revealing the slightest glimpse about herself," may be an exaggeration, it clearly points to a problem (for a different view see Shirav, *Ktivah lo' tamah*, chapter 1). Interestingly, this masqueraded autobiography was followed by a collection of stories, *Kesef katan* (Small Change, 1988) and almost a decade later another collection, *'Aruḥat boker temima* (An Innocent Breakfast), 1996) whose protagonists are mostly women, with themes and style that waver between the "feminine" and the "feminist."

In some sense the direction of Hendel's artistic evolution is diametrically opposite to that of Kahana-Carmon: she first explored social "otherness" in general, way ahead of her time (*'Anashim aḥerim hem* [They Are Different/Other People], 1950; and see Gertz's forthcoming "I Am the Other"), and only slowly began to cut closer home, probing artistic "difference" (1984) and female otherness (1988, 1996). Beyond these thematic variations, however, Hendel's work exhibits a constant, rather morbid fascination with death and mourning. This preoccupation links her stories with other recent books in which she explores nationally explosive issues such as the search for the past in post-Holocaust Poland (1987) and the Israeli heavy burden of bereavement and mourning (1991). On the latter as an expression of a specifically Israeli "mother tongue," see Naveh, "On Loss, Bereavment, and Mourning in the Israeli Experience."

46. As the 1977 essay that gave its name to the first collection of essays made clear, the author saw Israeli public opinion as ruled by the dynamics of a Don Quixotic "denial," which she vehemently criticized. See *The Dulcinea Syndrome* (unfortunately not available in English). For a critique of the critique see Margalit's ironically titled review, "Treasured Criticism."

The title of her next volume, *Messiah or Knesset*, contrasts the values of religious mythos, the messianic in particular, of which she is intensely critical, with the ethos of a democratic society. In this she is very close to the Israeli author A. B. Yehoshua, who used an analogous dichotomy in his 1987 essay "The Wall and the Mountain," which similarly became the title essay of his own collection of essays (Tel Aviv: Zmora-Bitan, 1989). The different (though related) metaphor used by Yehoshua contrasts the Wailing Wall with Mount Herzl, the site of the Israeli military graveyard. For further affinities between these two writers, see notes 54, 63, this chapter.

47. See press coverage in the *New York Times* where Fein writes about new books by Hareven (*Loneliness*, renamed *Twilight and Other Stories*) and Tatyana Tolstaya under the heading, "Two Writers Who Keep Their Fiction Free of Political Realities." Cf. a somewhat jaundiced view of this very idea in Shortt's review of the book, "Refugees from Reality." For supportive reviews, see Rubin; Cohen; Solomon and Starkman, "Twilight."

48. Hareven, *Eyeless in Gaza*. For the growing urgency of her political concerns in this collection, see an extensive interview with Ilan Sheinfeld, "To See a Different Order Here." This interview also clarifies, however, several of the author's narrative and poetic principles, which are especially relevant to the *Desert Trilogy* discussed later in this chapter. For a review, see Heda Boshes, "An Uncompromising Essayist."

The English collection of essays, *The Vocabulary of Peace*, is a selection mostly from the last two Hebrew volumes, plus some later essays. It is named after a 1994 lecture given at an Israeli-Arab meeting sponsored by UNESCO, which appropriately closes the book.

49. Hareven, *Sone' hanissim* and *Navi'*. The English translations, by Hillel Halkin, were published by North Point, in 1988 and 1990, respectively. References below are to these editions.

50. Hareven, "My Position, Almost in Principle," interview with Yael Admoni; cf. Hareven, "To See a Different Order Here," her interview with

Ilan Sheinfeld, where the Palestinian *woman* is the focus of her eyewitness reports from the refugee camps in Gaza and Samaria.

51. Hareven, *'Aḥarei hayaldut*. The English translation by Hillel Halkin is the last story in the volume *Thirst: The Desert Trilogy*, which includes all three novellas. It appeared in Hebrew under the same title, *Tsima'on: Shlishiyat hamidbar*.

52. We cannot do justice here to the stylistic affinity Hareven claims with authors like Yasunari Kawabata and Par Lagerqvist (personal communication; cf. her lecture at the Hebrew University in 1990, "To See and Not to See," Hareven, *Eyelss in Gaza*, pp. 128–129). See her argument in her interview with Sheinfeld: "We do not need Berdichevski, we need Kawabata and Lagerqvist to teach us a different aesthetics." Hareven, "To See a Different Order Here."

A detailed treatment of the innovative Hebrew style used in this trilogy will take us too far afield. Some valuable clues can be gathered, however, from her 1990 lectures on literature; see especially her comment on writing "without adjectives," *Eyeless in Gaza*, p. 151.

One point should be made here, however, concerning Hareven's Hebrew and the unavoidable limits of translation. Although the English version reads very well, and was received with great enthusiasm, the translation often misses the author's exceptional (in this day and age) linguistic innovations. These range from new usages of common Hebrew words (*tadhema*, "shock," her name for a tornadolike sand storm, is translated as "whirl storm," totally losing the reader's jolt of surprise and "disrecognition") to the author's own newly coined words, which are, however, readily assimilated because they follow the internalized morphological and semantic rules of the literate Hebrew reader (e.g., *ma'azeva* for a "dump").

53. The subversive implication of *Prophet*, the second title, is less transparent (save for the missing article). Its subversiveness does surface, however, when we find out that the prophet is a Gibeonite, a fact that automatically makes him a "false" prophet (at least from the traditional perspective of the Hebrew Bible).

54. A. B. Yehoshua's *Mr. Mani* (1990), the archetypal Israeli "counternovel," was actually begun in 1984 despite its later date of publication. See my essay "Back to Genesis"; see also Netiva Ben Yehuda's novels (1981, 1985, 1991), discussed in chapter 7, this volume.

55. Published in *Yediot Aḥaronot*; see Hareven, *The Vocabulary of Peace*, pp. 191–196. Cf. Shamir's review of *After Childhood*, "Carved in Rock."

56. See Alter, *The Art of Biblical Narrative*, which popularized this aspect of biblical narratology.

57. See Elboim, "Stories as Modern Midrash." The comparison with Thomas Mann's *Joseph and His Brothers*, suggested by some readers, creates a historical irony, of course, as Mann himself learned his "shuffling" techniques from Jewish midrash. For another view of the trilogy as a whole see Avishai,

"People and Nation Between Myth and Daily Routine." For reviews of the English collection (*Thirst*), see Abrahamowitz; Olson.

58. Early reviews latched on the "allegorical" meaning of the novella, e.g., Oryan, "The Daily Truth of the Grey Man." For a theological interpretation, see Sheinfeld, "The Power of Sealed Issues." A full endorsement was offered by Hillel Halkin (the translator) who interpreted it, once again, as an allegory about the dangers of an unrestrained revival of religious myth and faith in miracles: "A Multifaceted Miniature." After the warm reception of the English translation, five (!) years later, and the publication of *Prophet* soon after, Hareven's innovations began to make some inroads into the Israeli cultural imagination. See an interview with Toren, "Consensus with 3 S's," where the author refuses the allegorical interpretations of the interviewer and restates her claim that *Prophet* is a modern midrash. Cf. the enthusiastic American reviews of *The Miracle Hater* in the same year: Mendelson; Lelchuk.

A deft structural analysis of the midrashic elements used (and reworked) by Hareven was performed by Nave, "In Those Days and at This Time." Her conclusion is nevertheless that "it is also possible to view the story as an allegory of the historical development of the Jews during the last century. . . . In contrast to the biblical narrative they [the Israelis] are seen as pragmatists, not fundamentalists" (pp. 85, 87). Shaked points out several "oppositions" that were unavoidably meaningful to contemporary Israelis (*Hebrew Narrative Prose* 4:135). Both Nave and Shaked suggest Freud's *Moses and Monotheism* as a possible inspiration for the revisionist portrayal of Moses—a plausible possibility in view of our analysis below of Hareven's evolving psychopolitics.

59. Hareven, "Fraternal or Filial Society?" in Hareven, *The Dulcinea Syndrome*, pp. 248–255.

60. The idealized portrait of that era was subsequently undermined by the "post-Zionist" writings of the 1980s. See especially Netiva Ben Yehuda's Palmach trilogy, chapter 7.

In 1981 Hareven revisited this idea ("Dor haplaga" [The Tower of Babel Generation], *The Dulcinea Syndrome*, pp. 260–268), arguing, much more problematically, for an overlap between the fraternal/filial opposition and the Labor (Ashkenazi)/Likkud (Sephardi) opposition. I very much doubt that she would repeat this essentializing analogy today . . .

61. Feldman, "Back to Vienna," p. 317. See also my recent "Isaac or Oedipus?"

62. See note 46, this chapter.

63. Yehoshua's notorious Freudian analysis of Jewish history and Zionist ideology is aptly included in a collection of essays entitled *Bizkhut hanormaliut*. Although published as *Between Right and Right*, the title literally means "In Praise of Normalcy"; however, the Hebrew connotations of *normali* are strongly psychological, almost synonymic with *shafui*, "sane" (*lo' normali*

means "crazy"). Cf. Hareven's statement in a recent interview with Edna Evron: "To my mind, insanity is not interesting: It is predictable, and its vocabulary is predictable. . . . I find sanity much more intriguing, because one always walks a very thin line, without losing balance." Hareven, "Literature is Not the Stock Market."

64. The initial incomprehension of *Prophet* resulted in typically bewildered reviews, on the one hand (see Drimmer, "Prophecy by Fools," who "does not understand what she wants") and overwritten "postmodernist" interpretations, on the other. For the latter see Sheinfeld, "What is Glittering?" and "Writing to the Past." Sheinfeld made the first attempt, however, to define the linguistic achievement of Hareven's "new Hebrew." Cf. the warm review of the English translation, *Prophet* by Kaganoff.

65. Can we escape the association of *Hanibal ante portas*, or, in its modern version, *Barbarians at the Gate* (Leonard Woolf's 1939 novel)? Interestingly, this association is stronger in the English translation, which "supplements" the Hebrew "likhnos hakol pnima" (get everything inside) with the word *gate* ("get everyone inside the gate," p. 8; p. 5).

Alternatively, the *in*appropriateness of the Gibeonites' fear and desperation while waiting for a calamity that is never to take place is reminiscent of Constantinos Cavafis's famous poem, "Waiting for the Barbarians," a Hebrew translation of which, by Yoram Bronovsky, was published in 1978 by Sifriat Poalim (*Shirim*, p. 14).

66. See the interview with Toren, Hareven, "Consensus with 3 S's."

67. See Hareven, "'Alimut" (Violence) and "A Secret Ancient Guilt." Reprinted in *The Dulcinea Syndrome*, pp. 221–231 and 160–165, respectively. More about this later in this chapter.

68. A lecture at the Van Leer Institute (Jerusalem), published in *Yediot Aḥaronot* (December 1989) and in *Eyeless in Gaza*, pp. 157–170. References are to Hareven, *The Vocabulary of Peace*, pp. 14–29.

69. See Hareven, *Eyeless in Gaza*, pp. 146–147.

70. See Shamir, "Carved in Rock"; Avishai, "Layers of Language and Meaning"; Lapid, "Myth: Succinct and Stimulating"; Sheinfeld, "God is a Matter of Quantity." The only renegade in this chorus of praises is Navot, "In Well-Chosen Words," but even he cannot refrain from complimenting the author for adopting the "wisdom of erasure"—a precious stone "that only few authors can flaunt."

71. See Hareven, *The Vocabulary of Peace*, pp. 88–94.

72. Hareven, "Shivḥei lea," *The Dulcinea Syndrome*, pp. 128–135.

73. See Campbell, *The Hero with a Thousand Faces*.

74. See Shamir "Carved in Rock"; Avishai, "Layers of Language"; Sheinfeld, "God is a Matter of Quantity."

75. See note 67 in this chapter.

76. The depth and spread of "the motif of the akedah" in Israeli literature has been discussed time and again; for a full bibliography see my recent "Isaac or Oedipus?"

77. Shoham, "The Isaac Syndrome." The essay got wide visibility in Hebrew and in English: it was published in 1975 in the Israeli daily *Ha'aretz*, in 1976 in the Israeli Journal for Education, *Megamot*, and in *American Imago*; in 1977 as a chapter in Shoham's Hebrew book *Halikhei tantalus*, and in 1979 in the English translation, *The Myth of Tantalus*. My references are to the last publication.

78. Quoted from Hareven, *The Dulcinea Syndrome*, p. 222.

79. Wellisch, *Isaac and Oedipus*. For details see Feldman, "Isaac or Oedipus?"

80. I am thinking primarily about novelist A. B. Yehoshua—to whom we soon return—and dramatist Hanoch Levin; for more, see Feldman, "Isaac or Oedipus?"

81. Spiegel, *The Last Trial*. The original Hebrew essay was published in 1950. For a comparison of Spiegel's and Shoham's interpretations of Genesis Rabbah, see Feldman, "Isaac or Oedipus?"

82. In her 1985 lecture on "Language as Midrash" Hareven revisits "violence," this time from a linguistic perspective, again echoing Giora Shoham's latest book at the time. She traces the derivation of the Hebrew word for violence, *'alimut*, to the biblical verbal root that means "tie" (*'.l.m.*) and, by derivation, "mute," "tongue-tied" (*'ilem*). Significantly, the semantic extension to "violence" derives from the later Aramaic usage (Second Temple period), where *'alim* or *'alam* means "strong and demanding." The psychological "wisdom" of this semantic development was probed, appropriately enough, by Shoham in his book *'Alimut ha-'elem* (The Silence of Violence). His untranslatable pun establishes a psychological causality between mental "muteness" (*'elem*), namely, the inability to express emotions and communicate, and violence (*'alimut*). Hareven's essay is reprinted in *Messiah or Knesset*, pp. 175–193.

83. Hareven, *The Dulcinea Syndrome*, pp. 160–165.

84. Hareven, *The Vocabulary of Peace*, p. 27. The last clause of my quote is missing in the English; I supplemented it from *Eyeless in Gaza*, p. 168.

85. See my essays "Back to Genesis" [Hebrew] and "Isaac or Oedipus?"; for earlier Laius-Abrahamic fathers who raise a knife over their sons, see my "Back to Vienna."

86. See Hareven, "Against Charisma," in Hareven, *The Vocabulary of Peace*, pp. 199–214. Originally published in *Yediot Aharonot* (October 1 and 6, 1993).

87. There is an ambiguity in the Hebrew in this passage that the translation can not adequately represent. Since *'elohim* (God) is morphologically plural in Hebrew, despite its consistent usage as a singular noun (with a verb in the sin-

gular conjugation), Hareven can afford to play with it, using it alternatively in singular (God) and in plural (gods).

88. Hareven, "Laius, the Father Repressed by Freud." By pure coincidence, my own "biblical" critique of Freud was published earlier that year; see Feldman, " 'And Rebecca Loved Jacob.' "

89. No other essay has aroused such a barrage of responses. Six counteressays and letters to the editor were published in *Ha'aretz*, December 23, 1994, p. B6.

90. Hareven, "Woman's Talent for Sanity"; delivered at a conference, "Women Write and Speak Peace," Tel Aviv, March 26, 1997; published in May 1997 in *Yediot Aharonot* (a few months after the publication of the trilogy as a whole).

91. See Barrett, *Virginia Woolf: Women and Writing*, an edited collection of essays.

7. 1948 — HEBREW "GENDER" AND ZIONIST IDEOLOGY: NETIVA BEN YEHUDA

1. Ben Amotz and Ben Yehuda, *Milon le'ivrit meduberet*.

2. Ben Yehuda, *1948—Bein hasfirot* (1948—Between Calendars); *Miba'ad la'avotot* (Through the Binding Ropes); *Keshepartzah hamedinah* (When the State Broke Out).

3. See Poole, " 'We all put up with you Virginia,' " p. 93.

4. Margalit, "The *Palmach* According to Netiva," for example, rejects the "immediacy" of the narrative, claiming that, in spite of its effectiveness, it lacked the enriched reevaluation expected after thirty-five years; she totally accepts Ben Yehuda's own "judgment," concluding that *1948—Bein hasfirot* is neither history nor literature. Einat, "The Portrait of an Israeli Macho," goes even further. It is impossible, she charges, to weave a broad canvas of internal and external impressions on the basis of an "elementary" language like the one used by Ben Yehuda.

5. Or, "Between the Sheaves and the Sword," calls the book "a literary bombshell," "literature without quotation marks"; Golan, "The Last *Palmakhnikit*," although critical of the monotony of the narrator's slang, properly evaluates the rhetorical "contradictions" and the major motifs and labels the book "a social historical novel," part of the Palmach literature; the title of Oren's review, "Nevertheless: Real Literature," speaks for itself: she points out correctly the suspense quality of the ostensibly associative narration, believing that the author is *un*aware that "there is method in her madness;" I beg to differ, as I argue below.

More extensive (and fully appreciative) analyses, to which we shall return, were offered later by Miron, "Had It Been Written Then"; Tzemah, "Three Who Wrote."

6. In many reviews of *Miba'ad la'avotot* attention is given to both the literariness and the "gender trouble" of Ben Yehuda's "project." See, especially, Bar-Yosef, "Several Things At Once"; Bahur, "The Myth-Breaking Slang"; Shehori, "The Youthful and the Not So Beautiful." Less enthusiastic, but still upholding the experiential intensity of the book, are Boshes, "An Argument with History"; and Nitzan, "A Long Reckoning with the War."

7. See, on this issue, Kartun-Blum, "Don't Play Hide and Seek with Mothers."

8. Quoted in Golan, *'Al 'atzman*, p. 17, thirteen interviews with Israeli women. This response is narrated by the first interviewee, Rachel Barda, who—under the pseudonym MIRKA—is one of the major female protagonists in Ben Yehuda's narratives, a courageous fighter, "the second woman demolition officer of the Palmach" (Ben Yehuda being the first), who was severly wounded in the war, almost losing her leg.

9. See Ben Yehuda, "Netiva Ben Yehuda," an interview with Gil Hovav.

10. Ibid. We can add to this the personal testimony of a young colleague, Doron Lamm, who responded to my first essay on Ben Yehuda (in Hebrew) with a very vivid and telling anecdote:

> In 1978, as an education officer, I called Netiva and asked her to lecture to a *kurs ktzinot* [female officers in training] about her 1947–1948 experiences after reading about her in a small book that I once found at my friend's house. . . . She was totally surprised, and for fifteen minutes was convinced that I was an old friend from the Palmach who was trying to pull her leg. Then she objected, saying that it was too personal and that she never talked about it, "not even to my own daughter." . . . Finally, I persuaded her to come. When she arrived at the base, she was very agitated. She swore to the cadets that it was her first (and last) talk on the subject. . . . One of the cadets had to pour the water into her glass because her hands shook so violently (she is also a highly theatrical figure). She gave a magnificent talk, though not as personal as she got later in her books.
>
> At times, I like to flatter myself thinking that this talk served as a catalyst to her willingness to articulate and publish her memories. (Personal communication, November 4, 1998)

11. Yoffe, *Nikhtav betashah*.

12. The short list of women also includes the veteran poet Yocheved Bat-Miriam (1902–1980), who lost her only son in that war, and Edna Kornfeld, the only writer about whom no biographical information is given, except for the fact that "her poem 'Pogrom' is a response to the murder of her husband, Beni Rosenberg" (by an Arab mob, who besieged his car in 1947), and "was reprinted in her book *Eyes at Night* (1954)."

13. Ben Yehuda, *1948—Between Calendars*, p. 271.

14. Cf. her later anthology, *Autobiography Through Songs and Lyrics.* See also Fuchs, "Gender and Characterization."

15. Cf. de Lauretis, *Technologies of Gender,* pp. 3–5. For recent critiques of "gender," see chapter 2, this volume.

16. See chapter 5, pp. 20–33.

17. Golan, "The Last *Palmachnikit.*"

18. Miron, *Facing the Silent Brother.*

19. Although the identification of the male Jew as feminine goes back to medieval times, it reached new heights in the nineteenth century, when it was "scientifically" rationalized; see on this issue studies by Gilman, *Jewish Self-Hatred* and *Freud, Race, and Gender;* Harrowitz, *Antisemitism, Misogyny, and the Logic of Cultural Difference;* and Boyarin, *Unheroic Conduct.* Zionism has no doubt internalized this identification even as it attempted to eradicate its ostensible causes. A case in point is the presence of Otto Weininger's sexual racism in the works of the proponents of Zionism early in this century (Brenner, Agnon, etc.); see Hoffman, "Bodies and Borders."

On the psychopolitical implications of this Zionist complex in Israeli literature, see my "Back to Genesis."

20. A major theme in the third sequel, *When the State Broke Out,* is the ridicule felt and expressed by the young palmachniks toward the new immigrant soldiers, who embodied all the negative qualities of the Diaspora Other propagated by the "meta-Zionist narrative." Again, Ben Yehuda anticipated here one of the main preoccupations of Israeli scholarship in the last decade.

8. BEYOND THE FEMINIST ROMANCE: RUTH ALMOG

1. Almog, *Shorshei 'Avir.* All translations are mine. Portions of the following analysis were presented in a number of lectures between March 1991 (at Yale University) and May 1993 (at Brandeis University); see also my "From Feminist Romance to an Anatomy of Freedom."

2. An interview in *Na'amat,* "Writing Creates an Awareness of Negative Phenomena." Cf. her question, "How long can we live with the suppression of another people?" in an interview with Gideon Engler, "Literature Has No Justification Without Subversiveness." In that interview she also said that *Shorshei 'Avir* expressed the feeling that "it is impossible to scratch one's conscience without asking questions clearly and directly."

3. Shammas, *Arabesques;* see my essay, "Postcolonial Memory, Postmodernist Intertextuality."

4. Hirschfeld, "A Metaphor for the Design of the Soul." Cf. Ya'akov Siman-Tov, "The Person, the Design, the Homeland Landscape"; Alex Zehavi, "A Breakthrough Beyond the Familiar"; Netzer, "A Sunset Red as Blood." For a structural analysis of the reading process the novel demands see

Wolf, especially in her second review, "Roots of Air." Her first, "Madness Is the Wisdom of the Individuum," is more schematic.

5. See Almog, "An Interview with Ruth Almog," by Leah Fuchs. In other interviews Almog revealed the identity of her model: the late Livia Rokah, the daughter of a former mayor of Tel Aviv, who in the 1960s was a New Left activist in Israel and later became a radical extremist in Italy, where she stayed in exile until she committed suicide. See Almog's interview with Hadassah Wolman: Almog, "Inventing One's Own Life" (a translation of an interview originally published in *Yediot Aharonot*); and with Gideon Engler: Almog, "Literature Has No Justification Without Subversiveness."

6. Almog, "An Interview with Ruth Almog." Cf. Almog's feminist critique of Israeli culture in her lecture "On Being a Writer."

7. The emphasis is on *Israeli*, not *Hebrew*. For there are several treatments—rather ambivalent—of this issue in Dvora Baron's stories, while Leah Goldberg epitomized it not only in her autobiographic novel *Vehu ha'or* (see the introduction and chapter 1, this volume) but in her life as well (see also note 10 below). However, if this novel can be at all considered a forerunner of Almog's it is not so much for its mother-daughter relations, which are quite different—almost the opposite—but rather for its preoccupation with the effect on the daughter of parental "madness." However, the fact that in Goldberg's case it is the father who is the "carrier" of the mental disease leaves it out of the particular feminist discourse we follow below.

8. On the general shift from the oedipal to the preoedipal in psychoanalytic theory, see chapters 2 and 5.3. Cf. Rich, "Motherhood and Daughterhood," in her *Of Woman Born*; Friday, *My Mother/My Self*, which was published in Hebrew in 1980, rather early in the history of the translation of feminist work from English (Rich was translated only in 1988). On the literary representation of this paradigm see Davidson and Broner, *The Lost Tradition*; Abel, Hirsch, and Langland, *The Voyage In*; Hirsch, *The Mother/Daughter Plot*; and Heilbrun, "*To the Lighthouse*." Recent reevaluations include Johnson, *Strong Mothers, Weak Wives*; and Mens-Verhulst, Schreurs, and Woertman, *Daughtering and Mothering*.

9. See interviews with Orah Zarnitzki, Almog, "The Price is Erosion"; Naomi Aviv, Almog, "Love's Defeat"; and Billie Moskona-Lerman, Almog, "Father Complex."

10. Most notoriously, Gur's *Afterbirth* and Lev's *The First Morning in Paradise*; but see also Zilberman's *Woman Inside Woman*; Bernstein's *Provision*; and short stories by Savyon Liebrecht, Hana Bat-Shahar, Shulamit Gilboa and Ofra Ofer. Some of the latter appeared in the anthology, Dvash and Modan, *Mothers and Daughters* (1997), the first Israeli "statement" on the topic, a lag of two decades after its American emergence. This anthology includes also poems (several by Shulamit Lapid and Zvia ben Yosef Ginor), as well as Leah

Goldberg's classic on the subject, the 1930s poem, "To My Mother's Portrait." Typically, it is mostly the daughter's perspective that is represented; the mother's story is still untold. A little-known, small anthology was published a decade earlier, borrowing Nancy Friday's title; see Binyamini, *'Imi va'ani.*

Jewish American feminists may have had an earlier start (e.g., Chernin, *In My Mother's House*), as attested by the recent study by Burstein, *Writing Mothers, Writing Daughters.* But see, more recently, Jong, *Inventing Memory.*

11. Elizabeth R. Baer, "The Sisterhood of Jane Eyre and Antoinette Cosway," in Abel, Hirsch, and Langland, *The Voyage In*, pp. 131–148. Baer lists six recent re-visions of *Jane Eyre*, from Elizabeth Hardwick's to Gilbert and Gubar's notorious *The Madwoman in the Attic*. As Almog has related, Jean Rhys (1894–1979) is one of her favorite authors, and *Wide Sargasso Sea* one of her favorite novels (personal communication, March 1998; see also an earlier interview with Aviv, Almog, "Love's Defeat."

12. Adrienne Rich, "When We Dead Awaken: Writing as Re-Vision," in Rich, *On Lies, Secrets, and Silence*, p. 148.

13. Rhys, *Yam sargasso haraḥav*, trans. Aharon Amir.

14. Almog, "Love's Defeat."

15. Geldman, "An Essay on the Blocking of the Soul"; Zarhi, "On Elisheva's Loss [Destruction]." A more traditional reader saw the book as portraying "the disfigured image of the 'liberated' woman, who builds and destroys towers [in the air] on the basis of her mental instability [*sic!*]; Blatt, "A Woman in Crisis."

16. A note about the treatment of lesbianism in this novel is in order. This is the only time it is mentioned in Almog's work, curiously published contemporaneously with Hareven's *Loneliness* (see chapter 5.3). In both stories homoeroticism is viewed as a substitute for failed heterosexuality; however, while Hareven fully develops the psychosexual dynamics involved, Almog's protagonist only toys with the idea but rejects it out of hand as an unacceptable violation of the norm, which she upholds even as she is left on its margins.

17. Almog, *Mavet bageshem; Death in the Rain*, trans. Dalya Bilu. Reviews of this novel includes Gershon Shaked's enthusiastic article ("It has been a long time since I have read such a tender, sensitive, and humane book"), "Pain, Love, Death"; Zehavi, "Fate and Sophistication"; Domb's analysis of the function of Greece in this novel, chapter 3 of her *Home Thoughts from Abroad*, pp. 62–78; and Gila Ramras-Rauch's review in *World Literature Today*, which highlights the Mediterranean flavor of the novel as part of the spatial orientation in Israeli literature.

18. See Shaked, "Pain, Love, Death"; and Domb, *Home Thoughts from Abroad*.

19. Levitt, "The Creator as an Anarchist."

20. Almog, "Love's Defeat."

21. Gelbetz, "Ruth's Nightly Charities." Kenaz's exploration of "decay and stagnation" in Petaḥ Tikva, *After the Holidays*, was published in 1967, during Almog's formative years as a writer.

22. Reviews of *Nashim* (Women) typically identified its existentialist and psychologist underpinnings, but sometimes denied its "feminist" implications; e.g., Oren, "Like a Bolted Window, as a Closed Fist." Cf. Shamir, "A Woman in Her Four Square Feet"; Ben-Zion, "Her Heroine, in Her Own Foreign City." The first feministically oriented analysis (of a single story, "Hitztamtzemut") was suggested only in 1993; see Lubin, "A Woman Reading a Woman." For a rebuttal see Rattok, *Theory and Interpretation*. For the traditional nexus of suicide and the feminine see Higonnet, "Suicide."

23. Attention should be paid to this parenthetical comment—this is an early indication of the orientation of Almog's "postfeminist" fiction, as we shall see below.

24. Cf. Showalter,"Hysteria, Feminism, and Gender," on male hysteria; and see note 43 below.

25. See Gutkind, "Roots of Air or Roots in the Land?"; Oren, "Like Roots in the Air and a Worm in the Dark"; Brenner, "Reflections of/on Zionism in Recent Hebrew Fiction"; and, most recently, Shaked, "Between a Daughter and Her Fathers." See also notes 2 and 4. For a late recognition of the novel's feminist import, see Schwartz, "Hebrew Fiction."

26. See her lecture "On Being a Writer." Almog's early short story collections, *Marguerita's Nightly Charities, After Tu Bishvat*, were received warmly, e.g., Yoram Bronovsky. She also published a number of collections for children—for which she won two literary prizes—and one thriller, coauthored (see the introduction, note 17).

27. The proximity of the fiction to the life was made "public" when the writer Ehud Ben-Ezer identified himself in the child Udi (a nickname for Ehud) in the second collection. See his "Everyone with His Own Petaḥ-Tikva." Cf. Shamir, "Childhood in Petaḥ-Tikva."

28. Some hesitant scenes of childhood were later ventured by Heda Boshes (1981), Shulamit Gilboa (1993), and Sh. Shifra (1994), though most of their autobiographical retrospections do not regress all the way back to early childhood.

29. See chapter 5, note 33. Barring any deep psychological motivation, for which we have no data, I can offer the following conjecture. In her attempt to disassociate her poetics from that of the literary corpus of the Palmach, Kahana-Carmon also erased thematic markers that would have betrayed her generational "place"—among them the kibbutz, which was of course highly represented in this literature. For her childhood and parents, see the interview with Yaakov Besser: Kahana-Carmon, "Actually, It Writes Itself." The only

author of that generation with whom she has been aligned is S. Yizhar (b. 1917), who also "skipped over" his childhood until the 1990s, when, at age seventy-five, he made a miraculous comeback with a series of early childhood reconstructions.

For Hareven our conjecture leads in the opposite direction. Avid Zionist that she is, she may have been trying to construct a semi-native biography (not as extreme, but similar to that of Dahn Ben Amotz [1924–1990]; see his "disclosure" in *To Remember and Forget*) by repressing her European childhood on the eve of the Holocaust, with all the traumatic memories and the ideological discomfort it evidently aroused (on her essay, "On Being a Levantine," see chapter 5).

As for Lapid, no persuasive explanation for the absence of the autobiographic impulse in her writing presents itself. Except for some early stories, her generic choices (thrillers bordering on social farce) do not, as a rule, allow for personal introspection.

30. Chapter 5, note 33.

31. See the introduction in Abel, Hirsch, and Langland, *The Voyage In*.

32. Almog, "Just a Person Who Writes"; emphasis is mine.

33. We have little extratextual evidence for this particular family dynamics. Almog repeatedly recounted her family history: her parents, both of them physicians, immigrated to Palestine from Germany in 1933 (!). The moving force behind this step was her mother, about whom Almog is usually reticent. In Petah Tikva, the medical profession not being much of a source of income, they made their living by raising bees (for honey). The family was Orthodox, and apparently strictly so—until her father's early death when she was fourteen.

34. Especially in the story of Hagar (chapter 1), whose father was killed in (military) action, who is said to have been oedipally attracted to "father substitutes." While "the psychology of orphans" is openly thematized in the dialogue between Hagar and her mother, it is latently present throughout the book, making orphanhood a figurative "Jewish/Israeli condition."

35. Almog, "Libraries of (in) My Life."

36. Billie Moskona-Lerman's interview, titled "A Father Complex," in which the writer of the present study is quoted as telling the author that her heroines (in the collection *Women*) suffer from an Oedipal complex.

37. In Almog's case this is only a fictional representation—nowhere has she corroborated this extratextually; herself an avid student of classical philology, she may have endowed her father figures with her beloved subject in an attempt to heal the narcissistic wound that her own father's early death, and, perhaps, stern (German) parenting, inflicted on her.

38. Freud, "Creative Writers and Day-Dreaming."

39. In Leviticus 16:22 this phrase, *be'eretz gzera*, describes the wilderness into which the ritual "scapegoat," bearing all the sins of the community, is

"exiled." In later Hebrew, however, *gzera* (*mishamaim*) has come to mean a "divine decree" or a "fateful judgment," whereas *gzerot* stands for "persecutions." For the modern Hebrew reader, then, the name of the book literally means "In the Land of Decree/Fate/Persecution." Given the author's penchant for Greek mythology, I would even add *ta Moira*.

40. For the use of this metaphor, see Boose and Flowers, *Daughters and Fathers*, section 2, "*In Nomine Patris*: The Daughter in Her Father's House." The next step in the development of the woman artist is naturally metaphorized in the transition to "*In Nomine Filiae*" (ibid., section 3), namely, "The Artist as Her Father's Daughter," which is the "title" claimed for Woolf in chapter 4, this volume. Elizabeth Abel's somewhat different interpretation of the same argument, "Cam the Wicked," is included in this section (pp. 326–343).

41. The linkage between Germany and Crete, obviously based on the Germans' Romantic cult of the classics, is a motif that also anticipates *Mr. Mani*— where it is once again given a "national" rather than a personal interpretation.

42. See on this point Trible, *God and the Rhetoric of Sexuality*.

43. The reference, of course, is to Gilbert and Gubar, *The Madwoman in the Attic* (1979), which deals with *nineteenth*-century "mad" heroines. Feminist scholarship on this heavily loaded issue of *Women and Madness* ranges from Chesler's book through Felman's 1975 essay by this name, subtitled, "The Critical Phallacy," to Yalon's *Maternity, Mortality and the Literature of Madness*. Within this general theme, hysteria holds a special position, ever since its "discovery" by the nineteenth-century medical establishment. Its Freudian career and its post-Freudian reevalution by Foucault, Lacan, and French feminism (especially Cixous and Clement, *The Newly Born Woman*) is well-known and need not be documented here. A most useful summary is Gilman, King, Porter, Rousseau, and Showalter, *Hysteria Beyond Freud*. See, especially, Showalter's "Hysteria, Feminism, and Gender," for a different position on this issue: pp. 327, 333, 334. Cf. Logan, *Nerves and Narratives*. The theory of madness most relevant to our text, however, is R. D. Laing's. Romantically interpreting madness as existential freedom, this approach— developed in the stormy 1960s and available in Hebrew since 1977—was absorbed into the revolutionary discourse of the 1960s. The feminist interpretation of madness made its way into Hebrew discourse only in 1987, with the translation of Chesler's book, *Nashim veshiga'on*.

44. Not that clear, apparently, to judge from the superficial treatment of the subject in the critical reception of the book. It is also missing from Dan Miron's very short list of Hebrew literary works that deal with psychosis "without using it allegorically"; see his *Haḥole hamedume* (*Le Médecin Imaginaire*), p. 177.

45. See her interview with Orah Zarnitzki: Almog, "The Price Is Erosion."

46. For an exposition of the evolution of Laing's theories and a critique of their implication for female psychology and feminist ideology, see Mitchell, *Psychoanalysis and Feminism*, pp. 227–273. On the literary representation of "Women's Narratives of Departure" in general, see Stout, *Through The Window, Out the Door.*

47. An interview with Avraham Balaban: Almog, "Real Life Takes Place Elsewhere," which was conducted after the publication of *Mavet bageshem.*

48. Poole," 'We all put up with you Virginia' " p. 79.

49. See Showalter, "Introduction"; "Hysteria, Feminism, and Gender."

50. She apparently does base herself on one of the early pioneers (*biluyim*), by whom and about whom she found some documents, but soon gave up and let her imagination take over. See Gutkind, "Roots of Air or Roots in the Land?"

51. Oren, "Like Roots in the Air and a Worm in the Dark."

52. See *European Literature*, pp. 766–768.

53. Hebrew scholarship on Brenner is too voluminous to be cited here. For a small window into his psychosexual complexes in English see my "From Dostoyevsky to Brenner" (for a revised version in Hebrew see "Between the Mythic and the Tragic"); and Mintz, *Banished from Their Father's Table.*

54. As I have argued above, Almog anticipated this resemblance in one of her autobiographical literary columns in *Ha'aretz*, a decade earlier. See note 35, this chapter and text there.

55. Mitchell, *Psychoanalysis and Feminism*, p. 285 ff.

56. The self-consciousness of the protagonists, here and elsewhere in the novel, is in fact one of its weaknesses. Whether in dialogues or inner monologues, the characters are often (particularly in book 2) too transparent to themselves and to the reader—as if the author had very little trust in her readers' ability to infer and generalize.

57. In addition to reverberations of John Irving's *The World According to Garp*, "Jacques" evokes the name of Jean Jacques Rousseau, the father of the romantic philosophies of freedom, the source of "liberté, egalité" etc. Mutatis mutandis, it also brings to mind the other two Jacques of the 1960s, Lacan and Derrida. This plethora of intellectual intertexts has not fared well with readers and critics, who as a rule preferred the autobiographical (= "authentic") charm of part 1 over the harsh realities and the "unrealized" complex relationships of part 2!

58. Mira's experience bears out Robin Morgan's analysis of "the sexuality of terrorism" in her *The Demon Lover*. The presence of rape in narratives of female subjectivity demands a separate discussion. There are differences, however, between the extratextual rape in *Gei Oni*, the half-metaphorical one in *Up in Montifer*, and the grimly realistic rape in the present text. Its centrality to the plot resembles the one that takes place in *The Women's Room*.

59. In English see Almog's essay "On Being a Writer."
60. See Feldman, "Feminism Under Siege."
61. E.g., Amos Oz, Hanoch Bartov, David Shahar . . . and see my "Gender In/Difference."
62. Showalter, "Hysteria, Feminism, and Gender," pp. 327, 334.
63. Mitchell, *Women, the Longest Revolution*, p. 289 ff.
64. See note 23, this chapter.

AFTERWORD: THE NINETIES — PRELUDE TO A
POSTMODERNIST MILLENNIUM?

1. Personal communication, November 1998.
2. See chapter 5, note 36.
3. See Berlowitz, "Is Israeli Literature Being Feminized?" who argues that contemporary Israeli women's fiction lacks the subversiveness and protest typical of women's fiction around the world. Cf. Israel, "Feminine Writing and Israeli Writers."
4. London, "Four Religious Women Novelists Who Topped the Best-Seller Lists."
5. Some of the most original fiction defies any of these categories: see Gabriella Avigur-Rotem, Shulamit Gilbo'a, Zippi Keller.
6. Cf. Rabinyan, *Persian Brides*.
7. See Lazovski, "Running with She-Wolves."
8. Kahana-Carmon, "Do You (f.) Want to Write a Book?"
9. The debate has been cogently summarized in Ginor's forthcoming essay, "The Zionist Dystopia," which convincingly defines the particular slant of Castel-Bloom's Israeli postmodernism.
10. Lyotard, *The Postmodern Condition*, pp. 32–37.
11. For a critique of the Israeli version of the postmodernist culture of PC, see Taub, *Hamered hashafuf*. Cf. Miron, "The Unholy Trinity"; and Schwartz's rejoinder, "Hebrew Fiction." For more partisan views, see Balaban, *Hagal ha'aḥer*; and see especially the work of Gurevitch: "Postmodernism in Israeli Literature"; "Recycled Dreams."
12. In *Te'oria vebikoret* 5:165–182, under the title *Viku'aḥ: sifrut nashim* (A Debate: Women's Literature), Lily Rattok, Orly Lubin, and Rivka Feldhai argue over Kristevan and other subversive readings of Kahana-Carmon's early stories, while each forcefully holds on to a hegemonic position within the critical discourse.
13. Kahana-Carmon, "Do You (f.) Want to Write a Book?"

Selected Bibliography

Abel, Elizabeth. "(E)merging Identities: The Dynamics of Female Friendship in Contemporary Fiction by Women." *Signs* 6 (1981): 413–435.
— "Narrative Structure(s) and Female Development: The Case of *Mrs. Dalloway.*" In Elizabeth Abel, Marianne Hirsch, and Elizabeth Langland, eds., *The Voyage In: Fictions of Female Development*, pp. 161–185. Hanover: University Press of New England, 1983.
— " 'Cam the Wicked': Virginia Woolf's Portrait of the Artist as Her Father's Daughter." In Jane Marcus, ed., *Virginia Woolf and Bloomsbury: A Centenary Celebration.* Bloomington: Indiana University Press, 1987.
— *Virginia Woolf and the Fictions of Psychoanalysis.* Chicago: University of Chicago Press, 1989.
Abel, Elizabeth, Marianne Hirsch, and Elizabeth Langland, eds. *The Voyage In: Fictions of Female Development.* Hanover: University Press of New England, 1983.
Abrahamowitz, Molly. *Thirst* (book review). *Library Journal* 121, no. 6 (April 1, 1996): 120.
Abrahamsen, David. *The Mind and Death of a Genius.* New York: Columbia University Press, 1946.
Abramson, Glenda, ed. *The Oxford Book of Hebrew Short Stories.* Oxford: Oxford University Press, 1996.
Adar, Avraham. "Simone de Beauvoir: Her Own Person." *Ma'ariv*, April 18, 1986.
Adler, Ruth. "Dvora Baron: Daughter of the Shtetl." In Judith Baskin, ed., *Women of the Word: Jewish Women and Jewish Writing*, pp. 91–110. Detroit: Wayne State University Press, 1994.
Agnon, S. Y. *'Ad hena* [Until Now]. Tel Aviv and Jerusalem: Schocken, 1964.
— *'Al kapot haman'ul* [On the Handles of the Lock]. Tel Aviv and Jerusalem: Schocken, 1975.
— *Sefer hama'asim* [The Book of Deeds]. Tel Aviv and Jerusalem: Schocken, 1974.
Almog, Ruth. *Hasdei halailah shel margaretah* [Marguerita's Nightly Charities; stories]. Tel Aviv: Tarmil, 1969.
— *Be'eretz gzerah* [The Exile]. Tel Aviv: Am Oved, 1971.
— "Libraries of (in) My Life." *Ha'aretz*, December 17, 1976.
— *'Aharei tu bishvat* [After Tu Bishvat; stories]. Tel Aviv: Tarmil, 1979.

— *'Et hazar veha'oyev* [The Stranger and the Foe: A Report on a (Writer's) Block]. Tel Aviv: Sifriat Poalim, 1980.

— *Mavet bageshem.* Jerusalem: Keter, 1982.

— "Real Life Takes Place Elsewhere." Interview with Avraham Balaban. *Yediot Aharonot,* May 14, 1982.

— *Nashim* [Women; stories]. Jerusalem: Keter, 1986.

— "Love's Defeat." Interview with Naomi Aviv. *Kol Ha'ir Jerusalem,* October 10, 1986.

— "Father Complex." Interview with Billie Moskona-Lerman. *Ma'ariv,* November 21, 1986.

— *Shorshei 'Avir* [Roots of Air]. Jerusalem: Keter, 1987.

— "The Creator as an Anarchist." Interview with Anat Levitt. *Ha'aretz,* May 8, 1987.

— "The Price Is Erosion." Interview with Orah Zarnitzki. *Devar Hashavu'a,* December 4, 1987.

— "Literature Has No Justification Without Subversiveness." Interview with Gideon Engler. *Ma'ariv,* December 11, 1987.

— "Writing Creates an Awareness of Negative Phenomena." Interview. *Na'amat,* January 1988.

— "Inventing One's Own Life." Interview with Hadassah Wolman. *Modern Hebrew Literature* 1 (1988): 58–62.

— "An Interview with Ruth Almog." Leah Fuchs. *HaDoar,* January 13, 1989, pp. 14–15.

— "On Being a Writer." In Naomi B. Sokoloff, Anne Lapidus Lerner, and Anita Norich, eds., *Gender and Text in Modern Hebrew and Yiddish Literature,* pp. 227–234. New York: Jewish Theological Seminary, 1992.

— "Just a Person Who Writes." Interview with Wendy Zierler. *Jerusalem Post Magazine,* May 22, 1992, p. 19.

— *Tikkun 'omanuti* [Artistic Mending]. Jerusalem: Keter, 1993.

— *Death in the Rain.* Trans. Dalya Bilu. Santa Fe: Red Crane, 1993.

Aloni, Shulamit. *Nashim kivnei 'adam* [Women as Human Beings]. Jerusalem: Keter, 1976.

Alonso, Harriet Harman. *Peace as a Woman's Issue: A History of the U.S. Movement for World Peace and Women's Rights.* Syracuse: Syracuse University Press, 1993.

Alper, Rivka. *Hamitnahalim bahar* [The Settlers on the Mountain]. Tel Aviv: Am Oved, 1962.

Alter, Robert. *Defenses of the Imagination: Jewish Writers and Modern Historical Crisis.* Philadelphia: Jewish Publication Society, 1977.

— *The Art of Biblical Narrative.* New York: Basic, 1981.

— *The Invention of Hebrew Prose.* Seattle: University of Washington Press, 1988.

— "A Sensitive and Subtle Receptor" [on Kahana-Carmon's *Kan nagur*]. *Ha'aretz/Sfarim*, May 8, 1996, p. 8.

Amichai, Yehuda. *Yehuda Amichai: A Life of Poetry, 1948–1994*. Trans. Benjamin and Barbara Harshav. HarperCollins, 1994.

Aschkenasy, Nehama. *Eve's Journey: Feminine Images in Hebraic Literary Tradition*. Philadelphia: University of Pennsylvania Press, 1986.

Avishai, Mordekhai. "Life in Crisis in Shulamith Hareven's Stories." *Ma'ariv*, May 22, 1970.

— "Layers of Language and Meaning." *Al Hamishmar*, February 24, 1995.

— "People and Nation Between Myth and Daily Routine." *Moznaim* 70, no. 3 (December 1996): 52–54.

Azaryahu, Sara. *Hit'aḥdut nashim 'ivriyot leshivuy zekhuyot be'eretz israel, 1947* [The Association of Hebrew Women for Equal Rights in Eretz Israel: Chapters in the History of Women in the Land, 1900–1947]. Introduction by Marcia Freedman. Haifa: Fund for Support of Women, 1977.

Azmon, Yael, ed. *'Eshnav leḥayehen shel nashim beḥevrot yehudiyot* [A Window Onto Women's Lives in Jewish Communities]. Jerusalem: Zalman Shazar Center, 1995.

— "War, Mothers, and a Girl with Braids: Involvement of Mothers' Peace Movements in the National Discourse in Israel." *ISSR* 12, no. 1 (1997): 109–128.

Azmon, Yael and Dafna N. Izraeli, eds. *Women in Israel: A Sociological Anthology*. New Brunswick and London: Transaction, 1993.

Bahur, Yona. "The Myth-Breaking Slang." *Ha'aretz*, August 2, 1985.

Bair, Deirdre. *Simone de Beauvoir: A Biography*. New York: Summit, 1990.

Balaban, Avraham. *Hakadosh vehadrakon* [The Saint and the Dragon]. Tel Aviv: Hakibbutz Hameuchad, 1979.

— *Hagal ha'aḥer* [The Other/Different Wave]. Jerusalem: Keter, 1996.

Baron, Dvora. *Parshiyot* (Collected Stories). Jerusalem: Mossad Bialik, 1951.

— *The Thorny Path*. Trans. Joseph Schachter. Jerusalem: Israel Universities Press, 1969.

Barrett, Eileen and Patricia Cramer, eds. *Virginia Woolf: Lesbian Readings*. New York: New York University Press, 1997.

Barrett, Michele, ed. *Virginia Woolf: Women and Writing*. London: Women's Press, 1979.

Bartana, Orzion. "A Grey Reality." *Davar*, November 28, 1980.

Bar-Yosef, Hamutal. "Several Things at Once—Literature Too." *Yediot Aharonot*, April 21, 1985.

— "Trapped in the Equation 'Woman = Nature, Man = Culture' and Esther Raab's Poem 'Holy Grandmothers in Jerusalem.' " In Yael Azmon, ed., *'Eshnav leḥayehen shel nashim beḥevrot yehudiyot* [A Window on Women's Lives in Jewish Communities], pp. 337–347. Jerusalem: Zalman Shazar Center, 1995.

Baskin, Judith R., ed. *Women of the Word: Jewish Women and Jewish Writing.* Detroit: Wayne State University Press, 1994.

Bat Oren, Teḥiya. *Shiḥrur ha'isha—le'an?* [Women's Liberation—Where to?] Tel Aviv: Bustan, 1975.

Baym, Nina. "Melodramas of Beset Manhood: How Theories of American Fiction Exclude Women Authors." In Elaine Showalter, ed., *The New Feminist Criticism: Essays on Women, Literature, and Theory.* New York: Pantheon, 1985.

Beauvoir, Simone de. *Hamandarinim* [Les mandarins]. Trans. Zvi Arad. Tel Aviv: Sifriat Poalim, 1958 [1954].

— *The Second Sex* [Le deuxième sexe]. Penguin, 1974 [1949].

— *Mavet kal me'od* [Une mort très douce]. Trans. Mira Frankel. Jerusalem: Keter, 1983 [1964].

— *'Isha shvura* [La femme rompue]. Trans. Miryam Tiv'on. Tel Aviv: Zmora-Bitan, 1984 [1968].

— *Damam shel 'aḥerim* [Le sang des autres]. Trans. Miryam Tiv'on. Tel Aviv: Zmora-Bitan, 1985 [1945].

Beer, Gillian. "The Island and the Aeroplane: The Case of Virginia Woolf." In Homi K. Bhabha, ed., *Nation and Narration,* pp. 265–290. London: Routledge, 1990.

Bell, Quentin. *Virginia Woolf: A Biography.* 2 vols. London: Hogarth, 1972.

— *Virginia Voolf: biografia.* Trans. Leah Dovev. Tel Aviv: Schocken, 1988.

Ben Amotz, Dahn. *Lizkor velishko'aḥ.* Tel Aviv: Zmora-Bitan, 1968.

— *To Remember, to Forget.* Trans. Zeva Shapiro. Philadelphia: Jewish Publication Society, 1973.

Ben Amotz, Dahn and Netiva Ben Yehuda. *Milon le'ivrit meduberet* [Dictionary for Hebrew Slang]. Part 1. Tel Aviv: Zmora-Bitan, 1972.

— Part 2. Tel Aviv: Zmora-Bitan, 1982.

Ben-Ari, Nitza. *Roman 'im he'avar* [An Affair with the Past: The Jewish-German Historical Novel in the Nineteenth Century and the Creation of National Literature]. Tel Aviv: Dvir–Leo Baeck, 1997.

Ben-Ezer, Ehud. "Stories of Loneliness." *Al Hamishmar,* November 14, 1980.

— "Everyone With His Own Petaḥ-Tikva." *Iton 77* (January/February 1980).

— *Yamim shel la'anah udevash* [Days of Gall and Honey: The Life Story of the Poet Esther Raab]. Tel Aviv: Sifriat Poalim, 1998.

Benhabib, Selya and Drucilla Cornell, eds. *Feminism as Critique: On the Politics of Gender.* Minneapolis: University of Minnesota Press, 1987.

Benjamin, Jessica. *The Bonds of Love: Psychoanalysis, Feminism, and the Problem of Domination.* New York: Pantheon, 1988.

Benstock, Shari, ed. *The Private Self: Theory and Practice of Women's Autobiographical Writings.* Chapel Hill: University of North Carolina Press, 1988.

Ben Yehuda, Netiva. *1948—Bein hasfirot* [1948—Between Calendars]. Jerusalem: Keter, 1981.

— *Miba'ad la'avotot* [Through the Binding Ropes]. Jerusalem: Domino, 1985.

— *Keshepartzah hamedinah* [When the State Broke Out]. Jerusalem: Keter, 1991.

— *Otobiografiah beshir ubezemer* [Autobiography Through Songs and Lyrics]. Jerusalem: Keter, 1991.

— "Netiva Ben Yehuda." Interview with Gil Hovav. *Kol Ha'ir*, April 26, 1991, pp. 39–41.

Ben-Yehudah, Hemda. *Ben Yehudah, hayav umif'alo* [Ben-Yehudah, His Life and Work]. Jerusalem: Mossad Bialik, 1990 [1940].

Ben-Zion, Dina Katan. "Her Heroine, in Her Own Foreign City." *Al Hamishmar*, March 6, 1987.

Ben-Zvi, Rachel Yanait. *Before Golda*. Trans. Sandra Shurin. New York: Biblio, 1988.

Berg, Nancy. "*Oleh hadash* (New Immigrant): The Case of the Israeli Mystery." *Edebiyat* 5 (1994): 279–290.

Bergmann, Emilie L. "Dreaming in a Double Voice." In Emilie L. Bergmann, Janet Greenberg, Gwen Kirkpatrick, Francine Masiello, Francesca Miller, Marta Morello-Frosch, Kathleen Newman, Mary Louise Pratt, *Women, Culture, and Politics in Latin America*, pp. 151–172. Berkeley: University of California Press, 1990.

Berlovitz, Yaffa. "The Literature of the Early Pioneer Women." *Proza* 66–67 (July 1983): 31–33.

— *Sippurei nashim* [Stories by Women of the First Aliyah]. Tel Aviv: Tarmil, 1984.

— "Is Israeli Literature Being Feminized? On the Contemporary Boom in Fiction by Women." *Moznaim* (August 1992): 47–48.

— *Lehamtzi' 'eretz, lehamtzi' 'am* [Inventing a Land, Inventing a People: Literature of the First Aliyah]. Tel Aviv: Hakibbutz Hameuchad, 1996.

Bernstein, Deborah. "The Women Workers' Movement in Pre-State Israel, 1919–1939." *Signs* 12 (1987): 454–470.

— *The Struggle for Equality: Urban Women Workers in Prestate Israeli Society*. New York: Praeger, 1987.

Bernstein, Deborah S., ed. *Pioneers and Homemakers: Jewish Women in Pre-State Israel*. Albany: State University of New York Press, 1992.

Bernstein, Ilana. *She'erah, kesutah, 'onatah* [Provision]. Tel Aviv: Am Oved, 1991.

— *Daya Henig*. Tel Aviv: Am Oved, 1992.

Bhabha, Homi K., ed. *Nation and Narration*. New York: Routledge, 1990.

— *The Location of Culture*. New York: Routledge, 1994.

Biale, David. *Eros and the Jews: From Biblical Israel to Contemporary America.* New York: Basic, 1992.

Binyamini, Yaffa, ed. *'Imi va'ani* [My Mother and Myself: A Selection of Fiction and Essays]. Tel Aviv: Ḥorev, 1988.

Blackburn, Regina. "In Search of the Black Female Self." In Estelle C. Jelinek, ed., *Women's Autobiography,* pp. 133–148. Bloomington: Indiana University Press, 1980.

Blatt, Avraham. "A Woman in Crisis." *Hatzofe,* August 28, 1981.

— "The Fiction and the Captivity." *Hatzofe,* July, 13. 1984.

Blumert, Ruth. *Hatzariaḥ* [The Tower]. Jerusalem: Keter, 1984.

Bokser, Yokheved. "A Room of Your Own." *Ma'ariv/Signon,* February 10, 1988, pp. 14–16.

Boose, Lynda E. and Betty Flowers, eds. *Daughters and Fathers.* Baltimore: Johns Hopkins University Press, 1989.

Boshes, Heda. "Moments of Still Silence." *Ma'ariv,* December 28, 1980.

— *Hahar hashlishi* [The Third Hill; stories]. Tel Aviv: Sifriat Poalim, 1981.

— "Simone de Beauvoir—with No Delusions." *Ha'aretz,* March 18, 1985.

— "An Argument with History." *Ha'aretz,* May 20, 1985.

— "An Uncompromising Essayist." *Ha'aretz,* January 2, 1992.

Bowlby, Rachel, ed. *Virginia Woolf.* London and New York: Longman, 1992.

Boyarin, Daniel. *Carnal Israel: Reading Sex in Talmudic Culture.* Berkeley: University of California Press, 1993.

— *A Radical Jew: Paul and the Politics of Identity.* Berkeley: University of California Press, 1994.

— "Jewish Masochism." *American Imago* 51, no. 1 (Spring 1994): 3–36.

— *Unheroic Conduct: The Rise of Heterosexuality and the Invention of the Jewish Man.* Berkeley: University of California Press, 1997.

Brée, Germaine. "Autogynography." In James Olney, ed., *Autobiography: Essays Theoretical and Critical,* pp. 171–179. Princeton: Princeton University Press, 1980.

Brenner, Rachel Feldhay. "The Reception of Holocaust Testimony in Israeli Literature: Shulamith Hareven's 'The Witness' and 'Twilight.' " In Leon Yudkin, ed., *Hebrew Literature in the Wake of the Holocaust,* pp. 108–124. Rutherford, NJ: Fairleigh Dickinson University Press, 1993.

— "Reflections of/on Zionism in Recent Hebrew Fiction: Aharon Megged's *Foiglman* and Ruth Almog's *Dangling Roots.*" *Shofar* 13, no. 1 (Fall 1994): 68–69.

Brodzki, Bella and Celeste Schenck, eds. *Life/Lines: Theorizing Women's Autobiography.* Ithaca: Cornell University Press, 1988.

Bronovsky, Yoram. *Marguerita's Nightly Charities* (book review). *Ha'aretz,* May 8, 1970.

— *After Tu Bishvat* (book review). *Ha'aretz,* September 10, 1980.

Brownstein, Rachel M. *Becoming a Heroine: Reading About Women in Novels.* New York: Columbia University Press, 1994.

Bruss, Elizabeth W. *Autobiographical Acts: The Changing Situation of a Literary Genre.* Baltimore: Johns Hopkins University Press, 1976.

Burstein, Janet Handler. *Writing Mothers, Writing Daughters: Tracing the Maternal in Stories by American Jewish Women.* Urbana and Chicago: University of Illinois Press, 1996.

Butler, Judith. "Gender as Choice." In Selya Benhabib and Drucilla Cornell, eds., *Feminism as Critique: On the Politics of Gender,* pp. 128–142. Minneapolis: University of Minnesota Press, 1987.

— *Gender Trouble: Feminism and the Subversion of Identity.* New York: Routledge, 1990.

— *Bodies That Matter: On the Discursive Limits of "Sex".* New York: Routledge, 1993.

Butler, Judith and Joan W. Scott, eds. *Feminists Theorize the Political.* New York: Routledge, 1992.

Campbell, Joseph. *The Hero with a Thousand Faces,* 2d ed. Princeton: Princeton University Press, 1968.

Cadava, Eduardo, Peter Connor, and Jean-Luc Nancy, eds. *Who Comes After the Subject.* New York and London: Routledge, 1991.

Caramagno, Thomas C. *The Flight of the Mind: Virginia Woolf's Art and Manic-Depressive Illness.* Berkeley: University of California Press, 1992.

Cardinal, Marie. *Les mots pour le dire.* Paris: Grasset, 1975.

— *The Words to Say It: An Autobiographic Novel.* Trans. Pat Goodheart. Cambridge, Mass.: Van Vactor and Goodheart, 1983.

— *Milim kedei lomar zot.* Trans. Miriam Tiv'on. Tel Aviv: Adam, 1985.

Carrol, Berenice A. "Women and Peace Politics: The Powers of the 'Powerless.' " *Forum* 16, no. 3 (Spring 1990): 1–5.

Carrol, Berenice A. and Jane E. Mohraz, eds. *In a Great Company of Women: Nonviolent Direct Action.* New York: Pergamon, 1989.

Castel-Bloom, Orly. *Doli siti.* Tel Aviv: Zmora-Bitan. 1992.

— *Dolly City.* Trans. Dalya Bilu. London: Loki. 1997.

Caughie, Pamela L. *Virginia Woolf and Postmodernism.* Urbana and Chicago: University of Illinois Press, 1991.

Cavafis, Constantinos. *Shirim* [Poems]. Trans. Yoram Bronovsky. Tel Aviv: Sifriat Poalim, 1978.

Caws, Mary Ann. *Women of Bloomsbury.* New York: Routledge, 1990.

Cervetti, Nancy. "In the Breeches, Petticoats, and Laughter of *Orlando.*" *Journal of Modern Literature* 20, no. 2 (Winter 1996): 165–176.

Chazan, Naomi. "Gender Equality? Not in a War Zone!" *Israel Democracy* (Summer 1989): 4–7.

Chernin, Kim. *In My Mother's House.* New York: Ticknor and Fields, 1983.

Chertok, Haim. *We Are All Close: Conversations with Israeli Writers.* New York: Fordham University Press, 1989.

Chesler, Phyllis. *Women and Madness.* New York: Doubleday, 1972.

— *Nashim veshiga'on.* Trans. Sara Sykes. Tel Aviv: Zmora-Bitan, 1987.

Chodorow, Nancy. *The Reproduction of Mothering: Psychoanalysis and the Sociology of Gender.* Berkeley: University of California Press, 1978.

Church, Margaret. "Joycean Structure in *Jacob's Room* and *Mrs. Dalloway.*" *International Fiction Review* 4, no. 2 (July 1977): 101–129.

Cixous, Hélène. "The Laugh of the Medusa." *Signs* 1 (1975): 875–893.

Cixous, Hélène and Catherine Clement. *The Newly Born Woman.* Trans. Betsy Wing. Minneapolis: University of Minnesota Press, 1986.

Cohen, George. *Twilight* (book review). *Booklist* 88, no. 12 (February 15, 1992): 1087.

Cohen, Mabel Blake. "Personal Identity and Sexual Identity." In Jean Baker Miller, ed., *Psychoanalysis and Women,* pp. 156–182. New York: Penguin, 1973.

Cohen, Zafrira. "Loosen the Fetters of Thy Tongue, Woman: A Study in the Poetics of Yona Wallach." Ph.D. diss., New York University, 1997.

Coltun, Elizabeth, ed. *The Jewish Woman: New Perspectives.* New York: Schocken, 1976.

Cornell, Drucilla and Adam Thurschwell. "Feminism, Negativity, Intersubjectivity." In Selya Benhabib and Drucilla Cornell, eds., *Feminism as Critique: On the Politics of Gender,* pp. 143–162. Minneapolis: University of Minnesota Press, 1987.

Culler, Jonathan. *On Deconstruction.* Ithaca: Cornell University Press, 1983.

Davidman, Lynn and Shelly Tenenbaum, eds. *Feminist Perspectives on Jewish Studies.* New Haven: Yale University Press, 1995.

Davidson, Cathy N. and E. M. Broner, eds. *The Lost Tradition: Mothers and Daughters in Literature.* New York: Ungar, 1980.

Davies, Miranda, ed. *Third World—Second Sex: Women's Struggles and National Liberation.* London: Zed, 1983.

Davis, Natalie Zemon. *Women on the Margins: Three Seventeenth-Century Lives.* Cambridge: Harvard University Press, 1995.

Dayan, Yael. *New Face in the Mirror.* Cleveland and New York: World, 1959.

Defromont, Francoise. "Mirrors and Fragments." In Rachel Bowlby, ed., *Virginia Woolf,* pp. 62–76. London and New York: Longman, 1992.

De Lauretis, Teresa. *Technologies of Gender.* Bloomington: Indiana University Press, 1987.

Deleuze, Gilles and Felix Guattari. *Kafka: Toward a Minor Literature.* Trans. Dana Polan. Minneapolis: University of Minnesota Press, 1986.

Derrida, Jacques. "The Law of Genre." *Glyph* 7 (Spring 1980): 202–232.

DeSalvo, Louise A. *Virginia Woolf: The Impact of Childhood Sexual Abuse on Her Life and Work.* Boston: Beacon, 1989.

Diament, Carol and Lily Rattok, eds. *Ribcage: Israeli Women's Fiction.* New York: Hadassah, 1994.

Diamond, Irene and Lee Quinby, eds. *Feminism and Foucault: Reflections on Resistance.* Boston: Northeastern University Press, 1988.

Dinnerstein, Dorothy. *The Mermaid and the Minotaur: Sexual Arrangements and Human Malaise.* New York: Harper, 1976.

Doane, Janice and Devon Hodges. *From Klein to Kristeva: Psychoanalytic Feminism and the Search for the "Good Enough" Mother.* Ann Arbor: University of Michigan Press, 1992.

Domb, Risa. *Home Thoughts from Abroad: Distant Visions of Israel in Contemporary Hebrew Fiction.* London: Vallentine Mitchell, 1995.

Domb, Risa, ed. *New Women's Writing from Israel.* London: Vallentine Mitchell, 1996.

Drimmer, Nehemi. "Prophecy by Fools." *Kol Ha'ir Jerusalem,* February 3, 1989.

Dunn, Jane. *A Very Close Conspiracy: Vanessa Bell and Virginia Woolf.* Jonathan Cape, 1990.

Durrell, Lawrence. *Pope Joan.* Adapted from the Greek of Emmanuel Royidis. Penguin, 1974.

Dvash, Maya and Shula Modan, eds. *'Imahot ubanot* [Mothers and Daughters: An Anthology]. Tel Aviv: Modan, 1997.

Eakin, Paul John. *Fictions in Autobiography: Studies in the Art of Self-Invention.* Princeton: Princeton University Press, 1985.

— *Touching the World: Reference in Autobiography.* Princeton: Princeton University Press, 1992.

Edwards, Lee. "The Labors of Psyche: Toward a Theory of Female Heroes." *Critical Inquiry* 6 (1979): 33–49.

Eichenbaum, Louise and Susie Orbach. *What Do Women Want: Exploding the Myth of Dependency.* New York: Berkeley, 1984.

Eilam, Esther. "Women and War." *Women for a Renewed Society: Newsletter of the Israeli Feminist Movement* 4 (September 1974): 3.

Einat, Amela. "Portrait of an Israeli Macho." *Ha'aretz,* April 30, 1981.

Elboim, Yaakov. "Stories as Modern Midrash." *Yediot Aharonot,* July 12, 1996, p. 28.

El-Or, Tamar. *Maskilot veburot.* Tel Aviv: Am Oved, 1992.

— *Educated and Ignorant: Ultraorthodox Jewish Women and Their World.* Trans. Haim Watzman. Boulder, Colo.: Lynne Rienner, 1994.

Emmett, Ayala. *Our Sisters' Promised Land: Women, Politics, and Israeli-Palestinian Coexistence.* Ann Arbor: University of Michigan Press, 1996.

Engler, Gideon. "Without Subversiveness." *Ma'ariv,* December 11, 1987.

Erikson, Erik. "The Eight Ages of Man." In Erik Erikson, *Childhood and Society,* pp. 247–274. New York: Norton, 1950.

Estés, Clarissa Pinkola. *Women Who Run with the Wolves: Myths and Stories of the Wild Woman Archetype.* New York: Ballantine, 1992.

— *Ratzot ʿim ze'evim.* Trans. Adi Ginsburg Hirsh. Tel Aviv: Modan, 1997.

Ettinger [Esther and], Almog [Ruth]. *Me'ahev mushlam* [A Perfect Lover]. Jerusalem: Keter, 1995.

European Literature: The Penguin Companion to World Literature. Ed. Anthony Thorlby. New York: McGraw-Hill. 1969.

Eytan, Rachel. *Barakiʿa haḥamishi.* Tel Aviv: Am Oved, 1962.

— *The Fifth Heaven.* Trans. Philip Stimpson. Philadelphia: Jewish Publication Society, 1985.

— *Shidah veshidot.* Tel Aviv: Am Oved, 1974.

Ezer, Nancy. *Sifrut ve'ideologya* [Literature and Ideology]. Tel Aviv: Papyrus, 1992.

Fein, Esther B. "Two Writers Who Keep Their Fiction Free of Political Realities." *New York Times*, March 17, 1992, p. C13.

Feldhai, Rivka. "Drash nashi" [A Feminine Midrash]. *Te'oria vebikoret* [*Theory and Criticism*] 2 (1992): 69–89.

Feldman, Yael S. "From Dostoyevsky to Brenner." *Hebrew Annual Review* (1979): 91–104.

— "Between the Mythic and the Tragic." *Maḥbarot Brenner* [Essays on Brenner] 3–4:217–238. Tel Aviv: Hakibbutz Hameuchad, 1984.

— "Poetics and Politics: Israeli Literary Criticism Between East and West." *PAAJR* 52 (1985): 9–35.

— "Inadvertent Feminism: The Image of Frontier Women in Contemporary Israeli Fiction." *Modern Hebrew Literature* 10, nos. 3–4 (1985): 34–37.

— *Modernism and Cultural Transfer: Gabriel Preil and the Tradition of Jewish Literary Bilingualism.* Cincinnati: Hebrew Union College Press, 1986.

— "Historical Novels or Masked Autobiographies?" *Siman Kri'ah* 19 (1986): 208–213.

— "Zionism—Neurosis or Cure: The 'Historical' Drama of Y. Sobol." *Prooftexts* 7, no. 2 (May 1987): 145–162.

— "Gender In/Difference in Contemporary Hebrew Fictional Autobiography." *Biography: An Interdisciplinary Quarterly* 11, no. 3 (1988): 189–209.

— " 'Living on the Top Floor': The Arrested Autobiography in Israeli Fiction." *Modern Hebrew Literature* n.s. 1 (Fall/Winter 1988): 72–76.

— "Reconstructing the Past in Israeli Fiction." *Ariel: A Review of Arts and Letters in Israel* 71–71 (1988): 52–62.

— "Back to Vienna: Zionism on the Literary Couch." In Ruth Kozodoy, David Sidorsky, and Kalman Sultanik, eds., *Vision Confronts Reality: Historical Perspectives on the Contemporary Jewish Agenda*, pp. 310–335. London and Toronto: Associated University Presses, 1989. Repr. *Tikkun* (November 1989): 31–34, 91–96.

— "New Psychoanalytic Models for Theory of Comparative Study of Autobiography." In Mario J. Valdes, ed., *Toward a Theory of Comparative Literature*, pp. 125–133. New York: Lang, 1989.

— "Feminism Under Siege: The Vicarious Selves of Israeli Women Writers." *Prooftexts* 10, no. 3 (September 1990): 493–514.

— "Ideology and Self-Representation of Women in Israeli Literature." In Colette Hall and Janice Morgan, eds., *Redefining Autobiography in Twentieth-Century Women's Fiction*, pp. 281–301. New York: Garland, 1991.

— "The 'Other Within' in Israeli Fiction." *Middle East Review* 22, no. 1 (Fall 1991): 47–53. A modified version repr. Gerald Gillespie, ed., *The Force of Vision*, pp. 330–337. Tokyo: Proceedings of the ICLA '91 Tokyo Congress, 1996.

— "Whose Story Is It, Anyway? Ideology and Psychology in the Representation of the Shoah in Israeli Literature." In Saul Friedlander, ed., *Probing the Limits of Representation: Nazism and the "Final Solution"*, pp. 223–239, 380–384. Cambridge: Harvard University Press, 1992.

— " 'And Rebecca Loved Jacob,' But Freud Did Not." In Peter Rudnytsky and Ellen Handler Spitz, eds., *Freud and Forbidden Knowledge*, pp. 7–35. New York: New York University Press, 1994.

— "Back to Genesis: Toward the Repressed and Beyond in Israeli Identity." In Nitza Ben-Dov, ed., *Bakivun hanegdi: Critical Essays on Mr. Mani*, pp. 204–222. Tel Aviv: Hakibbutz Hameuchad, 1995.

— "The Ability to Speak Entirely New Phrases." *Seneca Review* 27, no. 1 (1997): 36–41.

— "From Feminist Romance to an Anatomy of Freedom: Israeli Women Novelists." In Alan Mintz, ed., *The Boom in Contemporary Israeli Fiction*, pp. 71–113. Hanover: University Press of New England, 1997.

— "Isaac or Oedipus? Jewish Tradition and the Israeli Aqedah." In Sheryl Exum and Stephen Moore, eds., *Biblical Studies/Cultural Studies*, pp. 159–189. Sheffield Academic Press, 1998.

— " 'Anu, anu hapalmach': A Subversive View from the Women's Gallery." *Moznaim* 72, no. 9 (June 1998): 41–44.

— "Postcolonial Memory, Postmodernist Intertextuality: Anton Shammas's *Arabesques* Revisited." *PMLA* 114 (May 1999): 373–389.

Felman, Shoshana. "Women and Madness: The Critical Phallacy." *Diacritics* (Winter 1975): 2–10.

— *What Does a Woman Want?* Baltimore: Johns Hopkins University Press, 1993.

Ferguson, Margaret and Jennifer Wicke, eds. *Feminism and Postmodernism*. Durham: Duke University Press, 1994.

Fisch, Harold. *A Remembered Future: A Study in Literary Mythology*. Bloomington: Indiana University Press, 1984.

Fishman, Sylvia Barack. *A Breath of Life: Feminism and the American Jewish Community.* Hanover: Brandeis University Press, 1995.

Flax, Jane. *Thinking Fragments: Psychoanalysis, Feminism, and Postmodernism in the Contemporary West.* Berkeley: University of California Press, 1990.

Foucault, Michel. *Discipline and Punish.* Trans. Alan Sheridan. New York: Vintage, 1977.

— *Madness and Civilization: A History of Insanity in the Age of Reason.* Trans. Richard Howard. New York: Vintage, 1965.

Fox, Everett. *In the Beginning.* New York: Schocken, 1983.

Freedman, Marcia. *Exile in the Promised Land: A Memoir.* Ithaca, NY: Firebrand, 1990.

French, Marylin. *The Women's Room.* New York: Summit, 1977.

— *Ḥeder hanashim.* Trans. Shulamit Ariel. Tel Aviv: Sifriat Poalim and Sh. Friedman, 1980.

Frenkel, Naomi. *Sha'ul veyohana* [Saul and Yohana; trilogy]. Tel Aviv: Sifriat Poalim, 1956, 1962, 1969.

Freud, Sigmund. "Creative Writers and Day-Dreaming" [1908]. Standard edition. Trans. and ed. James Strachey. 24 vols. 9:141–153. London: Hogarth, 1953–1974.

— "Beyond the Pleasure Principle" [1920]. Standard edition. Trans. and ed. James Strachey. 24 vols. 18:3–64. London: Hogarth, 1953–1974.

— "Some Psychical Consequences of the Anatomical Distinction Between the Sexes" [1925]. Standard edition. Trans. and ed. James Strachey. 24 vols. 19:248–258. London: Hogarth, 1953–1974.

— *Civilization and Its Discontents* [1929]. Standard edition. Trans. and ed. James Strachey. 24 vols. 21:57–145. London: Hogarth, 1953–1974; New York: Norton, 1962.

— "Female Sexuality" [1931]. Standard edition. Trans. and ed. James Strachey. 24 vols. 21:221–243. London: Hogarth, 1953–1974.

— "Femininity" [1932]. Standard edition. Trans. and ed. James Strachey. 24 vols. 22:112–135. London: Hogarth, 1953–1974.

— *Moses and Monotheism* [1938]. Standard edition. Trans. and ed. James Strachey. 24 vols. 23:7–56. London: Hogarth, 1953–1974.

Friday, Nancy. *My Mother/My Self: The Daughter's Search for Identity.* New York: Delacorte, 1977.

— *'Imi ve'ani: Ḥabat meḥapeset 'et zehutah.* Trans. Amasai Levin. Tel Aviv: Zmora-Bitan-Modan, 1980.

Friedan, Betty. *The Feminine Mystique.* New York: Dell, 1963.

Friedman, Susan Stanford. "Women's Autobiographical Selves: Theory and Practice." In Shari Benstock, ed., *The Private Self: Theory and Practice of Women's Autobiographical Writings,* pp. 34–62. Chapel Hill: University of North Carolina Press, 1988.

Frye, Northrop. *Anatomy of Criticism: Four Essays.* Princeton: Princeton University Press, 1957.

Fuchs, Esther. "Gender and Characterization in the Palmach Narrative Fiction." *World Congress of Jewish Studies* 9, c (1986): 179–184.

— *Israeli Mythogynies: Women in Contemporary Hebrew Fiction.* New York: State University of New York Press, 1987.

— "Amaliah Kahana-Carmon and Contemporary Hebrew Women's Fiction." *Signs* 13 (1988): 299–310.

— "Amaliah Kahana-Carmon's *And Moon in the Valley of Ayalon*: A Feminist Reading." *Prooftexts* 8 (1988): 129–141.

Furbank, P. N. "Portrait of a Lady." [Review of Mona Ozouf's *Women's Words: Essays on French Singularity*]. *New York Review of Books*, March 5, 1998, p. 30.

Furstenberg, Rochelle. "Israeli Thrillers: Second Generation." *Modern Hebrew Literature* 17 (Fall/ Winter 1996): 3–5.

Fuss, Diana. *Essentially Speaking: Feminism, Nature, and Difference.* New York and London: Routledge, 1989.

Galchinsky, Michael. *The Origin of the Modern Jewish Woman Writer: Romance and Reform in Victorian England.* Detroit: Wayne University Press, 1996.

Gay, Peter. *Freud: A Life for Our Time.* New York: Norton, 1988.

Gelbetz, Tamar. "Ruth's Nightly Charities." *Kol Ha'ir*, May 23, 1986.

Geldman, Mordekhai. "An Essay on the Blocking of the Soul." *Ha'aretz*, January 2, 1981.

Gertz, Nurit. *Ḥirbet ḥiz'a vehaboker shelemoḥorat* [Generation Shift in Literary History: Hebrew Narrative Fiction in the Sixties]. Tel Aviv: Porter Institute, 1983.

— *Sifrut ve'ideologya* [Literature and Ideology in *Eretz Israel* During the 1930s]. Tel Aviv: Open University, 1988.

— *Shvuya baḥaloma* [Captive of a Dream: National Myths in Israeli Culture]. Tel Aviv: Am Oved, 1995.

— "I Am the Other: The Holocaust Survivor in Yehudit Hendel's Story *'Anashim 'aḥerim hem.*" In Ziva Ben Porat, ed., *Harshav Festschrift.* Tel Aviv: Porter Institute, forthcoming.

Gilbert, Sandra M. "Costumes of the Mind: Transvestism as Metaphor in Modern Literature." *Critical Inquiry* 7 (1980): 391–417.

Gilbert, Sandra M. and Susan Gubar. *The Madwoman in the Attic: The Woman Writer and the Nineteenth-Century Literary Imagination.* New Haven: Yale University Press, 1979.

— *No Man's Land.* Vol. 1: *The War of the Words.* New Haven: Yale University Press, 1987.

Gilboa, Shulamit. *Hasheker harevi'i* [The Fourth Lie]. Tel Aviv: Hakibbutz Hameuchad, 1993.

Gillespie, Diane Filby. *The Sisters' Art: The Writing and Painting of Virginia Woolf and Vanessa Bell.* Syracuse: Syracuse University Press, 1988.

Gilligan, Carol. *In a Different Voice: Psychological Theory and Women's Development.* Cambridge: Harvard University Press, 1982.

Gilman, Sander L. *Jewish Self-Hatred: Anti-Semitism and the Hidden Language of the Jews.* Baltimore: Johns Hopkins University Press, 1986.

— *Freud, Race, and Gender.* Princeton University Press, 1993.

— "Hysteria, Race, and Gender." In Sander L. Gilman, Helen King, Roy Porter, G. S. Rousseau, and Elaine Showalter, *Hysteria Beyond Freud,* pp. 402–436. Berkeley: University of California Press, 1993.

Ginor, Zvia. "The Zionist Dystopia According to Orly Castel-Bloom." In Y. Bar-El, Y. Schwartz, and T. Hess, eds., *Sifrut vehevrah batarbut ha'ivrit bame'ah ha'esrim* [Literature and Society in Hebrew Culture in the Twentieth Century]. Jerusalem: Magnes, forthcoming.

Ginossar, Ya'ira. "A Delicate Hand." *Iton 77* (September 1985).

Gluzman, Michael. "The Exclusion of Women from Hebrew Literary History." *Prooftexts* 11:3 (1991): 259–278.

Golan, Avirama. *'Al 'atzman* [Women About Themselves]. Tel Aviv: Am Oved, 1988.

Golan, Yaron. "The Last *Palmachnikit.*" *Davar,* June 5, 1981.

— "Yearnings in Search of an Address." *Davar,* July 6, 1984.

Gold, Nili Scharf. "To Reach the Source." *Modern Hebrew Literature* 10 (Spring/Summer 1993): 43–46.

— "Rereading *It Is the Light,* Lea Goldberg's Only Novel." *Prooftexts* 17 (September 1997): 245–265.

— "On *With Her on Her Way Home* by Amalia Kahana-Carmon." In Y. Bar-El, Y. Schwartz, and T. Hess, eds., *Sifrut vehevrah batarbut ha'ivrit bame'ah ha'esrim* [Literature and Society in Hebrew Culture in the Twentieth Century]. Jerusalem: Magnes, forthcoming.

Goldberg, Leah. "'Aharei 'esrim shana" [After Twenty Years]. In Leah Goldberg, *Mukdam ume'uhar* [Early and Later Poetry], p. 184. Tel Aviv: Sifriat Poalim, 1958.

— *'Omanut hasippur* [The Art of the Short Story]. Tel Aviv: Sifriat Poalim, 1963.

— *Vehu ha'or* [It/He Is the Light]. Tel Aviv: Sifriat Poalim, 1994 [1946].

Goldstein, Jan Ellen. "The Woolfs' Response to Freud: Water Spiders, Singing Canaries, and the Second Apple." *Psychoanalytic Quarterly* 43 (1974): 438–476; repr. in Edith Kurzweil and William Phillips, eds., *Literature and Psychoanalysis,* pp. 232–255. New York: Columbia University Press, 1983.

Gordon, Lyndall. *Virginia Woolf: A Writer's Life.* Oxford: Oxford University Press, 1986.

Govrin, Michal. *Hashem.* Tel Aviv: Hakibbutz Hameuchad, 1994.
— *The Name.* Trans. Barbara Harshav. New York: Riverhead, 1998.
Govrin, Nurit. *Dvora Baron: hamahatzit harishona* [The First Half: The Life and Work of Dvora Baron, 1887–1922]. Jerusalem: Bialik Institute, 1988.
— *Dvash misela'* [Honey from the Rock: Studies in Eretz Israel Literature]. Tel Aviv: Ministry of Defense, 1989.
Gubar, Susan. "The Birth of the Artist as Heroine." In Carolyn G. Heilbrun and Margaret R. Higonnet, eds., *The Representation of Women in Fiction: Selected Papers from the English Institute,* pp. 1–20. Baltimore: Johns Hopkins University Press, 1983.
Gunn, Janet. *Autobiography: Toward a Poetics of Experience.* Philadelphia: University of Pennsylvania Press, 1982.
Gur, Batya. *Retzah beshabat baboker.* Jerusalem: Keter, 1988.
— *Retzah bahug lesifrut.* Jerusalem: Keter, 1989.
— *Linah shitufit.* Jerusalem: Keter, 1991.
— *Murder on Saturday Morning.* Trans. Dalya Bilu. New York: Harper-Collins, 1992.
— *A Literary Murder.* Trans. Dalya Bilu. New York: HarperCollins, 1993.
— *Lo' kakh te'arti li* [Afterbirth]. Jerusalem: Keter, 1994.
— *Murder on a Kibbutz.* Trans. Dalya Bilu. New York: Harper and Collins, 1994.
Gurevitch, David. "Feminism and Postmodernism." *Alpayim* 7 (1993): 27–58.
— "Postmodernism in Israeli Literature." *Modern Hebrew Literature* 15 (Fall/Winter 1995): 10–13.
— "Recycled Dreams: New Trends in Israeli Literature." *Iton* 77 (March 1996): 38–44.
— *Postmodernism: Tarbut vesifrut besof hame'ah ha'esrim* [Postmodernism: Culture and Literature at the End of the Twentieth Century]. Tel Aviv: Dvir, 1997.
Gusdorf, Georges. "Conditions and Limits of Autobiography." In James Olney, ed., *Autobiography: Essays Theoretical and Critical,* pp. 28–48. Princeton: Princeton University Press, 1980.
Gutkind, Naomi. "Roots of Air or Roots in the Land?" *Hatzofe,* December 25, 1987.
Hadary, Amnon. "*City of Many Days.*" *Shdemot* 51 (Spring 1973): 149–156.
Hagorni, Avraham. "Reshut netunah." *Hapo'el Hatza'ir,* April 14, 1970.
Halkin, Hillel. "A Multifaceted Miniature." *Ha'aretz,* November 9, 1984.
Handelsaltz, Michael. "The Miraculous Revival of the Israeli Canon." *Ha'aretz/Sfarim,* April 17, 1998, p. 3.
Harcourt, Wendy. "Feminism, Body, Self: Third-Generation Feminism." In Joseph H. Smith and Afaf Mahfouz, eds. *Psychoanalysis, Feminism and the Future of Gender,* pp. 70–90. Baltimore: Johns Hopkins University Press, 1994.

Har'el, Shlomo. "Around the Settlement—Between Myth and Historicism." In Nurit Govrin, ed., *Bein historia lesifrut* [Between History and Literature], pp. 134–150. Tel Aviv: Tel Aviv University Press, 1983.

Hareven, Shulamith. *Yerushalayim dorsanit* [Predatory Jerusalem, poems]. Tel Aviv: Sifriat Poalim, 1962.

— *Baḥodesh ha'aharon* [In the Last Month; stories]. Tel Aviv: Daga, 1966.

— *Mekomot nifradim* [Separate Places; poems]. Tel Aviv: Sifriat Poalim, 1969.

— "A Question of Identity." *Keshet* 11, no. 4 (Summer 1969): 5–26.

— *Reshut netuna* [Freedom of Choice; stories]. Tel Aviv: Massada, 1970.

— "Shonim ve-shavim" [Different and Equal]. *Ma'ariv*, September 24, 1971.

— *'Ir yamim rabim*. Tel Aviv: Am Oved, 1972.

— "A Struggle for Sanity." Interview with Sh. Shifra. *Davar*, February 16, 1973.

— "Wordsworth's Sister." *Ma'ariv*, January 23, 1976, p. 35.

— "'Alimut" [Violence]. *Ma'ariv*, July 9, 1976.

— *City of Many Days*. Trans. Hillel Halkin. New York: Doubleday, 1977.

— "A Secret Ancient Guilt." *Ma'ariv*, October 11, 1978.

— *Bedidut* [Loneliness; stories]. Tel Aviv: Am Oved, 1980.

— *Tismonet dulsine'a* [The Dulcinea Syndrome; essays]. Jerusalem: Keter, 1981.

— *Sone' hanissim*. Tel Aviv: Dvir, 1983.

— "'Ani levantinit" [I Am a Levantine]. *Al Hamishmar*, April 5, 1985.

— *The Miracle Hater*. Trans. Hillel Halkin. Berkeley: North Point, 1988.

— *Haḥulya* [The Link]. Tel Aviv: Zmora-Bitan, 1986.

— "My Position, Almost in Principle, Is That of the Minority." Interview with Yael Admoni. *Davar*, June 20, 1986, p. 19.

— *Mashiaḥ 'o knesset* [Messiah or Knesset]. Tel Aviv: Dvir/Zmora-Bitan, 1987.

— "The First Forty Years." *Jerusalem Quarterly* 48 (Fall 1988: 3–28.

— "Professional Questions." *Al Hamishmar*, February 12, 1988.

— "Consensus with 3 S's." Interview with Orly Toren. *Jerusalem*, December 12, 1988.

— *Navi'*. Tel Aviv: Dvir, 1989.

— *Prophet*. Trans. Hillel Halkin. Berkeley: North Point, 1990.

— *'Ivrim be'aza* [Eyeless in Gaza]. Tel Aviv: Zmora-Bitan, 1991.

— "To See a Different Order Here." Interview with Ilan Sheinfeld. *Al Hamishmar*, January 24, 1992.

— *Twilight and Other Stories*. Trans. Hillel Halkin. San Francisco: Mercury House, 1992 [New York: Doubleday, 1977].

— *City of Many Days*. Trans. Hillel Halkin. San Francisco: Mercury House, 1993.

— "Against Charisma." *Yediot Aharonot*, October 1, 6, 1993.

— *'Aharei hayaldut*. Tel Aviv: Dvir, 1994.

— "Laius, The Father Repressed by Freud." *Ha'aretz*, December 9, 1994, p. B7.
— "Literature Is Not the Stock Market." Interview with Edna Evron. *Yediot Aharonot*, December 9, 1994, p. 30.
— *The Vocabulary of Peace.* Trans. Marsha Weinstein et al. San Francisco: Mercury House, 1995.
— *Tsima'on: Shlishiyat hamidbar.* Tel Aviv: Dvir, 1996.
— *Thirst: The Desert Trilogy.* Trans. Hillel Halkin. San Francisco: Mercury House, 1996.
— "Woman's Talent for Sanity." *Yediot Aharonot*, May 2, 1997, pp. 26–27.
Harnik, Ra'ya. "More About Montifer: Enchantment in an Old Mirror." *Al Hamishmar*, August 3, 1984.
Harris, Adrienne and Ynestra King, eds. *Rocking the Ship of State: Toward a Feminist Peace Politics.* Boulder, Col.: Westview Press, 1989.
Harrowitz, Nancy. *Antisemitism, Misogyny, and the Logic of Cultural Difference.* Nebraska: Nebraska University Press, 1994.
Harshav, Benjamin. "About Yosef Ha'efrati's Contribution to Literary Research." *Hasifrut [Literature]* 17 (September 1974): 40.
— *Language in Time of Revolution.* Berkeley: University of California Press, 1993.
Hassan, Ihab. *The Postmodern Turn: Essays in Postmodern Theory and Culture.* Columbus: Ohio State University Press, 1987.
Hazak, Ravit. "The Woman Who Broke Frameworks." *Davar Sheni*, April 30, 1996.
Hazan-Roken, Galit. "Like a Person Stumbling Over a Mirror." *Hasifrut* 30–31 (April 1981): 184–192.
Hazleton, Lesley. *Israeli Women: The Reality Behind the Myth.* New York: Simon and Schuster, 1977.
Heilbrun, Carolyn G. *Toward the Recognition of Androgyny.* New York: Harper, 1973.
— *Reinventing Womanhood.* New York: Norton, 1979.
— *Writing a Woman's Life.* New York: Norton, 1988.
— *"To the Lighthouse*: The New Story of Mother and Daughter." In Carolyn G. Heilbrun, *Hamlet's Mother and Other Women*, pp. 134–139. New York: Ballantine, 1990.
Heilbrun, Carolyn G. and Margaret R. Higonnet, eds. *The Representation of Women in Fiction: Selected Papers from the English Institute.* Baltimore: Johns Hopkins University Press, 1983.
Hendel, Yehudit. *'Anashim aherim hem* [They Are Different People; stories]. Tel Aviv: Sifriat Poalim, 1950.
— *Rehov hamadregot.* Tel Aviv: Am oved, 1956.
— *The Street of Steps.* Trans. Rachel Katz and David Segal. New York and London: Herzl and Thomas Yoseloff, 1963.

— *Haḥatzer shel momo hagdolah* [The Yard of Momo the Great]. Tel Aviv: Am Oved, 1969.

— *Hako'aḥ ha'aḥer* [The Different/Other Power]. Tel Aviv: Hakibbutz Hameuchad, 1984.

— *Kesef katan* [Small Change; stories]. Tel Aviv: Hakibbutz Hameuchad, 1988.

— *Har hato'im* [The Mountain of Losses]. Tel Aviv: Hakibbutz Hameuchad, 1992.

— *'Aruḥat boker temima* [An Innocent Breakfast; stories]. 1996.

Herzig, Hana. *Amalia Kahana-Carmon* [Israeli Fiction in the 1960s]. Tel Aviv: Open University, 1983.

Heschel, Susannah, ed. *On Being a Jewish Feminist.* New York: Schocken, 1983.

Higonnet, Margaret. "Suicide: Representations of the Feminine in the Nineteenth Century." *Poetics Today* 6, nos. 1/2 (1985): 103–118.

Hirsch, Marianne. *The Mother-Daughter Plot: Narrative, Psychoanalysis, Feminism.* Bloomington: Indiana University Press, 1989.

Hirschfeld, Ariel. "A Metaphor for the Design of the Soul." *Ha'aretz*, May 13, 1988.

Hoffman, Anne Golomb. "Constructing Masculinity in Yaakov Shabtai's *Past Continuous.*" *Prooftexts* 11, no. 3 (September, 1991): 279–295.

— "Oedipal Narrative and Its Discontents: A. B. Yehoshua's *Molkho* (Five Seasons)." In Naomi B. Sokoloff, Anne Lapidus Lerner, and Anita Norich, eds., *Gender and Text in Modern Hebrew and Yiddish Literature*, pp. 195–215. New York: Jewish Theological Seminary, 1992.

— "Bodies and Borders: The Politics of Gender in Contemporary Israeli Fiction." In Alan Mintz, ed., *The Boom in Contemporary Israeli Fiction*, pp. 35–70. Hanover: University Press of New England, 1997.

Horowitz, Daniel. *Betty Friedan and the Making of the "Feminine Mystique": The American Left, the Cold War, and Modern Feminism.* University of Massachusetts Press, 1998.

Hussey, Mark. *The Singing of the Real World: The Philosophy of Virginia Woolf's Fiction.* Columbus: University of Ohio Press, 1986.

Hussey, Mark, ed. *Virginia Woolf and War: Fiction, Reality, and Myth.* Syracuse: Syracuse University Press, 1991.

Hutcheon, Linda. *A Poetics of Postmodernism.* New York: Routledge, 1988.

Irigaray, Luce. *Speculum of the Other Woman.* Trans. Gillian C. Gill. Ithaca: Cornell University Press, 1985.

— *This Sex Which Is Not One.* Trans. Catherine Porter. Ithaca: Cornell University Press, 1985.

— *The Ethics of Sexual Difference.* Trans. Carolyn Burke and Gillian C. Gill. Ithaca: Cornell University Press, 1993.

— *Sexes and Genealogies.* Trans. Gillian C. Gill. New York: Columbia University Press, 1993.

Irving, John. *The World According to Garp.* New York: Pocket, 1976.

Israel, Shulamit. "Feminine Writing and Israeli Writers—Are They Aware?" *Massa'*, December 24, 1993.

Izraeli, Dafna N. "The Zionist Women's Movement in Palestine, 1911–1927: A Sociological Analysis." *Signs* 7 (1981): 87–115.

— "The Status of Women in Israel Today." *Encyclopedia Judaica Yearbook 1986/1987.* Jerusalem: Keter, 1987.

Izraeli, Dafna N. and Ephraim Tabori. "The Political Context of Feminist Attitudes in Israel." In Yael Azmon and Dafna N. Izraeli, eds., *Women in Israel: A Sociological Anthology*, pp. 269–286. New Brunswick: Transaction, 1993.

Izraeli, Dafna N., Ariella Friedman, Ruth Schrift; with the participation of Frances Radai and Yehudit Buber-Agassi: *Nashim bemilkud* [The Double Bind: The Status of Women in Israel]. Tel Aviv: Hakibbutz Hameuchad, 1982.

Jacobs, Mary. *First Things: The Maternal Imaginary in Literature, Art, and Psychoanalysis.* New York: Routledge, 1995.

Jardine, Alice. A. "Gynesis." *Diacritics* (Summer 1982): 54–65.

— *Gynesis: Configurations of Woman and Modernity.* Ithaca: Cornell University Press, 1985.

Jay, Martin. *Downcast Eyes: The Denigration of Vision in Twentieth-Century French Thought.* Berkeley: University of California Press, 1993.

Jay, Paul. *Being in the Text: Self-Representation from Wordsworth to Roland Barthes.* Ithaca: Cornell University Press, 1984.

Jayawardena, Kumari. *Feminism and Nationalism in the Third World.* London: Zed, 1986.

Jelinek, Estelle C., ed. *Women's Autobiography.* Bloomington: Indiana University Press, 1980.

Johnson, Miriam M. *Strong Mothers, Weak Wives: In Search for Gender Equality.* Berkeley: University of California Press, 1994.

Jones, Ann Rosalind. "Writing the Body." *Feminist Studies* 7, no. 2 (Summer 1981): 247–263.

Jong, Erica. *Inventing Memory: A Novel of Mothers and Daughters.* Harper-Collins, 1997.

Joplin, Patricia. "The Authority of Illusion: Feminism and Fascism in Virginia Woolf." *South Central Review* 6, no. 2 (1989): 88–10.

Kaganoff, Penny. *Prophet* (book review). *Voice Literary Supplement* 33, no. 15 (May 1990): 11.

Kahana-Carmon, Amalia. *Bikhfifah 'ahat* [Under One Roof; stories]. Tel Aviv: Sifriat Poalim, 1966.

— *Veyare'ah be'emek 'ayalon* [And Moon in the Valley of Ayalon]. Tel Aviv: Hakibbutz Hameuchad, 1971.

— "Keta' labamah, beta'am hasignon hagadol" [A Piece for the Stage, in the Grand Manner; monodrama]. *Siman Kri'ah* 5 (1976): 241–272.

— *Sadot magnetiyim* [Magnetic Fields]. Tel Aviv: Hakibbutz Hameuchad, 1977.

— "High Stakes." *Siman Kri'ah* 10 (1980): 31–56.

— "The Right Password." Interview with Orly Lubin. *Ha'aretz*, March 9, 1984.

— *Lema'lah bemontifer* [Up in Montifer]. Tel Aviv: Hakibbutz Hameuchad/ Siman Kri'ah, 1984.

— "Here Is the Book." *Moznaim* 58, no. 5–6 (1984): 12–13.

— "To Be a Woman Writer." *Yediot Aharonot*, April 13, 1984, pp. 20–21.

— "To Be Wasted on the Peripheral." *Yediot Aharonot*, September 15, 1985, pp. 22–23.

— "Brenner's Wife Rides Again." *Moznaim* 59, no. 4 (October 1985): 10–14.

— "She Writes Rather Pleasingly, But About the Insignificant." *Yediot Aharonot*, February 4, 1988, pp. 20, 25.

— "The Song of the Bats in Flight." *Moznaim* (November/December 1989): 3–7.

— *Liviti 'othah baderekh leveitah* [With Her on Her Way Home]. Tel Aviv: Hakibbutz Hameuchad/Siman Kri'ah, 1991.

— "The Song of the Bats." Trans. Naomi Sokoloff. In Naomi B. Sokoloff, Anne Lapidus Lerner, and Anita Norich, eds., *Gender and Text in Modern Hebrew and Yiddish Literature*, pp. 235–245. New York: Jewish Theological Seminary, 1992.

— "How Does the Elephant Imagine Itself?" *Massa' (Davar)*, April 23, 1992.

— "Actually, It Writes Itself." Interview with Yaakov Besser. *Al Hamishmar*, September, 5, 1994.

— "Why There Is a Sudden Boom of Women Writers." *Ha'aretz*, March 8, 1996.

— *Kan nagur* [Here We'll Live: Five Short Novels]. Tel Aviv: Hakkibutz Hameuchad/Siman Kri'ah, 1996.

— "Do You (f.) Want to Write a Book?" *Ma'ariv*, October 3, 1997, p. 15.

Kahane, Claire. *Passions of a Voice: Hysteria, Narrative, and the Figure of the Speaking Woman, 1850–1915*. Baltimore: Johns Hopkins University Press, 1995.

Kahanoff, Jacqueline. *Mimizrah shemesh* [From the East; essays]. Tel Aviv: Yariv, 1978.

Kaminer, Wendy. *A Fearful Freedom: Women's Flight From Equality*. Reading, Mass.: Addison-Wesley, 1990.

Kamuf, Peggy. *Signature Pieces: On the Institution of Authorship*. Ithaca: Cornell University Press, 1988.

Kaniuk, Yoram. "Mountain, Stone, and Beauty." *Devar Hashavu'a*, February 23, 1973.

Kartun-Blum, Ruth. "Don't Play Hide and Seek with Mothers: Mothers' Voice and the Binding of Isaac." *Jerusalem Review* 3 (March 1999), forthcoming.

— "A Modern Mystical Experience: Intertextuality and Deconstruction in Israeli Women's Poetry," in Ruth Kartun-Blum, *Profane Scriptures: Reflections on the Dialogue with the Bible in Modern Hebrew Poetry*. Cincinnati: Hebrew Union College Press, forthcoming.

Katz, Susan. "Singleness of Heart: Spinsterhood in Victorian Culture." Ph.D. diss., Columbia University, 1988.

Katzir, Yehudit. *Sogrim 'et hayam*. Tel Aviv: Hakibbutz Hameuchad, 1990.

— *Closing the Sea*. Trans. Barbara Harshav. New York: Harcourt, Brace, Jovanovich, 1992.

Katznelson-Shazar, Rachel. *'Adam kemo shehu* [The Person as She Was]. Tel Aviv: Am Oved, 1989.

Keisari, Uri. "A Woman Recipient of the Prize." *Ha'aretz*, December 31, 1954, p. 3.

Kenaz, Yehoshua. *'Aharei hahagim*. Tel Aviv: Am Oved, 1967.

— *After the Holidays*. Trans. Dalya Bilu. San Diego: Harcourt Brace Jovanovich, 1987.

Kennard, Jean. "Woolf, the *Dreadnought* Hoax, and Sexual Ambiguity." *Journal of Modern Literature* 20, no. 2 (Winter 1996): 149–164.

Kerett, Etgar. *Tzinorot* [Pipelines]. Tel Aviv: Am Oved, 1992.

— *Ga'agu'ay lekissinger* [My Longings for Kissinger]. Tel Aviv: Zmora-Bitan, 1994.

Klein, Kathleen Gregory. *The Woman Detective: Gender and Genre*. Urbana and Chicago: University of Illinois Press, 1995 [1988].

Koren, Yehuda. "Is the Airport-Literature Landing?" *Yediot Aharonot* [weekend supplement], February 27, 1998, p. 24.

Kristeva, Julia. *Revolution in Poetic Language*. Trans. A. Waller. Columbia University Press, 1984 [1974].

— *The Kristeva Reader*. Ed. Toril Moi. New York: Columbia University Press, 1985.

— "Women's Time." In Toril Moi, ed., *The Kristeva Reader*, pp. 187–213. New York: Columbia University Press, 1985.

Kronfeld, Chana. *On the Margins of Modernism: Decentering Literary Dynamics*. Berkeley: University of California Press, 1996.

Kubovi, Miri. "From Slavery to Freedom and from Darkness to a Great Light: Another Reading of *Up in Montifer*." *Davar*, September 21, 1987.

Kuykendall, Eleanor H. "The Subjectivity of the Speaker." In Arleen B. Dallery and Charles E. Schott, eds., *The Question of the Other: Essays in*

Contemporary Continental Philosophy, pp. 145–155. Albany: State University of New York, 1989.

Lacan, Jacques. *Ecrits*. Trans. Alan Sheridan. London: Tavistock, 1977.

— *Feminine Sexuality*. Eds. Juliet Mitchell and Jaqueline Rose. New York: Norton, 1982.

Laing, R. D. *The Divided Self*. Penguin, 1960.

— *The Politics of The Family*. New York: Vintage, 1969.

— *The Politics of Experience*. New York: Ballantine, 1970.

— *Ha'ani hahatzui*. Trans. Rivka Yehoshua. Tel Aviv: Hakibbutz Hameuchad, 1977.

Laing, R. D. and A. Esterson. *Sanity, Madness, and the Family: Families of Schizophrenics*. London: Tavistock, 1964.

Laor, Yitzhak. *'Am, ma'akhal melakhim* [The People, Food Fit for a King]. Tel Aviv: Hakibbutz Hameuchad, 1993.

Lapid, Shulamit. "The Order of the Garter." *Mazal dagim* [Pisces; stories]. Tel Aviv: Eked, 1969.

— *Shalvat shotim* [The Calm of Fools; stories]. Tel Aviv: Massada, 1974.

— "Haroman haromanti" [The Harlequin Novel]. *Ma'ariv*, October 17, 1975.

— *Kadahat* [Fever; stories]. Tel Aviv: Yahdav, 1979.

— *Gei Oni*. Jerusalem: Keter, 1982.

— *Kaheres hanishbar* [As a Broken Vessel]. Jerusalem: Keter, 1984.

— *Mekomon* [Local Paper]. Jerusalem: Keter, 1989.

— *'Akavishim semehim* [Happy Spiders; stories]. Jerusalem: Keter, 1990.

— *Rehem pundaki* [Surrogate Mother; play]. Tel Aviv: Or Am, 1990.

— *Rekhush natush* [Abandoned Property; play]. Tel Aviv: Or Am. 1991.

— *Pitayon* [The Bait]. Jerusalem: Keter, 1991.

— *Hatakhshit* [The Jewel]. Jerusalem: Keter, 1992.

— "Myth: Succinct and Stimulating." *Shishi/Tikshoret: Tarbut*, December 30, 1994.

— *Hol ba'einaim* [Sand in the Eyes]. Jerusalem: Keter, 1996.

— *'Etzel Babou* [Chez Babou]. Jerusalem: Keter, 1998.

Lawrence, Patricia. "The Facts and Fugue of War: From *Three Guineas* to *Between the Acts*." In Mark Hussey, ed., *Virginia Woolf and War: Fiction, Reality and Myth*, pp. 225–245. Syracuse: Syracuse University Press, 1991.

Lazovski, Eli'an. "Running with She-Wolves." *Ma'ariv/Culture*, October 3, 1997, pp. 12–14.

Lee, Hermoine. *Virginia Woolf*. London: Chatto and Windus, 1996.

Le Guin, Ursula. *The Wind's Twelve Quarters*. London: Victor Gollantz, 1975.

— *The Left Hand of Darkness*. London: Virago, 1997 [1969].

Lejeune, Phillip. *On Autobiography*. Trans. Katherine Leary. Minneapolis: University of Minnesota Press, 1989.

Lelchuk, Alan. "Stumbling to Canaan" (book review). *New York Times Book Review*, June 12, 1988, p. 16.

Lerner, Anne Lapidus. " 'A Woman's Song': The Poetry of Esther Raab." In Naomi B. Sokoloff, Anne Lapidus Lerner, and Anita Norich, eds., *Gender and Text in Modern Hebrew and Yiddish Literature*, pp. 17–38. New York: Jewish Theological Seminary, 1992.

— "The Naked Land: Nature in the Poetry of Esther Raab." Baskin, Judith R., ed. *Women of the Word: Jewish Women and Jewish Writing*, pp. 236–257. Detroit: Wayne State University Press, 1994.

Lev, Eleanora. *Haboker harishon began eden* [The First Morning in Paradise]. Tel Aviv: Keshet, 1996.

Levitt, Laura. *Jews and Feminism: The Ambivalent Search for Home*. New York: Routledge, 1997.

Lieblich, Amia. *Rekamot*. Jerusalem: Schocken, 1991.

— *'El Lea* [To Leah]. Tel Aviv: Hakibbutz Hameuchad, 1995.

— *Conversations With Dvora: An Experimental Biography of the First Modern Hebrew Woman Writer*. Eds. Chana Kronfeld and Naomi Seidman. Trans. Naomi Seidman. Berkeley: University of California Press, 1997.

Liebrecht, Savyon. *Sinit 'ani medaberet 'eleikha* [It's All Greek to You]. 1992. Jerusalem: Keter.

— *Apples From the Desert*. Trans. Jeffrey M. Green, Marganit Weinberger-Rotman, Gilead Morahg, Riva Rubin. New York: Feminist Press, 1998.

Lilienfeld, Jane. " 'The Deceptiveness of Beauty': Mother Love and Mother Hate in *To the Lighthouse*." *Twentieth Century Literature* 23 (1977): 345–376.

Litvin, Rina. "The Tangle and the Way." *Yediot Aharonot*, May 9, 1985, pp. 1, 7.

Lloyd, David. *Nationalism and Minor Literature*. Berkeley: University of California Press, 1987.

Lloyd, Genevieve. *The Man of Reason: "Male" and "Female" in Western Philosophy*. Minneapolis: University of Minnesota Press, 1984.

Logan, Peter Melville. *Nerves and Narratives: A Cultural History of Hysteria in Nineteenth-Century British Prose*. Berkeley: University of California Press, 1997.

London, Yaron. "Battered Women (on *Up in Montifer*)." *Ha'ir Tel Aviv*, April 20, 1984.

— "Four Religious Women Novelists Who Topped the Best-Seller Lists." *Yediot Aharonot*, October 15, 1997, pp. 54–57.

Lubin, Orly. "A Woman Reading A Woman." *Te'oria vebikoret [Theory and Criticism]* 3 (1993): 65–79.

— "The Forerunners of a Revolution." *Ha'aretz/Sfarim*, September 1, 1993, p. 7.

— "The Woman as Other in Israeli Cinema." In Laurence J. Silberstein and Robert L. Cohn, eds., *The Other in Jewish Thought and History: Constructions of Jewish Culture and Identity*, pp. 305–325. New York: New York University Press, 1994.

— "A Feminist Reading of Nehama Puhashevski's Stories." Conference on Women in the Yishuv and Early State. Hebrew University, Jerusalem, June 2–4, 1998.

Luchtenstein, Esti. "The Form Hidden in the Chaos." *Ma'ariv*, October 30, 1981.

Luz, Zvi. *Shirat Esther Raab* [Esther Raab's Poetry]. Tel Aviv: Hakibbutz Hameuchad, 1997.

Lyotard, Jean-Francois. *The Postmodern Condition: A Report on Knowledge.* Trans. Geoff Bennington and Brian Massumi. Minneapolis: University of Minnesota Press, 1984.

McHale, Brian. *Postmodernist Fiction*. New York: Methuen, 1987.

Man, Paul de. "Autobiography as Defacement." *Modern Language Notes* 94 (1979): 919–930.

Marcus, Jane. " 'No More Horses': Virginia Woolf on Art and Propaganda." *Women's Studies* 4 (1977): 265–290.

— *Virginia Woolf and the Languages of Patriarchy*. Bloomington: Indiana University Press, 1987.

Marcus, Jane, ed. *New Feminist Essays on Virginia Woolf*. Lincoln: University of Nebraska Press, 1981.

— *Virginia Woolf and Bloomsbury: A Centenary Celebration*. Bloomington: Indiana University Press, 1987.

Margalit, Naomi. "The Palmach According to Netiva." *Ma'ariv*, March 29, 1981.

— "Treasured Criticism." *Ma'ariv*, December 25, 1981.

Marsh, Jan. *Bloomsbury Women*. New York: Henry Holt, 1995.

"Mashehu feministi zaz" [A Feminist Something Is Stirring]. *Yediot Aharonot/Seven Days*, December 1987, pp. 19–20, 45.

Mason, Mary G. "The Other Voice: Autobiographies of Women Writers." In James Olney, ed., *Autobiography: Essays Theoretical and Critical*. Princeton: Princeton University Press, 1980.

Matalon, Ronit. *Zeh 'im hapanim 'eleinu*. Tel Aviv: Am Oved, 1995.

— *The One Facing Us*. Trans. Marsha Weinstein. New York: Henry Holt, 1998.

Megged, Aharon. *Duda'im me'eretz hakodesh* [Mandrakes from the Holy Land]. Tel Aviv: Am Oved, 1998.

Megged, Eyal. *Barbarossa*. Jerusalem: Keter, 1993.

Mehlman, Jeffrey. *A Structural Study of Autobiography*. Ithaca: Cornell University Press, 1974.

Meisel, Perry. *The Absent Father: Virginia Woolf and Walter Pater.* New Haven: Yale University Press, 1980.

Melamed, Ariana. "No Man Is God." *Ḥadashot,* November 16, 1990.

— "Who is Afraid of *Orlando?*" *Ha'ir,* February 28, 1997.

Mendelson, Jane. *The Miracle Hater* (book review). *Voice* 33, no. 15 (April 12, 1988): 5.

Mens-Verhulst, Janneke, Karlin Schreurs, and Liesbeth Woertman, eds. *Daughtering and Mothering: Female Subjectivity Reanalyzed.* New York: Routledge, 1993.

Mepham, John. *Virginia Woolf: A Literary Life.* London: Macmillan, 1991.

Miller, Jean Baker, ed. *Psychoanalysis and Women.* New York: Penguin, 1973.

Miller, Nancy K. *The Heroine's Text.* New York: Columbia University Press, 1980.

— *The Poetics of Gender.* New York: Columbia University Press, 1986.

Mintz, Alan. *Banished from Their Father's Table: Loss of Faith and Hebrew Autobiography.* Bloomington: Indiana University Press, 1989.

Mintz, Alan, ed., *The Boom in Contemporary Israeli Fiction.* Hanover: University Press of New England, 1997.

Miron, Dan. "Had It Been Written Then." *Siman Kri'ah* 16/17 (1983): 519–521.

— *'Im lo' tihye yerushalayim* [If There Is No Jerusalem: Essays on Hebrew Writing in a Cultural-Political Context]. Tel Aviv: Hakibbutz Hameuchad, 1987.

— "Lizzie Badiḥi's Innocence." *Siman Kri'ah* 20 (May 1990): 166–185.

— *Noge'a badavar* [Essays on Literature and Society]. Tel Aviv: Zmora-Bitan, 1991.

— *'Imahot meyasdot, 'aḥayot ḥorgot* [Founding Mothers, Stepsisters]. Tel Aviv: Hakibbutz Hameuchad, 1991.

— "Why Was There No Women's Poetry in Hebrew Before 1920?" (a partial English rendition, by Naomi Sokoloff, of *Founding Mothers*). In Naomi B. Sokoloff, Anne Lapidus Lerner, and Anita Norich, eds., *Gender and Text in Modern Hebrew and Yiddish Literature,* pp. 65–94. New York: Jewish Theological Seminary, 1992.

— *Mul ha'aḥ hashotek* [Facing the Silent Brother: Essays on the Poetry of the War of Independence]. Tel Aviv and Jerusalem: Open University and Keter, 1992.

— "The Unholy Trinity." *Yediot Aḥaronot,* June 3, 1994.

— *Haḥole hamedume* [*Le Médecin Imaginaire*: Studies in Classical Jewish Fiction]. Tel Aviv: Hakibbutz Hameuchad, 1995.

Mitchell, Juliet. *Psychoanalysis and Feminism.* New York: Vintage, 1974.

— *Women, the Longest Revolution.* London: Virago, 1984 [1966].

Mohanty, Chandra, Anne Russo, and Lourdes Torres, eds., *Third World Women and the Politics of Feminism.* Bloomington: Indiana University Press, 1991.

Moi, Toril. *Sexual/Textual Politics: Feminist Literary Theory*. London and New York: Routledge, 1985.

— *Simone de Beauvoir: The Making of An Intellectual Woman*. Oxford and Cambridge: Blackwell, 1994.

Moked, Gabriel. "I-Thou Encounters" (on *Up in Montifer*). *Ha'aretz*, June 8, 1994.

Morgan, Robin. *The Anatomy of Freedom: Feminism, Physics, and Global Politics*. Oxford: Martin Robertson, 1982.

— *The Demon Lover: On the Sexuality of Terrorism*. New York: Norton: 1989.

— ed. *Sisterhood is Powerful: An Anthology of Writings from the Women's Liberation Movement*. New York: Vintage, 1970.

Morgan, Thais E., ed. *Men Writing the Feminine: Literature, Theory, and the Question of Gender*. Albany: State University of New York Press, 1994.

Morris, Benny. *The Birth of the Palestinian Refugee Problem*. Cambridge: Cambridge University Press, 1987.

Mosse, George L. *The Image of Man: The Creation of Modern Masculinity*. Oxford: Oxford University Press, 1996.

Mulvey, Laura. "Visual Pleasure and Narrative Cinema." *Screen* 16, no. 3 (Autumn 1975): 6–18.

Murphy, Ann B. "The Borders of Ethical, Erotic, and Artistic Possibilities in *Little Women*." *Signs* 15 (Spring 1990): 562–585.

Nash, Stanley. "Character Portrayal and Cultural Critique in Shulamit Hareven's Work." *Modern Judaism* 16 (1996): 215–228.

Natoli, Joseph and Linda Hutcheon, eds. *A Postmodern Reader*. Albany: State University of New York Press, 1993.

Nave, Yudith. "In Those Days and at This Time: Lyric and Ideology in Shulamith Hareven's Short Stories." *HAR* 13 (1991): 77–87.

Naveh, Hannah. "On Loss, Bereavment, and Mourning in the Israeli Experience." *Alpayim* 16 (1998): 85–120.

Navot, Amnon. "Up in Montifer of the Rococo." *Ma'ariv*, June 15, 1984.

— "Not One Needless Word." *Yediot Aḥaronot*, December 20, 1991.

— "In Well-Chosen Words." *Ma'ariv*, December 23, 1994.

Negev, Ayelet. "Dearest, I Have the Feeling That I Shall Go Mad Again." *Yediot Aḥaronot/Seven Days*, May 10, 1991, pp. 40–42.

Netzer, Ruth. "A Sunset Red as Blood." *Alei-Si'aḥ* (1988): 59–67.

Neumann, Erich. *Amor and Psyche: The Psychic Development of the Feminine*. Princeton: Princeton University Press, 1952.

— *The Great Mother*. Princeton: Princeton University Press, 1955.

— *The Origins and History of Consciousness*. Princeton: Princeton University Press, 1973 [1949].

Nicholson, Linda J., ed. *Feminism/Postmodernism*. New York: Routledge, 1985.

Nicolson, Nigel. *Portrait of a Marriage.* New York: Atheneum, 1973.

— *Dyokan nisu'im.* Trans. Oded Peled. Tel Aviv: Schocken, 1994.

Nirad, Yorgan. "Nationalism and Humanism." *Ha'aretz/Sfarim*, March 18, 1998.

Nitzan, Shlomo. "A Long Reckoning with the War." *Al Hamishmar*, September 29, 1985.

Niv, Kobi. *'Ani feminist* [I Am a Feminist (m.)]. Tel Aviv: Kineret, 1990.

Nye, Andrea. *Feminist Theory and the Philosophies of Man.* London and New York: Routledge, 1988.

O'Brien, Mary. *The Politics of Reproduction.* New York: Routledge, 1980.

Offen, Karen. "Defining Feminism: A Comparative Historical Approach." *Signs* 14 (Autumn, 1988): 119–157.

Olney, James, ed. *Autobiography: Essays Theoretical and Critical.* Princeton: Princeton University Press, 1980.

— *Studies in Autobiography.* Oxford: Oxford University Press, 1988.

Olson, Ray. *Thirst* (book review). *Booklist* 92, no. 15 (April 1, 1996): 1342.

Or, Shulamit. "Between the Sheaves and the Sword." *Na'amat* (May 1981).

Oren, Miriam. "Nevertheless: Real Literature." *Moznaim* (December 1981): 53–55.

Oren, Yosef. "*Up in Montifer*—Up!" *Moznaim* (August-September, 1984): 69–71.

— "Like a Bolted Window, as a Closed Fist." *Ma'ariv*, November 14, 1986.

— "Like Roots in the Air and a Worm in the Dark." *Apirion* 12 (1988–1989): 7–8.

— "Ruth Almog's *Roots of Air.*" *Hatzda'ah lasifrut haisraelit* [Salute to Israeli Literature], pp. 91–97. Rishon Lezion: Yahad, 1991.

Oryan, Yehudit. "Clarissa's Adventures." *Ma'ariv*, March 28, 1975, pp. 29, 31.

— "The Wild East." *Yediot Aharonot*, April 16, 1982, pp. 22, 26.

— "The Daily Truth of the Grey Man on Whose Back History Takes Place." *Yediot Aharonot*, June 10, 1983.

— "Boredom Has Many Faces." *Yediot Aharonot*, August 20, 1993.

Ostriker, Alicia Suskin. *Stealing the Language: The Emergence of Women's Poetry in America.* Boston: Beacon, 1986.

Oz, Amos. *'Ad mavet.* Tel Aviv: Sifriat Poalim, 1971.

— *Unto Death.* Trans. Nicholas de Lange. San Diego: Harcourt Brace Jovanovich, 1975.

— *Lada'at 'ishah.* Jerusalem: Keter, 1989.

— *To Know a Woman.* Trans. Nicholas de Lange. San Diego: Harcourt Brace Jovanovich, 1991.

Pardes, Ilana. *Countertraditions in the Bible.* Cambridge: Harvard University Press, 1992.

— "Yocheved Bat Miriam: The Poetic Strength of a Matronym." In Naomi

B. Sokoloff, Anne Lapidus Lerner, and Anita Norich, eds., *Gender and Text in Modern Hebrew and Yiddish Literature*, pp. 39–64. New York: Jewish Theological Seminary, 1992.

Paz, Miri. "The Death of the Princess Beauvoir." *Davar*, April 20, 1986.

— "The Observers of an Ethical Double Standard." *Na'amat* 89 (June 1986): 44–45.

Paz, Octavio. *Sor Juana: The Traps of Faith*. Trans. Margaret Sayers Peden. Cambridge: Harvard University Press, 1988.

Perlis, Isa. "One Woman's Problem." *Davar*, September 1985.

Peskowitz, Miriam and Laura Levitt, eds. *Judaism Since Gender*. New York: Routledge, 1996.

Pierson, Ruth Roach. *Women and Peace: Theoretical, Historical, and Practical Perspectives*. London: Croom Helm, 1987.

Pinkney, Makiko M. *Virginia Woolf and the Problem of the Subject*. Harvester, 1987.

Plaskow, Judith. *Standing Again at Sinai*. New York: Harper and Row, 1990.

Plath, Sylvia. *The Collected Poems*. Ed. Ted Hughes. New York: Harper and Row, 1981.

Pogrebin, Letty Cottin. *Deborah, Golda, and Me: Being Female and Jewish in America*. New York: Crown, 1991.

Poole, Roger. *The Unknown Virginia Woolf*. Cambridge: Cambridge University Press, 1978.

— "We all put up with you Virginia: Irreceivable Wisdom About War." In Mark Hussey, ed., *Virginia Woolf and War: Fiction, Reality, and Myth*, pp. 79–100. Syracuse: Syracuse University Press, 1991.

Pridmore-Brown, Michele. "1939–40: Of Virginia Woolf, Gramophones, and Fascism." *PMLA* 113, no. 3 (May 1998): 408–421.

Probyn, Elsbeth. *Sexing the Self*. New York and London: Routledge, 1993.

Raab, Esther. *Kol hashirim* [Collected Poems]. Ed. Ehud ben Ezer. Tel Aviv: Zmora-Bitan, 1994.

Rabinyan, Dorit. *Simtat hashkediot be'omrijan*. Tel Aviv: Am Oved, 1995.

— *Persian Brides*. Trans. Yael Lotan. New York: Braziller, 1998.

Ragen, Naomi. *Sotah*. New York: Crown, 1992.

— *Ve-'el 'ishekh teshukatekh*. Trans. Adah Feldor. Jerusalem: Keter, 1995.

Raitt, Suzanne. *Vita and Virginia: The Work and Friendship of Victoria Sackville-West and Virginia Woolf*. Oxford: Clarendon Press, 1993.

Ramras-Rauch, Gila. *Death in the Rain* (book review). *World Literature Today* 69, no. 1 (Winter 1995): 215.

Rapoport-Albert, Ada. "On Women in Hasidism, S. A. Horodecky and the Maid of Ludmir Tradition." In Ada Rapoport-Albert and Steven J. Zipperstein, eds., *Jewish History: Essays in Honor of Chimen Abramsky*, pp. 495–525. London: Peter Halban, 1978.

Rattok, Lily. *Amalia Kahana-Carmon*. Tel Aviv: Sifriat Poalim, 1986.

— "Woman Is the Jew of the World." *Modern Hebrew Literature* 4 (1990): 6–8.

— "Two Responses." *Te'oria vebikoret [Theory and Criticism]* 5 (1994): 165–177.

— *Mal'akh ha'esh* [Angel of Fire: The Poetry of Yona Wallach]. Tel Aviv: Hakibbutz Hameuchad, 1997.

Rattok, Lily, ed. *Hakol ha'aher* [The Other Voice: Women's Fiction in Hebrew]. Tel Aviv: Hakibbutz Hameuchad, 1994.

Ravikovitch, Dahlia. *'Ahavat tapu'ah hazahav* [The Love of an Orange; poems]. Tel Aviv: Mahbarot Lesifrut, 1959.

— *Horef kasheh* [A Hard Winter; stories]. Tel Aviv: Dvir, 1964.

— *The Window: Poems*. Trans. Chana and Ariel Bloch. Sheep Meadow Press, 1989.

Rein, Natalie. *Daughters of Rachel: Women in Israel*. Penguin, 1979.

Reinharz, Shulamit. "Manya Wilbushewitz-Shohat and the Winding Road to Sejera." In Deborah S. Bernstein, *Pioneers and Homemakers: Jewish Women in Pre-State Israel*, pp. 95–118. Albany: State University of New York Press, 1992.

Renan, Yael. "On the Principles of Human Existence and Their Artistic Embodiment in Virginia Woolf's *Mrs. Dalloway*." *Siman Kri'ah* 5 (February 1976): 103–109.

— "Facts: On Virginia Woolf's *The Years*, Upon the Publication of a Hebrew Translation." *Siman Kri'ah* 10 (January 1980): 488.

— "Virginia Woolf's Poetics and Ideology." *Hasifrut* n.s. 1, no. 1 (33), (Summer 1984): 42–50.

Rhys, Jean. *Wide Sargasso Sea*. New York: Norton, 1966.

— *Yam sargasso harahav*. Trans. Aharon Amir. Tel Aviv. Zmora-Bitan, 1981.

Rich, Adrienne. *Of Woman Born: Motherhood as Experience and Institution*. New York: Norton, 1976.

— *On Lies, Secrets, and Silence*. New York: Norton, 1979.

— "Compulsory Heterosexuality and Lesbian Existence." *Signs* 5 (1980): 631–660.

— *Yelud 'ishah*. Trans. Karmit Gai. Tel Aviv: Am Oved, 1989.

Riding, Alan. "The World Reintroduces Beauvoir to the French." *New York Times*, January 31, 1999, pp. B9, B11.

Riffaterre, Michael. *The Semiotics of Poetry*. Bloomington: Indiana University Press, 1978.

— *Text Production*. Bloominton: Indiana University Press, 1982.

Ringel-Hoffman, Ariela. "The Four Mothers Movement." *Yediot Aharonot* [weekend supplement], March 27, 1998, pp. 10–11.

Rotem, Yehudit. "Dvora Baron Is Not Alone Anymore." *Devar Hashavu'a*, November 18, 1994, pp. 8–10.

Rowbotham, Sheila. *Woman's Consciousness, Man's World*. London: Penguin, 1973.

Rubin, Emmanuel. *Twilight* (book review). *World Literature Today* 68, no. 1 (Winter 1994): 206.

Rubin, Gayle. "The Traffic in Women: The Political Economy of Sex." In Rayna R. Reiter, ed., *Toward an Anthropology of Women*, pp. 157–210. New York: Monthly Review, 1975.

Rudavsky, T. M., ed. *Gender and Judaism: The Transformation of Tradition*. New York: New York University Press, 1995.

Ruddik, Sara. *Maternal Thinking: Toward a Politics of Peace*. Boston: Beacon, 1989.

Sacks, Maurie, ed. *Active Voices: Women in Jewish Culture*. Urbana and Chicago: University of Illinois Press, 1995.

Said, Edward. *Orientalism*. New York: Vintage, 1978.

Sarna, Igal. *Yona Wallach: Biografia* [A Biography]. Jerusalem: Keter, 1993.

Scholem, Gershom G., ed. *Zohar: Basic Readings from the Kabbalah*. New York: Schocken, 1974 [1949].

Schwab, Gabriele. *Subjects Without Selves*. Cambridge: Harvard University Press, 1994.

Schwartz, Nina. *Dead Fathers: The Logic of Transference in Modern Narrative*. Ann Arbor: University of Michigan Press, 1994.

Schwartz, Yigal. "Hebrew Fiction: The Era After." *Efes Shtayim* 3 (Winter 1995): 7–15.

Scott, Bonnie Kime. *Refiguring Modernism*. Vol. 2: *Postmodern Feminist Readings of Woolf, West, and Barnes*. Bloomington: Indiana University Press, 1995.

Sedgwick, Eve Kosofsky. *The Epistemology of the Closet*. Hemel Hempstead, 1991.

Segal, Lynne. *Straight Sex: Rethinking the Politics of Pleasure*. London: Virago, 1994.

Seidenberg, Robert. "Is Anatomy Destiny?" In Jean Baker Miller, ed., *Psychoanalysis and Women*, pp. 306–329. New York: Penguin, 1973.

Shaked, Gershon. *Gal ḥadash basifrut ha'ivrit* [A New Wave in Hebrew Literature]. Tel Aviv, 1971.

— "Pain, Love, Death." *Moznaim* 58, nos. 3/4 (August/September 1984): 21–25.

— *Gal 'aḥar gal* [Wave After Wave in Hebrew Narrative Fiction]. Jerusalem: Keter, 1985.

— *'Ein makom 'aḥer* [No Other Place: On Literature and Society]. Tel Aviv: Hakibbutz Hameuchad, 1988.

— *Hasipporet ha'ivrit 1880–1980*. [Hebrew Narrative Prose]. 5 vols. Tel Aviv and Jerusalem: Hakibbutz Hameuchad and Keter, 1977–1999.

— "Between a Daughter and Her Fathers." *Moznaim* 71, no. 6 (March 1998): 8–12.

Shaked, Gershon, ed. *Hebrew Writers: A General Directory*. Tel Aviv: Institute for the Translation of Hebrew Literature, 1993.

Shalev, Meir. *Keyamim 'ahadim* [As a Few Days]. Tel Aviv: Am Oved, 1994.

Shalvi, Alice. *Networking for Women* 8, no. 1 (January 1995): 6.

Shamir, Moshe. *Hu halakh basadot* [He Walked in the Fields]. Tel Aviv: Sifriat Poalim, 1947.

— *Tahat hashemesh* [Under the Sun]. Tel Aviv: Am Oved, 1951.

— *Rohok mipninim* [More Than Rubies; a trilogy]. Tel Aviv: Am Oved, 1975, 1985, 1991.

Shamir, Ziva. "Childhood in Petah-Tikva." *Ma'ariv*, November 30, 1979.

— "And He Saw a Woman of Beauty." *Iton 77* (June 1984): 66.

— "A Woman in Her Four Square Feet." *Ha'aretz*, December 26, 1986.

— "Carved in Rock." *Yediot Aharonot*, January 13, 1995, p. 28.

Shammas, Anton. *Arabeskot*. Tel Aviv: Av Oved, 1986.

— *Arabesques*. Trans. Vivian Eden. New York: Harper and Row, 1988.

Shapiro, Yonatan. *'Elit lelo' mamshikhim* [An Elite Without Successors]. Tel Aviv: Sifriat Poalim, 1984.

Sharfman, Dafna. "The Status of Women in Israel—Facts and Myths." *Israeli Democracy* (Summer 1989): 12–14.

Sharoni, Simona. *Gender and the Israeli-Palestinian Conflict: The Politics of Women's Resistance*. Syracuse: Syracuse University Press, 1995.

Shehori, Dalia. "The Youthful and the Not So Beautiful." *Al Hamishmar*, June 28, 1985.

Sheinfeld, Ilan. "The Power of Sealed Issues." *Al Hamishmar*, June 10, 1983.

— "What Is Glittering?" *Dapim Lesifrut*, January 20, 1989.

— "Writing to the Past." *Apirion* (Fall 1991).

— "God Is a Matter of Quantity." *Ha'aretz/Sfarim*, December 28, 1994, p. 6.

Shemer, Sarah. *Doh 'intimi 'al nashim beisrael* [An Intimate Report on Women in Israel]. Tel Aviv: Ma'ariv, 1992.

Sherzer, Dina. "Postmodernism and Feminisms." In Edmund J. Smyth, ed., *Postmodernism and Contemporary Fiction*, pp. 156–168. London: Batsford, 1991.

Shifra, Shin. *Rehov hahol* [The Sand Street; stories]. Tel Aviv: Hakibbutz Hameuchad and Yediot Aharonot, 1994.

Shilo, Margalit. "The Woman—A 'Worker' or A 'Member' in the National Renaissance? Woman's Place in the First Aliyah (1882–1909)." *Yahadut zemanenu* 9 (1995): 121–147.

— "The Double or Multiple Image of the New Hebrew Woman." *Nashim* (Winter 1998): 73–94.

Shirav, Pnina. *Ktivah lo' tamah* [Noninnocent Writing: Discourse Position and Female Representations in Works by Yehudit Hendel, Amalia Kahana-Carmon, and Ruth Almog]. Tel Aviv: Hakibbutz Hameuchad, 1998.

Shoham, Shlomo Giora. "The Isaac Syndrome." *American Imago* 33, no. 4 (1976): 329–349.

— *Halikhei Tantalus*. Tel Aviv: Tcherikover, 1977.

— *The Myth of Tantalus*. St Lucia, Queensland: University of Queensland Press, 1979.

— *'Alimut ha'elem* [The Silence of Violence]. Tel Aviv: Tcherikover, 1984.

Shortt, Barbara. "Refugees from Reality." *Women's Review of Books* 9, nos. 10/11 (July 1992): 27.

Showalter, Elaine. *A Literature of Their Own: British Women Novelists From Bronte to Lessing*. Princeton: Princeton University Press, 1978.

— *The Female Malady: Women, Madness, and English Culture, 1830–1980*. New York: Pantheon, 1985.

— "Toward a Feminist Poetics." In Elaine Showalter, ed., *New Feminist Criticism*, pp. 137–141. New York: Pantheon, 1985.

— "Introduction." In Virginia Woolf, *Mrs Dalloway*. London: Penguin, 1991.

— "Hysteria, Feminism, and Gender." In Sander L. Gilman, Helen King, Roy Porter, G. S. Rousseau, and Elaine Showalter, *Hysteria Beyond Freud*, pp. 286–344. Berkeley: University of California Press, 1993.

Silva, N. Takei da. *Modernism and Virginia Woolf*. Windsor: Windsor, 1990.

Silverman, Kaja. *Male Subjectivity at the Margins*. New York: Routledge, 1992.

Siman-Tov, Yaakov. "The Person, the Design, the Homeland Landscape." *Yediot Aharonot*, May 13, 1988.

Singer, Isaac Bashevis. *The Collected Stories*. New York: Farrar Strauss Giroux, 1982.

Singer, June. *Androgyny: Toward a New Theory of Sexuality*. Anchor, 1977.

Sivan, Emmanuel. *Dor tashah: mitos, dyokan vezikaron* [The 1948 Generation: Myth, Profile and Memory]. Tel Aviv: Ministry of Defense, 1991.

Smith, Barbara Herrenstein. *Poetic Closure*. Chicago: University of Chicago Press, 1968.

Smith, Paul. "Julia Kristeva et al.; or, Take Three or More." In Richard Feldstein and Judith Roof, eds., *Feminism and Psychoanalysis*, pp. 84–104. Ithaca: Cornell University Press, 1982.

Smith, Sidonie. *A Poetics of Women's Autobiography*. Bloomington: Indiana University Press, 1987.

Snider, Clifton. "A Single Self." *Modern Fiction Studies* 25 (1979): 263–268.

Sokoloff, Naomi B. "Feminist Criticism and Modern Hebrew Literature." *Prooftexts* 8, no. 1 (1988): 143–156.

— "Gender Studies in Modern Hebrew Literature." In Naomi B. Sokoloff, Anne Lapidus Lerner, and Anita Norich, eds., *Gender and Text in Modern*

Hebrew and Yiddish Literature, pp. 257–264. New York: Jewish Theological Seminary, 1992.

— "Modern Hebrew Literature: The Impact of Feminist Research." In Lynn Davidman and Shelly Tenenbaum, eds., *Feminist Perspectives on Jewish Studies*, pp. 224–243. New Haven: Yale University Press, 1995.

Sokoloff, Naomi B., Anne Lapidus Lerner, and Anita Norich, eds. *Gender and Text in Modern Hebrew and Yiddish Literature*. New York: Jewish Theological Seminary, 1992.

Solomon, S. and E. Starkman, "Twilight" (book review). *Prairie Schooner* 69, no. 1 (Spring 1995): 173.

Spengemann, W. C. *The Forms of Autobiography*. New Haven: Yale University Press, 1980.

Spiegel, Shalom. *The Last Trial*. Trans. Judah Goldin. New York: Behrman House, 1967.

Spivak, Gayatri Chakravorty. *In Other Worlds: Essays in Cultural Politics*. New York: Methuen, 1987.

— "Political Commitment and the Postmodern Critic." In H. Aram Verset, ed., *The New Historicism*, pp. 243–277. New York: Routledge, 1989.

Stanton, Donna C., ed. *The Female Autograph: Theory and Practice of Autobiography from the Tenth to the Twentieth Century*. Chicago: University of Chicago Press, 1987.

— "Difference on Trial: A Critique of the Maternal Metaphor in Cixous, Irigaray, and Kristeva." In Nancy K. Miller, ed., *The Poetics of Gender*, pp. 157–182. New York: Columbia University Press, 1987.

Stimpson, Catharine R. "The Androgyne and the Homosexual." *Women's Studies* 2 (1974): 237–248.

— "The Female Sociograph: The Theatre of Woolf's Letters." In Domna C. Stanton, ed., *The Female Autograph: Theory and Practice of Autobiography from the Tenth to the Twentieth Century*, pp. 168–179. Chicago: University of Chicago Press, 1987.

— "Woolf's Room, Our Project: The Building of Feminist Criticism." In Ralph Cohen, ed., *The Future of Literary Theory*, pp. 129–143. New York: Routledge, 1989.

Stimpson, Catharine R. and Ethel Spector Person, eds. *Women: Sex and Sexuality*. Chicago: University of Chicago Press, 1980.

Stories from Women Writers of Israel. New Delhi: Star, 1995.

Stout, Janis P. *Through the Window, Out the Door: Women's Narratives of Departure*. Tuscaloosa: University of Alabama Press, 1998.

Sturrock, John. "The New Model Autobiographer." *Modern Language Notes* 9 (1977): 51–63.

Styron, William. *Darkness Visible*. New York: Random House, 1990.

Suleiman, Susan Rubin. *Subversive Intent: Gender, Politics, and the Avant-Garde.* Cambridge: Harvard University Press, 1990.

Suleiman, Susan Rubin, ed. *The Female Body in Western Culture.* Cambridge: Harvard University Press, 1985.

Swerdlow, Amy. *Women Strike for Peace: Traditional Motherhood and Radical Politics in the 1960s.* Chicago: University of Chicago Press, 1993.

Swirski, Barbara. "Israeli Feminism New and Old." In Barbara Swirski and Marilyn P. Safir, eds., *Calling the Equality Bluff: Women in Israel,* pp. 285–302. New York: Teachers College Press, 1993.

Swirski, Barbara and Marilyn P. Safir, eds. *Calling the Equality Bluff: Women in Israel.* New York: Teachers College Press, 1993.

Taub, Gadi. *Hamered hashafuf* [A Dispirited Rebellion: Essays on Contemporary Israeli Culture]. Tel Aviv: Hakibbutz Hameuchad, 1997.

Tishbie, Yeshayahu. *Pirkei Zohar* [Chapters from the Zohar]. Tel Aviv: Mossad Bialik, 1972.

Todorov, Tzvetan. *Mikhail Bakhtin: The Dialogical Principle.* Trans. Wlad Godzick. Minneapolis: University of Minnesota Press, 1984.

Topping, Nancy Bazin. *Virginia Woolf and the Adrogynous Vision.* New Brunswick, N.J.: Rutgers University Press, 1973.

Torgovnick, Marianna. *The Visual Arts, Pictorialism, and the Novel.* Princeton: Princeton University Press, 1985.

Tremper, Ellen. "In Her Father's House: *To the Lighthouse* as a Record of Virginia Woolf's Literary Patrimony." *Texas Studies in Literature and Language* 34, no. 1 (Spring 1992): 1–40.

— *"Who Lived in Alfoxton?" Virginia Woolf and English Romanticism.* Bucknell University Press, 1998.

Trible, Phyllis. *God and the Rhetoric of Sexuality.* Philadelphia: Fortress, 1978.

Trinh T. Minh-ha, *Woman, Native, Other: Writing, Postcoloniality, and Feminism.* Bloomington: Indiana University Press, 1989.

Tzemah, Adah. "Three Who Wrote." *Siman Kri'ah* 16/17 (1983): 522–529.

Ulman-Margalit, Edna. "A Different Face in the Mirror." *Mikarov* 2 (1998): 153–161.

Warner, Eric. "Some Aspects of Romanticism in the Work of Virginia Woolf." Thesis, Oxford University, 1980.

Warner, Marina. *Alone of All Her Sex: The Myth and the Cult of the Virgin Mary.* New York: Pocket, 1976.

Watson, Julia. "Shadowed Presence: Modern Women Writers' Autobiographies and the Other." In James Olney, ed., *Autobiography: Essays Theoretical and Critical,* pp. 180–189. Princeton: Princeton University Press, 1980.

Weil, Kari. *Androgyny and the Denial of Difference.* Virginia: Virginia University Press, 1992.

Weininger, Otto. *Sex and Character.* New York: Putnam, 1908 [1903].

Wellisch, Erich. *Isaac and Oedipus: A Study in Biblical Psychology of the Sacrifice of Isaac, the Akedah.* London: Routledge and Kegan Paul, 1954.

Wilson, J. J. "Why is *Orlando* Difficult?" In Jane Marcus, ed., *New Feminist Essays on Virginia Woolf,* 170–184. Lincoln: University of Nebraska Press, 1981.

Winthrup, Christiane. *Women's Bodies, Women's Wisdom: Creating Physical and Emotional Health and Healing.* Rev. ed. New York: Bantam, 1998.

Wirth-Nesher, Hana. "Final Curtain on the War: Figure and Ground in Virginia Woolf's *Between the Acts.*" *Style* 28, no. 2 (Summer 1994): 183–200.

Wittig, Monique. "One Is Not Born a Woman." *Feminist Issues* 1, no. 2 (1978): 47–54.

Wolf, Tami. "Madness Is the Wisdom of the Individuum." *Moznaim* 61, no. 9 (January 1988): 48–49.

— "Roots of Air." *Davar,* April 22, 1988.

Wolfson, Elliott. "Woman—The Feminine as Other in Theosophic Kabbalah: Some Philosophical Observations on the Divine Androgyne." In Laurence J. Silberstein and Robert L. Cohn, eds., *The Other in Jewish Thought and History,* pp. 166–204. New York: New York University Press, 1994.

— *Circle in the Square: Studies in the Use of Gender in Kabbalistic Symbolism.* Albany: State University of New York Press, 1995.

Woolf, Leonard. *Barbarians at the Gate.* London: Golantz, 1939.

Woolf, Virginia. *The Voyage Out.* New York: Harcourt, Brace and World, 1920 [1915].

— *Mrs. Dalloway.* London: Penguin, 1991 [1925].

— *To the Lighthouse.* New York: Harcourt, Brace and World, 1927.

— *Orlando: A Biography.* New York: Penguin, 1946 [1928].

— *A Room of One's Own.* London: Penguin, 1945 [1929].

— *The Waves.* New York: Penguin, 1951 [1931].

— *Flush: A Biography.* New York: Harcourt Brace, 1933.

— *Three Guineas.* New York: Penguin, 1977 [1938].

— "The Leaning Tower." In Virginia Woolf, *The Moment and Other Essays,* pp. 128–154. New York: Harcourt, Brace, 1948 [1940].

— *Between the Acts.* New York: Harcourt Brace Jovanovich, 1941.

— *The Moment and Other Essays.* New York: Harcourt, Brace, 1948.

— *A Writer's Diary.* Ed. Leonard Woolf. London: Hogarth, 1953.

— *Collected Essays.* 4 vols. London: Hogarth, 1966–1967.

— *The Letters of Virginia Woolf.* 6 vols. Eds. Nigel Nicolson and Joanne Trautman. New York: Harcourt Brace Jovanovich, 1975–1980.

— *The Diary of Virginia Woolf.* 5 vols. Eds. Anne Olivier Beel and Andrew McNeillee. New York: Harcourt Brace Jovanovich, 1976–1984.

— *The Complete Short Fiction of Virginia Woolf.* Ed. Susan Dick. London: Hogarth, 1985.

— *Moments of Being: Unpublished Autobiographical Writings.* 2d ed. Ed. Jeanne Schulkind. New York: Harcourt Brace Jovanovich, 1985.

Yaglin, Ofra. "Up by Amalia." *Al Hamishmar,* April 20, 1984.

Yalon, Marilyn. *Maternity, Mortality, and the Literature of Madness.* University Park: Pennsylvania State University Press, 1993.

Yehoshua, A. B. *Bizkhut hanormaliut.* Jerusalem and Tel Aviv: Schocken, 1980.

— *Between Right and Right.* Trans. Arnold Schwarz. New York: Doubleday, 1981.

— *Molkho.* Tel Aviv: Hakibbutz Hameuchad, 1987.

— Five Seasons. Trans. Hillel Halkin. New York: Doubleday, 1989.

— *Mar Mani.* Tel Aviv: Hakibbutz Hameuchad, 1990.

— *Mr. Mani.* Trans. Hillel Halkin. New York: Doubleday, 1992.

Yoffe, A. B., ed. *Nikhtav betashah* [Written in 1948]. Tel Aviv: Reshafim, 1989.

Young, Iris. "Is Male Gender Identity the Cause of Male Domination?" In Joyce Treblicot, ed., *Mothering: Essays in Feminist Theory.* Totowa, N.J.: Rowman and Allenheld, 1983.

Yudkin, Leon. *Escape Into Siege: A Survey of Israeli Literature Today.* London, Boston: Routledge and Kegan Paul, 1974.

Zarhi, Nurit. "On Elisheva's Loss [Destruction]." *Ma'ariv,* January 16, 1981.

— "She Is Joseph." In Nurit Zarhi, *'Oman hamasekhot* [The Mask Maker], pp. 7–13. Tel Aviv: Zmora-Bitan, 1993.

Zehavi, Alex. "Fate and Sophistication." *Modern Hebrew Literature* 8, nos. 1/2 (1982–1983): 41–47.

— "A Breakthrough Beyond the Familiar." *Ma'ariv,* May 27, 1988.

Zevuloni, Shalom. "Hame'ah vehamakor" [The Centenary and Original (Literature)]. *Ha'aretz/Sfarim,* November 5, 1997, p. 13.

Zilberman, Dorit. *'Ishah betokh 'ishah betokh 'ishah* [A Woman Inside Woman Inside Woman]. Tel Aviv: Tarmil, 1991.

Zilberman, Dorit and Zippi Shahrur, eds. *Nimfa bejins* [Nymph in Jeans; stories]. Tel Aviv: Ma'ariv, 1997.

Zwerdling, Alex. *Virginia Woolf and the Real World.* Berkeley: University of California Press, 1986.

Index